The Fourth Estate

MANCHESTER 1824

Manchester University Press

The Fourth Estate

Journalism in twentieth-century Ireland

Mark O'Brien

Manchester University Press

Published by Manchester University Press
Altrincham Street, Manchester M1 7JA
www.manchesteruniversitypress.co.uk

British Library Cataloguing-in-Publication Data
A catalogue record for this book is available from the British Library

First published by Manchester University Press in hardback 2017
This edition first published 2018

ISBN 978 0 7190 9613 6 hardback
ISBN 978 1 5261 3478 3 paperback

Typeset by Out of House Publishing
Printed in Great Britain
by CPI Group (UK) Ltd, Croydon, CR0 4YY

Contents

Acknowledgements

I wish to acknowledge the support given to this publication by the Faculty of Humanities and Social Sciences, Dublin City University. The book was completed while I was the recipient of the Faculty's Research Fellowship and published with the assistance of the Faculty's book publication scheme. I extend my gratitude to the staff of Manchester University Press for their enthusiasm in bringing this volume to fruition. I am grateful to Independent Newspapers and the National Library of Ireland for their provision of the cover image.

Over the past decade much work on media and journalism history has been prompted, developed, and facilitated by the Newspaper and Periodical History Forum of Ireland. The Forum has held an annual conference since 2008 and I had the pleasure of serving as its chairperson between 2013 and 2016.

Numerous people facilitated the research by granting access to papers, translating documents, pointing me in the right direction, sharing their own research and insights with me, and reading drafts of the manuscript. Their generous help is very much appreciated. Needless to record, any omissions or errors remain the responsibility of the author.

My thanks in particular to Sheila Ahern, Joe Breen, Pat Brereton, Ray Burke, Martin Conboy, Farrel Corcoran, Mary Corcoran, Yvonne Daly, Séamus Dooley, John Doyle, Declan Fahy, Michael Foley, Justin Furlong, John Horgan, Anthony Keating, Colum Kenny, Felix Larkin, Martin Molony, Gary Murphy, Pádraig Murphy, Donnacha Ó Beacháin, Mark O'Connell, Kevin Rafter, Helena Sheehan, Brian Trench, Maurice Walsh, Regina Uí Chollatáin, and Aoife Whelan. For his endless patience, this book is dedicated to Brian Cotter.

Abbreviations

AIB	Allied Irish Banks
AIJ	Association of Irish Journalists
BMHWS	Bureau of Military History Witness Statement
CIU	Congress of Irish Unions
CMI	Clerical Medical International
CP	Communist Party
CPGB	Communist Party of Great Britain
CRO	Companies Registration Office
CYMS	Catholic Young Men's Society
DDA	Dublin Diocesan Archives
DED	Dáil Éireann Debates
DIRT	Deposit Interest Retention Tax
DNMC	Dublin Newspaper Managers' Committee
EEC	European Economic Community
GAA	Gaelic Athletic Association
HCRC	Historic Collections Research Centre, Dublin City University
IJA	Irish Journalists' Association
IRA	Irish Republican Army
IRB	Irish Republican Brotherhood
ITGWU	Irish Transport and General Workers' Union
ITUC	Irish Trade Union Congress
IWLM	Irish Women's Liberation Movement
JIC	Joint Industrial Council
NAI	National Archives of Ireland
NEC	National Executive Council
NFA	National Farmers' Association
NIB	National Irish Bank
NLA	National Library of Australia
NLI	National Library of Ireland
NUJ	National Union of Journalists
SED	Seanad Éireann Debates

SPUC	Society for the Protection of the Unborn Child
TUC	Trade Union Congress
UCD	University College Dublin
UCDA	University College Dublin Archives

Glossary

Áras an Uachtaráin	official residence of the President of Ireland
Ard Fheis	party conference
Bord Fáilte	tourist board
Ceann Comhairle	speaker of parliament
Dáil Éireann	lower house of parliament
Garda Síochána	Irish police force
Gardaí	police officers
Oireachtas	collective term for both houses of parliament
Radio Telefís Éireann	national broadcaster
Seanad Éireann	upper house of parliament
Taoiseach	prime minister
Tánaiste	deputy prime minister
TD	Teachta Dála (member of parliament)

Introduction

It was, by any measure, a sensational court case: a prominent solicitor suing a Catholic priest for damages after the cleric had allegedly stalked, hypnotised, and slept with the man's wife. The case was heard before the President of the High Court over several days in May 1943 and provided much copy for the journalist who worked as a stringer for the London-based *Daily Mirror*. As the case progressed, the *Mirror* continued to report developments and published photographs of the priest and the lady in question. However, the only mention the case ever received in the Irish media was an innocuous listing in the *Irish Times*'s daily court diary. Both the *Irish Independent* and the *Irish Press* ignored the case altogether, while the government-monitored Radio Éireann would certainly not have reported on the proceedings. Undoubtedly aware of the case, the national media chose not to report on it. As late as 1964, a report complied for the Archbishop of Dublin, John Charles McQuaid, concluded that many journalists believed the Catholic Church enjoyed 'a special protection from criticism in the editorial and letter columns of newspapers' and that it was 'well known among journalists that certain newspapers have a policy of keeping off issues in which the Church may be involved'.[1] Fast forward to October 2002, and the national broadcaster, RTÉ, airs *Cardinal Secrets*. The programme, which in stark terms reveals the sexual abuse perpetrated by clergy in the Dublin archdiocese over several decades and the failure of successive bishops and archbishops to report the abuse to the Garda Síochána, prompts unprecedented public outrage. The then Minister for Justice, Michael McDowell, declares that, as far as the state is concerned, canon law holds the same status as 'the internal rules of a sporting organisation', and, shortly afterwards, the government establishes an inquiry into the archdiocese's handling of abuse complaints.[2] Though fifty-nine years apart, these two incidents illustrate the transformation of journalism in Ireland over the course of the twentieth century – from a time when, as Seán O'Faolain put it, 'the Catholic Church was felt, feared and courted on all sides as the dominant power' to a time when television documentaries revealed the moral abyss of clerical child sex abuse and government commissions of inquiry criticised the state's deferential and submissive attitude towards the church.[3] It is this transformation that forms the core of this book.

As noted by Tom Garvin, for much of the twentieth century, the Catholic Church held an ideological monopoly wherein political parties were submissive and 'theological orthodoxies isolated, marginalised and stifled dissent and opposition'.[4] Where, one may reasonably ask, was journalism situated within this power structure? And how did this relationship evolve over time? While many media institutions and newspaper titles have been the subject of historical scrutiny, the professional and organisational development of journalists, the practices of journalism, and the contribution of journalists and journalism to the evolution of modern Ireland have remained unexamined.[5] And, while historiography recognises the centrality of the media in the development of Ireland over the course of the twentieth century and frequently makes use of the press as a primary source, it often fails to peel back the coverage to examine the conditions under which the journalism being cited was conducted. Indeed, the term 'journalism' is remarkable for its absence in the indexes of the works of Irish historiography.[6]

It is such deficits that this book aims to rectify. It seeks to put the experiences of journalists and the practice of journalism at the heart of its analysis in the belief that such a focus sheds valuable light on the development of Ireland over the course of the twentieth century. It argues that the position of journalists and the power of journalism are products of their time and are shaped by ever-shifting political, economic, social, technological, and cultural forces. Beginning with the rise of the new journalism in the 1880s and concluding at the onset of the twenty-first century, it examines how journalists organised, worked, and related to the primary centres of power – in particular the state, political parties, and the Catholic Church. Conversely, it examines how these centres of power related to journalists amid the ebbs and flows of an ever-evolving Ireland. Ultimately, it examines how, over the decades, the prevailing conditions facilitated or constrained the work of journalists and how their work impacted on the processes of social stasis and social change.

The book was prompted by the questions posed about journalism amid the political corruption and clerical abuse scandals of the late 1990s and early 2000s. How, these questions went, could such corruption and abuse have remained hidden for so long? And why had journalists not exposed this misconduct earlier? Was Irish journalism the dog that would not bark? If it was, others answered, it was because it was muzzled for much of the twentieth century by state censorship and clerical dominance. The aim of this book is to tease out these questions and answers by looking at what the surviving records tell us about the condition of journalism – and journalists – as Ireland moved through the twentieth century.

Several caveats are in order as seeking to write a book on the development of journalism in any nation is akin to determining a precise measurement for the proverbial piece of string: the more that is examined, the greater the sense that more is being omitted. First, the book is a case study: its aim is to examine how journalism developed in the Irish case, and, while international influences are acknowledged and examined, the primary focus remains on the Irish situation. Second, by Ireland is meant what is nowadays the Republic of Ireland. While Northern Ireland and the Troubles loom large in the text, the North – given the differences in political culture and the specific circumstances prevailing there – is worthy of its own detailed analysis. Third, this research does not seek to replicate the substantial work on the history of media institutions or the history of Irish-language journalism that has been published in recent years. Fourth, journalism is examined in its broadest sense: the emphasis is on journalism in the round rather than on detailed analysis of specific strands of journalism. Fifth, some strands of journalism, specifically photojournalism and political cartoons, are not examined as they require specialised publications very different to this book.[7] Sixth, notwithstanding the presence of a vibrant provincial press – and the fact that it served as a training ground for many journalists who rose to national prominence – the analysis focuses primarily on how national journalism interacted with centres of power. Seventh, there is a strong focus on the Catholic Church: this is because Catholicism was the most prevalent faith within the state and the Catholic Church sought to intervene in the journalistic sphere more regularly than other churches. Last, it is not an attempt to list every journalist or editor who worked in Irish journalism during the twentieth century: rather, the primary emphasis is on examining the key inflection or turning points in the relationship between journalism and the state and journalism and the Catholic Church.

As with any research that takes 'the long view', along with social, political, and economic change, certain inflection points make themselves clear: the new journalism of the 1880s, the development of representative organisations for journalists in the early 1900s, the Censorship of Publications Act 1929, the 'Red Scare' of the 1950s, the advent of television, the introduction of free second-level education, the rise of the women's movement, the Northern Ireland Troubles, broadcast censorship, and the rise of the periodical press of the 1970s all loom large in how journalism related to centres of institutional power over the course of the twentieth century. The author is aware that, as with all books, different researchers would, perhaps, have placed greater or less emphasis on certain events or persons. This, ultimately, is a matter of interpretation, and if this work prompts further analysis of any topic or trend examined herein, then that is only to be welcomed.

Notes

1 Dublin Diocesan Archives (DDA), AB8/B/XXVI/e/78 (Public Image Committee), 'The journalist and the church', undated but most likely late 1963 or early 1964.
2 *Irish Times*, 24 Oct. 2002, p. 8.
3 S. O'Faolain, *Vive Moi! An Autobiography* (London, 1965), p. 264.
4 T. Garvin, *Preventing the Future: Why Was Ireland So Poor for So Long?* (Dublin, 2004), pp. 70–1.
5 Notable exceptions are K. Rafter (ed.), *Irish Journalism before Independence: More a Disease than a Profession* (Manchester, 2011) and H. Oram, *The Newspaper Book: A History of Newspapers in Ireland, 1649–1983* (Dublin, 1983).
6 A rare exception is T. Brown, *Ireland: A Social and Cultural History* (Dublin, 2004).
7 See F. M. Larkin, *Terror and Discord: The Shemus Cartoons in the Freeman's Journal, 1920–24* (Dublin, 2009). For an account of the difficulties encountered by cartoonists in the nascent Irish state, see C. E. Kelly, 'May we laugh please?', *The Furrow*, 4:12 (1953), 697–705.

1

A new age

Since daily newspapers have doubled their sheets and multiplied their numbers - since men took to travelling by steam and corresponding by telegraph - since the world has begun to live so fast, that it takes its news like its meals, regularly four times a day, with a latest edition, by way of nightcap after supper - the functions of the monthly magazine have undergone a remarkable alteration.[1]

— The Daily Express on changes in media production, 1851

The second half of the nineteenth century brought profound change to journalism in Ireland. The gradual abolition of the knowledge taxes - the long-standing stamp duty on newspapers and taxes on newsprint and advertising - gave a new lease of life to the printed word by lowering prices, encouraging competition, and making newspapers a more viable business enterprise.[2] The expansion of the railway - from 428 miles in 1849 to 1,909 miles in 1866 - encouraged urbanisation and provided secure routes for telegraph wires. In turn, urbanisation encouraged the development of the provincial press by creating core readerships for such titles. Technological innovations, such as the completion of submarine cables from Howth to Holyhead in 1852, and from Valentia Island to Newfoundland in 1866, allowed for the transmission of news almost instantaneously. Other technological advances, such as the typewriter and the rotary press in the 1860s, the telephone in the 1870s, and the Linotype machine in the 1880s, allowed for a more efficient production process. Rising literacy levels meant more people were capable of reading newspapers: between 1841 and 1881, the percentage of the population over five years of age that was literate rose from 47 to 75 per cent.[3] Electoral reform increased the number of voters and changed how they voted. While the 1884 Reform Act trebled the number of voters by extending the franchise to cottiers and labours, the Ballot Act 1872 introduced the secret ballot, lessening the hold landlords had over their tenants' votes. These technological, social, and political developments prompted huge growth in the demand for news. As L. M. Cullen has recorded, sales of Irish daily newspapers through the country's main distributor, Eason's, jumped from 99,558 in 1878 to 119,442 in 1894 while sales of weekly newspapers increased from 26,859 in 1878 to 42,864 in 1883.[4]

Political events also transformed journalism. The 'new departure' of the late 1870s, whereby constitutional and militant nationalists and agrarian agitators united in a campaign for land reform and Home Rule, politicised journalism as never before. The Land League, led by Michael Davitt and Charles Stewart Parnell, sought to address the grievances of tenant farmers, and, since land was at the heart of the new political struggle, it also became the centre of journalistic life. As Christopher Morash and Felix Larkin have pointed out, one of the first pieces of what would later be called investigative journalism was published at this time. In 1878, the *Freeman's Journal* published William O'Brien's series 'Christmas on the Galtees' that exposed the plight of the rack-rent tenants of the Buckley estate in County Tipperary.[5] As the 1880s unfolded, Land League meetings, land sales, evictions, boycotts, crop raids, demonstrations, and attacks on landlords and their agents dominated the work of journalists. Reporting on these events was a hazardous task for journalists as they ran the risk of being mistaken for government officials or being accused of being unsympathetic to the aims of the League – or, in extreme cases, being injured in the disturbances that occasionally erupted. Interestingly, journalists were originally hired by Dublin Castle to report on such meetings and give evidence in court, but when this practice was condemned by the *Freeman's Journal*, the Castle resorted to using policemen who had been trained in the use of shorthand. The most noted of these policemen was one Jeremiah Stringer and so famous did he become that 'his name was often applied derisively to other Constabulary note-takers'.[6] Stringer is mentioned consistently in the newspaper reports of the prosecutions of Land League leaders during the 1880s and is also mentioned in House of Commons debates on Ireland. When, in 1881, Parnell challenged William Gladstone's account of a speech he (Parnell) had made at an eviction, Gladstone retorted that he had 'authentic evidence' – to which T. M. Healy cried, amid much laugher, 'Jeremiah Stringer'.[7] On his death, the *Weekly Irish Times* noted that 'in the days of the Land League there were few names more prominently mentioned in connection with the preservation of law and order than his, the knowledge of shorthand he possessed being of invaluable service to the Government'.[8] In time, the term 'stringer' came to be used to describe local correspondents who reported on events for national media.

New journalism

But the biggest change in journalism in the latter half of the nineteenth century was undoubtedly the advent of 'new journalism'. As Joel Wiener has pointed out, the new journalism emerged in America in the 1830s and significantly influenced the development of journalism in Britain and Ireland. It did so by introducing significant changes in typography and makeup, in content, and by encouraging greater commercialisation.[9] The shape of newspapers changed with the introduction of headlines and summary leads, and there was a greater emphasis on display adverts, illustrations, and, later, photographs. There occurred a changed definition of what constituted news – 'a rejection of the older view that the press existed primarily to record and disseminate high politics' and the adoption of 'a modern tabloid sensibility'. Out went the emphasis on verbatim parliamentary reportage and page-length leading articles, and in came an emphasis on 'gossip, display advertising, sports news, human interest features, articles aimed at women and children and, above all, fast-breaking stories transmitted by wire agencies'.[10] As viewed by prominent proponent of the new journalism T. P. O'Connor, its distinguishing feature was 'the more personal tone of the more modern methods'. While previously 'any illusion to the personal appearance, the habits, the clothes, or the home and social life of any person would have been resented as an impertinence and almost as an indecency', new journalism advocated that 'the desire for personal details with regard to public men is healthy, rational, and should be yielded to'. The public, O'Connor declared, 'suffer a great deal more from the cowardice than from the audacity of journalism, from the suppression than from the publication of awkward facts'.[11] In terms of his own newspaper, *The Star*, O'Connor promised to 'do away with the hackneyed style of obsolete journalism': there would be no place 'for the verbose and prolix articles to which most of our contemporaries still adhere'.[12] Thus, personalised reporting, interviews, serialisations, crime news, and investigative pieces were staples of the new journalism. In Britain, the new journalism was inextricably linked with W. T. Stead, Editor of the *Pall Mall Gazette*, whose pioneering investigation into London childhood prostitution in 1885 has achieved iconic status.[13] But while this series is often highlighted as the first sex scandal that typified the scandalmongering approach of new journalism, Margot Gayle Backus has pointed out that William O'Brien's exposé, in *United Ireland*, of the Dublin Castle sex scandal, which involved sexual impropriety among government officials, predates Stead's series. She also noted that the failed libel suits that arose from the series would have been closely monitored by editors and journalists in London. Their timing, argues Backus, 'strongly implies a connection between … O'Brien's right to publish and the new mode of investigative scandal that Stead launched the following year'. Prior to O'Brien's series, Stead's actions, Backus concludes, 'would have been unthinkable'.[14]

Within the new journalism, crime and divorce stories loomed large: the blanket coverage devoted to the so-called 'Jack the Ripper' murders in London's Whitechapel area in 1888 and the tales of adultery and cruelty that emanated from the divorce courts typified the new journalism. By 1896, with the establishment of the halfpenny *Daily Mail* by Alfred Harmsworth (later Lord Northcliffe), the new journalism had been appropriated as a mean of selling mass-circulation daily newspapers – a process decried by Stead as 'purposeless sensationalism, sham heroics, and opportunism'.[15] Indeed, many scholars draw a distinction between the initial and later stages of the new journalism: while Stead's new journalism represented 'a moral thrust, social conviction, directness of language and political ambition', Harmsworth's incorporation of new journalism represented monetisation and commercial gain.[16]

In Ireland, this use of crime and scandal to sell newspapers manifested itself in the British Sunday titles that arrived every week. The idea of newspapers reporting gossip, scandal, crime, and conducting investigations was one far removed from Irish journalism at the turn of the century. These topics were taboo, and the publication of such stories in imported British titles was viewed by the Catholic Church as contributing to the moral degeneration of the local population. In 1899, the hierarchy called for action against the 'printing presses in Great Britain [that] daily pour out a flood of infidel and immoral publications some of which overflows into this country'. There followed the establishment of the Catholic Truth Society of Ireland, the aim of which was to distribute 'cheap publications of sound Catholic literature in popular form [to] remove the temptation of having recourse to filthy garbage'.[17] By 1902, the Society had 120 branches nationwide and had sold over 800,000 penny books.[18]

The following year, among the attendees at the Society's first annual conference at Dublin's Mansion House was William Martin Murphy, former MP and owner of the *Irish Daily Independent*. Reminding those assembled of the Society's origins, its secretary, John Rochford, stated that it existed 'for the purpose of providing sound and wholesome literature for their people, and thus preventing them from the moral poison of the infidel and foul and immoral publications imported into Ireland weekly in such vast quantities from England'.[19] Another speaker, Revd Peter Finlay, delivered a talk on 'The Catholic Journalism of To-day' in which he effectively described what would later become the *Irish Independent*. A Catholic newspaper would be, he stressed, 'written and edited in the main by Catholics, for readers mostly Catholics, and on Catholic principles'. Such a paper would 'not deal with religious topics only … it should provide news, discuss men and manners, further special interests, promote literature, and even take sides in controversial political questions'. It should, Finlay continued, 'be conducted on Catholic principles, and be at one with ecclesiastical authority in religious questions'. Such a daily press existed elsewhere he concluded, and in Ireland 'they had numbers on their side, a rightful cause and a crying need, and there was nothing in the way which persistence and ability could not conquer'.[20]

Whether coincidence or not, fifteen months later, William Martin Murphy launched the new-look *Irish Independent*. Established as the *Irish Daily Independent* in 1891, it had been the organ of those within the Irish Parliamentary Party who had continued to support Charles Stewart Parnell in the wake of the O'Shea divorce saga.[21] Acquired by Murphy in 1900, he considered selling the title and found a potential buyer who commissioned newspaper experts to conduct a review of its business prospects. Murphy was intrigued with the advice received: to make the title a halfpenny paper and run it as a business venture rather than a political organ. Having observed another Irish-born businessman, Alfred Harmsworth, make a success of the *Daily Mail* in London, Murphy decided to emulate the *Mail*'s low price and emphasis on condensed news, serials, interviews, features, and competitions. Wary of Harmsworth's business prowess, Murphy contacted him to enquire whether he intended to expand his newspaper empire to Ireland. Harmsworth had no such intention; he even advised Murphy on the proposed relaunch of the *Independent*.[22]

In essence, the redesigned *Irish Independent* emulated Harmsworth's *Daily Mail* – with certain very important differences. Murphy not only selected, applied, and adapted elements of the new journalism to suit his own commercial objectives but also paid particular attention to the constraints of the society in which the reinvented title would be published.[23] To this end, Murphy adopted the new marketing strategies and the elements of the new journalism that seemed safe – display advertising, condensed reportage, illustrations, and serials – but he studiously rejected any element – gossip, scandal, crime reportage, and investigative journalism – that would cause controversy or attract condemnation from the Catholic Church. The paper's first edition announced that it would present news 'in a form which the public will appreciate as a departure from traditions of journalism which are now outworn'. It aimed to be 'brightly written and attractively presented [but] free from un-wholesome sensationalism and sustaining a character for truthfulness and good faith'. News would 'be given without colouring or prejudice', and, while reports would be condensed, 'the greatest care will be taken that their essence shall be retained'.[24]

Murphy's choice of editor was crucial in making the *Irish Independent* a successful commercial enterprise, and, as Felix Larkin has pointed out, the appointment of the strong-willed T. R. Harrington ensured that the paper was no longer the political plaything of Murphy's political friends.[25] Murphy also added one more innovation: that of independently audited circulation figures. In the early 1900s, most newspapers simply published what they believed to be the number of copies sold, but these tended to be print runs rather than circulation figures. The *Independent* changed all that: from 1909, it made a big play out of publishing its independently verified sales figures as a promotional tactic to attract advertising. In 1931, it noted that it had been 'the first paper outside the USA to give the public these figures'.[26] From an initial circulation of 22,608 copies in 1905, it sold 56,462 copies a day in 1913.[27]

To state that Murphy sanitised his newspaper's content for purely business reasons would be untrue: he, like many other businessmen, was a product of his time, and he was 'intensely Catholic, nationalist and conservative'.[28] It was, however, fortuitous that his world view chimed with that of the Catholic Church in relation to what constituted proper journalism, a world view that was reflected in his newspaper and that helped establish the *Independent* as the very profitable voice of middle-class conservative Ireland. In the early 1900s, the *Independent* devoted considerable space to reporting the hierarchy's annual Lenten pastorals that addressed the issue of objectionable newspapers.[29]

It is impossible that Murphy or Harrington would have been unaware of the consequences of adopting all the tenets of the new journalism – as evidenced by the controversy that the *Independent* strayed into in 1911. It was in that year that the Dublin Vigilance Committee emerged from various branches of the Catholic Young Men's Society (CYMS) to 'defend the people against the insidious attempts of modern journalism to corrupt them' and draw attention to 'the gross pandering of some of their Irish newspapers to that tendency of the sensational and shady'. Those newspapers had, it was claimed by the group's spiritual director, Revd Myles V. Ronan, published 'the intimate details of the private lives of the unfortunate victims of the Divorce Courts', and it was 'outrageous and degrading for the Irish press to lavishly imitate their fellow-pressmen across the Channel in that vile pandering to a depraved taste and low moral sense'. What was needed was 'a great

Crusade – a Holy War against the enemies of Christian morality and against the diabolical campaign carried on by mischievous publications'.[30] Addressing the meeting, P. J. Daniel, secretary of the St Laurence branch of the CYMS, noted that he had previously contacted the editors of the Dublin newspapers and 'two of them point blank refused to comply with the demand of the Committee'. He identified the two papers as the *Independent* and the *Daily Express*. There then followed 'a strong attack' on the *Independent* by one Revd Canon Dowling for publishing matter on five days of the week to which he objected and 'then on the last day dishing up sermons'.[31] At a subsequent Vigilance Committee meeting in Galway, one Father Davis stated that, unlike the *Freeman's Journal* and the *Irish Times*, 'the *Irish Independent* refused – as far as he could see from the paper – to comply to leave out those [divorce] cases'.[32]

Having had his newspaper so publicly criticised, Harrington argued in a leading article that the *Independent* had not been asked to exclude reports of divorce cases. Instead, it had been requested to 'discontinue publishing the details of evidence of divorce, and other cases which were calculated to undermine public morals', and his reply to that request had been 'that such details did not appear in the "Irish Independent" as the greatest care was exercised to exclude them'. Every effort, he asserted, had been made to present such reports 'in such a way as to render them entirely free from objection'.[33] Harrington had every reason to be cautious. The previous month, in Limerick, under pressure from the Holy Family sodality, twenty-two newsagents signed a pledge not to sell copies of 'undesirable publications', and newsboys undertook not to sell the 'objectionable prints'.[34] When pressure did not work, other methods were used. A few days later, a large crowd gathered at Limerick train station and intercepted the delivery of Sunday newspapers. According to one account, 'the papers were solemnly burned, amidst a scene of great enthusiasm, the band playing hymns while the obnoxious journals burned, and then the Dead March (Saul) over their ashy remains'.[35] Ultimately, the Vigilance Committee had its way: a report of a meeting held in early December 1911 recorded that 'the replies from the editors of the Dublin papers re the publishing of objectionable details of divorce cases and other scandals were read and considered satisfactory, the committee expressing the hope that the editors would adhere faithfully in the future to their promises'.[36]

Titles, politics, and circulation

The *Independent*'s primary competitors were the *Freeman's Journal*, the *Daily Express* and the *Irish Times*. In his work on the *Freeman's Journal*, Felix Larkin notes that the paper was published continuously from 1763 to 1924 and was originally associated with the 'patriot' opposition in the Irish parliament, with Charles Lucas and Henry Grattan being instrumental in its establishment. Through many changes of ownership it became, as Larkin points out, the 'foremost nationalist newspaper in Ireland in the nineteenth century'. It supported Home Rule and, after some initial reservations, Charles Stewart Parnell, but only after Parnell established his own weekly newspaper, *United Ireland*. The fall of Parnell in 1891 marked the beginning of the *Freeman*'s decline. Caught between the feuding factions of the Irish Parliamentary Party, it first supported Parnell and then denounced him when the anti-Parnellites established their own newspaper, the *National Press.* If the feuding within the Irish Parliamentary Party was a fatal blow to the paper, then the launch of the *Irish Independent* in 1905 was the death knell. With a circulation of 35,000 copies per day, it could not cope with the more keenly priced and lively *Independent.* After the demise of the Irish Parliamentary Party in the 1918 general election, the *Freeman* was sold to a prominent Dublin businessman, Martin FitzGerald, who kept it going until 1924, when his business partner absconded, leaving FitzGerald and the *Freeman's Journal* laden with debt.[37] Unable to continue publication, the title was purchased by Independent Newspapers.

On the other end of the political spectrum was the *Daily Express.* Established in 1851, it sought 'to reconcile the rights and impulses of Irish nationality with the demands and obligations of imperial dominion'.[38] It viewed the rise of the Land League and its challenge to the landlord system with horror. The paper is best remembered for its role in the Captain Boycott saga of 1880 when it published an extensive account of the travails of Boycott at the hands of the Land League in County Mayo. The article prompted an anonymous reader to write a letter suggesting the creation of a fund to recruit a body of men to save Boycott's crops – a suggestion endorsed wholeheartedly by the paper.[39] The government subsequently spent £10,000 saving £500 worth of crops, and the word 'boycott' became synonymous with blacklisting. In 1898, the *Express* took part in what it described as 'an experiment of the greatest interest to journalism and science' when it reported on the annual Kingstown (Dun Laoghaire) regatta by using 'Marconi's new system of Wireless Telegraphy'. A steamboat charted by the paper followed the race and sent messages to a station on land; it in turn sent the reports to the newspaper's offices, which printed them in successive editions of its sister title, the *Evening Mail.*[40] In its subsequent report, headlined 'Wireless Telegraphy Applied to Journalism', it noted that the experiment was 'successfully carried out'.[41] This event is believed to have been the first time that a newspaper published news received by radio.

Following the deaths of its long-term proprietor James Poole Maunsell in 1897 and its long-time editor George V. Patton in 1898, the paper passed into the ownership of Horace Plunkett, and, as one contemporary put it, 'it shone quite brilliantly as an organ of Progressive Ireland – the Ireland of industrial development and literary renaissance'.[42] It subsequently passed into the ownership of Lord Ardilaun (Sir Arthur Edward Guinness) and Henry L. Tivy of the *Cork Constitution* who again revitalised its unionist identity. As late as 1918 it described itself as 'the organ of the landed gentry, clergy, the leading professional and commercial classes' and its mission as being 'to maintain intact the Imperial union', while its sister title, the *Evening Mail*, was described simply as 'Independent'.[43] In June 1921, during the War of Independence, the *Daily Express* was discontinued due to declining circulation although the *Evening Mail*, later famous for its hugely popular Letters to the Editor page, continued publication until 1962.[44]

Also representing the unionist tradition was the *Irish Times*, which was established in 1859 by Lawrence E. Knox as the voice of southern unionism. Its first leading article declared that 'As Irishmen we shall think and speak; but it shall be as Irishmen loyal to the British connection.'[45] In June 1862, it claimed a daily circulation of 16,988. When Knox died in 1873, the paper was purchased by the Scottish businessman Sir John Arnott, and it remained in the ever-diluting ownership of the Arnott family until 1974 when it was reconstituted as a trust. Its politics were unionist, and, while it editorialised against Home Rule, it was sympathetic to the aims (though not the methods) of the Land League in its campaign for land reform. In 1879, it described the League's campaign against rack rents as 'fair and desirable': the fact that the paper was aimed at the Protestant mercantile community rather than the landed class may explain this stance.[46] In appearance, it was austere, and by 1907 its layout had not altered dramatically: each page was still printed in eight single columns of dense type. Classified adverts and three-column-width display adverts for Dublin department stores dominated the front page (and would do so until 1941), while the 'Court Circular' column – embossed with the royal coat of arms – kept readers informed of the latest happenings at Buckingham Palace. The 'London Letter' summarised proceedings at Westminster, while 'Fashionable Intelligence' listed the doings and the comings and goings of nobility. In the 1922 *Newspaper Press Directory*, it claimed to hold 'the premier position in Ireland [as] the organ of the monied community'.[47] In terms of circulation, it averaged daily sales of 25,500 during the 1920s and remained roughly at this level until its reinvention in the 1960s.[48]

All these companies also published evening or weekly titles. Independent Newspapers published the *Evening Herald*, the *Irish Weekly Independent*, the *Saturday Herald*, and the *Sunday Independent*. The Freeman's Journal Ltd published the *Evening Telegraph*, the *Weekly Freeman*, the *Sunday Freeman*, and a weekly sports newspaper, *Sport*. The Daily Express Company published the *Evening Mail* and the weekly *Sports Mail and Irish Weekly Mail*, while the Irish Times Ltd published the *Weekly Irish Times* and a weekly sports newspaper, the *Irish Field*. As L. M. Cullen has observed, the prevalence of weekly papers was explained by the fact that not everyone could afford a daily paper or only had access to a retailer in the course of a weekly visit to a market or mass.[49] Outside of Dublin, the two main urban centres, Belfast and Cork, also had thriving newspaper industries. In Belfast, the industry was characterised by daily newspapers that mostly described themselves as unionist, including the *Belfast Evening Telegraph* ('advocates Unionist political opinions'), the *Belfast News-letter* ('advocates Unionist principles'), the *Northern Whig* ('Unionist') and the *Ulster Echo* ('Unionist'). The only daily paper that described itself as 'National' was the *Irish News and Belfast Morning News*. In Derry, the industry was more balanced, with the *Derry Journal* and *Derry People*, both described as 'Nationalist', competing with the *Derry Standard* ('Unionist') and the *Londonderry Sentinel* ('Conservative and Unionist'). In Cork, the industry was dominated by Thomas Crosbie's *Cork Examiner*, *Evening Echo*, and *Weekly Examiner and Weekly Herald*, all described as 'National'. Representing the 'Conservative' viewpoint was the *Cork Constitution*. Unfortunately, with the exception of the Independent titles, newspapers did not commonly issue circulation figures. While the *Irish Independent* first published its figures in 1910, the *Irish Times* first published its circulation figures in 1960.[50] In the annual *Newspaper Press Directory and Advertisers' Guide*, newspapers simply indicated their political stance and the geographical areas they circulated within.

Ireland also had a vibrant provincial press. As Maire-Louise Legge has pointed out, the Land War of the 1880s and the new unity among the formerly disparate elements of Irish nationalism created a potent political movement and delivered a huge boost to provincial newspapers, many of which were owned and edited by members or supporters of Parnell's Irish Parliamentary Party.[51] Such proprietors/editors included Thomas Cleary of the *Clare Independent*, James Daly of the *Connaught Telegraph*, Luke Hayden of the *Roscommon Messenger*, Timothy Harrington of the *Kerry Sentinel*, Edmund Walsh of the *Wexford People*, Patrick McHugh of the *Sligo Champion*, Jasper Tully of the *Roscommon Herald*, James Carew of the *Leinster Leader*, John Hayden of the *Westmeath Examiner*, John O'Donnell of the *Connaught Champion* and Daniel Sheehan of the *Southern Star*.[52] These newspapers spread the news of Land League meetings and played a crucial role in the development of political consciousness among the farming and labouring classes. This phenomenon was summed up by one *Freeman's Journal* reporter when he noted that:

> Print had become for the first time an actuality for the Catholic peasants and part of their everyday life, speaking to them in a thrilling, palpitating language, intelligible – and there lay the marvel – yet different from anything previously known, for it enabled them to hear their friends at a distance talking to them in accents of power about the wondrous doings of the Land League.[53]

But the provincial press was not exclusively nationalist: the 1917 *Newspaper Press Directory* also records the existence of provincial newspapers that advocated the conservative or unionist position, including the *Carlow Sentinel*, the *Galway Express*, the *Meath Herald*, the *Kilkenny Moderator*, the *Limerick Chronicle*, the *Longford Journal*, the *Sligo Independent*, the *Waterford Standard*, and the *Wicklow News-letter*.

There existed also a very lively periodical press, and, while it is beyond the scope of this work to survey each title, from the late 1880s onwards the establishment of organisations such as the Gaelic League, the cooperative movement, the Irish Transport and General Workers' Union, the Irish Women's Franchise League, and Sinn Féin, resulted in a plethora of new publications espousing such causes as the Irish language, trade unionism, feminism, and nationalism. Their radicalism lay in the independence they possessed. Often produced on a shoestring budget, they were free to challenge orthodoxy without fear or favour, and some published seminal pieces of journalism that changed the course of Irish history. Arthur Griffith, Editor of the *United Irishman*, first published his *Resurrection of Hungary* as a series of articles in that journal in 1904; it provided the blueprint for the final phase of Ireland's struggle for independence. In 1913, Eoin MacNeill's article, 'The North Began', which called for and led to the foundation of the Irish Volunteers, was published in *An Claidheamh Soluis*. Such periodicals were 'the fulcrum on which the intellectual foundations of Irish society moved – slowly, but irrevocably'.[54]

Journalists and journalistic life

Corresponding with the increase in newspaper and periodical titles was an increase in the number of people working as journalists. The 1901 Census for the island of Ireland lists 509 journalists (472 male, thirty-seven female), 111 reporters (109 male, two female) and fifty-nine editors (fifty-seven male, two female). In 1911, the respective figures are: 613 journalists (578 male, thirty-five female), 129 reporters (129 male) and seventy-four editors (seventy-one male, three female).[55] The work they did was, for the very most part, poorly paid and anonymous, and the few surviving accounts of life as a journalist in the late 1880s and early 1900s tend to be anecdotal in nature. In his memoir, Matthias McDonnell Bodkin, who worked at the *Freeman's Journal* during this period, gave an account of what was expected of the working journalist:

> In England press work is specialised, the Irish reporter is a Jack of all trades. Within an hour he must be gay at a wedding and sad at a funeral, he must know something about everything or must at least successfully 'assume a knowledge if he hath it not'. He must lecture learnedly on every theme ... There is nothing he must not be ready to describe at a moment's notice, and he must write just as much and just as little as may be required by his editor, dilute his thoughts into three columns or concentrate them into a paragraph. The length or brevity of his description is not to be regulated by his experience, knowledge or imagination, or by his belief in the importance or triviality of the subject, but simply by the amount of available space. He must measure his thoughts with the editor's rule, and simply provide three inches or three yards as the occasion may require.[56]

Each morning, Bodkin recounted, the paper's reporters would gather in what would nowadays be called a newsroom, and there they would meet the paper's chief reporter (nowadays titled the news editor), whose duty it was to keep a record of all public events and assign the reporters – senior and junior – to cover these events.[57] Specialist beats – such as crime reporter or sports reporter – did not exist and would only evolve in the 1960s. Political meetings and important events were assigned to those who had the best shorthand. The importance of shorthand to a journalist could not be overstated. Bodkin observed, 'if a man can write even a hundred words a minute and read them at sight he is worth a trial as a reporter', while Andrew Dunlop, whose memoir also provides a valuable insight into journalism during this period, described it as the 'open sesame' to journalistic work.[58]

As the census figures indicate, journalism at this time was very much a male preserve. One of the main columns aimed at women during this period was the 'Women and Their World' column in the *Weekly Irish Times*, which presented a collection of society news, descriptions of society marriages and balls, and cookery and fashion tips. The *Weekly Irish Independent* also had a women's column, 'Women's World', written by Mary E. Butler, a member of the executive of the Gaelic League and a member of Sinn Féin. In her column, Butler concerned herself with two central themes: the importance of domestic education and the relationship between domesticity and public life. She argued that by perfecting their domestic skills Irishwomen could have a wider influence in terms of promoting Irish industry, national identity, and the Irish language – 'that great bulwark against the denationalising and demoralising influences'.[59]

Other prominent female journalists at the turn of the century included Nannie Lambert Power O'Donoghue, who wrote for the *Irish Times* and *Irish Society*, which styled itself as 'the leading society and fashion magazine in Ireland … conducted [edited] by Ladies who are specially capable of dealing with the subjects upon which they write'.[60] According to her biographer, O'Donoghue frequently used her column to highlight social issues. She reported 'on the success of the Kevin Street Penny Dinners scheme which provided cheap nourishing meals for the poor of that district' and pointed out that 'wealthy ladies, who often wore dresses only once or twice, could make them available to the poor at certain collection points'.[61] Also working for the *Irish Times* at this time was Annie Bethune Maguire. A member of the Dublin Unionist Women's Club, according to her obituary she was 'among the first women in this country to become attached to a newspaper'. Having joined the paper's staff in 1905 as its social correspondent, she remained in that position until 1937 and was 'a well-known and popular figure at the Viceregal Lodge and the Castle under several vice-royalties'.[62] Writing about female journalism in 1902, Gertrude Crowe, an occasional contributor to the *Weekly Irish Times*, observed that with 'adaptability and powers of perception, with perseverance, pluck, and physical strength … a really capable woman will find that she can earn the living wage of an educated person sooner as a journalist than as an artist, teacher or nurse'.[63] With the exception of Alice Milligan and Anna Johnson, who edited the nationalist monthly *Shan Van Vocht* in Belfast between 1896 and 1899, for the most part journalism remained the preserve of men, and those women who became journalists were mostly pigeonholed into writing about what men considered to be topics of female interest.[64]

Representation and professionalism

Alongside the new journalism, other journalistic developments in Britain had an impact in Ireland. In 1884, the National Association of Journalists of Great Britain was established with the aim of 'uniting and organising the profession of journalism'.[65] This movement was replicated in Ireland by the establishment of the Association of Irish Journalists (AIJ) in 1887, the object of which was to 'incorporate the profession of journalists in Ireland for their mutual advantage [and] to represent the status of the profession and protect its interests'. Only working journalists, whose qualifications for membership would be judged by a governing council, were eligible for membership.[66] Among the editors and proprietors who attended its inaugural meeting were James A. Scott, Editor of the *Irish Times*; Edward Byrne, Editor of the *Freeman's Journal*; Thomas Cleary of the *Clare Independent*; Frederick Potter of the *Skibbereen Eagle*; Arthur Malley of the *Sligo Independent*; Edmund Walsh of the *Wexford Standard*; Thomas Crosbie of the *Cork Examiner*; and William Copeland Trimble of the *Impartial Reporter* (Enniskillen). Among the senior journalists present were Thomas A. Stodart (*Irish Times*), John

Wyse Power (*Freeman's Journal*), John B. Hall (*Freeman's Journal*), and Andrew Dunlop (*Irish Times*) – the latter two men being the authors of prominent journalistic memoirs of the period. Oddly, neither Hall nor Dunlop made any references in their memoirs to the association or their involvement in it.[67] While the records of the association no longer exist, newspaper reports of its proceedings give a partial insight into the machinations of journalism in Ireland at the end of the nineteenth century. Upon his election as the association's president, James A. Scott noted that before it came into being, journalists were:

> utterly unknown to each other; they were jealous of each other; they were often looked upon as in antagonism to one another – they were regarded as people who had no recognised positions. The term Bohemian was very frequently applied to them. Now they had got beyond that. They considered themselves entitled to be regarded as a profession as well as other professions.[68]

One of the first initiatives undertaken by the association was the establishment of a benevolent fund, financed by voluntary subscriptions and donations, which was used to cover members' loss of income through illness or death. But, while such attempts at unity were laudable, the politically partisan nature of nineteenth-century journalism in Ireland meant that attempts to keep the volatile politics of the period out of the AIJ were not always successful. Indeed, at the association's first AGM in April 1888, Scott noted that while its membership 'comprised gentlemen of very great difference of opinion on many matters', they met as an association simply to advance the interests of journalism. They would, he warned, 'be shattered into many fragments if they did not meet together on the assumption that everything was to be excluded except that which concerned the interests of the profession as a profession'.[69] Scott made reference to an incident earlier in the year in which two journalists, one from a unionist newspaper and one from a nationalist newspaper, had been injured. The injuries had been sustained at a meeting held to protest against the banning of a Land League meeting that was to have been addressed by Michael Davitt. The meeting concluded without incident until the attendees attempted to leave the building and found it surrounded by police and military personnel. The police insisted on taking the names of those present, but some of the journalists declined to give their names, offering instead the names of the newspapers they represented. Eventually, a baton charge occurred, and two journalists, one from the *Irish Times* and one from the *Freeman's Journal*, were injured.[70] Scott implored those present to confine any resolution concerning the incident to one of regret at the injuries caused to the journalists. The politics surrounding the incident were to be left aside: what mattered were the interests of the journalistic profession. Pressmen had, he maintained, been injured at all sorts of meetings, and it was the association's business to 'see that they would protect their interests in every way – not in one place, but in every place – not against men of one opinion, but of men of every opinion – and not against one form of incident, but against every form of incident'. The resolution that was passed thus confined itself to an expression of sympathy to the reporters who had been injured.

But, having survived this wobble by a masterful display of diplomacy, the association then elected one of the most divisive journalists and politicians as its incoming president. William O'Brien, MP, former editor of *United Ireland* and Land League activist and agitator, was an odd choice of president for an association that was at pains to stress its non-political nature.[71] In his inaugural speech, O'Brien declared that when asked to be president he was greatly delighted but 'also terrified for the Association', which he recognised as 'a non-political organisation, which required a good deal of delicate handling in its tender years'.[72] His election was, however, an indication that, as on the island as a whole, nationalist journalists composed the association's majority membership. The following year, the association split when, at a meeting of its Dublin branch, Matthias McDonnell Bodkin proposed an unscheduled motion of sympathy for O'Brien who had been imprisoned for Land League agitation. When the motion was adopted, several journalists resigned on the basis that the non-partisan nature of the association had been violated. The sentiments expressed by association member and editor of the *Northern Whig*, Thomas MacKnight, encapsulated the views of those who had resigned. He declared that nationalists such as Bodkin were not 'satisfied with equality … They wish to dictate, just as an Irish Nationalist majority in a Dublin parliament would do.'[73] In response, Bodkin, writing in *United Ireland*, was equally scathing of those who had resigned. He noted that O'Brien was 'President of the Association for the present year, duly elected', and those journalists who had resigned appeared to have 'no sense of professional dignity'.[74]

Shortly afterwards, in February 1890, the National Association of Journalists of Great Britain was granted a royal charter and changed its name to the Institute of Journalists. In time, the journalists who had comprised the AIJ would all join the institute, which established three districts in Ireland. The Dublin district was chaired by George Patton (Editor, *Daily Express*), and its 1890 AGM noted that it had fifty-seven members, with its membership drawn primarily from the *Irish Times*, *Daily Express*, *Dublin Evening Echo*, and *Evening Mail*.[75] Two years later, it had sixty members, including two ladies; ten associates, including two ladies; and four pupil associates.[76] The Ulster district was chaired by Thomas MacKnight (Editor, *Northern Whig*), and its members were drawn from the *Belfast News-letter*, *Ulster Echo*, *Belfast Evening Telegraph*, and the *Ballymena Weekly Telegraph*.[77] The third district, the Irish Association district, was the largest of the three and was populated by what might be described as nationalist-leaning journalists. Describing itself as 'the parent district' in Ireland, in 1890 it had 113 members, which gave it the distinction of being the largest district with the exception of London. Its first chairman was Thomas Crosbie of the *Cork Examiner*, and among its proprietor/editor members were Edward Byrne (Editor, *Freeman's Journal*), Edward Walsh (Editor, *Wexford People*), Patrick McHugh (Editor, *Sligo Champion*), Jasper Tully (Editor, *Roscommon Herald*), William O'Brien, MP (*United Ireland*), Edward Harrington (Editor, *Kerry Sentinel*), William Roddy (Editor, *Derry Journal*), and Luke Hayden (Editor, *Roscommon Messenger*).[78]

In terms of promoting its belief that journalism was a profession, the institute's charter declared that its mission was 'the promotion of whatever might tend to the elevation of the status and the improvement of the qualifications of all members of the journalistic profession'. Its first president, Hugh Gilzean-Reid, viewed journalists as being on a professional par with lawyers, doctors, and theologians:

> They stood with the law; for their function was that of judges and advocates; they reported, they examined, they condemned, and they absolved, and in all great cases the country awaited their final judgment. They might class themselves with the medical profession, for they examined the body morally, socially, and materially, and if they sometimes gave pain in their examination, their diagnosis was accompanied by remedial prescription which at least were meant to carry healing in their application ... They stood with the theologian, for it was their providence, according to the light that was in them, to preach justice and truth and mercy and righteousness.[79]

Membership of the institute was open to journalists, editors, and proprietors, and leading members of both the Dublin and Irish Association districts played key roles in its development. At the institute's 1890 AGM, both Thomas Crosbie and James A. Scott were elected as vice-presidents of the institute.[80] Crosbie served as its president between 1894 and 1895, while Andrew Dunlop, Thomas Stodart, John B. Hall, and Edward Tuomy served, at various times, as vice-presidents. The decision by the Dublin and Irish Association districts to jointly invite the institute to hold its 1891 annual conference in Dublin resulted in both districts appointing a joint committee to organise the conference.[81] Dublin again hosted the conference in 1906. Held at Trinity College, this conference was an international affair, with journalists from France, Sweden, Belgium, the United States, India, Africa, and New Zealand in attendance. Addressing the conference, Trinity's Provost, Dr Anthony Traill, invited the delegates to consider the 'possible relations which might or ought to exist between the universities and the profession of journalism'. He saw 'no reason why a university education on the literary and historical side should not raise the status and add to the learning' of journalists.[82] He returned to this theme at the Dublin district's 1908 AGM, when he again stressed that 'those who are to lead public opinion should have a wide general education to enable them to grapple with those great social problems which are looming up before us so rapidly'.[83] His persistence paid off: later that year, the institute and Trinity College held a series of lectures 'suitable for undergraduates who may decide to join the journalistic profession'. Not everyone was supportive of the idea: writing in the *Evening Mail*, William J. Lawrence expressed his agreement with an editor who had privately asserted that journalism was 'not so much a profession as a disease. It can be caught – not taught. Knack presses the button and experience does the rest. The greatest desideratum is aptitude, and that is precisely the one thing that cannot be evolved.'[84]

Nonetheless, the lecture series went ahead, and among the topics addressed were the joys and pitfalls of being a London correspondent, drama criticism, and financial journalism.[85] On the topic of journalism and education, the Editor of the *Westminster Gazette*, J. A. Spender, suggested that a combination of history, law, natural science, and political philosophy would be suitable for aspiring journalists.

If, he declared, there ever came into existence a university for journalists, the 'Professor of Public Opinion' would be the principal post.[86] The ideas of a diploma in journalism and a school of journalism were later floated by Trinity's Provost, but neither developed into workable propositions.[87] In 1910, University College Cork introduced a short-lived 'special course for journalists': students took a wide range of humanities and science subjects as well as journalistic seminars on topics such as 'descriptive article writing, leading article writing, paragraphing, and reviewing' and lectures on the professional aspects of journalism.[88]

In matters of professional practice, neither the Dublin nor the Irish Association districts were shy in defending the integrity of journalists. When, in November 1903, the organisers of a reception for the Lord Lieutenant failed to make any accommodation for journalists, they simply walked out and his speech went unreported. This action led to a special joint meeting of both districts at which support for the journalists' action was expressed by the President of the Institute.[89] Shortly afterwards, both districts amalgamated as the Dublin and Irish Association district.[90] Initially chaired by William A. Locker (Editor, *Irish Times*), by 1910 its membership stood at 104 members, twelve associates and two pupil associates, 'making it the strongest district of the Institute, with the exception of London'.[91] In 1904, it resolved to take legal action against the editor of a local (unnamed) publication for continuously lifting material from other newspapers without acknowledgement or payment, and in 1905 it announced its intention to promote a parliamentary Bill to exempt 'practising journalists who are members of the Institute from serving on juries'.[92] In 1909, after journalists who had attended a rowdy political convention at Dublin's Mansion House were subpoenaed as witnesses in a subsequent court case, the district's executive declared that 'reporters who attend meetings in a professional capacity should not be subpoenaed as witnesses to events that took place or speeches delivered at such meetings'.[93]

But for all this the institute was not, and could not be, by virtue of its royal charter, a trade union. As the years passed, there developed a gulf between its proprietor members who were concerned with professionalism and its working journalist members who were concerned with improving their terms and conditions of employment. As Mark Hampton has pointed out, 'critics of the Institute constantly insisted that the organisation benefited only proprietors and (perhaps) editors, largely by providing social opportunities for them'.[94] There eventually occurred within the ranks of the institute in Britain 'the ultimate rejection of any pretence towards the "professional ideal" by a large number of journalists, who chose instead to think of themselves as "mental labourers" who could benefit more from a trade union than from a professional organisation'.[95] The same tensions were obvious in the Irish branches. At the Dublin district's 1901 AGM, William Locker had observed that the institute was not a trade union: its main objective, he stressed, 'was to raise the status of the members of the profession'.[96] At the district's 1904 AGM, Count George Noble Plunkett annoyed his fellow members when he declared the institute 'the first attempt made amongst English-speaking people towards "Trades Unionism" for the protection of journalists'. To loud cries of 'No, No', he hastily conceded that 'the historic knowledge of others went back further than his'.[97] In short, the institute was powerless to improve its members' terms and conditions of employment. Its membership did not distinguish ordinary working journalists from proprietors, editors, and management. Thus, journalists who wished to raise issues relating to their employment regularly found that their employer, or their employer's peers, dominated the committees of the institute.

Out of this impossible situation emerged the National Union of Journalists (NUJ). Established in Birmingham in 1907, as a trade union its sole objective was to improve its members' terms and conditions of employment. In 1909, two of the union's founding fathers, general secretary William Watts and J. H. Harley, National Executive Council member for London, visited Ireland. They established branches in Dublin, Waterford, Derry, and Newry and recruited nearly 100 members. In Cork, which was a stronghold of the institute (a legacy from Thomas Crosbie's involvement in the institute that would live on until the late 1960s), no members were recruited.[98] The arrival of the NUJ set Irish journalists thinking and encouraged them to again consider the lack of representation for ordinary journalists. From such concerns emerged the Irish Journalists' Association.

Notes

1 *Daily Express*, 3 Feb. 1851, p. 3.

2 The tax on advertisements was abolished in 1853; stamp duty was abolished in 1855; and the tax on newsprint was abolished in 1861.

3 L. M. Cullen, *Eason & Son: A History* (Dublin, 1989), pp. 39 and 5–7.

4 Cullen, *Eason & Son*, pp. 77 and 79. Individual circulation figures are not available for this period.

5 C. Morash, 'Ghosts and wires: the telegraph and Irish space', and F. M. Larkin, 'Green shoots of the new journalism in the *Freeman's Journal*, 1877–90', in K. Steele and M. de Nie (eds), *Ireland and the New Journalism* (New York, 2014), pp. 21–33 and pp. 35–55; quote at p. 39.

6 A. Dunlop, *Fifty Years of Irish Journalism* (Dublin, 1911), p. 120.

7 *The Times*, 29 Jan. 1881, p. 6.

8 *Weekly Irish Times*, 22 Apr. 1905, p. 15. Stringer's death is reported in the *Irish Independent*, 17 Apr. 1905, p. 5.

9 J. Wiener, 'How new was the new journalism?', in J. Wiener (ed.), *Papers for the Millions: The New Journalism in Britain, 1850s–1914* (London, 1988), pp. 47–71.

10 J. Wiener, 'The Americanization of the British press, 1830–1914', in M. Harris and T. O'Malley (eds), *Studies in Newspaper and Periodical History* (Westport, Conn., 1994), pp. 61–74.

11 T. P. O'Connor, 'The new journalism', *The New Review*, 1 (1889), 423–34.

12 H. Fyfe, 'The new journalism', in *T. P. O'Connor* (London, 1934), pp. 137–58, at p. 140.

13 See L. Brake, E. Hill, R. Luckhurst, and J. Mussell (eds), *W. T. Stead: Newspaper Revolutionary* (London, 2012).

14 M. Gayle Backus, *Scandal Work: James Joyce, the New Journalism, and the Home Rule Newspaper Wars* (Notre Dame, Ind., 2013), pp. 62–3. For an account of the Dublin Castle scandal, see M. Dungan, *Mr Parnell's Rottweiler: Censorship and the United Ireland Newspaper, 1881–91* (Dublin, 2014).

15 J. O. Baylen, 'The new journalism in late Victorian Britain', *Australian Journal of Politics and History*, 18:3 (1972), 367–85, at p. 385.
16 Baylen, 'The new journalism', p. 375. See also Wiener, 'How new was the new journalism?' and Steel and de Nie, *Ireland and the New Journalism*.
17 *Irish Times*, 4 Dec. 1899, p. 6.
18 *Irish Times*, 28 Jun. 1902, p. 10.
19 *Irish Times*, 15 Oct. 1903, p. 7.
20 *Irish Times*, 16 Oct. 1903, p. 3.
21 For a full account of the genesis of the *Irish Daily Independent*, see P. Maume, 'Parnellite politics and the origins of Independent Newspapers', in M. O'Brien and K. Rafter (eds), *Independent Newspapers: A History* (Dublin, 2012), pp. 1–13.
22 *Irish Independent*, 2 Jan. 1909, p. 4.
23 M. O'Brien and K. Rafter, 'Commerce and the church: the factors that shaped new journalism in the *Irish Independent*', *Media History*, 21:3 (2015), 252–64.
24 *Irish Independent*, 2 Jan. 1905, p. 4.
25 F. M. Larkin, 'No longer a political side show: T. R. Harrington and the "new" *Irish Independent, 1905–31*', in O'Brien and Rafter (eds), *Independent Newspapers: A History*, pp. 26–38.
26 *Irish Independent*, 12 Sep. 1931, p. 8.
27 C. Kenny, 'Tom Grehan: advertising pioneer and newspaperman', in O'Brien and Rafter (eds), *Independent Newspapers: A History*, pp. 52–66, at p. 59.
28 P. Yeates, 'The life and career of William Martin Murphy', in O'Brien and Rafter (eds), *Independent Newspapers: A History*, pp. 14–25, at p. 14.
29 See *Irish Independent*, 2 Mar. 1908 and 7 Feb. 1910.
30 *Irish Independent*, 6 Nov. 1911, p. 6.
31 *Weekly Irish Times*, 11 Nov. 1911, p. 18.
32 *Irish Independent*, 17 Nov. 1911, p. 4.
33 *Irish Independent*, 17 Nov. 1911, p. 4.
34 *Irish Times*, 26 Oct. 1911, p. 5.
35 *Freeman's Journal*, 31 Oct. 1911, p. 9.
36 *Irish Independent*, 4 Dec. 1911, p. 6.
37 F. M. Larkin, 'A great daily organ: the *Freeman's Journal*, 1763–1924', *History Ireland*, 14:3 (2006), 44–9.
38 *Daily Express*, 3 Feb. 1851, p. 3.
39 *Daily Express*, 28 Oct. 1880, p. 7; 29 Oct. 1880, p. 4; and 30 Oct. 1880, p. 7.
40 *Daily Express*, 19 Jul. 1898, p. 4.
41 *Daily Express*, 21 Jul. 1898, p. 5.
42 *Irish Independent*, 2 Jul. 1921, p. 4.
43 *Newspaper Press Directory and Advertisers' Guide* (London, 1918), p. 211.
44 See *Irish Times*, 20 Jul. 2002, p. 15.
45 *Irish Times*, 29 Mar. 1859, p. 2.
46 *Irish Times*, 22 Oct. 1879, p. 8.
47 *Newspaper Press Directory* (London, 1922), p. 205.
48 For a history of the *Irish Times*, see M. O'Brien, *The Irish Times: A History* (Dublin, 2008).
49 Cullen, *Eason & Son*, p. 5.
50 *Irish Independent*, 1 Jan. 1910, p. 7; *Irish Times*, 27 Aug. 1960, p. 4.
51 For a detailed analysis of the provincial press in Ireland in the late 1800s, see M. L. Legg, *Newspapers and Nationalism: The Irish Provincial Press, 1850–92* (Dublin, 1998).

52 For an account of the interplay between journalism and politics in the Irish Parliamentary Party, see F. M. Larkin, 'Double helix: two elites in politics and journalism in Ireland, 1870–1918', in C. O'Neill (ed.) *Irish Elites in the Nineteenth Century* (Dublin, 2012), pp. 125–36.
53 M. J. F. McCarthy, *The Irish Revolution* (Edinburgh, 1912), p. 129.
54 M. O'Brien and F. M. Larkin (eds), *Periodicals and Journalism in Twentieth Century Ireland* (Dublin, 2014), p. 11.
55 The 1901 and 1911 censuses are searchable at www.census.nationalarchives.ie.
56 M. McDonnell Bodkin, *Recollections of an Irish Judge: Press, Bar and Parliament* (London 1914), p. 28.
57 Bodkin, *Recollections of an Irish Judge*, pp. 28–9.
58 Bodkin, *Recollections of an Irish Judge*, p. 28; Dunlop, *Fifty Years*, p. 3.
59 *Irish Weekly Independent*, 21 Oct. 1899, cited in D. A. J. MacPherson, 'Mary Butler, domesticity, housewifery, and identity in Ireland, 1899–1912', in C. J. Litzenberger and E. Groth Lyon (eds), *The Human Tradition in Modern Britain* (Lanham, Md., 2006), pp. 171–85, at p. 179.
60 *Irish Times*, 13 Feb. 1895, p. 4.
61 O. Lockley, *Nannie Lambert Power O'Donoghue: A Biography* (Preston, 2001), p. 106.
62 *Irish Times*, 10 May 1913, p. 7; 2 Mar. 1937, p. 8.
63 *Weekly Irish Times*, 19 Apr. 1902, p. 16.
64 See C. Morris, *Alice Milligan and the Irish Cultural Revival* (Dublin, 2012).
65 *Irish Times*, 7 Feb. 1887, p. 6.
66 *Weekly Irish Times*, 12 Feb. 1887, p. 6.
67 See J. B. Hall, *Random Records of a Reporter* (Dublin, 1928); and Dunlop, *Fifty Years*.
68 *Irish Times*, 19 Sep. 1887, p. 7.
69 *Irish Times*, 23 Apr. 1888, p. 3.
70 *Irish Times*, 9 Apr. 1888, p. 5.
71 *Irish Times*, 23 Apr. 1888, p. 3.
72 *Irish Times*, 16 Jun. 1888, p. 6. O'Brien makes no reference to the AIJ or his presidency of it in his memoirs, *Recollections* (London, 1905) and *Evening Memories* (Dublin, 1920). There are also no references in his papers held in the Special Collections Department, University College Cork Library.
73 *Irish Times*, 26 Feb. 1889, p. 6.
74 *United Ireland*, 2 Mar. 1889, p. 1; M. O'Brien, 'Journalism and emerging professionalism in Ireland: the Association of Irish Journalists, 1887–90', *Journalism Practice*, 10:1 (2016), 109–22.
75 *Irish Times*, 22 Feb. 1890, p. 6 and 25 Aug. 1890, p. 7.
76 *Irish Times*, 25 Jul. 1892, p. 6.
77 *Irish Times*, 24 Feb. 1890, p. 6.
78 *Freeman's Journal*, 26 Apr. 1890, p. 6 and 28 Apr. 1890, p. 7.
79 *Irish Times*, 27 Sep. 1890, p. 6. Reid was Editor of the *Edinburgh Weekly News*.
80 *Irish Times*, 29 Sep. 1890, p. 6.
81 *Irish Times*, 10 Dec. 1890, p. 7.
82 *Irish Times*, 4 Sep. 1906, p. 6.
83 *Irish Times*, 20 Jan. 1908, p. 10.
84 *Evening Mail*, 17 Dec. 1908, p. 7.
85 For a full list of the lectures delivered, see *Irish Times*, 10 Nov. 1908, p. 5.
86 *Irish Independent*, 8 Mar. 1909, p. 3.

87 *Irish Times*, 18 Jan. 1909, p. 9 and 15 Jan. 1912, p. 9.
88 *Irish Times*, 26 May 1910, p. 7. See also Larkin, 'Double helix: two elites'.
89 *Weekly Irish Times*, 5 Dec. 1903, p. 2.
90 *Irish Times*, 11 Dec. 1903, p. 3.
91 *Irish Times*, 24 Jan. 1910, p. 10.
92 *Irish Times*, 27 Apr. 1904, p. 9; 25 Feb. 1905, p. 5.
93 *Irish Times*, 9 Mar. 1909, p. 6.
94 M. Hampton, 'Journalists and the "professional ideal" in Britain: the Institute of Journalists 1884–1907', *Historical Research*, 72:178 (1999), 183–201, at p. 195.
95 Hampton, 'Journalists and the "professional ideal"', p. 183.
96 *Irish Times*, 18 Feb. 1901, p. 6.
97 *Irish Times*, 16 Jan. 1904, p. 11. Plunkett had occasionally written articles for magazines and had edited a short-lived magazine, *Hibernia*, in 1882.
98 F. Mansfield, *Gentlemen, the Press! Chronicles of a Crusade* (London, 1943), p. 57.

2

High dignity and low salaries

His working week still consists of seven days, he is still expected to make the night joint labourer with the day, regular meal hours do not find any place in the conditions of his employment. His Saturday and Sunday, his night and day still belong entirely to his employer, and that without the slightest recompense in the way of what is universally known as overtime pay.[1]

— The Irish Journalists' Association on working conditions for journalists, 1913

While James Joyce famously captured the daily life of newspaper production in the Aeolus episode of *Ulysses*, little is known about the actual working lives of journalists in the early 1900s.[2] Very few relevant records from this era survive, and what does survive in the way of memoir is mostly anecdotal. In 1911, printers agitated for a forty-eight-hour working week instead of the existing fifty-two-hour week.[3] Since printers were highly unionised and better paid than journalists, it follows that their employment conditions were superior to those of journalists. In 1913, Dublin journalists passed a resolution calling for a basic salary of £160 per annum or roughly £3 per week.[4] In terms of working conditions, split shifts were the norm, and seven-day weeks were not unheard of. There was no salary scale or overtime payments, and individual wage levels were determined by time served, experienced gained, and what proprietors were willing to pay. In terms of representation, there existed the Institute of Journalists – but that admitted proprietors and management as members alongside ordinary journalists and did not concern itself with the bread-and-butter issues of wages and conditions of employment.[5]

The establishment of the NUJ in Britain in 1907 altered the journalistic landscape: that same year, Irish newspaper proprietors established the Irish Newspaper Society to facilitate 'mutual consultation and assistance' among proprietors and senior managers.[6] All the main national daily and weekly newspapers, north and south, were members, and among the issues of mutual concern were 'advertisement rates, railway carriage, the amendment of the law of libel, united action in case of strikes, fraudulent returns'.[7] Among the proprietors and managers who were members were George Crosbie (Proprietor, *Cork Examiner*), William J. Flynn (Manager, *Freeman's Journal*), John J. Simington (Manager, *Irish Times*), William Lombard Murphy (son of William Martin Murphy), William T. Brewster (Manager, *Irish Independent*), and Thomas A. Grehan (Advertising Manager,

Irish Independent). As there was a high degree of cross-membership between the Society and the Institute of Journalists, this further alienated rank-and-file journalists from the institute.

The appeal of a trade union for ordinary journalists that excluded proprietors was too strong to resist, and, in November 1909, the NUJ established branches in Dublin, Waterford, Derry, and Newry and recruited nearly 100 members. The first meeting of the NUJ in Dublin took place at Wynn's Hotel, Abbey Street, when the union's general secretary, William Watts, addressed a gathering of Dublin journalists. A resolution that a Dublin branch be formed was passed, and, at a subsequent meeting, an organising committee was convened.[8] Very little is known about the founding fathers of the union in Ireland other than their names. The first chairman of the Dublin branch was A. C. Cummings; also sitting on the first committee were C. V. Crosby, W. Redmond (*Daily Express*), J. R. Wright, Andrew W. Garbutt (*Daily Express*), F. C. Kidd (*Daily Express*), and H. L. Pichard.[9] There may be a reason as to why so many of its original membership hailed from the *Daily Express*. It appears that working conditions at the paper were very poor: one journalist later observed that it paid 'miserably small salaries' and was 'responsible for introducing "sweat" wages into Dublin'.[10]

Since the NUJ was based in London, this prompted other Dublin journalists, less than a month later, to establish an Irish representative organisation for journalists that excluded proprietors. In December 1909, at a meeting held in the Minerva Hotel in Dublin's Rutland Square, the Irish Journalists' Association (IJA) was established. Among those who organised the inaugural meeting were John B. Hall, a former vice-president of the institute and journalist with the *Freeman's Journal*; John D. Collins (*Daily Express*); Matthew M. O'Hara (*Irish Times* and later editor of the *Weekly Freeman*); William J. Ryan, later editor of the *Evening Telegraph*; and a young journalist, Pierce Beazley, then a reporter with the *Freeman's Journal*.[11] Hall was elected its first president, and sometime later the association declared that its mission was 'to advance the interests of working Journalists and to improve the conditions of their employment, especially in regard to salary, hours, and tenure of office'.[12] Unfortunately, the records of the IJA were destroyed, along with its premises at 65 Middle Abbey Street, during the 1916 Rising. But newspaper reports of its meetings and the journal it published, the *Irish Journalist*, give a unique – if partial – insight into the working lives of journalists in the early 1900s.

While the IJA had aspirations to be a nationwide organisation, over the course of its existence it had mixed fortunes in convincing provincial journalists to join, and, given its support for Home Rule, very little success in recruiting northern journalists. Only 'ordinary working journalists', including editors, could join, and to do so they had to prove that journalism had been their main source of income for at least three years. This neatly excluded newspaper managers, directors, and proprietors from its membership. At its first AGM in 1911, Hall declared that the association's main objective 'was to do something practical in the direction of improving the condition under which journalists are employed'. He also reported that the association had 106 members.[13] Among its members were Maurice Linnane (chief reporter, *Irish Independent*); George MacDonagh (later news editor, *Irish Independent*); John M. O' Keefe (later director of the Government Information Bureau);[14] Thomas F. O'Sullivan (later London correspondent of the *Freeman's Journal* and later again, news editor, *Irish Press*); Michael Knightly (later editor of the Oireachtas Debates and later again, press censor during the Emergency); Michael F. Brunicardi (later editor, *Evening Herald*); Edward (Ned) Lawler (later political reporter, *Irish Independent*, and later again, director of the Government Information Bureau); Joseph Harrington (later editor, *Sligo Champion*); Frank Geary (later editor, *Irish Independent*); David Boyd (later editor, *Waterford Standard*); and Seumas O'Kelly (editor, *Leinster Leader*, and later editor, *Dublin Saturday Post*).[15] Another prominent member was John (Seán) Lester (chief reporter, *Daily Express* and, subsequently, the *Freeman's Journal*, later director of publicity for the Free State government and later again, secretary general of the League of Nations), who was a member of the Irish Republican Brotherhood (IRB) and who was elected to the IJA's executive committee at its 1916 AGM.

Such success in recruiting members attracted the attention of the NUJ, and, from the surviving correspondence, it is clear that both organisations entered into discussions about how they might work together. In February 1912, representatives of the association's committee met with a delegation from the NUJ 'for the purpose of considering proposals with a view to both associations coming to a working arrangement in furtherance of their respective interests'. An agreement was reached, which was to be put before the members of both organisations for ratification.[16] In May 1912, the NUJ's general secretary, William Watts, invited the IJA's secretary, Pierce Beazley, to attend the union's annual delegate conference in Manchester. Beazley attended the conference, and, in a later letter to Watts, informed him 'that the IJA fell in speedily with the idea of a conference of spheres of the National Union Executive, the union's Belfast branch and the IJA executive'.[17] Despite the fraternal intentions, no working arrangement was agreed upon as the NUJ made it a condition that the IJA become a trade union before any joint venture could be embarked upon.[18] In a similar vein, when, in 1914, the Dublin district of the Institute of Journalists proposed an amalgamation, the IJA noted that while its principal objective was 'the improvement of the wages of the working journalist', the institute 'does not trouble about the wage question'.[19]

The IJA and trade unionism

Despite opting not to do business with the NUJ, the issue of trade unionism remained on the agenda. The establishment of the Irish Transport and General Workers' Union (ITGWU) by James Larkin in 1909 and its successful tactics of boycotts and sympathetic strikes radicalised trade unionism. It also startled newspaper proprietors. In 1911, the Irish Newspaper Society was among numerous employer bodies that wrote to Prime Minister Herbert Asquith expressing concerns on picketing, which was described as 'a form of tyranny', and the amalgamation of trade unions, which was described as 'a conspiracy against individual freedom, industrial peace, and national well-being'.[20] The growing strength of the trade-union movement also prompted some within the IJA to consider whether the organisation should become a trade union.

However, its new president, Matthew O'Hara, viewed matters differently. In his address to the association's AGM in January 1913, he declared that the IJA's sole aim was 'the welfare and betterment of the Pressmen of Ireland'. He noted that there was 'nothing aggressive' in the IJA's objectives and that it desired to improve its members' conditions 'by appealing to the fair play of employers'. While he did not feel 'a throwing in of their lot with the other workers of the country [... was] beneath their dignity', he did object to 'the rigid discipline, the levelling process, the detailed regulation of the Trades Union'. As president, he felt that by being 'reasonable and just in their claims, yet firm in pressing them, they should be able to better the condition of the Irish journalist on lines more consonant with the traditions of our calling than those adopted by [the] mass of the workers in the cities and towns of Ireland'.[21] Indeed, it seems there was no love lost between the upper echelons of the IJA (editors, chief reporters, and senior reporters), who viewed journalism as a profession, and the trade-union movement, who sought to represent unskilled workers. In April 1913, at a public meeting to discuss the progress of a dockers' strike, the President of the Trades Council, Thomas McPartlin, declared that the council 'considered that the Press of Dublin had dealt with merely one side of the question, and that side the side of the employers'.[22] In response, the IJA criticised the 'insulting treatment experienced by reporters' and called for a boycott of such meetings 'until an ample public apology has been made by the council'.[23]

Later that year, O'Hara reported that representations to newspaper proprietors had resulted in pay increases for several members.[24] By this time, the showdown between the ITGWU and the Dublin Employers' Association was looming. The latter body was headed by William Martin Murphy, proprietor of Independent Newspapers, and it is quite possible that the pay increases reported by O'Hara were made by newspaper proprietors in appreciation of the importance the press would play in the impending battle with Jim Larkin's union. Murphy himself noted that all employees in Independent Newspapers except the unskilled labourers were 'in trades unions, with whom we have always the best relations, and who, so far from resenting our action with regard to Larkin's bogus union have cordially supported us'.[25] Regardless of whether or not rank-and-file journalists were sympathetic to Larkin during the Great Lockout, the editorial positions of the *Independent* and the *Irish Times* were not. Murphy himself took to the pages of his paper to describe how Larkin 'had the imprudence to endeavour to bring pressure on the composing staff of the Independent papers [... but] it was rather too much for these men to be asked to associate with scum like Larkin and his followers'.[26] For its part, the *Irish Times* accused the ITGWU of 'exercising an abominable tyranny over the working classes of the city'.[27] As a result, Larkin had little time for the Dublin press. Writing shortly after the end of the Lockout, he castigated the press for its coverage of events:

> We wonder if the press of Dublin have a shred of decency left. If so, there is still a suitable bed left for the repose of their dirty foul carcasses. We refer to the

> residual tanks of the Pigeon House sewerage works. Surely for their carnival of lying during the lock-out they deserve eternal rest. What mendacious, brazen-faced monsters they are.[28]

Aware of what had happened in Dublin, provincial journalists seemed wary of joining the IJA for fear of being viewed as trade unionists or troublemakers. In 1914, the association noted that many provincial journalists were 'afraid of [the] movement with reference to the salaries question, and offered the wishy-washy suggestion that if this question of salaries was deleted from our programme "for the present" more members might be induced to come in at that particular centre'.[29] Given its continued emphasis on wages and conditions of employment, in 1914 the association again received unsuccessful overtures from William Watts of the NUJ to work together.[30]

The *Irish Journalist* and journalistic practices

In October 1914, the IJA launched a journal, the *Irish Journalist*, and within its pages its members wrote on the issues that concerned them most. While some wrote in a conciliatory manner, others wrote more provocatively: nonetheless, the journal gives a unique insight into what journalists in the early 1900s were thinking about. A monthly journal, it was established 'to secure the redress of outstanding grievances affecting Irish newspaper workers in the discharge of their onerous and responsible duties: to bring about such reforms as may be considered desirable in their status, their rates of remuneration, their conditions of service'.[31] Edited by Michael F. McGrenahan (*Irish Independent*), it was a platform for members to write about the frustrations they encountered on a daily basis.[32]

The recruitment by Dublin newspapers of rural reporters who took 'an inadequate salary just for the sake of getting to Dublin' was one such issue. One leading article described such reporters as 'our worst foe on the salary question' and noted that if they were 'more careful not to accept salaries below or merely on the edge of the living wage … then the supply will regulate itself automatically along the line of good wages'.[33] The practices of 'blacking' (whereby journalists sent a copy of a story to more than one title) and 'milking' (whereby editors rewrote copy for London titles in return for a fee that reporters did not share in) were criticised numerous times. One correspondent asserted that 'one man with a sheet of carbon keeps a number of other men out of work' and declared that milking was a 'peculiarly mean form of larceny'. If the IJA were a trade union, he concluded, such practices 'would not be permitted for a moment'.[34] The publication of 'outsider copy' – published not because of some 'innate or surface merit but because of the position, social, public, or political, held by the writers' – was decried by another correspondent as 'unfair to the working journalist and detrimental to the status of journalism itself'. Such a practice arose from society's belief 'that the value of an article is to be measured by the name of the person that produces it'. 'Personality', he concluded, had 'largely usurped the place of principle and merit'.[35] Under the IJA's rules, all members were expected to 'discourage in every legitimate way in their power the regular and continuous employment of amateurs and outsiders in newspaper journalism'.[36]

The position of women journalists, virtually invisible at this time, was also discussed. A correspondent, 'Helen', observed that most of the content aimed at female readers came 'from English or Foreign agencies, and that the same "copy" and the same ideas appear simultaneously in various Irish newspapers'. She declared such content as 'monotonous to the readers' and expressed the hope that Irish newspapers would take a lead by employing female journalists:

> Why not give clever Irish girls a chance to enter into the field of journalism in Ireland – not as active competitors with their male fellow-workers, but as co-operators in departments that women can best conduct for women readers? … The Irish Journalists' Association would do a good service to journalism by keeping this fact in mind and it would be to their everlasting credit if they would endeavour to open the way to the profitable employment of brainy young Irishwomen in a field that admirably suits their temperament and talents.[37]

The following month, another correspondent, 'E.M.D.', expressed qualified support for this proposal. While he did not believe that 'women should usurp the places that properly belong to men in Irish journalism', they did have a role to play:

> just as there is a sphere for men so is there one for women, and only a woman knows best how to interpret the mind of her own sex … Let a woman with a capable mind set up a special page or special columns for women; let her pick out the little chatty items that would appeal alike to the grande dame in Merrion Square, or her less fortunate sister in Marlborough Street; let her give the woman's point of view in connection with the latest books or the latest happenings on the Irish stage; let her do these, and the hundred and one other things that women can do well for women, and Irish newspapers will have taken a big step forward in the right direction.[38]

In April 1915, the professional standing of journalists became an issue when the Lord Lieutenant made a speech at the Royal Dublin Society show grounds. No facilities were provided for the journalists assigned to cover the marking. Having made a protest, a table was provided, but it was not allowed to be positioned within the space marked off from the audience and no chairs were provided. In an article, John B. Hall described this treatment as 'humiliating' and asserted that had the speaker not provided the journalists with copies of his speech, 'not one word of it would or could have appeared in any newspaper'. Should the same thing happen again, he declared, 'the reporters present should – as they have done before with good effect – leave in a body and let the blame lie on the shoulders of the official or officials who neglect what they must be taught to regard as one of their primary duties'.[39] Some months later, the lack of reciprocation between officialdom and journalists was highlighted. One correspondent noted that very few of

> the judges, the magistrates the officials and the rest … are in the least shy about seeking favours which may place them in the proper perspective before the

> public; but once they have got their 'whack' out of the obliging Pressmen, the transaction is quite complete, so far as they are concerned.[40]

The issue of Home Rule and what this might mean for journalists in terms of workload and practices also loomed large. Following the passing of the Home Rule Bill in 1912, the IJA and the Dublin and Irish Association branch of the Institute of Journalists established a joint committee 'for the purpose of considering, reporting upon and safeguarding the interests of Irish journalists in connection with the forthcoming establishment of Home Rule'.[41] The first edition of the IJA's journal noted that Home Rule would mean 'much in the way of progress and prosperity in every direction for our neglected and impoverished country' and expressed the hope that the arrangements for reporting debates in the new parliament would be given careful consideration.[42] From a reference in the journal, it seems that an IJA deputation met with Irish Parliamentary Party leader John Redmond to discuss this issue before the First World War broke out.[43] For many journalists in the North, the IJA's support for Home Rule was off-putting; in 1914, its journal noted the 'aloofness of the majority of Belfast Pressmen from what may be described as a national journalistic movement'.[44] As late as July 1916, despite the unsuccessful post-Rising negotiations between John Redmond and David Lloyd George about the immediate implementation of Home Rule, the IJA's president, Matthew O'Hara, was still planning for a Dublin parliament. To his mind, there were many issues to be considered, including 'the size of staffs, the duration of labour demanded, details such as the holding of "boxes" in the Houses and of "gallery" tickets by journalists, the amount of copy to be esteemed a fair day's or night's work in Parliament'.[45]

The *Irish Journalist* and trade unionism

The *Irish Journalist* was also the medium through which those for and against the association becoming a trade union did battle. In his first message to the membership, its president, Matthew O'Hara, acknowledged that the greatest issue for members was 'remuneration for their labour' but noted the issue 'should not be approached in any spirit of hostility to employers' because there was 'no business in which the loyal and friendly partnership of employed and employer is more requisite for mutual success than in the business of the Press'.[46] However, the following month he had strong words on the working conditions of journalists:

> the death-rate of journalists, in Dublin, say, is perfectly appalling … It is largely because their business duties are flung at them in such an unintelligent fashion that all methodological life is impossible; they cannot have fixed regular hours for meals; their day may just as readily end at two o'clock in the morning as at six o'clock in the evening, and their working week is as often one of seven days as of six. Needless to say, a healthy, thrifty, methodical, regular life is out of the question under such conditions.[47]

He insisted that a six-day week and 'a definite number of hours for the working day should be secured for journalists' and noted that this had been achieved in New Zealand.[48] In an unsigned series of articles on working conditions, the journal noted that, in relation to wages, 'the salary of no small number of Irish journalists is little better than that of the scavengers employed by the Dublin Corporation'. It also observed that the journalist – 'more and more a specialised man' – was paid less than the newspaper compositor who, having his trade revolutionised by machinery, was now just 'a glorified type-writing machine manipulator'. The difference in wages was the result of compositors being 'a well-organised body of men', and demands for better wages for journalists would, it concluded, 'remain something resembling a pious opinion unless it has a real genuine effective organisation behind it'.[49] In February 1915, it suggested a minimum weekly salary of £3 10s for all Dublin journalists. It also addressed what it viewed as the unacceptable expenses incurred by journalists in the course of their work:

> he cannot make one collar serve him three days running … On the contrary, when he goes up to the Castle to report a Viceregal deputation, he must be spic and span, as neat and presentable as any of the J.P.s [justices of the peace] or D.L.s [deputy lieutenants] or Knights present. And when he has to report the dinner at the College of Surgeons he must command a 'boiled suit' somehow … The heads of the Metropolitan newspapers expect their reporters to live respectably, to turn out in presentable fashion, to be creditable to their concerns.[50]

Despite such sentiments it again declared that, since journalism was a profession, trade unionism for journalists was not appropriate:

> The necessity in journalism of a perfect understanding between proprietor and journalist, the necessity for some closer and more intimate approach than that of merely wage payer and wage earner must often have struck the thoughtful journalist. The power and influence and success of the Press depend on a nicer and more fraternal adjustment of relations between our employers and ourselves that trades unionism would, perhaps, permit … instead of levelling down to trades unionism, might we not try for a spell, at any rate, to level up? We hold many of the characteristics of a profession. There is a charter of journalism in existence. If we were to insist on professional status … the result all round, and especially from the financial point of view, would be good.[51]

The issue of wages, it concluded, would 'best be settled by a policy of moderation and friendly exchange of views with employers'.[52] It seems this approach did indeed yield some results. An undated (most likely 1915 or 1916) letter from the IJA's secretary to Sir John Arnott, Chairman of the Irish Times Ltd, mentions the increased cost of living caused by the First World War and seeks 'a more generous interpretation of the "sympathetic clause" of the agreement' entered into by proprietors, the IJA and the institute. The letter noted that senior reporters had been paid £3 10s. per week before the war, and, while this had risen to £5 per week, wages were again 'altogether out of proportion to the relative costs of living'.[53]

In June 1915, the *Irish Journalist* underwent a change of editor and editorial direction. Its new editor, Thomas F. O'Sullivan, declared his intention to make the journal 'a real live organ which will grapple with all the subjects that are of vital interest to working journalists, whose wages and conditions of employment in Dublin and throughout the country are simply appalling and degrading'.[54] In the July–August 1915 edition, an article, entitled 'Dublin Reporter's Life' by 'A Victim', referred to journalism as 'a form of refined slavery' and declared that journalists must have:

> the constitution of a steam engine, be full of energy, ability and resource, work long, anxious hours and under the most distressing conditions, carry out the most unreasonable markings, be prepared for attack from the public and those placed over him, and expect little or no appreciation of his work from employers, and all for a princely salary ranging from 35s to £3 10s a week. Who says slavery has been abolished in Ireland?[55]

From then on, the debate on trade unionism took a more dynamic form. In September 1915, the journal declared that 'if a paper cannot afford to give its employees fair wages and reasonable working conditions, the sooner it ceases to exist the better'. It also made a plea for more members in the belief that better organisation would mean grievances, including 'starvation wages and unending hours of labour', would end:

> Salaries would be increased; working hours, where they are excessive, would be reduced. Remuneration for overtime would become a recognised thing in every newspaper office. Undesirables would be prevented from entering our ranks. Journalists who bring discredit on themselves, and on their calling, would be drummed out with ignominy, and the whole prestige of our occupation would be raised. In a word, journalism would in reality become a profession, with all the dignity and emoluments of a profession. It would cease to be an occupation which commanded a lower wage than that paid to a third-rate mechanic, for half the working hours, with Sundays free. We have seen what organisation has done for labour. It can confer the same advantages on Journalism.[56]

One correspondent, 'Reformer', criticised what he viewed as the ease of entry into journalism of 'uneducated wasters and undesirables of all kinds'. Journalism was, he contended, wide open to 'every broken-down clerk, dismissed insurance agent, disbarred canvasser, disenfranchised political wire-puller, and discredited ward-heeler'. Such were 'illiterate bosthoons who talk of the dignity of the Press in tap-rooms, and who bring journalism into contempt every day of the year'.[57] The use of such provocative language drew a stinging rebuke from the association's first president, John B. Hall, who accused the journal of running 'perilously near the worst phases of the Larkinite variety'.[58] Thus began an animated debate on whether the association should become a trade union. In a signed article, Shán Ó Cuív of the *Evening Telegraph* called for trade unionism to be examined again, in place of the 'high dignity and low salaries' option of trying to improve conditions by stressing that journalism was a profession that deserved to be treated better by employers.[59] This call brought forth an anonymous letter from 'Journalist' who warned of 'the tyranny of trade union rules' and who declared that once a member of a trade union,

> the journalist would find himself fettered by rules which forbid him to do this or compel him to do that ... he will find himself hampered at every turn and the rate of his work regulated for him by the pace of the slowest of his fellows, until in the end he becomes a 'shirker' and a 'slacker' like the rest.[60]

This, in turn, prompted a retort from 'Union', who acidly asserted that 'Journalist' must be 'a small shareholder in some newspaper company ... in love with the "dignity" of his "profession"'.[61] The granting of a wage increase to compositors in autumn 1915 brought the issue to a head. As the journal noted, the compositors 'were too well organised to be successfully resisted, so their employers granted the increase with the best grace possible under the circumstances'. In contrast, journalists had 'been playing the part of the jelly-fish too long'; what was needed was 'a little manliness'.[62] It also reported that a motion for the forthcoming AGM had been received requesting that the association's executive committee 'be empowered and directed to have the Association registered as a trades union immediately'.[63]

At the AGM, Matthew O'Hara declared that while 'the salary question was one that would have to be tackled with seriousness and with something approaching finality in the near future', he still preferred 'working upwards' with the journalism-as-profession option rather than 'levelling downwards' towards trade unionism. Putting forward the unionisation motion, John G. Hill (*Freeman's Journal*), who had served on the committee of the Westminster NUJ branch, noted that 'the objection to trades unionism in the minds of some of its opponents was that it dared to try to tread in the path to prosperity beaten by the multitudinous feet of doctors, lawyers and members of other professions'. On the issue of dignity, Shán Ó Cuív declared that 'the dignity of the members of the Association depended on the way in which they conducted themselves in public and in private, and was in no way affected by whether they called themselves trades unionists or not'. To reinforce his point, he alluded to the NUJ, the membership of which, he noted, included most of the leading working journalists in Britain; he had 'never heard it suggested that its members were less respected now by themselves or by the public than they were before they joined the Union'. The motion was eventually carried by a division of fifteen to nine votes. The meeting also passed a motion, proposed by Ó Cuív, instructing the executive committee to consider the advisability of affiliating with the labour movement, or with particular units of the labour movement, and to effect such affiliation if considered desirable.[64]

But those against trade unionism did not take this result lying down. At a subsequent executive committee meeting, Matthew O'Hara gave notice of his intention to call a special general meeting to consider a motion that would rescind the motions passed at the AGM.[65] He also gave notice of a motion requesting the executive committee to consider changing the association into an Irish institute of journalists and obtaining a royal charter for it. This would have had the effect of ensuring that the association could never become a trade union.[66] However, at a subsequent quarterly meeting of the association, it was decided that a plebiscite of members on the issue of trade unionism should take place during the month of April 1916.[67] Political events, however, overtook the association's plans.

The 1916 Rising and the IJA

The Easter Rising of 1916 took everyone by surprise – no more so than the administration in Dublin Castle, which, just some months earlier, had arranged with the War Office in London for a party of Irish journalists to visit the Western Front. Among those who travelled were John E. Healy, Editor of the *Irish Times*, and William J. Flynn, Managing Editor of the *Freeman's Journal*, both of whom were involved in early efforts to coordinate recruitment through the Voluntary War Services League and the Central Council for Recruitment in Ireland.[68] Others who travelled included Cornelius Lehane of the *Irish Independent*; James Crosbie of the *Cork Examiner*; W. G. Anderson, Editor of the *Belfast News-letter*; T. P. O'Donoghue of the *Irish News*; and T. J. W. Kenny, Proprietor and Editor of the *Connacht Tribune*. Over the four-day tour in January 1916, the men visited the various Irish regiments – the 2nd Royal Irish Rifles, the 2nd Royal Irish Regiment, and the Ulster Division – in the trenches, witnessed an aerial battle, and visited the town of Albert, which had been destroyed by German shelling. In the feature articles that followed, of the national titles it was the *Irish Times* that was most effusive about the duty of able-bodied men to enlist. As Charles Townshend has noted, as the losses and injuries suffered by the 10th (Irish) Division at Gallipoli became public knowledge, the Irish Parliamentary Party's support for the war 'was gradually revealed to be a major political encumbrance' – a process that undoubtedly had knock-on effects on the *Freeman's Journal*.[69] For its part, the *Irish Independent*, always mindful of its circulation, remained wary of being too closely associated with recruitment – prompted in part by the July 1915 call by Irish bishops on John Redmond to withdraw Irish Parliamentary Party support for the war.[70] But whatever coverage the War Office secured as a result of the expedition, it dissipated rapidly in the aftermath of the Rising.[71]

As with all other publications, the *Irish Journalist* was affected by the events of Easter Week 1916. Its premises on Middle Abbey Street in Dublin's city centre were occupied by the Irish Volunteers and ultimately destroyed. Publication of the journal was suspended until August, and that edition listed the members of the IJA who had taken part in the Rising. The association's secretary, Piaras Béaslaí, as Pierce Beazley had recently begun styling himself, was sentenced to three years' penal servitude but was released in 1917, whereupon he again resumed his duties as secretary.[72] A member of the Gaelic League, Béaslaí sat on the provisional committee of the Irish Volunteers at its formation in 1913. In January 1916, he was dispatched to Liverpool by Seán Mac Diarmada to pass on a coded message to a contact who was helping to organise the ill-fated attempt by Germany to supply arms for the Rising.[73] Béaslaí later edited *An tÓglach*, the journal of the Irish Volunteers, and was elected to the first Dáil, at which he proposed the adoption of the Proclamation of Independence.[74] Indeed, it seems that the IJA premises were used as a safe space within which to progress some of the planning of the Rising.

Some days before the Rising, Michael Knightly, an IRB member and journalist with the *Irish Independent*, disturbed a meeting taking place in the building. When he was eventually allowed entry, he was introduced to several senior IRB members who had been consulting a Dublin street map. He was also pointedly asked whether he would be 'turning out on Sunday'.[75]

Béaslaí and Knightly were just two of several journalists imprisoned for taking part in the Rising. As the *Irish Journalist* put it, 'numbers of other equally brilliant young Pressmen and literary men have been identified with the movement which culminated in an effort to establish an Irish Republic and are to-day bravely paying the penalty in English dungeons and British detention camps'. Other journalists imprisoned included Robert Brennan and David Sears of the *Enniscorthy Echo*; Arthur Griffith, Editor of *Nationality*; James Murphy of the *Saturday Post*; and Herbert Pim, Editor of the *Irishman*.[76] In an attempt to remain an apolitical organisation, the journal noted that it was the duty of the association, 'without committing itself to approval or disapproval of the Rising, to take steps with the object of seeing that our colleagues in convict establishments are treated as political offenders and not as common criminals'.[77] However, it seems that not all Dublin journalists were on the side of the Volunteers; curiously, the journal noted that had an Irish republic been established, 'four journalists would have been asked to answer a charge of high treason'. The killing of Francis Sheehy-Skeffington – 'the brave young journalist who was the champion of all weak causes' – while in military custody was described as 'one of the saddest tragedies' of the Rising.[78] No mention was made of the two other journalists – Patrick McIntyre (*Searchlight*) and Thomas Dixon (*The Eye-opener*) – who were killed alongside Sheehy-Skeffington.[79]

Reporting the Rising was, the journal noted, 'a comparatively safe affair'. From the second day onwards, journalists were prevented by the military from venturing into the firing line. This, the journal remarked, was just as well 'as Dublin reporters have never been paid the salaries of war correspondents'.[80] It also briefly mentioned the death of a journalist, Patrick Reynolds, of the *Evening Mail*, who 'received three bullet wounds in Dame St on Easter Monday'.[81] Reynolds was, the *Evening Mail* observed, 'one of the innocent victims of the rebellion': as he tried to make his way out of the firing line, he had been caught in the crossfire between the rebels, who had seized the newspaper's building on Parliament Street, and the soldiers, who had attacked it from Dublin Castle.[82] On the military censorship that had been imposed on publications, the journal had some choice words:

> As Journalists, we believe that the people least qualified to censor Journalists' work are half-educated military officers and thick-skulled Co. Inspectors of police. Yet these are the very persons who sit in ignorant judgment on the work of competent Pressmen in this unfortunate country. Why Journalists have not been employed in connection with censorship is more than we can understand. The explanation probably is that it could not be done so stupidly by them, and that all sources of annoyance to Pressmen and the public might be removed.[83]

It also noted that one unnamed Dublin newspaper had been offered the job of supplying shorthand reporters to the trial of John (Eoin) MacNeill, the Chief of

Staff of the Irish Volunteers, who had not taken part in the Rising. However, no journalist would undertake the posting as 'the trial was of a political character, and involved the prisoner's life'.[84]

Trade unionism and dissolution

Despite the Rising, the debate on the association becoming a trade union continued. Those against the proposition viewed the Rising as an opportunity to stop such moves; the first edition of the *Irish Journalist* published after the Rising noted that while the association had agreed to hold a plebiscite on the trade-union issue, it could not afford 'for the present at least, to indulge in the luxury of even discussing subjects on which there is a sharp conflict of opinion amongst our members'.[85] But those who had succeeded in getting the trade-union motions passed at the February 1916 AGM did not take such sentiments lightly.

In the subsequent edition, Shán Ó Cuív, who had been elected to the executive committee at the 1916 AGM, returned to the fray with an article that was highly critical of the association's executive committee. He noted that the AGM had 'passed a resolution in favour of the registration of the Association. Notice of the resolution had appeared on the agenda and it was passed in a perfectly regular way at the meeting.' However, when the executive committee began to put this decision into practice, 'some members developed strong opposition to the proposal'. After many meetings, and possibly to avoid a split, a referendum had been agreed on, but, as Ó Cuív put it, 'the vote was to have been taken on May Day, but when May Day arrived journalists had something else to think about'. Calling for the association to embark on 'an active organising campaign', Ó Cuív asserted that if it could not do that before the next general meeting, 'some member ought to give notice of motion that the Association be dissolved'.[86]

Thereafter, the records of what happened to the association become scarce. The last edition of the *Irish Journalist* was published in October 1916, but within the national newspapers there are occasional references to the IJA's fortunes. At the association's 1917 AGM, Matthew O'Hara was replaced as president by John D. Collins (*Irish Times*).[87] Subsequent presidents included Shán Ó Cuív and Michael Knightly.[88] In February 1918, a special general meeting was held to consider whether or not the association should be dissolved.[89] It lived to fight another day; a report in the *Irish Independent* in October 1918 noted that a meeting of Dublin journalists 'unanimously decided' to request the association to summon an AGM 'to put into effect the terms of a resolution of 1919 [sic] forming the association into a trade union'. This, presumably, was meant to have read '1916'![90]

At the association's November 1918 AGM, Shán Ó Cuív was elected president.[91] A report of the meeting noted that the executive committee was empowered to register the association as a trade union and affiliate to the wider trade-union movement if so desired.[92] In 1919, it finally affiliated to the Dublin Printing and Kindred Trades Alliance and wrote to the newspaper proprietors' organisation, the

Irish Newspapers Managers' Association, requesting a review of journalists' salaries and the implementation of a six-day week.[93] This move prompted the Institute of Journalists to seek a discussion with the association on the subject of salaries.[94] This combined action resulted in 'some favourable results in improving conditions of service and increasing salaries'.[95]

With the establishment of the Irish Free State, the IJA was determined to position itself as the premier representative association for journalists. In January 1922, it wrote to Dáil Éireann describing itself as 'the only Irish organisation representing the overwhelming majority of Irish journalists and having no connection with a foreign body' and seeking official recognition 'as the only body entitled to speak for Irish journalists'.[96] The letter was forwarded to the Minister for Publicity, Desmond FitzGerald, who promised to deal with the matter. There the matter rested.[97] The following year, the accommodation and facilities afforded to journalists within the new parliament became an issue. In June 1923, political reporters walked out of the Dáil halfway through a debate in protest at the lack of facilities provided for them. This had an instantaneous effect: the Ceann Comhairle (speaker) wrote to the association with suggestions as to how parliament would properly accommodate journalists.[98] The following October, the Press Gallery Committee was established to liaise with the clerk of the Dáil on matters affecting the work of journalists in parliament. The first chairman of this committee was William Clarke (*Belfast Telegraph*), and its first secretary was Frank Geary (later editor of the *Irish Independent*).[99] In July 1924, Thomas Johnson, leader of the Labour Party, accused the political journalists of not giving 'an intelligent criticism or an intelligent summary of the work that is done in the Dáil'.[100] In response, the Press Gallery Committee and the IJA criticised the fact that a TD was 'permitted to abuse the privileges of the House by making such sweeping and unfounded charges'.[101] This protest was to be the IJA's swansong; with its membership declining, towards the end of 1924 it merged with the Dublin and Irish Association branch of the Institute of Journalists.[102] By then, the landscape of journalism in Ireland had changed fundamentally.

Notes

1 National Library of Ireland (NLI), Piaras Béaslaí papers, Ms. 33,981(9), text of Matthew O'Hara's speech to IJA, Jan. 1913.

2 See T. Killeen, 'From the "Freeman's General" to the "dully expressed": James Joyce and journalism', in K. Rafter (ed.), *Irish Journalism before Independence: More a Disease than a Profession* (Manchester, 2011), pp. 201–12.

3 *Irish Times*, 11 Jan. 1911, p. 9.

4 *Irish Times*, 9 Jun. 1913, p. 7. For comparison purposes, the salary scale for male national teachers in 1913 ranged from £84 to £192. See M. Moroney, *National Teachers' Salaries and Pensions, 1831–2000* (Dublin, 2007), p. 70.

5 The newspaper reports of the meetings of the Irish branches of the institute, while plentiful, are very sparse in detail other than listing the membership of its committee and the administration of its unemployment and orphan funds.

6 *Irish Times*, 25 Feb. 1907, p. 8. Its first president was R. H. H. Baird (*Belfast Evening Telegraph*), and its first secretary was W. T. Brewster (Manager, *Irish Independent*). For a list of its members, see *Irish Times*, 7 Apr. 1919, p. 6. In the Free State, this group would eventually become known as the 'Newspapers Managers' Committee'.
7 *Irish Times*, 15 Mar. 1910, p. 9.
8 *Irish Times*, 15 Nov. 1909, p. 6.
9 In the 1930s, Cummings wrote occasional articles for the *Irish Independent* about the politics of France (21 Nov. 1936, p. 10) and the military defences being constructed by France and Russia against Nazi Germany (15 Jul. 1938, p. 10); *Irish Times*, 22 Nov. 1909, p. 9 and 20 Dec. 1909, p. 5.
10 NLI, Piaras Béaslaí papers, Ms. 33,934(20), undated letter but most likely 1912 or 1913.
11 NLI, Piaras Béaslaí papers, Ms. 33,932(18), letter regarding general meeting of journalists, 11 Dec. 1909. Born in Liverpool in 1881, Percy Frederick Beazley was known in Ireland as Pierce Beazley and later, and more commonly, as Piaras Béaslaí. His father, P. L. Beazley, was editor of the *Catholic Times*; see *Irish Times*, 1 Dec. 1923, p. 6.
12 *Irish Times*, 21 Dec. 1909, p. 7. Hall makes no mention of the IJA in his memoir, *Random Records of a Reporter* (Dublin, 1928); *Irish Journalist*, 1:4 (Jan. 1915), p. 4.
13 *Irish Times*, 20 Jan. 1911, p. 9.
14 O'Keefe is variously mentioned in reports as Saun O'Keefe, Sean O'Keefe, Sean Ó Cuív and Shán Ó Cuív. He worked as a sub-editor at the *Evening Telegraph* and the *Freeman's Journal* and later joined the *Irish Independent* of which he became Irish editor in 1931. He was appointed the first director of the Government Information Bureau in 1934.
15 Names are taken from various newspaper reports of the IJA's meetings from 1909 onwards.
16 *Irish Times*, 26 Feb. 1912, p. 4.
17 NLI, Piaras Béaslaí papers, Ms. 33,932(19/20), Watts letter, dated 1 May 1912; Béaslaí reply undated but most likely Jul. 1912.
18 *Irish Journalist*, 1:12 (Oct. 1915), p. 2.
19 *Irish Journalist*, 1:4 (Jan. 1915), pp. 6–7.
20 *Irish Times*, 28 Oct. 1911, p. 8.
21 NLI, Piaras Béaslaí papers, Ms. 33,981(9), text of O'Hara speech, Jan. 1913.
22 *Irish Times*, 1 Apr. 1913, p. 8. (In the report, McPartlin's name is misspelled as McPartland.)
23 *Irish Times*, 7 Apr. 1913, p. 7.
24 *Irish Times*, 9 Jun. 1913, p. 7.
25 *Irish Independent*, 27 Aug. 1913, p. 7.
26 *Irish Independent*, 27 Aug. 1913, p. 7.
27 *Irish Times*, 29 Aug. 1913, p. 6.
28 *Irish Worker*, 4 Apr. 1914, cited in D. Keogh, *The Rise of the Working Class: The Dublin Trade Union Movement and Labour Leadership, 1890–1914* (Belfast, 1982), p. 224.
29 *Irish Journalist*, 1:2 (Nov. 1914), pp. 6–7.
30 *Irish Times*, 24 Jan. 1914, p. 10.
31 *Irish Journalist*, 1:1 (Oct. 1914), p. 1.
32 *Irish Independent*, 2 Nov. 1948, p. 6.
33 *Irish Journalist*, 1:5 (Feb. 1915), pp. 2–3.
34 *Irish Journalist*, 2:5 (May–Aug. 1916), p. 2.
35 *Irish Journalist*, 1:6 (Mar. 1915), pp. 1–2.
36 *Irish Journalist*, 1:4 (Jan. 1915), p. 4.
37 *Irish Journalist*, 1:6 (Mar. 1915), pp. 2–3.

38 *Irish Journalist*, 1:7 (Apr. 1915), p. 4.
39 *Irish Journalist*, 1:9 (Apr. 1915), pp. 6–7. In his memoir, *Random Records*, Hall gives examples of when reporters walked out of meetings due to lack of facilities being provided for them (pp. 226–9).
40 *Irish Journalist*, 1:9 (Jun. 1915), p. 2.
41 NLI, Piaras Béaslaí papers, Ms. 33,932 (20), letter dated 20 Aug. 1913.
42 *Irish Journalist*, 1:1 (Oct. 1914), pp. 1–3.
43 *Irish Journalist*, 2:5 (May–Aug. 1916), p. 2.
44 *Irish Journalist*, 1:1 (Oct. 1914), p. 4.
45 *Irish Journalist*, 2:5 (May–Aug. 1916), p. 3.
46 *Irish Journalist*, 1:1 (Oct. 1914), pp. 1–2.
47 *Irish Journalist*, 1:2 (Nov. 1914), p. 2.
48 *Irish Journalist*, 1:2 (Nov. 1914), p. 2.
49 *Irish Journalist*, 1:3 (Dec. 1914), p. 2.
50 *Irish Journalist*, 1:5 (Feb. 1915), pp. 2–3.
51 *Irish Journalist*, 1:5 (Feb. 1915), pp. 2–3.
52 *Irish Journalist*, 1:5 (Feb. 1915), pp. 2–3.
53 There is no copy of the agreement in the file. NLI, Piaras Béaslaí papers, Ms. 33,934(22), undated letter. Later NUJ files refer briefly to a 1919 agreement between journalists and proprietors, but, again, no copy was found (Historic Collections Research Centre [HCRC], NUJ, Dublin branch minutes, 8 Feb. 1930).
54 *Irish Journalist*, 1:11 (Sep. 1915), p. 1.
55 *Irish Journalist*, 1:10 (Jul. and Aug. 1915), pp. 4–5.
56 *Irish Journalist*, 1:11 (Sep. 1915), p. 1.
57 *Irish Journalist*, 1:11 (Sep. 1915), p. 5. The terms 'canvasser' refers to those men who sold advertising on behalf of newspapers.
58 *Irish Journalist*, 1:12 (Oct. 1915), p. 3.
59 *Irish Journalist*, 1:12 (Oct. 1915), p. 2.
60 *Irish Journalist*, 1:13 (Nov. 1915), p. 6.
61 *Irish Journalist*, 1:14 (Dec. 1915), p. 6.
62 *Irish Journalist*, 2:1 (Jan. 1916), p. 1.
63 *Irish Journalist*, 2:1 (Jan. 1916), pp. 1 and 5.
64 *Irish Journalist*, 2:2 (Feb. 1916), pp. 4–5.
65 *Irish Journalist*, 2:2 (Feb. 1916), p. 6.
66 *Irish Journalist*, 2:3 (Mar. 1916), p. 6.
67 *Irish Journalist*, 2:5 (May–Aug. 1916), p. 7.
68 *Irish Times*, 21 Apr. 1915, p. 10 and 24 Apr. 1915, p. 4. In later years, Flynn produced the first guide to membership of the Irish parliament. *The Oireachas Companion and Saorstát Guide* was first published in 1928 and continued in various guises until 1945.
69 C. Townshend, *Easter 1916: The Irish Rebellion* (London, 2005), p. 71.
70 M. Walsh, *The News from Ireland: Foreign Correspondents and the Irish Revolution* (London, 2011), p. 49.
71 Each of the titles published a series of articles based on the expedition between Jan. and Apr. 1916. See M. O'Brien, 'With the Irish in France: The national press and recruitment in Ireland 1914–1916' in *Media History*, 22:2 (2016), 159–73.
72 *Irish Independent*, 18 Jun. 1917, p. 4.
73 See Béaslaí's account of these activities in *Irish Independent*, 24 Apr. 1952, pp. 6 and 8. See also Bureau of Military History Witness Statement (BMHWS) 675 (Béaslaí).
74 *Weekly Irish Times*, 25 Jan. 1919, p. 1.

75 BMHWS 833 (Knightly), p. 2.
76 *Irish Journalist*, 2:5 (May–Aug. 1916), p. 1.
77 *Irish Journalist*, 2:5 (May–Aug. 1916), p. 6.
78 *Irish Journalist*, 2:5 (May–Aug. 1916), p. 1. The co-founder of the *Irish Citizen* (the journal of the Irish Women's Franchise League), Sheehy-Skeffington had been trying to prevent looting in the city centre when he was arrested and later shot dead for no apparent reason.
79 See H. Oram, *The Newspaper Book: A History of Newspapers in Ireland, 1649–1983* (Dublin, 1983), p. 128.
80 *Irish Journalist*, 2:5 (May–Aug. 1916), p. 1.
81 *Irish Journalist*, 2:5 (May–Aug. 1916), p. 7. See also *Irish Independent*, 26 Apr. 1916, p. 4.
82 *Evening Mail*, 4 Aug. 1916, p. 6.
83 *Irish Journalist*, 2:5 (May–Aug. 1916), p. 3.
84 *Irish Journalist*, 2:5 (May–Aug. 1916), p. 1.
85 *Irish Journalist*, 2:5 (May–Aug. 1916), p. 7.
86 *Irish Journalist*, 2:6 (Sep.-Oct. 1916), p. 4.
87 *Irish Independent*, 18 Jun. 1917, p. 4.
88 *Irish Independent*, 26 Nov. 1918, p. 4 and 14 Aug. 1940, p. 6; *Weekly Irish Times*, 6 Nov. 1920, p. 5 and *Irish Times*, 21 Dec. 1965, p. 12.
89 NLI, Piaras Béaslaí papers, Ms. 33,933(3), letter dated 12 Feb. 1918.
90 *Irish Independent*, 28 Oct. 1918, p. 4.
91 *Irish Independent*, 26 Nov. 1918, p. 4.
92 *Irish Independent*, 26 Nov. 1918, p. 4.
93 *Irish Times*, 13 Jan. 1919, p. 3.
94 *Irish Times*, 17 Feb. 1919, p. 7.
95 *Freeman's Journal*, 20 Jan. 1920, p. 4.
96 National Archives of Ireland (NAI), DE 4/11/55, letter dated 30 Jan. 1922.
97 NAI, DE 4/12/82. The letter was also forwarded to Piaras Béaslaí, former secretary of the IJA, who was by then working as a translator in Dáil Éireann. See NLI, Piaras Béaslaí papers, Ms. 33,914(5).
98 *Freeman's Journal*, 15 Jun. 1923, p. 5.
99 *Irish Times*, 13 Oct. 1923, p. 6.
100 Dáil Éireann Debates (DED), vol. 8 (col. 2288–90), 25 Jul. 1924.
101 *Irish Times*, 2 Aug. 1924, p. 5.
102 *Irish Times*, 7 Dec. 1942, p. 3 and 19 Jan. 1925, p. 5.

3

Free State – free press?

It is not the ordinary function of journalists to act as censors of public morals. That is the duty of the clergy and Vigilance Committees of which we heard so much a few years ago, but of which we hear so little now. But neither are journalists under any obligation to canonise filth. Yet, this they frequently do by lauding objectionable entertainments.[1]

— 'Self-Respect' on journalists and entertainment, 1915

As the momentum for Independence grew in the early 1900s, the mainstream press found itself caught between a new system being born out of violence and the old system dying – but not without an equally violent struggle to hold on. Editors and journalists found themselves in the same position. In such an environment, it was impossible to please both the British administration and the Irish Republican Army (IRA). Many proprietors, editors, and journalists found themselves bearing the brunt of threats and intimidation from both parties to the conflict. During the War of Independence, the British administration and the IRA viewed the support of the press as essential to their success. Suppression, intimidation, and the destruction of printing presses were the mechanisms by which both sides sought to bring editors and newspapers into line. The moves towards Independence did, however, result in some journalistic innovations. During the Easter Rising of 1916, it was from the Irish School of Wireless Telegraphy, based at the intersection of O'Connell and Lower Abbey Streets in Dublin's city centre, that radio was first used to address a mass audience. Working on an old 1.5-kilowatt transmitter, the rebels spent nineteen hours using Morse code to signal to passing ships that a republic had been declared. Given that up to then wireless telegraphy had been used only for point-to-point communication, it is believed that the rebels' message was the first broadcast; certainly it was the first live broadcast from a conflict zone.[2]

Indeed, it is important to acknowledge that many journalists were active republicans or supportive of the struggle for independence. Piaras Béaslaí, Secretary of the IJA, was also the IRA's director of publicity, while David Boyd (*Evening Mail*) had taken part in the Howth gunrunning.[3] In 1915, Larry de Lacy of the *Enniscorthy Echo* fled to America to escape arrest for rebel activities.[4] At the *Irish Independent*, David Sears, Ned Lawler, Joseph Harrington, and Martin Pender were all involved in the republican movement.[5] Also at the *Independent*, Michael Knightly used his position as a reporter to pass intelligence information to the IRA – particularly photographs of persons of interest.[6] At the *Freeman's Journal*, Thomas F. O'Sullivan and John (Seán) Lester were supporters of the republican movement.[7]

As the conflict intensified, so too did reactions to press coverage of it. In December 1919, the IRA took offence at the *Irish Independent*'s coverage of its attempted killing of the Lord Lieutenant, Viscount French: 'the office was taken possession of by about forty men [and] their leader lectured the editor [T. R. Harrington] for the use of the term "murder" when more harmless words like "assassination" were in use'. The men's leader then 'tossed a penny to determine whether they should shoot the editor or smash the company's machinery' before hammers and crowbars were used to smash the presses. In 1920, the Black and Tans raided the *Independent*'s premises and demanded to view the original of a letter that had been published. When the sub-editor refused, he was 'beaten with a revolver butt, and kicked about the room [and told] if he wasn't careful he might find his own body in the River Liffey [and] he left his job at once'.[8] At the *Freeman's Journal*, things were not much better. In December 1919, it was suppressed for publishing articles deemed offensive to the British military. The articles in question had criticised the planned establishment of a new auxiliary force.[9] Following the passing of the Restoration of Order in Ireland Act in August 1920 – which made it an offence for publications to 'spread false reports or make false statements; or spread reports or make statements' that might cause disaffection with the British government – the paper's proprietors, Martin FitzGerald and Hamilton Edwards, and its editor, Patrick Hooper, appeared before a military court in November 1920 charged with publishing what the military authorities deemed to be false reports of the conflict. They were sentenced to twelve months' imprisonment but were released in early 1921 on 'medical grounds' following the intervention of the British Prime Minister, David Lloyd George.[10] FitzGerald later played a central role as an intermediary between republicans and Dublin Castle as both sides negotiated a truce in the summer of 1921.[11]

Recalling this period much later, then *Irish Times* deputy editor Robert Smyllie remembered that on the night of Bloody Sunday (November 1920), he and then editor John E. Healy were arrested by a party of drunken auxiliaries who insisted they were 'Sinn Féiners and, consequently, must be shot'. Taken to a house and placed against a wall, their lives were spared when the householder recognised them and telephoned Dublin Castle, which rushed a group of officers to the house.[12] The *Cork Examiner* also suffered intimidation from both sides. In September 1919, it was suppressed by crown forces for three days for printing the Dáil Éireann loan prospectus, while in December 1920 it was forced at gunpoint to publish intimidating notices signed by the 'Black and Tans' and the 'Anti-Sinn Féin Society'. Later that month, a group claiming to be from the IRA severely damaged its printing press.[13] Such incidents prompted the paper's proprietor, George Crosbie, to reflect on the unpredictability of newspaper production: 'Between the Government and the Extremists, you cannot be sure how long you will be permitted to produce your newspapers.'[14]

The increasingly life-threatening nature of journalism prompted a monster meeting of journalists in Dublin's Gresham Hotel in December 1920. The meeting, convened jointly by the Institute of Journalists and the IJA, was also attended by British and American journalists. The meeting's chairman – 'the [unnamed] senior member of the Dublin Press' – declared that in the preceding weeks 'instances of absolute terrorism had occurred where individual Pressmen had been not only intimidated, but violently attacked when performing their duties'. It was essential, he concluded, that journalists let the public know 'something of the intolerable grievances which they labour under and have those grievances published … to the nations of the world'.[15]

In his address, the Chairman of the Dublin district of the Institute of Journalists, John P. Gaynor, asserted that 'with the solitary exception of Bolshevik Russia, there was nothing to compare with the system of terrorism at present carried on in Ireland'. He mentioned the armed raids on the three national titles as evidence of the methods by which journalists were being 'coerced and terrorised'. The press, he concluded, 'had always been the guardian and protector of popular liberties, and never was there a time when it was more necessary to exercise its functions freely in Ireland'. A resolution protesting against the use of force or threats towards newspapers or journalists and demanding that proprietors and journalists charged with offences be tried by civil tribunal was deemed by many attendees as not strong enough. Ultimately, it was the President of the IJA, Michael Knightly, who proposed the final, rather one-sided, resolution protesting 'in the strongest possible form the treatment of journalists in Ireland by the Crown forces'. The meeting also agreed to 'compile a detailed statement of the acts of terrorism, violence and intimidation perpetrated' against journalists working in Ireland and to send it to the 'Press associations and Governments of the world'.[16]

One impartial observer, Chris O'Sullivan, an Australian journalist who arrived in Dublin in autumn 1919 and acted as a special correspondent for the *Sydney Sun* while also writing for the *Irish Times*, later wrote of the hair-raising experiences of journalists during this period. While passing the offices of the *Freeman's Journal* one day, he noticed its staff being 'hauled out into the street by the Auxiliaries and cuffed and kicked':

> As I watched the raid from a footpath 30 yards away an Auxiliary ordered me off the street. I stood my ground, saying I was a newspaper man, and produced a military SHQ [Sector Headquarters] identification pass signed by an officer of the General Staff. The Auxiliary jabbed me in the stomach with a large Webley revolver, swung me about and kicked my hind parts. His argument was unanswerable.[17]

The official press pass, issued by military HQ was, according to O'Sullivan, worthless. Having arrived at the scene of a raid by regular British units with another reporter, they sought unsuccessfully to watch events unfold:

> A Tommy sergeant ordered us away, and when I produced my pass and asked for the officer in charge at that point, he told us to get right out of the street (50 yards back). We stood fast and the sergeant drew his revolver, promising faithfully to

> blow our brains out if we didn't leave the street at once. At such moments, one ceases to argue.[18]

Similar to Robert Smyllie and John E. Healy, O'Sullivan had a narrow escape on Bloody Sunday:

> I heard a rattle of machine gun fire at the football meeting at Croke Park. Approaching the oval with two other men I was fired upon by a Tommy who had apparently failed his marksmanship test. The three of us took cover, and after a while fled the spot. Other pressmen were actually warned they would be shot if they put in appearance at certain places.[19]

Having concluded that Dublin was becoming 'too sticky', after many months of convincing republican contacts of his *bona fides*, O'Sullivan secured an interview with Éamon de Valera that was syndicated around the world and that allowed him to secure work elsewhere.[20]

One interesting aspect of the role played by the press in the long struggle for independence is that it inspired a new phrase, 'the mosquito press', which has remained in use since to describe cheaply produced publications that sting at those in authority. According to the *Irish Times*, it was the journalist and poet Tom Kettle who coined the phrase to describe the early Sinn Féin periodicals, but, writing in *The Bell*, P. S. O'Hegarty attributed the phrase to Augustine Birrell, Chief Secretary for Ireland between 1907 and 1916.[21] The War of Independence was followed by a short but bloody civil war in which editors and journalists again endured much intimidation. In March 1922, having taken offence at its coverage of the conflict, anti-Treaty forces destroyed the printing presses of the *Freeman's Journal*. While the Editor of the *Irish Independent*, T. R. Harrington, was forced to sleep in the newspaper building because of threats to his life, shots were fired at the house of *Irish Times* editor John E. Healy.[22] In January 1923, Denis McGrath, office manager of the *Cork Examiner*, was shot on his way home from work, while the following month George Crosbie's home was burned to the ground.[23]

Censorship of publications

As the Free State emerged from the Civil War in 1923, Irish journalism began to adjust to the reality of Independence. Despite the revolutionary zeal with which the republican movement had brought about political independence, in social terms, the revolutionaries were, as justice minister Kevin O'Higgins described them in 1923, 'probably the most conservative-minded revolutionaries that ever put through a successful revolution'.[24] As the new state found its feet, this conservatism was reflected in the government's legislative programme. In 1923, the Intoxicating Liquor Act, which curtailed and regulated the opening hours of public houses, was passed, as was the Censorship of Films Act, which, as the *Irish Times* put it, sought to deal with 'the films which come from the neurotic studios of Los Angeles and Berlin'.[25]

The following year, dancing and the dress sense of females caught the eyes of the Catholic hierarchy. Cardinal Michael Logue declared that Ireland could no longer pride itself on 'the reserve and scrupulous modesty of her women and girls [as] there seems to be a rivalry among them to see how little dress they can wear without incurring universal reprobation'. Imported dances also caused anxiety: he thought their names were 'bizarre', and he viewed them as 'the outcrop of the corruption of the age, most objectionable on the score of morality'.[26] He was not alone: the Archbishop of Cashel, John Harty, condemned the 'abnormal craze for dancing and other amusements', while the Bishop of Galway, Thomas O'Doherty, condemned 'the evil craze of dancing' and went so far as to 'formally forbid' the people of his diocese from organising or taking part in Saturday night dances.[27]

Post-Civil War, the moral crusade against objectionable publications started anew. Crime journalism, in particular, moved centre stage. In an article in the *Irish Ecclesiastical Record*, Revd David Barry declared that the 'publication of every crime is, no doubt, more or less likely to lead those who are weak to its commission, by familiarising their minds with it, lessening their abhorrence of it, and showing them that the perpetration of it is not unthinkable'. Barry noted that journalists often justified crime coverage on the grounds that 'the fear of shame and disgrace incidental to publicity [exerted] a wholesome and restraining influence on those whose sense of propriety is not quite dead'. However, Barry did not believe this and declared that it was

> important for journalists to realise that reporting these lecherous cases cannot be defended on the plea of whetting the legitimate curiosity of the public, or as a warning against the commission of sin. Its sole justification or palliation is to be looked for in the financial return due to the appeal this species of journalism makes to the cruder sentiments or lower instincts of the public.[28]

An important factor in the revival of the crusade was the Catholic hierarchy's Lenten pastorals of the 1920s. In his 1925 pastoral, the Archbishop of Cashel, John Harty, noted the 'unhealthy influx of foreign immoral literature into many places' and how this was 'likely to pollute the minds and lives of our young men and women if stern measures [were] not taken to repress this evil'. He contended that the establishment of 'a flourishing branch of the Catholic Truth Society in each parish would go far to cure this festering sore'.[29] Around the same time, the Irish Vigilance Association and the Catholic Truth Society were reactivated.

At the centre of this renewed crusade was Revd Richard S. Devane, a passionate promoter of legislation devoted to, as his obituary put it, 'moral protection'. This legislation included the Censorship of Publications Act (1929), the Public Dance Halls Act (1935) and the Criminal Law Amendment Act (1935), section 17 of which banned the sale of contraceptives.[30] Devane was nothing if not prolific in his writings on indecent literature; he published three substantial articles on the topic in the *Irish Ecclesiastical Record* in the latter half of 1926 alone.

Devane was keen to point out that any legislation to deal with objectionable publications would not be directed against Irish journalism and publications as he believed 'Irish journalism and the Irish press are as near perfection in this matter as any press can be'. In contrast, English journalists had descended 'into a rivalry of filth'. Birth control was a central issue; in Devane's opinion, wherever birth-control adverts were tolerated there had 'arisen a crowd of filthy literary sharks, publishers, writers, sex-fanatics – each surpassing the other in so called "courage" and "daring", in other words, lewdness and filth'. Irish newspapers had, however, excluded such advertisements, refusing 'to barter personal honour and the nation's morals at such a price'.[31] In one article, he quoted with approval the Bishop of Clogher, Patrick McKenna, who had declared that 'it would be somewhat reassuring to our sense of moral rectitude if we read of an Irish Catholic newsagent being sentenced to imprisonment or the lash by an Irish Catholic Judge for purveying such filth'. He also quoted Bishop O'Doherty, who had declared that 'it was time that a great crusade was started … to save the soul of the Nation, which is being steadily destroyed by filthy publications'.[32] In another article, he outlined the remedies he viewed as necessary to combat indecent literature. These included a new legal definition of indecency or obscenity 'in harmony with the standards of sexual morality obtaining in Saorstát Éireann', the establishment of a censor attached to the Ministry of Justice, the banning of all 'so-called "Birth Control" propaganda', the registration of imported journals, and the licensing of newsvendors and booksellers.[33]

The government acts

As a result of all this activity, the Catholic Bishops' Standing Committee sought and was granted a meeting with Minister O'Higgins in January 1926. The arguments made by the bishops – shortly afterwards one bishop asserted that 'thirty tons of literature, consisting principally of the scandals of the world, reach the country every week' – were obviously persuasive.[34] O'Higgins was, noted one of his officials, 'being subjected to considerable pressure from vigilance associations, the Catholic Truth Society, and bishops to introduce legislation giving more effective and definitive power to the State to prevent the importation and distribution of indecent and meretricious literature'.[35]

The following month, O'Higgins announced the establishment of the Committee on Evil Literature to examine whether the state should take action to prohibit the sale of certain publications. The committee invited various professional bodies, youth associations, and other organisations to submit evidence.[36] Among those invited were the Catholic Truth Society, the Irish Vigilance Association, the Irish Christian Brothers, the Catholic Headmasters' Association, the Irish National Teachers' Organisation, and Revd Richard S. Devane.[37] The Christian Brothers, represented by its superior general, Brother J. L. Craven, made a particularly strong submission. In terms of indecent literature, he noted that the Free State had

> the vulgar and the course, the suggestive, the unsavoury, the offensive, the smutty, the ill-smelling; we have gilded filth, unvarnished filth, gross animalism, sex-knowledge series, sexual science … Is it any wonder that we should have so many houses of infamy – the resorts of night birds and wild cats? … At present the spiritualised Irishman is quickly passing away and all of the brute that is in him is being fed almost to the point of moral leprosy, to be followed by a tempest of fire from heaven.[38]

In its submission, the Irish Vigilance Association objected to the publication of 'revolting details of sexual crimes and of divorce cases'.[39] The Catholic Truth Society's submission listed the weekly circulation figures of the British Sunday newspapers to which it objected:

News of the World	132,444
Empire News	76,698
Sunday Chronicle	46,188
The People	30,660
Reynold's News	28,772
Sunday News	22,198
Sunday Herald	15,842
Total	352,802[40]

In relation to the *News of the World*, the Society noted that it was 'devoted almost entirely to reports of murders, suicides, divorces, bigamy cases, indecent assault, incest, affiliation cases and crime in general, but particularly sexual crime'. It illustrated its case by reproducing the headlines from the 14 February 1926 edition of the paper:

> Girl's terrible ordeal: exemplary sentence on emigrant, ten years' imprisonment and 21 lashes [rape case]
>
> Loveless bride: didn't know why she married: £500 for husband who spent night in the woods [divorce case]
>
> Indicted by family: grave allegations against septuagenarian [incest case].[41]

In spring 1927, the government received the committee's report which recommended the establishment of a censorship board and a clampdown on the availability of information relating to contraception.[42] As the government began drafting a censorship bill, the Archbishop of Dublin, Dr Edward Byrne, noted, 'with most lively satisfaction that the State has initiated measures to provide a remedy against the traffic in vile literature'.[43] Referring to the 'abundance of error and filth served up under cheap and attractive covers', the Archbishop of Tuam, Thomas Gilmartin, declared it the government's duty 'to pass with all haste such legislation that will deliver our country from a dire evil'.[44] Lay groups also kept up the pressure. In May 1927, the *Irish Times* reported that masked men armed with revolvers had taken over Dundalk railway station, unloaded several thousand copies of British Sunday newspapers from a train, stacked them on the station platform, sprinkled them with petrol and set them alight.[45] A week later, the same thing happened at Dublin's Killiney railway station.[46] In the south, the Cork Angelic Warfare Association led the charge by seizing copies of the *News of the World*. When proceedings were taken against one of those involved, a priest called as a character witness declared that there was nothing wrong with seizing objectionable newspapers. He had even done it himself: while walking on the quays he had stopped a newsboy, seized his copies of the *News of the World* and thrown them into the river Lee – 'the only congenial place for such filth'.[47] As the Censorship of Publications Bill made its way through the Dáil, the hierarchy requested prayers from the faithful for its safe passage through parliament.[48]

Ultimately, the Censorship of Publications Act would have serious implications for journalism. The Act created a censorship board and allowed for a permanent ban on any publication deemed by the board to be indecent, obscene or detrimental to or subversive of public morality. Several sections of the Act affected newspapers and, by extension, journalism. Crime journalism came in for particular attention. During the Dáil debate on the Act, several politicians had expressed their concerns about crime coverage. The Minister for Justice, James FitzGerald-Kenney, had asserted that reading too much about 'sexually unpleasant cases [must] have the effect of depraving a person's mind'. Another deputy had declared it 'demoralising that we should have the attention of the people continually directed to crimes of violence, to sordid, ugly, vulgar things, as to details, say, of divorce trials'. Deputy William Thrift, who had been a member of the Committee on Evil Literature, had noted the 'perfectly astounding circulation of newspapers … which simply set themselves out to describe crime, particularly sexual crime, with every kind of disgusting detail'. Another deputy had noted that readers were 'compelled to wade through pages of headlines dealing with this horror that took place in Paris and that horror that took place in New York, or how this man has committed suicide in a slum in one city, or another man has cut his sweetheart to pieces in another city'.[49]

To resolve the problem of imported newspapers that carried these types of stories, Section 7 of the Act allowed the Minister for Justice to ban for three months any publication that 'devoted an unduly large proportion of space to the publication of matter relating to crime'. Once the Act became law, this section was used vigorously: in November 1930, the Minister indicated that he had used the section to ban six imported newspapers.[50] In an attempt to clean up Irish journalism, or at least to prevent it following the lead set by British newspapers, the Act limited the descriptive nature of crime reporting. Section 14 imposed constraints on the details that newspapers could report on in relation to court cases. It declared it unlawful to print or publish 'any indecent matter … which would be calculated to injure public morals … or any indecent medical, surgical or physiological details … which would be calculated to injure public morals'. The aim of this section was to clean up the reporting of the 'sexually unpleasant cases' that the politicians had spoken of. While reports were allowed to carry the names of the parties involved, the charges put, the points of law argued on, the judge's summing up, and the findings of the jury, medical evidence that mentioned particular body parts was seen as a corrupting power that would damage public morality and so could not be reported on.[51]

The *Waterford Standard* case

It was into this journalistic minefield that David Boyd and the *Waterford Standard* were to stumble. Born in Dundonald, County Down, in 1892, Boyd began his career as a reporter on the *Belfast Telegraph* before moving to Dublin to join the *Evening Mail*. While in Dublin he was active in the IRB and the Irish Volunteers, was present at the Howth gunrunning in 1913, and, as his obituary put it, played an active part in the fight for Independence. In 1915, he took up a reporter's post on the weekly *Waterford Standard* and eventually became its proprietor in 1920. A straight-talking individual, he was noted for his forthright views on local and national affairs.[52]

In September 1929, under the headline 'Serious Charge Against Mr Laurence Breen', the *Waterford Standard* reported on an arraignment hearing against a local theatre proprietor who was accused of having unlawful and felonious carnal knowledge of a thirteen-year-old girl in his employment. According to the girl's evidence, on her first night of employment, as the play was drawing to a close, Breen instructed her to follow him to his office. Once inside, he locked the door and turned off the light. Having assaulted her, he turned on the light, opened the door and told her to go home. The same thing happened four nights later. On this occasion, the girl suffered pain as she walked home, and, when she went to the lavatory, she passed blood. The girl's family eventually established what had happened and complained to the Garda Síochána. Giving medical evidence, the doctor who had examined the girl stated that there were no abrasions on the outside, two abrasions in the vagina, and the hymen was dilated. He concluded that the conditions were consistent with what the girl had told him. In reply to all this evidence, Breen's barrister raised the issues of class and cash. He highlighted the legal costs being incurred by Breen in defending himself and declared that Breen 'could if he wished erect another barrier by putting his hand in his pocket for a fraction of the cost he is now put to stop the open mouths in this case'. This drew a strong rebuke from the judge who declared it 'a very improper observation to make'; he then sent Breen forward for trial.[53]

Given the nature of the case, Boyd's *Waterford Standard* devoted its entire front page to the hearing. Page two was also devoted to the case, and the reportage included the medical evidence given by the doctor. It also printed a special edition the following day – with the case again being the lead item. One of the first to react to this coverage was the Bishop of Waterford, Bernard Hackett. The following week, in a letter read at all masses in the diocese, Hackett declared it his 'painful duty to make a solemn protest against the action of a section of the local Press in giving extended publication to certain recent proceedings in the District Court'. Noting that he was associating himself 'with the universal view of the city', he condemned the *Waterford Standard* as 'as an outrage on public decency and morality'. While this 'outrage' remained unatoned for, he warned, 'parents cannot be expected to admit the offending newspaper to their households with the implicit confidence which they may have hitherto entertained'.[54] What this denunciation from the pulpit meant for the paper's circulation is lost to history, but it hardly helped in attracting advertising from local businesses – the lifeblood of every local newspaper.

The state also acted. In October 1929, Boyd was summoned before the District Court and charged – under Section 15 of the Censorship of Publications Act – with publishing indecent medical, surgical or physiological details calculated to injure public morals. He faced a fine of £500, or imprisonment with hard labour for six months, or, if the judge so decided, both.[55] Given that this was the first case under the Censorship Act, the evidence offered by the state against Boyd was sparse: it effectively consisted of a copy of the newspaper being presented to the court and two members of the Garda Síochána stating that they had purchased a copy of the newspaper and had heard people talking about the case. Detective Garda Bartholomew Dowling gave evidence that he had bought a copy of the paper marked 'special edition' on 4 October directly from the paper's offices. He had made the purchase there as he had tried all the shops in the city but the paper had sold out. He then stated that he was aware that the report was read, discussed, and talked about by practically every class of person in the city. This untested assertion was backed up by a second garda who subsequently stated that he had not actually read the article in question. This prompted the judge, Francis J. McCabe, to quip, 'You left out the bad parts, I suppose.' There ended the state's evidence.

In response to the rather thin case presented by the state, Justice McCabe noted that the legislation stated that there were certain details that should not be published if calculated to injure public morals. He then observed that the state had not presented any direct evidence that the details had, in fact, caused injury to public morals. He enquired whether the state was going to present such evidence, to which the State Solicitor replied that while it had made efforts to procure evidence of injured public morality, it had been unsuccessful and so would not be presenting such evidence. It subsequently emerged that the state's prosecution team had tried to convince the Catholic and Protestant bishops of Waterford to give evidence. Neither man made himself available. Bishop Hackett's concern for public morality was, it seems, confined to denunciations from the pulpit.

Justice McCabe noted that the case involved an important principle and maintained that while the details may well have injured public morals, he needed independent evidence that they had, in fact, caused injury. As he put it to the State Solicitor, 'I want someone to come here and tell me plainly the public morality of Waterford was injured by the publication of the details.' In reply to this, the State Solicitor conceded that, while the judge might require the assistance 'of some holy and learned Divine who will come up and say the publication of all the details was likely to injure public morals', he wished to know whether the defence team was going to produce 'equally holy and learned Divines to say the publication was a very wholesome thing for public morals'. This neatly sidestepped the judge's question while also ignoring the fact that the burden of proof lay solely with the prosecution. But the state was forced to concede that it could not produce the evidence the judge had asked for.

In his defence, Boyd declared that it was 'always the policy of the paper to give careful, verbatim, and authentic reports, and, according to that principle, it was always a well conducted paper'. In terms of journalism, he stated that it was his policy to have an independent attitude, and he had tried to make his newspaper as decent and independent as he could. In a swipe at the local establishment, he stated that attempts were often made to suppress reportage of such cases, and that he had often lost money (in terms of circulation or advertising) by refusing to bend to such pressure. He maintained he had a duty to society, declared that it was 'in the interests of the public that a newspaper should be free and independent', and expressed his belief that 'it was a very good thing that cases of this kind should be known'. He was, he continued, a married man with three children, and the last thing he would do would be to publish anything calculated to injure public morals.

Boyd acknowledged that he had been aware of the Censorship of Publications Act but not its provisions. Neither was he aware that it had become law. He believed he had performed a public duty in publishing the story and still held that belief. He asserted that the medical evidence had been published in 'clean scientific terms in which there was nothing smutty'. He reasoned that the publication of such evidence would 'have a restraining effect on vicious minds [and] in decent minded people it would create indignation that the child was treated in the way she alleged'. In neither instance would the story injure morals. If anything, it would have the reverse effect. 'Publicity', he declared, was 'good for morality.' It was what 'evil-doers fear most in offences of this kind' and was, he contended, 'the greatest punishment'. If only a summary of the case had been published, he reasoned, 'people would be more smutty in their minds about it. There would be more speculation in their minds as to what happened'. The offence he was alleged to have committed was, he concluded, a matter of opinion.

Despite not being able to convince Bishop Hackett to give evidence, the state still played the religious card in its cross-examination of Boyd. Would, the State Solicitor asked, he consider the story to be in the public interest had the defendant been a clergyman? Boyd replied that a clergyman would 'get full publicity for an offence of this nature'. Asked had he heard about Hackett's condemnation of his newspaper, he replied that he had. Was he, the State Solicitor asked, setting his opinion against the bishop and the legislature in terms of what details might be inappropriate to publish? Sensing that the prosecution was trying to set him in direct conflict with the church, Boyd asserted that it was not a fair question. Asked again, he replied that he was not; the bishop was entitled to his opinion.

In his judgment, Justice McCabe expressed regret that the prosecution had happened. But, despite not hearing any evidence that public morals in Waterford had been injured, he declared the publication of the medical details 'a scandal'. Boyd was found guilty and fined £25, a not inconsiderable amount of money at the time. Coincidentally, Justice McCabe had presided over the original arraignment hearing that had given rise to Boyd's prosecution. He noted that he had had the right to exclude the press from the original hearing and would have done so if he had anticipated reportage along the lines of that of the *Waterford Standard*. But, having made an example of Boyd, he felt that such an offence would not be repeated by the press.[56] This triple blow to press freedom, from the state (in terms of prosecution), the church (in terms of public denunciation), and the judiciary (threatening to bar the press from cases if they anticipated troublesome coverage) sent a clear signal to all newspaper proprietors and journalists.

Fallout and 'the kissing case'

Despite the treatment meted out to Boyd, and the manner in which the case impacted on press freedom, the hearing merited little or no response from the national media. The *Irish Independent* published an extensive report on the case but did not comment editorially on the case or its implications for press freedom.[57] The *Irish Times* published a sparse fifteen-line paragraph on the case but did not comment editorially on the case or its implications.[58] Somewhat belatedly, the Institute of Journalists expressed concern about what the Censorship Act might mean for journalism. At its 1930 AGM, one member, F. J. Keane, noted that the legislation allowed for the suppression of newspapers deemed to devote an unduly large amount of space to crime coverage. He asserted that the definition of crime was 'very vague and might be applied to local papers giving long reports of District and Circuit Courts'; it might also, he contended, 'give power to any Government to suppress papers which did not agree with its policy'.[59] To combat this, he felt the institute should make representations to the Minister for Justice to ensure a journalist sat on the censorship board. Sometime before, the Minister had indicated that he favoured having a journalist sit on the board but had not found anyone willing to serve.[60] While Keane's colleagues did not agree with his interpretation of the Act – one declared that such events would not happen as 'such a state of affairs would be monstrous' – all agreed that a journalist sitting on the board would be a good thing. However, when the chairman asked for volunteers, none were forthcoming.[61]

For its part, the still nascent NUJ had appointed a sub-committee 'to interview members of the Oireachtas and make such recommendations as might be advisable in order to maintain the established and customary rights of journalists in the courts and elsewhere'. In June 1929, it convened a special meeting 'to discuss certain matters arising out of the Censorship Bill' that was to have been addressed by independent senator (and former journalist) Patrick Hooper but 'owing to the unexpectedly small attendance only an informal discussion took place'. Indeed, press reports about 'the inability of the Minister for Justice to find a journalist able and willing to act [as] a member of the proposed Board of Censors' prompted the union's Dublin branch secretary, James O'Farrell, to observe that the Minister's 'quest must have been made in peculiar places [as] no member of the NUJ was approached by or on behalf of the Minister in this matter'.[62] There ended any journalistic opposition to the Censorship Act, and the campaign to purify the Free State continued. In a systematic examination of court records relating to sexual offences and related press coverage between 1923 and 1933, Anthony Keating found that just over 15 per cent of such trials received any coverage and concluded that, of these,

> the vast majority produced reports that ranged from those that completely obscured the sexual nature of the offence to those wrapped in language that was so oblique that the detail and nature of the crime was barely discernible. For most Irish editors, not to report on sexual crime seemed the lesser of two evils

> and the small percentage that chose to report developed strategies to minimise the impact on local sensitivities and the wider 'purity' agenda, so central to the Catholic hierarchy's mission.[63]

Indeed, in the *Irish Times*, the term 'sexual assault' only appears ten times between January 1930 and December 1959, with five of those mentions relating to one Dublin murder case in 1939.[64] Similarly, the term 'unlawful carnal knowledge' appears only six times over the same period, with five of those mentions relating to three court cases and one relating to legislation.[65] The term 'unnatural vice' appears only twelve times, none of which relate to court cases, while the catch-all phrase 'unnatural offences' appears a total of eleven times, five of which relate to three court cases.[66] The first mention of 'child abuse' (a relatively modern term) occurs in 1968.[67]

There were, however, occasions when the press, or certain newspapers, reported on the extremes that local vigilance committees went to – much to the chagrin of the judiciary. In 1937, a case centring on a charge of public indecency was heard at Blackrock, County Louth, and ended up being reported on worldwide. The case arose out of an incident whereby members of a local vigilance committee had witnessed a couple 'lying on the ground embracing' on church grounds and had called the Garda Síochána. When cautioned, the couple insisted they had merely been lying on the ground kissing.[68] What made headlines around the world was how the female involved was treated by the court. At the sentencing hearing for the male, who lived locally, it was stressed that he 'was respectable [and had got] more or less carried away by the appearance and get-up of his partner, who was on holiday from England'. It was also stated that 'there was nothing immoral in what had happened [and] in the sense that it might give scandal it was a moral [not criminal] offence'. While the male was fined £2, at a later sentencing hearing, the maximum sentence of one month's imprisonment was passed on the female, a Scottish lady who had been on holidays but who had returned to Glasgow before the case was heard.

In his summary, Justice B. J. Goff declared that the sentence was passed 'with a view to keeping this lady out of the State' and that the offence had been aggravated 'by being on church property'.[69] This judgment was somewhat at odds with a previous hearing in 1935 in which a male, charged with indecency for 'embracing and kissing a girl outside a dance hall' had been acquitted when the presiding judge had declared that 'kissing in public was not an indecent offence'.[70]

The 1937 case created considerable international interest – it was reported on in Britain, Canada, and Australia.[71] In Ireland, both the *Irish Times* and the *Irish Press*, but not the *Irish Independent*, reported on the case, but only the *Times* commented editorially. It noted somewhat wryly that since summer had turned to winter 'the sward of a churchyard will provoke not dreams of sweet ecstasy, but some rather vague apprehensions about rheumatism and arthritis'. Therefore, it continued, the vigilance committee should 'withdraw its forces from the countryside and to concentrate – with the strength that comes from consolidation of troops – upon the now more popular streets of the town [since] love is inclined to freeze in winter and humanity makes various questionable efforts to keep it warm'. During winter, the vigilance committee's members should be able 'to spot deportable young women arm in arm with their escorts; to round up couples who use the one umbrella ostensibly for reasons of economy, but actually in the interests of emotion; and to corral behind the bars the multitudinous and unsavoury pairs who share the same rugs at a football match'.[72] For its part, the *Daily Mirror* reported that one bachelors' club – in Ballymurphy, County Wexford – had congratulated the vigilance committee on its work. The club had noted that Irish bachelors had 'colleens and cranks, hags and harridans enough of our own to contend with without having to face importations from England, Scotland, or elsewhere'.[73]

Responding to the press coverage, Justice Goff criticised what he referred to as 'the scandalous treatment that was given by a section of the "Yellow Press", mostly imported, but including one notorious Dublin organ [the *Irish Times*]' to the case. Oddly, given that the sentencing hearing for the local male had stressed that 'nothing immoral' had transpired, Goff contended that the case had been 'distorted beyond all recognition by the omission of all the particulars that made it a serious case' and that the newspapers concerned had 'deceived the public by a case that they had concocted themselves [and] founded on it a campaign of calumny and ridicule', the intention of which was 'to intimidate the Guards … and so making the country safe for indecency'. He also took offence at a cartoon from a Scottish newspaper that showed a couple being marched by gardaí towards a boat; it was, he observed, 'intended to injure the tourist traffic of the State'. If such reportage occurred again, Goff declared, 'he would ask the Attorney General to put a couple of the offending editors, who were within his reach in the dock'.[74] The press coverage of what became known as 'the kissing case' was raised in the Dáil when local Fine Gael TD James Coburn asked the Minister for Justice to 'make a full statement of the charges in this case, and of the misconduct upon which these charges were based'. The Minister, P. J. Ruttledge, responded that, as the Attorney General was looking into the case, he could not say anything more.[75]

Shortly afterwards, citing the 'recent scandalous distortion of the facts of the Blackrock indecency case', Justice Goff announced that in future all indictable cases – including preliminary hearings and full trials – in his district would be heard *in camera* as 'it was fairer to both the State and the defendant that the evidence should not be read and discussed … by people who might ultimately be called to serve as jurors in the case [and] who might also read the evidence in a distorted form in the yellow press, principally the imported press'. The court was then cleared of both the public and the press so that it could hear a case of a man charged with 'serious offences'.[76] Little over a week later, the press and the public were again excluded from Dundalk courthouse as a Liverpool man was charged with serious motoring offences.[77] While the NUJ Dublin branch discussed the issue, no action was taken.[78] It seems there the matter ended as normal, restricted, reporting of cases resumed shortly afterwards. But the two cases – that of the *Waterford Standard* and that of the 'kissing case' – are indicative of the sensitivities of the relationship between the new state and journalism and how, through judicial outrage at press coverage of court cases, many of the more unpleasant aspects of life in the Free State were, for many years, kept out of the public arena.

Notes

1 *Irish Journalist*, 1:10 (Jul.–Aug. 1915), p. 3.
2 P. Mulryan, *Radio, Radio: The Story of Independent, Local, Community and Pirate Radio in Ireland* (Dublin, 1988), pp. 1–2.
3 *Irish Times*, 29 Oct. 1965, p. 4.
4 *Irish Journalist*, 1:13 (Nov. 1915), p. 3.
5 H. Oram, *The Newspaper Book: A History of Newspapers in Ireland, 1649–1983* (Dublin, 1983), pp. 139–40; and *Irish Times*, 4 Jul. 1945, p. 3.
6 Knightly's statement to the Bureau of Military History (BMHWS 833–5) gives a detailed account of his involvement in the republican movement.
7 O'Sullivan passed intelligence to the republican movement; see *Irish Press*, 11 Jul. 1961, p. 9. Lester was a member of the IRB and the Irish Volunteers; see D. Gageby, *The Last Secretary General: Seán Lester and the League of Nations* (Dublin, 1999), Chapter 2.
8 This account comes from Chris O'Sullivan, an Australian journalist who wrote of his Dublin experiences in the *Freeman's Journal* (Sydney), 4 May 1922, p. 12.
9 I. Kenneally, *Paper Wall: Newspapers and Propaganda in Ireland, 1919–21* (Cork, 2008), p. 9.
10 Kenneally, *Paper Wall*, pp. 14–15.
11 See F. M. Larkin, 'A great daily organ: the *Freeman's Journal, 1763–1924*', *History Ireland*, 14:3 (2006), 44–9. See also I. Kenneally, 'Truce to treaty: Irish journalists and the 1920–21 peace process', in K. Rafter (ed.), *Irish Journalism before Independence: More a Disease than a Profession* (Manchester, 2011), pp. 213–25. For an account of the *Freeman's Journal* during the War of Independence, see D. Ryan, *Remembering Sion* (London, 1934), pp. 256–81. See also BMHWS 724–5 (Ryan).
12 Bloody Sunday (21 Nov. 1920) is so called because of the killing of fourteen British spies and the subsequent raid by the auxiliaries on Croke Park, in which twelve people were killed. *Irish Times*, 17 Nov. 1945, p. 3.
13 Kenneally, *Paper Wall*, pp. 7 and 125–6.
14 *Irish Times*, 4 Feb. 1920, p. 5.
15 *Freeman's Journal*, 13 Dec. 1920, p. 7.
16 *Irish Independent*, 13 Dec. 1920, p. 4; *Irish Times*, 13 Dec. 1920, p. 6.
17 O'Sullivan published an account of his experiences in Ireland in the *Freeman's Journal* (Sydney), 4 May 1922, p. 12. For an account of how foreign correspondents reported the conflict, see M. Walsh, *The News from Ireland: Foreign Correspondents and the Irish Revolution* (London, 2008).
18 *Freeman's Journal* (Sydney), 4 May 1922, p. 12.
19 *Freeman's Journal* (Sydney), 4 May 1922, p. 12.
20 *Irish Times*, 22 Jun. 1976, p. 10.
21 *Irish Times*, 31 May 1940, p. 4; P. S. O'Hegarty, 'The mosquito press', *The Bell*, 12:1 (1946), 56–65.
22 Oram, *The Newspaper Book*, p. 152; *Irish Times*, 31 May 1934, p. 6.
23 *Irish Times*, 20 Jan. 1923, p. 7; 3 Feb. 1923, p. 5.
24 DED, vol. 2 (col. 1909), 1 Mar. 1923.

25 *Irish Times*, 6 Mar. 1924, p. 6.
26 *Weekly Irish Times*, 8 Mar. 1924, p. 5.
27 *Irish Times*, 2 Mar. 1925, p. 8. In 1927, the hierarchy was still calling for an end to 'forms of dancing which pander to the lower animal instincts'. See *Weekly Irish Times*, 5 Mar. 1927, p. 1.
28 D. Barry, 'The ethics of journalism', *Irish Ecclesiastical Record*, 19 (1922), 515–26, at pp. 524–6.
29 *Irish Times*, 2 Mar. 1925, p. 8.
30 The Public Dance Halls Act made it a requirement for anyone holding a public dance to apply for a licence: it effectively handed over control of dances to the Church, which then organised and policed dances in parish halls. *Irish Times*, 24 May 1951, p. 5.
31 R. S. Devane, 'The committee on printed matter: some notes of evidence', *Irish Ecclesiastical Record*, 28 (1926), 357–77, at pp. 370–2.
32 R. S. Devane, 'Indecent literature', *Irish Ecclesiastical Record*, 25 (1925), 182–204, at pp. 183–4.
33 R. S. Devane, 'The committee on printed matter: indecency in law', *Irish Ecclesiastical Record*, 28 (1926), 583–95, at pp. 593–4.
34 *Irish Times*, 15 Feb. 1926, p. 5. See M. Curtis, *A Challenge to Democracy: Militant Catholicism in Modern Ireland* (Dublin, 2010).
35 NAI, CEL/Jus/7/1/4, letter from Einri O'Frighil, Secretary of Department of Justice, to James McNeill, High Commissioner Irish Free State, London, 21 Jan. 1926, cited in K. Rafter, 'Evil literature: banning the *News of the World* in Ireland', *Media History*, 19:4 (2013), 408–20, at p. 415.
36 The committee membership was: Prof. R. Donovan, Professor of English, UCD; Prof. W. E. Thrift, TD, TCD; Thomas O'Connell, TD; Revd James Dempsey and Revd Sinclair Stephenson.
37 M. Adams, *Censorship: The Irish Experience* (Tuscaloosa, Ala., 1968), pp. 24–5.
38 Adams, *Censorship*, pp. 26–7. See *Irish Independent*, 11 Oct. 1927, p. 1, for Craven's front-page advert – 'Satan, Smut & Co.' – against such publications.
39 Adams, *Censorship*, p. 27.
40 Adams, *Censorship*, p. 28.
41 Adams, *Censorship*, p. 29.
42 Section 16 of the 1929 Censorship Act made it unlawful for anyone to print, publish, sell or distribute any book or periodical that advocated 'the unnatural prevention of conception or the procurement of abortion or miscarriage or any method, treatment, or appliance to be used for the purpose of such prevention or such procurement'.
43 *Weekly Irish Times*, 5 Mar. 1927, p. 1.
44 *Weekly Irish Times*, 5 Mar. 1927, p. 1.
45 *Irish Times*, 2 May 1927, p. 8.
46 *Irish Times*, 9 May 1927, p. 7.
47 L. M. Cullen, *Eason & Son: A History* (Dublin, 1989), p. 267.
48 *Irish Times*, 11 Feb. 1929, p. 5.
49 DED, vol. 26 (cols. 624–5, 630, and 643), 18 Oct. 1928.
50 DED, vol. 36 (col. 719–20), 28 Nov. 1930. The periodicals were *World's Pictorial News and Competitor's Guide*, *News of the World*, *Empire News*, *The People*, *Thomson's Weekly News*, and *Weekly Record*.
51 Censorship of Publications Act 1929, section 14.
52 *Irish Times*, 29 Oct. 1965, p. 4. The prosecution of David Boyd had faded from history until it was discovered by Anthony Keating while completing a Ph.D. at Dublin City

University. See Anthony Keating, 'Setting the agenda for the press: The 1929 case against the *Waterford Standard*', *New Hibernia Review*, 16:2 (2012), 17–32.

53 *Waterford Standard*, 28 Sep. 1929, pp. 1–2. At Breen's trial for the alleged offence, the local jury could not agree a verdict. At a second trial in Dublin, Breen was acquitted but was killed in a car crash while returning to Waterford.

54 *The (Catholic) Standard*, 26 Oct. 1929, p. 2.

55 Censorship of Publications Act 1929, section 15.

56 *Waterford Standard*, 26 Oct. 1929, pp. 8–9. See also *Irish Independent*, 19 Oct. 1929, p. 11. In 1945, Boyd was charged with contempt of court over his report of a county-council meeting which had heard remarks critical of a judge. While he was found guilty of contempt, no order was made against him. See *Irish Times*, 8 May 1945, p. 5 and 18 May 1945, p. 2.

57 *Irish Independent*, 19 Oct. 1929, p. 11.

58 *Irish Times*, 19 Oct. 1929, p. 10.

59 *Irish Times*, 20 Jan. 1930, p. 5.

60 *Irish Times*, 29 Oct. 1929, p. 7.

61 *Irish Times*, 20 Jan. 1930, p. 5.

62 HCRC, NUJ, Dublin branch minutes, 25 Jan. 1930.

63 A. Keating, 'Sexual crime in the Irish Free State, 1922–33: its nature, extent and reporting', *Irish Studies Review*, 20:2 (2012), 135–55, at p. 146.

64 Within the other five mentions, one relates to legislation (1934), two relate to murders in England (1947 and 1957), one relates to a letter to the editor (1955), and one relates to a US prisoner on death row (1959).

65 The reference to legislation occurred in 1934, while the cases occurred in 1947, 1950, and 1952.

66 The mentions relate to religious instruction, immoral publications, the dangers of communism, letters relating to banned books and letters on public morality and censorship, etc. The other mentions relate to Dáil questions, crime statistics, a medical conference, a British court case, etc.

67 The term was used in the context of a book review, 'The battered child', *Irish Times*, 5 Jul. 1968, p. 5.

68 *Irish Times*, 22 Oct. 1937, p. 5.

69 *Irish Times*, 22 Oct. 1937, p. 5. Justice Goff was a somewhat controversial figure: between 1936 and 1942, the government referred him to the Judicial Advisory Committee on four occasions for 'comments of a non-judicial nature by way of expression of his personal views', but no action was taken against him. He retired from the bench in 1944. See NAI, TSCH/3/S6642.

70 *Irish Times*, 30 Nov. 1935, p. 11.

71 *Glasgow Herald*, 6 Nov. 1937, p. 12; *Ottawa Citizen*, 13 Nov. 1937, p. 1; *The West Australian* (Perth), 23 Oct. 1937, p. 19.

72 *Irish Times*, 25 Oct. 1937, p. 8.

73 *Daily Mirror*, 4 Nov. 1937, p. 23.

74 *Irish Times*, 6 Nov. 1937, p. 9.

75 *Irish Times*, 10 and 11 Nov. 1937, p. 5.

76 *Irish Times*, 8 Nov. 1937, p. 5.

77 *Irish Times*, 18 Nov. 1937, p. 7.

78 HCRC, NUJ, Dublin branch minutes, 12 Nov. and 4 Dec. 1937.

4

Power in a union

But the press are more or less the sleuth hounds who are all the time looking for some advance information. They want to know everything in advance, whether it is or is not in the public interest … Their interest is to get information of one kind or another, and the more sensational it is, and the more premature it is, the better from their point of view … They hear that something is going on. They add more than two and two – they add two and two and make five of it very often.[1]

— Éamon de Valera on journalists, 1939

In 1926, the NUJ made its second attempt to establish itself in Ireland. As highlighted in Chapter 2, it had already made such an attempt in November 1909, when it established branches in Dublin, Waterford, Derry, and Newry and recruited nearly 100 members before being quickly eclipsed by the establishment of the IJA a month later. Nonetheless, the NUJ kept a close eye on the country, and, as the IJA began to decline in the early 1920s and amid the closure of the *Daily Express* in 1921 and the *Freeman's Journal* in 1924, the NUJ's executive council was informed by its general secretary, Henry Richardson, that 'there was a good prospect of forming branches in Dublin and Belfast'.[2] Thus, in 1926, the union's national organiser, Clement Bundock, visited Dublin and Belfast and established branches. The new Dublin branch attracted eighty members and the Belfast branch seventeen members. The first chairman of this second incarnation of the Dublin branch was James W. Good, a Belfast-born journalist who was a leader writer with the *Freeman's Journal* and later the *Irish Independent.*[3] Subsequent chairmen included the journalist and playwright David Sears and William Buttimer, the deputy chief reporter of the *Irish Times.*[4] Fittingly, Buttimer was no stranger to defending the integrity of journalists. When, in November 1926, the Governor General, T. M. Healy, accused two newspapers of misreporting a speech of his (in which he had made some choice remarks about Éamon de Valera and Fianna Fáil), the two reporters concerned, Buttimer and Ned Lawler of the *Irish Independent*, wrote to their newspapers and refuted Healy's assertion by releasing their full notes of his speech.[5]

However, as the union's first historian, Frederick Mansfield, has pointed out, the 'work of the branch in its early years was of an uphill nature, as the members lacked the stimulus of constant contact with the great mass of fellow members in Great Britain'.[6] Nonetheless, having formed an NUJ branch, the Dublin journalists were eager to improve their employment conditions. In 1927, the branch sought to open negotiations with newspaper proprietors; when the latter were unresponsive, advice from London was sought. The union's president, H. A. Raybould, and its general secretary, Henry Richardson, attended a meeting of the Dublin branch to consider what action might be taken. They quickly realised that the threat of industrial action was negated by the continued existence of the Institute of Journalists, which still retained a significant, if not a majority, of Dublin journalists in its membership. The suggestion by newspaper proprietors, whom by this time had organised themselves into the Dublin Newspaper Proprietors and Managers Committee (known more commonly as the Dublin Newspaper Managers' Committee), that the Dublin branch act jointly with the institute (which was not a trade union), was rejected by the NUJ officers.[7] As well as the institute not being a trade union, its membership was composed of editorial executives as opposed to working journalists, a situation starkly illustrated at a state reception at Dublin's Shelbourne Hotel in October 1929, when journalists walked out in protest at the accommodation provided for them. In contrast, the invited editorial executives, including John E. Healy of the *Irish Times* and J. W. Whitehead of the *Evening Mail*, remained behind.[8] The NUJ had more success in securing the right of journalists to travel independently to and from political meetings. In 1930, it complained to editors about 'the matter of reporters' markings especially with regard to the sending of men to the country in the cars of political parties' and shortly afterwards reported that the complaints 'had put an end to the practice'.[9]

The NUJ and the *Irish Press*

It was the establishment of the *Irish Press* in 1931 that finally gave the NUJ the boost it needed to establish itself.[10] Founded by Éamon de Valera, the paper's first leading article declared that it would not be 'the organ of an individual, or a group or a party' but would support Fianna Fáil because its philosophy and aspirations were the same as those espoused by the paper. On the eve of every general election, it called on its readers to vote for Fianna Fáil, a tradition that survived until the paper's demise in May 1995. The *Press* played a central role in bringing the party to power in 1932 and keeping it there; so much so that de Valera noted that 'if the paper were to disappear, the government would disappear with it'.[11] It made an immediate impact by putting news rather than advertisements on its front page, and it also pioneered the reportage of the Gaelic Athletic Association (GAA). The popularity of such coverage forced the other national titles to follow suit: in 1938, the *Press* noted that, since its launch, the *Irish Independent* had increased its GAA coverage tenfold.[12]

In its early days, it had a campaigning spirit: in October 1936, it published a series on the appalling conditions endured by those who inhabited Dublin's slum tenements. Interestingly, the series was the brainchild of two 'outsiders' – John J. Harrington (the paper's American general manager) and Chris O'Sullivan (the paper's Australian managing editor) – both of whom left the paper shortly after the series ended. The series revealed that the infant-mortality rate in the slums was 119 per 1,000 compared to ratios of sixty-three and fifty-nine per 1,000 in the Free State and England respectively. The *Press* was careful to stress that the articles were based on 'official statistics, medical officers' reports, reports of Royal Commissions, and the testimony of many trustworthy bodies and persons'. They were not, it was careful to add, 'an attack on any person, slum owner or otherwise, individually [but was] an exposure and an indictment of a system'.[13] The series continued throughout the month of October and ended when, as Jim Larkin TD put it, 'somebody came down with a hand … and said this thing has gone far enough'.[14] As recalled by Tim Pat Coogan, when he was appointed editor of the *Press* in 1968, the series was held up by then managing director Vivion de Valera as the type of journalism to avoid as it cost advertising and created 'a bad image, an impression of socialism'. According to Coogan, some of the journalists who had worked on the series told him that 'the problem stemmed from the fact that many of the slum properties excoriated by the series were owned by "important personages"; including those of the church'.[15] In an interview for an oral-history project recorded in 1978, one of the originators of the series, Chris O'Sullivan, described the Catholic Church as 'the biggest landlord in Ireland, and rack-renter' and recalled how clergy visited his home to insist that he send his children to church.[16]

Given the paper's association with Fianna Fáil, it was inevitable that opposition parties would target the paper's journalists. In one such incident, Richard Mulcahy asked de Valera whether it was true that the paper's journalists had 'their emoluments supplemented from the moneys voted for the Secret Service Fund'.[17] The NUJ's Dublin branch responded by criticising Mulcahy's use of Dáil privilege to make 'unsustainable and uncalled for attacks on newspaper employees'.[18] Whatever about the Secret Service, given the paper's ethos it was perhaps inevitable that its journalists would gravitate towards a trade union rather than the Institute of Journalists, which concerned itself solely with professional matters. According to NUJ historian Frederick Mansfield, the paper's first night editor, James [Seamus] O'Farrell, was a former secretary of the Dublin branch and was keen that the paper be staffed by NUJ members.[19] In his obituary, mention is made of O'Farrell being 'associated with the late Jim Larkin in the founding, in 1909, of the ITGWU'.[20] But the paper's first editor, Frank Gallagher, who had worked on the *Irish Bulletin* and *Poblacht na hÉireann*, was also well disposed towards trade unionism and joined the NUJ in February 1931.[21]

So numerous were NUJ members at the *Irish Press* that they established a newspaper branch, or chapel, distinct from the Dublin branch. In a significant move, the chapel was recognised by management: such recognition was a first for Irish newspapers. There may have been a pressing reason for this: the establishment of the chapel took place against the backdrop of the continuing 'Red Scare' that had characterised the 1932 general election and industrial unrest at the *Press*. A detailed report on communism in Ireland, written by the Garda Commissioner Eoin O'Duffy in 1932, noted how the Communist Party of Great Britain was 'responsible for sending selected agitators to Ireland'. The report makes reference to one 'Bryan' O'Neill (later employed at the *Irish Press*) as having 'only recently come under notice here when he was sent from England by the Communist Party, Great Britain, to push the sale of *The Workers' Voice* and to re-organise the Workers' Revolutionary Party'.[22]

The report also notes how 'the present dispute between the Workers' Union of Ireland and the Directors of the "Irish Press" has been taken advantage of by Communist agitators here'. In 1932, the Workers' Union of Ireland succeeded in organising newsboys into a section, and, as the report observes, 'these newsboys have refused to sell the "Irish Press" and have created an amount of disorder by attacks on vans conveying the paper to shops where it is sold'.[23] In fact, the newsvendors' strike affected only the *Evening Telegraph*, an evening title published by the Press company between June and October 1932, which newsboys refused to sell as a means of seeking a shorter working week. In a series of disturbances, dubbed 'The Charge of the Newsboys' Brigade', a Press delivery van was attacked on O'Connell Street and newspapers were flung into the river Liffey.[24] One member of the *Irish Press* chapel, future government minister Seán MacBride, unsuccessfully sought to convince its members to come out in support of the newsboys. The chapel's chairman, Geoffrey Coulter, who had worked with Frank Ryan at *An Phoblacht*, opposed the idea, and MacBride – 'much to the horror of the journalists and the management of the paper' – joined the picket line. Having already begun working as a barrister, MacBride left the paper shortly afterwards.[25]

In December 1932, a more serious issue arose when the paper's chief political reporter, Joseph Dennigan, was imprisoned for refusing to reveal his sources. Dennigan was summoned to appear before a military tribunal, where Commandant Edmond John Cronin was charged with membership of an illegal organisation, the Young Ireland Association, better known as the Blueshirts. Sometime before, Dennigan had written a story in relation to the Fianna Fáil government's plans to ban that organisation and 'to allow a short period to members of the organisation so as to provide them with an opportunity of ceasing their membership'.[26] This information had appeared only in the *Irish Press*, and Cronin's defence team argued that, as a non-reader of that newspaper, he had been unaware of the amnesty.[27]

When asked to identify the source of his story, Dennigan claimed privilege, a claim disallowed by the President of the Court. Dennigan then stated that he could not name his source without the joint permission of his source and his editor. Cronin's defence team then suggested that rather than having to reveal his source publicly, he could write down the name. Dennigan again replied that he needed permission from his source and his editor. He stated that the privilege of the press was involved in the case and that his editor had asked him to 'take a certain line of action'. The court then adjourned to allow Dennigan to consult with his editor, Frank Gallagher. Dennigan later told the court that Gallagher had agreed that it would be a breach of confidence for him to reveal his source and that he was unwilling to do so. He was then jailed for one month for contempt of court.[28] Appalled that one of its members should be imprisoned for upholding journalistic privilege, the NUJ's Dublin branch expressed its support for

Dennigan, who had 'upheld the traditional rights of his profession', and called on the de Valera-led Fianna Fáil government to release him.[29] The Dublin and Cork districts of the Institute of Journalists, Dublin Corporation, and the Dublin Trades Council passed similar resolutions.[30] However, the calls fell on deaf ears, as did an NUJ-financed appeal against the sentence.[31] Following Dennigan's release in January 1934, the *Irish Press* chapel held a dinner in his honour. In his after-dinner speech, Dennigan noted the 'striking unanimity among our own Irish newspapers. Though worshipping at different political shrines they are one in agreeing that confidences reposed in newspapermen ought to be respected at whatever cost.' He also revealed that a cell had been prepared for the paper's editor, Frank Gallagher, in case he too had been sentenced for contempt.[32]

Interestingly, no sooner had Dennigan been released than Frank Gallagher faced the prospect of going through a similar ordeal. In January 1934, Gallagher was summoned to give evidence in the case of three men who were before the same military tribunal, charged with membership of an illegal organisation. Called to the stand, Gallagher sought and was granted permission to address the tribunal on the appropriateness of his appearing before it. Reminding the tribunal of Dennigan's imprisonment, Gallagher declared that he had been called before them by those 'politically opposed' to him. He noted that since Dennigan's imprisonment public opinion had come to believe that Dennigan and now he (Gallagher) were brought before the tribunal 'not to assist in the administration of justice, but to receive a penalty from the Court which was really contrived for us by those who are politically opposed to us'. He asserted that what had happened to Dennigan would also happen to him and requested that the tribunal adjudicate on the relevance of any questions put to him by the men's defence team. Remarkably, the tribunal agreed. When the defence team sought to elicit the source for Dennigan's article from Gallagher, the tribunal decided, after much legal argument, that, in this particular case, such evidence was irrelevant and allowed Gallagher to avoid answering the question.[33]

Although the NUJ had not been able to secure Dennigan's release, the legitimacy that recognition by *Irish Press* management gave it was an important boost to its fortunes. At the Dublin branch's 1932 AGM, James O'Farrell was elected chairman, and it was noted that membership 'was increasing steadily'. The idea of forming an Irish district council to link up with the Belfast branch was also floated.[34] O'Farrell's successor as Dublin branch chairman was Geoffrey Coulter, another *Irish Press* journalist. Coulter was a former IRA intelligence officer and former assistant editor of *An Phoblacht*, and he played a key role in the union's development.[35] Among those who chaired the Dublin branch in its early years were James O'Farrell (*Irish Press*, 1932), Geoffrey Coulter (*Irish Press*, 1933, 1936), Patrick W. Little (*Irish Independent*, 1934), Gabriel Diskin (*Irish Press*, 1935), P. A. Sheehan (*Garda Review*, 1937), and John McGuire (*Licensed Grocer and Vintner*, 1938).

During Sheehan's chairmanship, the NUJ membership card was granted official recognition by the Garda Síochána.[36] However, gaining the recognition of newspaper proprietors (other than at the *Irish Press*) proved difficult. In May

1933, the Dublin branch became affiliated with the Printing Trades Group of the Dublin Trades Union Council.[37] It was through this affiliation, and an industrial dispute, that recognition of the union by all newspaper proprietors came about.

Between July and October 1934, all Dublin newspapers ceased publication for nearly ten weeks due to an industrial dispute initiated by the ITGWU, which represented transport and administrative staff. The print union (the Dublin Typographical Society) became involved when its members refused to set a statement that newspaper proprietors wished to have printed. All workers, including journalists, were subsequently locked out, with the newspapers paying journalists two-thirds of their salary intermittently and the NUJ paying out 'dispute benefit' to its members.[38] A march of 4,000 workers and their supporters followed, and Clement Bundock addressed the rally in the city centre. This act of solidarity, according to then *Irish Press* journalist R. M. Fox, 'was a pivotal point in the history of the Dublin branch. Our public expression of solidarity with the printing trade workers helped to teach our own members the wider implications of trade union membership.'[39] It also bore fruit in terms of employer recognition. When the dispute ended, a joint industrial council (JIC) was established to settle future disputes within the printing industry, and the NUJ secured one of the seven places afforded to trade unions. Geoffrey Coulter was the first NUJ representative on the JIC.[40]

All this activity prompted a visit to Dublin by the union's president, R. S. Forsyth, and Bundock. In December 1935, both men met with the Irish branches (Dublin and Belfast) and with the managements of the Dublin newspapers.[41] In April 1936, the union agreed to grant Ireland representation on its national executive council (NEC).[42] This move prompted closer cooperation between Dublin and Belfast, and the Irish District Council came into being in July 1936.[43] From then on, the union went from strength to strength. At the Dublin branch's 1937 AGM, it was reported that membership had increased throughout 1936 from eighty-one to 111 members. It was also reported that the union was now 100 per cent strong in one (unnamed but most likely the *Irish Press*) Dublin newspaper.[44] The following year, it was reported that membership had grown to 117 members.[45] Such was the union's growth that it joined the Irish Congress of Trade Unions in 1943.

Other stalwarts of the early Dublin NUJ included Maurice Liston, Dan Duffy, Michael McInerney, and Maurice Hickey. Liston, a staunch republican and journalist with the *Irish Press*, was chairman of the Dublin branch between 1938 and 1949, represented the Irish District Council on the union's NEC, and, in 1954, received the distinction of being the first Irish journalist to receive honorary membership of the union.[46] He was succeeded as branch chairman by Dan Duffy (*Irish Times*). Duffy had begun his journalism career on the *Northern Constitution*, and, along with journalists from the *Derry Journal*, *Derry Standard*, and *Derry Sentinel*, he established the Derry and North-West branch of the NUJ. He joined the *Irish Times* in 1945 and the following year established its first NUJ chapel.[47] Duffy was helped in this endeavour by Michael McInerney who had also just joined the paper and who would later become its long-time political correspondent.[48] Duffy was succeeded as Dublin branch chairman by Maurice Hickey (*Irish Independent*), who served as chairman throughout the 1960s.[49]

Journalism and the sexes

Amid the male-dominated journalistic world, it is important to note that several female reporters, including Nora O'Keefe and Marie Comerford (both *Irish Press*), sat on the Dublin branch committee throughout the 1930s.[50] By this stage, all three national daily titles had weekly women's pages, but, as a conservative climate developed post-Independence, the female journalists who had played key roles in the War of Independence were restricted to areas of journalism that male editors deemed suitable for them. During the revolutionary period, female activists such as Anna Kelly and Marie Comerford had been viewed as equals: Kelly had written for the *Irish Bulletin* while Comerford had been Frank Aiken's driver and an IRA courier. But by the 1930s their position had been relegated to generating female-oriented content for the *Irish Press* – much of which revolved around shopping, fashion, and cookery. While it is arguable that these women's pages maintained a media presence for women, it is equally arguable that such an approach was commercially driven, deprived women of a political voice, and relegated them to a house-bound citizenry. Relaunching itself in 1936, the women's page of the *Irish Press* observed that 'women think first in terms of clothes, food and general adornment of person and home, before they put their minds to outside matters'. Much of this content was motivated by the fact that women controlled much of any household's spending power, a point acknowledged by the *Press* when it noted that 'the main bulk of advertising is devised for women's eyes and for her interest. It may not be the woman who pays, but it is certainly the woman who buys.'[51]

Writing in 1939 about the confines placed on female journalists, Anna Kelly observed that they were all too often assigned to cover 'social events where the description of frocks and hats were considered essential to the readers' happiness'. Noting that there were only two or three women working as reporters in Dublin, she observed that the fallacy of this situation was 'based on the assumption that women readers take no interest in general news, that they will read only news that has a feminine appeal – a specialised appeal to the interests of their own sex'. Alluding to how female journalists had been sidelined, Kelly, in a manifesto that could easily have been written for the female journalists of the 1960s, advised against women reporters confining themselves to the 'feminine angle':

> In all our wars and politics they [men] never allowed us a feminine angle. We took the rough with the smooth – mostly the rough. We are politically educated more than the people of most countries. We pick our way through a newspaper just as a man does. We select and read according to our individual taste and not because of our sex. We are not mass thinkers. We are individualists. The ambitious women journalist would do well to dodge this feminine angle, for it will prove her undoing in the long run. Because her ultimate success in her profession

> depends not upon a deliberately cultivated feminine eye, but on the impartial outlook of an intelligent human being. There is no sex in good writing.

The male viewpoint had, Kelly concluded,

> been given prominence for a long time, and the women of today, who are as interested as their men folk in politics, industry, education, art, and economics, want to know what women like themselves think of this life, apart from the newest fashions and the sure way to cook an omelette.[52]

In later years at the *Irish Press*, Joan Kelly wrote a social/gossip column between 1958 and 1968 under the pen name 'Darina' before she left for London, where she later worked as an information officer with the Royal Navy.[53]

At the *Irish Independent*, its 1920s 'Women's World' column – compiled by the paper's 'Lady Editor' – concentrated on household tips and recipes. However, it too found occasional space to defend the rights of women. In 1925, it reported on a hospital's attempt to compel a female typist to resign from her position after she had married. The column noted the 'anomaly of male preachers, writers and critics upbraiding modern women for their tendency to shirk the marriage bond and the same time penalising marriage by dismissing them from their jobs the moment they are outside the church door'.[54] To compete with the *Irish Press*, in 1931 the *Independent* initiated its 'Leaves from a Woman's Diary'. Written by Gertrude Gaffney – described by Louise Ryan as 'an outspoken advocate of women's rights' – it was part social diary, part travelogue, part fashion column, but also found occasional space to examine contentious issues.[55] In 1932, Gaffney chastised Trinity College's Philosophical Society for continuing to hold 'men only' events. Was it, Gaffney wondered, 'fear of feminine competition that is eating at the heart of this masculine stronghold?'[56] In 1936, Gaffney wrote an eleven-part series on emigration to Britain. Based on a fact-finding mission, the series recounted the poverty, loneliness, and desperation that many of the emigrants encountered and revealed that many of the female emigrants were pregnant and had left Ireland 'to save their reputations'.[57] The following year, she travelled to Spain to report on its civil war.[58]

At the *Irish Times*, its women's editor, Barbara Dickson, wrote social features under her own name and fashion and cookery features under the pen name Caroline Mitchell. In 1949, Dickson initiated 'An Irishwoman's Diary' under the pen name 'Candida': its emphasis was on news relating to females who were active in the spheres of the arts, society, and the professions.[59] June Levine wrote a series of bylined articles for the *Times Pictorial* in 1948, including an article on twenty Jewish children who had survived Auschwitz and who now lived in Ireland as temporary refugees.[60] In 1947, another columnist, Mary Francis Keating, writing under the pen name 'A Woman Correspondent', initiated the 'Report to Housewives' column which concentrated on home economics, nutrition, and recipes. Occasionally, Keating covered contentious issues such as the obstacles housewives faced in securing part-time work, the need for legalised adoption, and the lack of support given by women to female candidates in local elections.[61] At the short-lived *Sunday Review* – published by the *Irish Times* between 1957 and

1963 – Patsy Dyke wrote a social column that transferred to the *Sunday Press* when the *Review* closed.

But it was de Valera's Constitution, Article 41 of which stated that mothers should not 'be obliged by economic necessity to engage in labour to the neglect of their duties in the home' that really irritated female journalists. Writing in the *Irish Independent*, Gertrude Gaffney declared that the article sounded 'the death knell of the working woman' and reduced them to being 'little more than a chattel'.[62] Such freedom of speech was not afforded to female journalists at the *Irish Press*. Claiming 'political victimisation', Hanna Sheehy-Skeffington, who contributed drama reviews to the paper, wrote to its NUJ chapel, stating that she would have to resign her membership since the paper had decided not to accept any more work from her due to her part in the agitation against Article 41. The chapel decided to investigate her complaint and if it was substantiated to write to the editor and de Valera to point out that 'it was not usual to penalise journalists for the expression of political views in their private capacity [and] that failing a satisfactory adjustment, the facts would be published'. Ultimately, the newspaper backed down, and the chapel reported that Sheehy-Skeffington's 'grievance against the *Irish Press* had been adjusted through NUJ intervention'.[63]

Female journalists did occasionally manage to speak their minds. Anna Kelly of the *Irish Press* was a particularly independently minded journalist. Writing in 1939, she observed that journalism could not expand beyond the restrictions placed upon it by the real influences – 'industrial, political, commercial' – that governed it. Within such confines, the journalist had to

> revolve like a squirrel in a cage [and] innocent-looking news goes under the microscope to see if it will please or annoy any faction, party, vested interest. Its fate will be decided, not by its value as news, but for its propaganda value in whatever game is being played at the moment.[64]

Kelly's independence of mind was tolerated at the *Press* because of her republican credentials, but even reporting social functions got her into trouble. In 1939, she wrote a devastating critique of President Douglas Hyde's annual garden party. Leaving the event, which she described with undisguised disdain, she had heard the Army Band playing 'The Men of Old' and concluded that she would have liked 'to have seen more of the men and women who made that party possible, under the Flag of Green, White and Gold [sic] over the ex-Viceregal Lodge'.[65] The President's office 'drew the attention of the Taoiseach to the article [because] the whole tone of the article seems designed to cast ridicule on the Presidential function and on the President himself and has caused a good deal of offence'.[66] The article was raised in the Dáil – Fine Gael's Richard Mulcahy accused the *Irish Press* of ridiculing the position of president – and the paper was forced to offer its 'sincere apologies to the President'.[67] The paper's board suspended Kelly, prompting Maud Gonne MacBride to write to Hyde asking him to intervene, but Hyde declined to become involved in the affair.[68] Ultimately, wiser counsel, in the form of the paper's Irish editor (and later president of Ireland) Cearbhall Ó

Dálaigh, prevailed, and Kelly was eventually allowed to contribute to the paper again.[69]

The IJA and the Institute of Journalists

While the NUJ made much headway in the Dublin and Belfast regions, it initially made little progress in rural Ireland. One of the main obstacles, according to Hugh Oram, was that the union's subscriptions proved too expensive for provincial journalists, who were paid less than their urban counterparts.[70] In April 1938, provincial journalists became organised and established the IJA. The inaugural meeting was held in Thurles, County Tipperary, and was attended by journalists from counties Kerry, Limerick, Tipperary, Kilkenny, Galway, Laois, and Offaly.[71] Among the leading lights of this new association was Con Cregan, Editor of the *Limerick Leader*, and Thomas Cleary, a reporter on the same paper.

The association's first congress, held in Galway in October 1938, was presided over by Cregan, who declared that the main aim of the association was 'to ensure that haphazard entry into Irish journalism should cease'. There was, he noted, 'no law or charter preventing any man from calling himself a journalist or practising as one if he could get somebody to employ him in such a capacity'. The new association sought to ensure that no person 'be allowed follow the profession of journalism in future unless he entered its ranks in a proper and legitimate way and went through the usual course of preparation and training for that calling'. What it proposed was a register of journalists and a charter under which it would be 'a punishable offence for anyone not registered as a journalist to practise as such'. Such governance would, according to Cregan, be similar to governance of the legal, medical, and dental professions.[72] Membership of the IJA was restricted to 'practising regular journalists' who had been associated for not less than five years with a newspaper or other periodical publication either on the office staff or as district reporters or who, in any other capacity, were living solely by journalism. Editors with no ownership interest were also eligible for membership.[73] Despite this ambitious start, the IJA would never register as a trade union, and its invitation to then president Douglas Hyde to become its patron was turned down.[74]

For its part, the NUJ was totally opposed to the IJA's idea of a register for journalists. It described the idea as 'the greatest possible menace to the freedom of the Press' and declared that 'any limitation or state interference with entry to the profession would be opposed to public interests'.[75] Nonetheless, on Good Friday of 1940, representatives of the NUJ, the IJA, and the Institute of Journalists met to discuss the idea of a register, after which the NUJ completely rejected the idea. As far as the NUJ was concerned, 'the only hope of improving the journalists' lot was by 100% trade unionism and that the card of a strong energetic union was a better safeguard than any charter or register'.[76] In July 1941, the IJA met with and presented its proposals to Taoiseach Éamon de Valera, who promised to consider them.[77] The IJA was subsequently informed that the government would not pursue the matter until the government-sponsored Commission on Vocational Organisation had issued its report.[78] There, rather abruptly, the matter ended.[79] But the increased interaction between the IJA and the NUJ led to Cleary and Cregan establishing one of the first provincial branches of the NUJ in Limerick in 1943. Shortly afterwards, the IJA amalgamated with the NUJ. After the war, Cleary moved to Dublin to work with the *Evening Mail*; he later joined the *Irish Independent* and became treasurer of the NUJ's Dublin branch.[80]

The Institute of Journalists also remained active but remained the domain of senior editorial staff. A briefing note prepared in 1945 for President Seán T. O'Kelly on the different journalist organisations in the country described the institute as 'an English Body with an Irish branch … mainly a professional organisation, its members consisting principally of senior Journalists of the standing of Assistant Editors, Leading writers, etc.'. In contrast, the NUJ (also 'an English Body') was described as 'more of a trade union and is affiliated to British TUC (Trade Union Congress)'. Its membership consisted of 'reporters, sub-editors etc., but it includes many senior journalists of the rank of editor'. The memo noted that while 'there is nothing to prevent Journalists from being members of both … in practice they are more or less distinct in personnel'.[81]

Throughout the 1930s, such was the prestige of the institute's membership that its annual dinner dance was regularly addressed by the head of government. In 1937, the *Irish Press* reported Éamon de Valera as having told the institute that 'Journalism is the greatest of the professions: it can do more than any other profession for humanity.' The following year, he returned and queried the accuracy of this report: had it not been the *Irish Press* that reported his speech he would have been inclined to say he had 'never made such an absolute statement'; he felt he must have 'said "one of the greatest" or something of that sort'.[82] On this occasion, de Valera took the opportunity to address concerns that had arisen in relation to the Constitution, which had been passed by referendum in July 1937. Article 40 related, in part, to the relationship between the state, the media, and, by extension, journalism. The new constitution guaranteed freedom of expression 'subject to public order or morality' but also empowered the state to ensure that the media, 'while preserving their rightful liberty of expression, including criticism of government policy, shall not be used to undermine public order or undermine public order or the authority of the state'.[83] In his speech, de Valera declared that freedom of the press 'if it is to have a meaning must have a reasonable meaning'. 'No reasonable man', he continued, 'would blame the public authority for restraining a newspaper that, for reason of commercial interest, had set itself to foster a war-fever, for example, or that callously pandered to unlawful passions, or that really endeavoured to overthrow the lawful authority of the State'. As a last resort, the protection of the public interest was given to the state, 'not to a private firm that might want to do certain things for commercial interest, or a private journalist who might have extraordinary views which are quite contrary to the general common-sense of what is right, just and moral'.[84]

The crisis of registration and the 1947 agreement

Competition between the NUJ and the Institute of Journalists for the ear of government continued throughout the 1930s and 1940s. In 1937, as the government was deciding the composition of the nominating bodies for the Seanad panels, Éamon de Valera met with an NUJ delegation that sought nominating-body status for the Cultural and Educational Panel.[85] As recorded in the NUJ account of the meeting, de Valera expressed the view that an obstacle to the representation of journalists in the Seanad 'was that both the NUJ and the Institute had their headquarters in England'.[86] For its part, the Department of Education refused the NUJ's application, expressing its doubt 'as to the desirability of the suggestion that journalism might be represented on the Cultural and Educational Panel, apart from the fact that so far as the Dept. is aware there is not at present in existence any organised body entitled to represent Irish journalism'. On the final list of nominating bodies, the NUJ was excluded while the Institute of Journalists was included.[87] By 1943, however, the NUJ was a nominating body through its affiliation with the Irish Congress of Trade Unions, and it nominated Joseph Dennigan and R. M. Fox as Seanad candidates.[88] Neither man was successful in his election bid.

Throughout the 1940s, the NUJ faced several challenges that could have killed it but that instead made it stronger. The Trade Union Act of 1941 provided for state regulation of trade unions; it required them to register, to acquire a negotiating licence, and to deposit a sum proportionate to membership with the High Court. Part III of the Act, later found to be unconstitutional, stated that only Irish-based unions would be given negotiation rights by the Minister for Industry and Commerce. This legislation did not sit well with NUJ headquarters in London. Having returned from a stormy NEC meeting at Leicester in October 1941, Irish delegate Geoffrey Coulter reported that the NEC had 'by 15 votes to 3 decided to chuck out the Dublin branch if and when the Irish Trade Union Bill became operative'. Coulter noted that 'the big argument put up against us was that the NUJ could not co-operate in operating Fascist legislation'.[89]

In February 1942, the Dublin branch proposed a motion for that year's annual delegate meeting instructing the NEC 'to register the NUJ as a negotiating body under the Éire Trade Union Act'.[90] Shortly afterwards, however, the NEC reaffirmed its decision 'that it would not be in the interests of the Union to seek to function as a registered and authorised body under the terms of the new Act, but that the utmost aid should be given to the members in Éire to organise themselves in the changed circumstances'. Thus, the NEC proposed that Irish journalists resign from the NUJ, establish their own trade union, and maintain 'cordial and reciprocal' relations with the NUJ. It proposed to provide this new union with the £1,000 needed to register and £600 to open an office and to cover various benefit claims for up to two years from the date of separation.[91] The NEC also circulated a notice to all members explaining its position in advance of the upcoming annual delegate meeting at which the issue would be decided. The notice described the legislation 'as an obnoxious piece of anti-trade union legislation designed to bring trade union activity in Éire under stricter government control'. It also noted that if the union were found to be in breach of the law then fines or damages would be deducted from the deposit, which would then have to be made whole again. The risks under this provision could not, it noted, 'be accurately gauged because the possible offences are not stated, and new regulations may be introduced at any time by the Éire government under its special powers'.[92] (The country was operating under emergency legislation introduced to deal with the Second World War.) To operate as a trade union the NUJ would 'have to invest in Éire at least £1,000 under the control of what is technically a foreign government and subject to the laws and special powers of that government'.[93]

The following month, representatives of the Dublin branch travelled to London to meet with NUJ President, Tom Foster. The delegates, Joe Dennigan (*Irish Press*) and Patrick Staunton (*Daily Express*), noted that while the separation terms were very generous, Irish journalists wished to remain within the NUJ. Staunton stated that it would be 'a terribly difficult task', even with the NUJ's financial support, to establish a trade union for journalists in Ireland as they were relatively few in number and so would have to pay very high subscriptions to provide for strike and other benefits. They could not afford this, and, according to Staunton, if the NUJ withdrew from Ireland then they would be left with no option but to join the Institute of Journalists, which had decided to register and seek a negotiating licence. Tensions over Ireland's neutrality also emerged in the discussions. According to Frederick Mansfield, 'information to support the belief that Nazi influence in Éire was being used to separate Éire and British trade unionists' was discussed. When Foster asked how Irish journalists felt about Britain, the Irish delegates replied, 'They are not pro-German. They just don't like the British.' This was, presumably, a reference to the fact that many of the union's Irish leaders had taken part in the War of Independence. Dennigan and Staunton also pointed out that other unions in a similar position to the NUJ had decided to register or to leave the issue to be decided by their Irish memberships. The sides parted without any decision being taken.[94]

At the union's annual delegate meeting in April, the Irish delegation proposed that the NUJ register under the Act and allow Irish journalists to remain in the union. Irish delegate R. M. Fox made a stirring speech in which he noted that 'the NEC proposed to abandon the Dublin branch and spend £1,600 to smash the NUJ in Dublin'. Unless the NUJ agreed to register, he concluded, the institute would 'automatically become the body speaking for journalists in Dublin'. In reply, Clement Bundock declared the matter as one of 'trade union principle': legislation that put trade unionism under state control was 'repugnant'. If Irish journalists could accept such legislation, he asserted, the NUJ would help them form a new union to operate under the Act. Ultimately it was agreed that the Dublin branch would operate in a holding position until the operation of the Act was better understood, with the NEC authorised to pay the £1,000 for a trial period if circumstances demanded it.[95]

In August 1942, the union's NEC received an urgent request from the Dublin branch to register and apply for a licence. In return for its support during the printers' strike of 1934, the union had been allocated a seat on the JIC established to resolve disputes within the newspaper sector. But it was now informed that as it was not a registered body it would have to vacate the coveted council seat. It was time to make a final decision on registration. The NEC subsequently decided by a majority of one (eleven votes to ten) to immediately register as a trade union in Ireland.[96] The decision to register paid off in terms of attracting new members and encouraging existing members to pay their membership subscriptions. In June 1943, the Dublin branch noted that 'the £1,000 lodged had already drawn about £300 in subs. and interest at 2.5% which was not a bad investment'.[97]

The NUJ's position was further boosted in June 1947 when the union and newspaper proprietors (represented by the Dublin Newspapers Managers' Committee) concluded an agreement on terms and conditions of employment for all Dublin journalists. The agreement was hammered out by John J. Dunne (Independent Newspapers), Robert Childers (Irish Press Group), Tynan O'Mahoney (Irish Times Ltd), and James Begg (Evening Mail Ltd) on the newspaper side; and by P. Fullerton Bustard, NUJ national organiser, and Brendan Malin, Irish NEC member, on the union side. It established, for the first time, minimum rates of payment, maximum hours of labour, and general conditions of employment for journalists, including photographers and creative offices and applied to all newspapers owned or controlled by the Dublin Newspapers Managers' Committee members. The agreement provided for a minimum weekly rate of £9 9s 0d for senior journalists (defined as aged twenty-four years or older with three years' experience, including one year on the metropolitan press), and a minimum scale for juniors (aged under twenty-four years) that ranged from £2 15s 0d at age eighteen to £7 10s 0d at age twenty-three. It also created a minimum daily rate for casual or freelance reporters at £1 11s 6d per day. In terms of employment conditions, it stipulated that the normal working week was to consist of not more than a five-and-a-half-day week of forty-four hours or an eleven-day fortnight of eighty-eight hours. The normal working day was not to exceed eight consecutive hours, and all journalists were to be awarded at least three weeks' holiday annually with pay and a day with pay in lieu of each bank holiday worked.[98]

The newspaper proprietors did not easily grant such improvements. The agreement took six months of negotiations, and, as the talks dragged on, the NUJ agreed that strike notice be served on all newspapers on 16 May 1947.[99] This focused the minds of the proprietors, and agreement was finally reached. As recalled by Gerry Mulvey, then with the *Irish Times*, proprietors mounted a serious attempt to block the introduction of an eight-hour day in the belief that newspapers could not function on such a system. According to Mulvey, 'the Independent and the Press fought very hard' to prevent the eight-hour day being introduced as they were concerned about whether a reporter would, 'when his time was up at four o'clock, walk out of a court and demand that another reporter take his place'. But the union had fought hard for the introduction of an eight-hour day to replace the long-standing practice of split shifts that had come to dominate journalism. Before the introduction of the eight-hour day, journalists usually worked from 10 a.m. to 4 p.m., had a gap of two to three hours, and then spent another few hours covering evening assignments. It was these working hours, particularly the gap between shifts, that encouraged and facilitated the drink culture endemic in Dublin newspaper circles at the time. There was, Mulvey recalled, 'simply nothing else to do'.[100] As the years progressed, this agreement was revised, and the minimum weekly rates were increased in 1951, 1953, and 1956.[101]

Such success in the capital did not go unnoticed in the provinces, and the NUJ launched an intensive membership campaign in local and provincial newspapers in 1948. The following year, negotiations with the Irish Master Printers' Association, which represented provincial newspaper proprietors, yielded results. In January 1949, both sides reached an agreement on terms and conditions of employment for provincial journalists. The agreement provided for the introduction of a minimum rate of £7 per week for senior journalists (defined as aged twenty-four years or older with four years' experience) and a minimum weekly scale for juniors (aged under twenty-four years) which ranged from £2 0s 0d at age eighteen to £5 10s 0d at age twenty-three. In terms of employment conditions, it stipulated that the normal working week was to consist of not more than a five-and-a-half-day week of forty-four hours or an eleven-day fortnight of eight-eight hours. When Sunday work was essential, it stipulated that, where possible, turns of duty should be worked on a rota system. All journalists were to be awarded at least two weeks' holiday annually with pay and a day with pay in lieu of each bank holiday worked.[102] Given that many provincial journalists had been working for as little as £3 per week, the agreement made a huge difference to their quality of life. Belfast proved a tougher nut to crack: the long struggle for recognition from the Belfast Newspaper Society (the organisation representing proprietors) only ended in 1951 when agreement on revised rates of pay was reached.[103]

Such success should have cemented the NUJ's claim to be the undisputed representative association for journalists in Ireland. But the tides of history turn suddenly, and, less than two years after the industry-wide agreements had had been achieved, the government announced its intention to declare a republic and leave the British Commonwealth. This prompted some journalists to consider, despite all that had been achieved, the desirability of being represented by a trade union that had its headquarters in London. In the heady days of the new republic, these journalists took matters into their own hands and, amid an acrimonious split, established a new, Irish, trade union for journalists, the Guild of Irish Journalists, which was to be a thorn in the side of the NUJ for nearly two decades.

Notes

1 DED, vol. 76 (col. 971), 14 Jun. 1939.

2 C. Bundock, *The National Union of Journalists: A Jubilee History* (Oxford, 1957), p. 110. For more on the closure of the *Freeman's Journal*, see F. M. Larkin, 'A great daily organ: the *Freeman's Journal*, 1763–1924', *History Ireland*, 14:3 (2006), 44–9.

3 *Irish Times*, 14 May 1930, p. 8; 10 May 1930, p. 1.

4 *Irish Times*, 13 Aug. 1928, p. 5; 12 Jan. 1931, p. 13.

5 *Irish Times*, 17 Nov. 1926, p. 8.

6 F. Mansfield, *Gentlemen, the Press! Chronicles of a Crusade* (London, 1943), p. 489.
7 Bundock, *National Union of Journalists*, pp. 110–11.
8 NAI, Tsch/S/5936, correspondence, Oct. and Nov. 1929.
9 HCRC, NUJ, Dublin branch minutes, 10 May and 12 Jul. 1930.
10 For histories of the Irish Press Group, see M. O'Brien, *De Valera, Fianna Fáil and the Irish Press* (Dublin, 2001) and R. Burke, *Press Delete: The Decline and Fall of the Irish Press* (Dublin, 2005).
11 University College Dublin Archives (UCDA), de Valera papers, File 1453/1, letter from de Valera to Archbishop Daniel Mannix, 1932.
12 M. de Búrca, *The GAA: A History* (Dublin, 1999), p. 217.
13 *Irish Press*, 1 Oct. 1936, p. 9.
14 *Irish Press*, 20 Dec. 1937, p. 3.
15 T. P. Coogan, *Ireland in the Twentieth Century* (London, 2003), p. 721.
16 National Library of Australia (NLA), Oral History Project, 637; O'Sullivan interviewed by Andrew Reeves, 26 Jul. 1978.
17 DED, vol. 49 (col. 2202), 11 Oct. 1933.
18 *Irish Times*, 12 Oct. 1933, p. 4; HCRC, NUJ, Dublin branch minutes, 14 Oct. 1933; *Irish Times*, 16 Oct. 1933, p. 5. The controversy arose from de Valera's false statement that Mulcahy had met the British Minister for War, Lord Hailsham in Glasgow. He later apologised, but Mulcahy repeatedly stated that the source of the false information was an *Irish Press* journalist.
19 Mansfield, *Gentlemen, the Press!*, p. 489.
20 *Irish Press*, 10 Dec. 1973, p. 7.
21 HCRC, NUJ, Dublin branch minutes, 7 Feb. 1931.
22 NAI, 97/9/73, memo on communism, 24 Nov. 1932, pp. 1–57, at pp. 1 and 5.
23 NAI, 97/9/73, memo on communism, p. 8.
24 *Irish Times*, 25 Oct. 1932, p. 8; 27 Oct. 1932, p. 2.
25 S. MacBride, *That Day's Struggle: A Memoir* (Dublin, 2005), pp. 119–20.
26 *Irish Press*, 9 Dec. 1933, p. 1.
27 *Irish Times*, 30 Dec. 1933, p. 8.
28 NAI, S2380, Constitution: special powers tribunal; *Irish Times*, 30 Dec. 1933, p. 8.
29 *Irish Times*, 1 Jan. 1934, p. 7.
30 *Irish Times*, 2 Jan. 1934, p. 4; 3 Jan. 1934, p. 7; 9 Jan. 1934, p. 5.
31 *Irish Times*, 16 Jan. 1934, p. 2; HCRC, NUJ, Dublin branch minutes, 13 Jan. 1934.
32 UCDA, Joseph Dennigan papers, P188/28.
33 *Irish Times*, 16 Jan. 1934, p. 8; 17 Jan. 1934, p. 7.
34 *Irish Times*, 19 Jan. 1932, p. 11.
35 *Irish Times*, 13 Mar. 1981, p. 7.
36 *Irish Times*, 10 Jan. 1938, p. 2.
37 *Irish Times*, 16 May 1933, p. 2; 9 Aug. 1933, p. 15.
38 O. Curran, *Two Hundred Years of Trade Unionism* (Dublin, 2009), p. 59; HCRC, NUJ, Dublin branch minutes, 7, 11, 14, 18 Sep. 1934.
39 Mansfield, *Gentlemen, the Press!*, p. 490. R. M. Fox was a prolific author on trade-union history. See his obituary in the *Irish Press*, 29 Dec. 1969, p. 4.
40 *Irish Times*, 21 Nov. 1934, p. 2.
41 *Irish Times*, 14 Dec. 1935, p. 10.
42 *Irish Times*, 20 Apr. 1936, p. 8. The first Irish representative on the union's council was *Irish Press* sports reporter, Patrick McKenna.
43 *Irish Times*, 28 Jul. 1936, p. 5; 21 Dec. 1951, p. 5.

44 *Irish Times*, 18 Jan. 1937, p. 5.
45 *Irish Times*, 10 Jan. 1938, p. 2.
46 *Irish Times*, 20 Apr. 1973, p. 5.
47 *Irish Times*, 14 Mar. 1983, p. 11.
48 *Irish Times*, 28 Jan. 1980, p. 8.
49 *Irish Times*, 18 Nov. 1988, p. 13.
50 *Irish Times*, 6 Feb. 1933, p. 9; 18 Jan. 1937, p. 5.
51 *Irish Press*, 21 Mar. 1936, p. 5.
52 *Irish Press*, 10 Feb. 1939, p. 8.
53 *Irish Press*, 10 Oct. 1969, p. 11.
54 *Irish Independent*, 27 Jan. 1925, p. 7.
55 L. Ryan, *Gender, Identity and the Irish Press 1922–37: Embodying the Nation* (New York, 2002), pp. 100–1.
56 *Irish Independent*, 11 Nov. 1932, p. 5.
57 The series ran in the *Irish Independent*, 7–18 Dec. 1936.
58 Gaffney's series, 'In war-torn Spain', was published during Feb. and Mar. 1937. A second series was published in Oct. and Nov. 1937. For Gaffney's obituary see *Irish Independent*, 10 Dec. 1959, p. 13.
59 *Irish Times*, 20 Apr. 1994, p. 2.
60 *Times Pictorial*, 8 Jan. 1948, p. 5.
61 *Irish Times*, 22 Jan. 1949, p. 4; 3 Dec. 1949, p. 5; 30 Sep. 1950, p. 5.
62 *Irish Independent*, 7 May 1937, p. 5.
63 HCRC, NUJ, Dublin branch minutes, 7 Aug. 1937 and 2 Oct. 1937.
64 *Irish Press*, 2 Feb. 1939, p. 7.
65 *Irish Press*, 20 Jun. 1939, p. 8.
66 NAI, Pres/1/P969, memo dated 22 Jun. 1939.
67 DED, vol. 76 (cols. 1515–19), 22 Jun. 1939; *Irish Press*, 23 Jun. 1939, p. 8.
68 NAI, Pres/1/P969, letter dated 27 Jul. 1939.
69 *Irish Press*, 22 Mar. 1978, p. 4.
70 H. Oram, *The Newspaper Book: A History of Newspapers in Ireland, 1649–1983* (Dublin, 1983), p. 192.
71 *Irish Independent*, 12 Apr. 1938, p. 12.
72 *Irish Independent*, 10 Oct. 1938, p. 12.
73 *The Leader*, 18 Oct. 1941, pp. 270–1.
74 NAI, P 1437, letters dated 30 Nov. 1939 and 8 Dec. 1939.
75 *Irish Times*, 14 Feb. 1939, p. 8.
76 HCRC, NUJ, Dublin branch minutes, 5 Apr. 1940 and 7 Feb. 1943.
77 *Weekly Irish Times*, 5 Jul. 1941, p. 5.
78 *Irish Independent*, 4 Dec. 1941, p. 4. The report was published in 1944.
79 A similar bill, the Journalists (Registration) Bill, had been unsuccessfully put before the British parliament in Jul. 1936. See *Irish Times*, 25 Feb. 1935, p. 4 for details of the Bill.
80 *Irish Times*, 22 Feb. 1989, p. 9 and 2 Mar. 1989, p. 11; HCRC, NUJ, Dublin branch minutes, 7 Nov. 1943.
81 NAI, P 1071, briefing note dated 10 Oct. 1945.
82 NAI, 97/9/160; see also *Irish Press*, 31 Jan. 1938, p. 1.
83 Bunreacht na hÉireann, Article 40, 6, 1, i.
84 NAI, 97/9/160, Institute of Journalists. See also, *Irish Independent*, 31 Jan. 1938, p. 11.
85 NAI, Tsch/3/S10089; the meeting occurred on 16 Aug. 1937.
86 HCRC, NUJ, Dublin branch minutes, n/d Sep. 1937.

87 NAI, Tsch/3/S10264, memo dated 11 Oct. 1937.
88 NLI, R. M. Fox papers, Ms. 40,327 (9); *Irish Times* 17 Jul. 1943, p. 1; HCRC, NUJ, Dublin branch minutes, 6 Jul. 1943.
89 HCRC, NUJ, Dublin branch minutes, 9 Nov. 1941.
90 HCRC, NUJ, Dublin branch minutes, 2 Feb. 1942.
91 HCRC, NUJ, Dublin branch minutes, 8 Mar. 1942.
92 Mansfield, *Gentlemen, the Press!*, pp. 490–1.
93 HCRC, NUJ, Dublin branch minutes, 8 Mar. 1942.
94 Mansfield, *Gentlemen, the Press!*, pp. 491–2.
95 Mansfield, *Gentlemen, the Press!*, pp. 491–2; HCRC, NUJ, Dublin branch minutes, 3 May 1942.
96 Mansfield, *Gentlemen, the Press!*, pp. 491–2; Bundock, *National Union of Journalists*, p. 222; HCRC, NUJ, Dublin branch minutes, 6 Sep., 4 Oct. and 6 Dec. 1942.
97 HCRC, NUJ, Dublin branch minutes, 6 Jun. 1943.
98 NLI, Piaras Béaslaí papers, Ms. 33,981 (9). See also *Irish Times*, 10 Jun. 1947, p. 3. For comparison purposes, the salary scale for single male national teachers in 1947 ranged from £210 to £386 and for married male national teachers from £225 to £525, all depending on length of service. See *Report of the Dept. of Education, 1946–7* (Dublin, 1947), p. 85.
99 HCRC, NUJ, Dublin branch minutes, n/d, 1947.
100 Interview with Gerry Mulvey.
101 Bundock, *National Union of Journalists*, pp. 222–3. See also *Irish Times*, 10 June 1953, p. 1.
102 NLI, Piaras Béaslaí papers, Ms. 33,981 (9). See also *Irish Times*, 1 Feb. 1949, p. 7.
103 Bundock, *National Union of Journalists*, pp. 223–4.

5

A red republic

At Rest: We mourn the death of Joseph V. Stalin, beloved and brilliant leader of the peoples of the Soviet Union and champion of peace and freedom among the peoples of all lands.[1]

— Death notice published in the Evening Mail, March 1953

As noted by political scientist Gary Murphy, 'the dismal economic conditions of the post-war period brought with it significant political uncertainty [and] the fluidity of politics during this period saw successive changes of government in the four elections between 1948 and 1957'.[2] Between 1951 and 1961, over 400,000 people emigrated, and the decade witnessed three changes of government. During the summer of 1953, marches and sit-down protests by the Dublin Unemployed Association became a frequent occurrence and a worry for the government and the Catholic Church, both of which perceived such activity as the first signs of communism. As Brian Fallon, then with the *Irish Times*, recalled, the church was 'almost insanely obsessed with international communism which was never even a shadow-threat in Ireland'.[3] Newspaper proprietors were also worried: the Unemployed Association had plans to launch its own newspaper. They were also wary at what was perceived as the growing power of the trade-union movement. As John Kelly of the *Irish Press* remembered, the atmosphere at that newspaper was tense: 'editorial executives had to watch every trade union story on the orders of the de Valeras. They studied them in microscopic detail and had to be careful of the various groups. They were scared of the political left, which was still minor enough at the time.'[4]

Over the preceding decade, the growing influence of the NUJ had not gone unnoticed by politicians or the Catholic Church. Against the background of the Cold War and the growing fear of communism, the politics of those involved in leading the NUJ in Ireland caused increased concern, particularly among the Catholic hierarchy, and fears that the union was a Communist front grew stronger as the 1950s progressed. As the unofficial organ of the Catholic Church, *The Standard* kept a wary eye on developments and never missed an opportunity to warn its readers about the dangers of communism. The paper, described by one writer as 'a rabidly right-wing and quite influential lay Catholic paper', was edited by Peadar O'Curry.[5] Educated at the National Seminary in Maynooth, O'Curry had been in charge of the church's public-relations team during the 1932 Eucharistic Congress. He was, as his obituary put it, 'a man of very strong right-wing views'.[6] He became editor of *The Standard* in 1938 and built up its weekly circulation from 8,000 copies in 1938 to 78,000 copies in 1954. According to one review of his editorship, during his reign the paper was virulent in its condemnation of communism, high in its praise for the 'Portuguese patriot' Salazar and Franco of Spain, staunch in its denunciations of strikers, and virulent in its attacks on bodies such as the People's College, the Workers' League and the World Federation of Trade Unions. No hint of communism escaped its attention. In one edition, the paper condemned the library of the Irish Bakers' Union because it contained books written by Karl Marx and James Connolly. Was the cost of buying such books, it enquired, 'included in the price of bread?'[7]

The backdrop to the allegations of communism levelled against the NUJ's Irish officers during the late 1940s and early 1950s was the appointment of Michael McInerney as an *Irish Times* reporter in 1946. McInerney, a Limerick-born journalist, had lived in London during the late 1930s, had contributed articles to the Communist Party's newspaper, the *Daily Worker*, and had, in 1938, co-founded the Connolly Club in London. As its name suggests, the club, which was originally the London branch of the Republican Congress, espoused the teachings of James Connolly and campaigned for Irish unity. McInerney was its secretary and also, in 1939, established and edited its first newspaper, *Irish Freedom* (later the *Irish Democrat*).[8] Against the backdrop of the IRA's bombing campaign in Britain in 1939 and 1940, McInerney was refused re-entry into Britain in 1941 after a holiday at home in Ireland. He moved to Belfast and worked on the railway where he also immersed himself in trade-union organisation, becoming industrial organiser of the Communist Party and editor of the party's newspaper *Unity*. Having joined the *Irish Times*, McInerney helped organise the paper's first NUJ chapel. His reporting of trade-union matters soon attracted the attention of military intelligence: it believed he was slanting coverage in favour of the trade-union movement.[9] He became the paper's industrial correspondent in 1951 and its political correspondent in 1953.[10]

McInerney was not the only journalist under suspicion. The employment of one Brian O'Neill by the *Irish Press* in 1942 had also raised eyebrows. In a Department of Justice memorandum dated 1936, O'Neill is mentioned as having lectured in the Workers' College, where he taught 'the ABC of Communism'. It also noted that O'Neill was on the Central Executive Committee of the Communist Party of Ireland, but the report is sketchy on his background: 'was at UCD [University College Dublin]? and is thought to be a native of Manchester: he is a professional Communist pamphleteer and is regarded as a paid agitator'.[11] A supplementary file noted he was

> believed to have been sent to Ireland by the CPGB [Communist Party of Great Britain] and first came to notice by reason of his association with the Revolutionary Workers' Groups towards the end of 1931. He is a prominent member of the Dublin branch of the National Union of Journalists … was at one

> time editor of the *Irish Workers' Voice* and is one of the principal Communist pamphleteers in this country.[12]

O'Neill is also mentioned in the reports of Dublin's Archbishop John Charles McQuaid's vigilance committee which kept a close eye on journalists. O'Neill was described in one such report as having 'trained in Moscow, "Pravda"; Worked in Arcos House, Soviet Trade & Espionage Agency in London until broken up by police in 1927. Came here [Dublin] in 1931 when in trouble with police in Glasgow, took high-sounding name of B. O'N. and later joined IP [*Irish Press*] staff. Organised here as a paid man for CP [Communist Party] (Britain).'[13] Whatever his origins were, O'Neill continued to work at the *Irish Press* until the early 1970s.[14] In a report on journalism and communism compiled in 1948 by the Knights of Columbanus – an exclusively male conservative lay organisation that often organised vigilance committees and engaged in media monitoring for the hierarchy – for Archbishop McQuaid, both McInerney and O'Neill are mentioned as suspected Communists, as are Anna Kelly and Tony Molloy, both *Irish Press* journalists during the 1940s.[15]

The fear of communism

In June 1948, the Irish delegates to the NUJ annual delegate meeting, Michael McInerney and Maurice Liston, voted for Allen Hutt in the election for the editorship of the union's newsletter, *The Journalist*. Hutt, the night editor of the *Daily Worker* and a typography expert, was a well-known Communist, but, according to Clement Bundock, never 'permitted his political view to obtrude into his conduct of the union's journal'.[16] However, the action of the Irish delegates prompted reactions from several quarters. In a speech, the Bishop of Galway, Michael Browne, observed that 'the indication of the great value of trade unions were the desperate efforts that Communists were making to get control of them … and to use them as a weapon of political aggression and revolution'. He had heard of a union 'which concerned newspapermen which had elected a Communist as Editor of its trade journal' and called on people to 'take an active interest in their trade unions, and endeavour to keep them on sound lines'.[17] This rebuke was enough to prompt the NUJ's Dublin Trade and Periodical branch to write to Archbishop McQuaid and the *Irish Independent* to declare that it had 'nominated and voted for a non-communist journalist in opposition to Mr Hutt [and had] no sympathy whatsoever with any form of communism'.[18]

However, controversy erupted when Hutt supposedly boasted that he had been elected 'with the support of the solid Irish bloc'. At a meeting of the NUJ's Dublin branch in September 1948, one journalist, Gabriel Diskin, queried Hutt's assertion. In reply, Brendan Malin, the Irish delegate to the union's NEC, stated that McInerney and Liston 'had voted for Hutt not because he was a communist but because he was the best man for the job, being an expert in types and that he was friendly to the Irish NUJ'. Malin also observed that, if the matter were pursued, 'it would split the branch from stem to stem'. At the branch's November meeting, a resolution proposed by Diskin accepting the delegates' motives but describing Hutt's election as 'unfortunate' was defeated by twenty votes to four. This led one source (most likely Diskin) to inform Archbishop McQuaid that the branch had 'an active "left" of at least 15 members. Some were communists.'[19]

With a meeting of the NUJ's Irish District Council imminent, Bishop Browne took a swipe at the political pedigree of Michael McInerney and his involvement in the Connolly Club. Browne noted that the British Trade Union General Council had issued a statement to all unions declaring that it had 'evidence that the Communists were deliberately seeking to obstruct economic recovery and to disrupt the trade union movement'. In Browne's view, there were two organisations that were of 'particular interest for Irish Catholics – the Connolly Association and Connolly Clubs and the *Irish Democrat* paper in England'. It was common knowledge, Browne observed, 'that well-known Communists are connected with this Association as founders and members of the Executive' and that the clubs were 'used to bring Irish boys and girls into the Communist recruiting net and propaganda'. The main objective of the *Irish Democrat* was, according to Browne, 'to infect Irish workers with the Communist Party line'. He thus called on all Irish trade unionists 'to open their eyes to the malignant nature of Communist agitation and its evil machinations' and noted that 'the vast body of our trade unions – especially those which have their headquarters in Ireland have resisted Communist infiltration'.[20] It was against this backdrop that the Irish District Council met to review Hutt's election. The meeting was a stormy one, and the Limerick branch proposed a motion that left no one in any doubt as to where its members stood:

> That the Irish District Council enters a most emphatic protest against the appointment of an avowed Communist to the important position of Editor of the official organ of the Union, as such an appointment is tantamount to a challenge to Christian and democratic principles. That this Council hereby disassociates itself from an appointment that has outraged our Christian feelings and our sense of appreciation of true freedom; fully realising as we do that the primary allegiance of a Communist is to the Marxist doctrines enunciated from Moscow.[21]

In response, one journalist branded Limerick 'a sodality city'.[22] After a long debate, the Dublin branch stood by McInerney and Liston; it accepted their argument that they had voted for Hutt not because he was a Communist but because he was the best candidate. The Belfast branch declared for the freedom of the individual to belong to any political party he wished.[23] It fell to the Derry branch to propose a compromise motion designed to prevent a damaging split from occurring:

> That this Council, representative of all Irish Branches of the NUJ, calls on the National Executive Council of the Union to declare its total opposition to Communism and to endeavour by every means in its power to defeat all future proposals for the appointment to any office at the disposal of the Executive of Branches of the Union, of members of the Communist Party, and all other attempts at Communist infiltration into the Union.[24]

This motion was passed, though not unanimously. The lack of unanimity prompted Peadar O'Curry of *The Standard* to observe that while 'Irish Catholics … will be glad to see that a majority of the men on whom they depend for information and interpretation of home and foreign events in these perilous days, are opposed to Communism', they were also entitled to ask who had voted against the motion and what newspapers they worked for.[25] Three days after the meeting, O'Curry wrote a memorandum for the Garda Special Branch (intelligence section) in relation to a meeting that had been held between the NUJ and the Minister for Justice. The purpose of that meeting had been to foster closer relations between journalists and the force. O'Curry saw it as his duty to warn the Special Branch of the dangers of establishing relationships with certain journalists. It was not possible, he stated, to assume that journalists were 'themselves adherents of the principles of democracy'. In particular, he drew attention to Michael McInerney, whom he described as 'a recent import into journalism', founder of the 'so called "Connolly Association"' and one of 'the triumvirate running the Communist Party in the Six Counties'. The NUJ's Dublin branch, O'Curry believed, 'contains quite a few active Communists'. What guarantee was there, he asked,

> that information, perhaps not necessarily of a confidential and political character, given to journalists in the course of co-operation with the Ministry of Justice ... will not be communicated ... to organisations which have the declared object of destroying the democratic Government of the Irish Republic and replacing it with a Godless totalitarianism?[26]

The Guild of Irish Journalists

The following year, the Communist scare continued to put a strain on the NUJ's Dublin branch. The imprisonment of Cardinal József Mindszenty by the Hungarian Communist government was condemned by the branch; it noted that, 'as Christians and as trade unionists', it wished the Hungarian people 'a speedy end to their tribulation and tyranny'.[27] In February 1949, the compromise motion agreed at the Irish District Council meeting came up for discussion at the NUJ's NEC meeting: it was emphatically rejected by nineteen votes to one.[28] This was the final straw for several Dublin journalists. In March 1949, at a meeting of the Dublin branch, a proposal that a new union be established was defeated by thirty-five votes to five.[29] Undaunted, those who had lost faith with the NUJ pressed ahead, and, shortly afterwards, Comhaltas Nuachtóirí Éireann, or the Guild of Irish Journalists, made its existence known in a statement to Dublin newspapers. The language used was unambiguous, with a neat reference to Moscow:

> We consider it inconsistent with the dignity of a sovereign independent state that its newspaper men and writers who play such a vital part in moulding public opinion should be controlled from outside. What would be thought in Paris if it were proposed that French journalists should be controlled from Berlin, or what would be said in Moscow if it were proposed to control Russian journalists from Rome? Why should Irish journalists be controlled from London?[30]

This declaration is remarkably similar to sentiments expressed by Revd Richard Devane, who, in an article in *Hibernia* earlier that month, had criticised the situation whereby 'newspaper men in the free and independent Irish State find themselves organised in two foreign trade organisations [the NUJ and the institute], each of which has its headquarters in a foreign state'. No one could contemplate, he observed, 'the journalists of a small national *independent* State on the Continent having its journalists organised in a foreign Union and with its headquarters in a foreign State – for instance, the Swiss journalists in a German Union, having its headquarters in Berlin'.[31]

The split also mirrored events in the wider trade-union movement in which a damaging division had occurred. The membership of the Irish Trade Union Congress (ITUC) had originally been comprised of Irish branches of London-based unions as well as Irish unions such as the ITGWU. In May 1945, fifteen Irish unions, including the ITGWU, had established their own congress, the Congress of Irish Unions (CIU), membership of which was restricted to unions that had their headquarters in Ireland.[32] The wider political environment was also a factor. The Republic of Ireland Act 1949, by which the Irish state left the British Commonwealth, and the corresponding British legislation, the Ireland Act, which guaranteed that Northern Ireland would remain within the United Kingdom, aroused passions over Partition that intensified as the Irish government embarked on an international anti-Partition campaign. This was a period characterised by what Conor Cruise O'Brien described as 'anti-partition propaganda [that] became hyper-excited and stridently anti-British after the Ireland Act'.[33]

It is clear that those who established the guild had the backing of senior trade unionists. An advert placed in the national press declared that the relatively new CIU had given the guild 'written assurance of its full support and co-operation'. It listed Owen Hynes, President, and Leo Hynes, Secretary of the CIU, as well as William McMullen, President of the ITGWU, as among those who would address the guild's inaugural meeting.[34] The following day, the NUJ responded with its own advert, stating that neither the Irish District Council nor any of its nine branches had been informed by the ITGWU that it proposed 'the organisation of NUJ members into a new union'. Neither had the NUJ 'approved the holding of a meeting … for the purpose of launching a break-away journalistic organisation'.[35] In a letter to all NUJ branches, Brendan Malin alerted them to 'the attack on the National Union of Journalists which is being sponsored by certain Trade Union leaders in Dublin aided by a minority of the members of the Dublin Branch'. The plan, Malin continued, was 'to split the Union, to sap its strength and inveigle its membership into the politically dominated Irish Transport and General Workers' Union'. The NUJ, he concluded, was being 'attacked, wantonly stabled before the ink on its latest Irish Agreement was dry, and while its representatives were on their way back to the negotiating table to finish the provincial job': the only response was to 'to fight back at this attack on the flank of the Union'.[36] A meeting of the Dublin branch unanimously carried a resolution that strongly deplored 'the action of a small minority of branch members in conducting secret negotiations with outside organisations for the setting up of a new "union" for journalists against the declared wishes of the overwhelming majority of the branch members' and called on all NUJ members to 'disassociate themselves from the break-away "union"'.[37]

At the guild's inaugural meeting, which was attended by forty journalists, James J. MacSweeney, an *Irish Press* journalist and a senior member of the Knights of St Columbanus, was elected chairman.[38] Among those elected to its first executive committee were news editor of the *Irish Press*, William Redmond; *Irish Press* sub-editor and later political correspondent of the *Sunday Independent*, Liam Skinner; *Irish Independent* sports editor, Mitchel Cogley; *Irish Independent* racing correspondent and sports broadcaster Micheál O Hehir; *Irish Press* sub-editor Gabriel Diskin; and *The Standard*'s Peadar O'Curry.[39] So pleased was O'Curry with developments that he declared that 'the principles of social policy set out in the Guild's Manifesto were more advanced than any hitherto set out by any Irish Union or English Union operating in this country'.[40] Addressing the meeting, William McMullen, President of the ITGWU, stated that there was a 'fundamental principle involved – control of their own trade unions by Irish workers' and assured those gathered of the ITGWU's 'ample protection'.[41] Leo Crawford, Secretary of the CIU, declared that 'the ultimate object of the Guild should be to become the sole union for journalists in Ireland'.[42] There was, however, at least one dissenting voice. Noting that the guild's newspaper statement had expressed solidarity with James Connolly's view that while the interests of labour are worldwide, each country had to work on its own salvation, *Irish Press* journalist Liam MacGabhann pointedly queried whether the guild members 'were really followers of James Connolly or would they be turned back by a man with a mitre'.[43]

In May 1949, the guild intensified its battle with the NUJ. The second edition of its newsletter, *Bulletin*, reported that the Dublin Printing Trades Group, the consultative body to which all trade unions in the Dublin printing industry sent delegates, had dissolved itself. The reason given by the Irish unions was stark; having affiliated to the CIU, they 'refused to sit any longer with representatives of British-controlled unions' that were members of ITUC.[44] As the guild found its feet, its leading members received letters from the NUJ threatening their expulsion from the union. The letters were issued after the Dublin branch complained to the union's NEC. The basis of the complaint was that those who had established the guild had 'conducted negotiations with outside organisations for the setting up of a new union of journalists'. Not short of hyperbole, the *Bulletin* described the NUJ letters as 'impertinent an edict as was ever sent into this country by an Englishman' and considered the NUJ's action as a mere continuation of British oppression:

> Just as in the political sphere the British Government still attempts to legislate for Ireland, as in the Ireland Bill, attempting to perpetuate the unjust and unnatural Partition of our country, so in the industrial sphere, a British Trade Union warns that Irish Journalists may never have an organisation of their own here except at their peril.[45]

Having considered the Dublin branch's complaint, the NEC concluded that, under Rule II of the union, the actions of those members who had established the guild constituted 'conduct detrimental to the union' that was punishable by expulsion. The council decided to consider the complaint at its forthcoming meeting and invited those who had been the subject of the complaint to appear at that meeting in London if they so wished. The *Bulletin* noted that the guild members who had received this letter were 'highly honoured that they had been chosen for attack as the vanguard of the final drive which will end the interference of the British trade union movement in this country's affairs'.[46] The NUJ subsequently expelled ten of its members for their involvement in establishing the guild.[47]

In July 1949, the CIU's annual conference launched a thinly veiled attack on the NUJ. The meeting recorded its 'indignant protest against the continued operation of foreign unions in Ireland' and called on the government to cease granting negotiating licences to them. One trade unionist stated that 'the existence of foreign unions created a partition that was even more serious than the border between North and South'. William McMullen of the ITGWU appealed 'to the patriotism and the good-will of Irishmen in British unions to leave them and to join the appropriate Irish organisation'. The time had come, McMullen concluded, 'when members of the British trades unions should realise that the game was up'. A resolution supporting the formation of the Guild of Irish Journalists was also passed.[48] In October 1949, the guild became affiliated with the CIU, which entitled it to representation on the reconstituted Printing Trades' Group.[49] Despite having the strong backing of the wider trade-union movement, the guild was to find it impossible to displace the NUJ in Ireland.

An Glór

From February 1952 onwards, the guild published a monthly newsletter entitled *An Glór* (*The Voice*). Its first edition proclaimed that the guild was 'a national trade union, founded and controlled by Irishmen, with a place in its ranks for each and every Irish journalist'. It appealed to journalists to work 'for the implementation of a progressive Social policy, based on Christian principles and having as its aim a fairer division of profits and a voice in the management of and a share in the ownership of industry' – a fairly liberal policy given the Red Scare then ongoing.[50]

In terms of aims and objectives, the guild positioned itself between the institute (professional matters) and the NUJ (employment terms). It declared itself interested in:

- the regulation of the relations between Newspaper Managements and Guild members,
- the promotion of the welfare and the safeguarding of the interests of the members,
- the consideration of questions affecting the professional conduct of its members,
- the promotion of activities for the social and economic welfare of its members,
- and the regulation of entry into, and qualifications for, the profession.[51]

The guild never missed an opportunity to remind its members that it was an Irish union while the NUJ had its headquarters in London. It noted that in a speech to the Dublin branch of the NUJ the Minister for Industry and Commerce Seán

Lemass had declared that 'We shall always be in danger so long as we are relying on outsiders to provide us with the things which we can quite well provide for ourselves.' 'No doubt', the guild's newsletter declared, 'the Minister had the Guild in mind when he spoke thus!'[52]

Not so enamoured with the guild was President Seán T. O'Kelly. In August 1952, Riobard Bramham, the general secretary of the guild, wrote to O'Kelly's secretary, Michael McDunphy, to complain that 'the usual courtesies, by way of invitations, to Official Presidential and State functions, enjoyed by kindred organisations, are not extended to the Guild of Irish Journalists'. Bramham attributed this omission to 'an oversight' and felt that it was only necessary for him to draw this to McDunphy's attention to 'ensure that the usual invitations will be issued in the normal way for the future'. McDunphy showed the letter to O'Kelly, who declared that 'it would appear that these people thought they had a right to an invitation to functions at the Áras – a right which no one had'. McDunphy was directed by O'Kelly to 'do nothing more in the matter'.[53] Undeterred, Bramham wrote again the following year. Describing the guild as 'a Truly Irish Trade Union for all the Journalists of Ireland', Bramham declared that its founders had considered it 'an embarrassment that all the Journalists of Ireland – on whom the whole population of the country always so heavily relies, to give them guidance on matters of nationalism, politics, and economics – were under the influence of the leaders of a Trade Union which was, and still is, based in England'. To raise funds, the guild intended to hold an annual gala variety concert in Dublin's Theatre Royal, and, given O'Kelly's 'great connection to, and interest in, journalism', Bramham requested that he be 'patron of these concerts'.[54] While the records do not indicate whether or not this letter was answered, press coverage of the guild's annual 'press parade ball' indicate that Dublin's Lord Mayor, Alfie Byrne, was its patron.[55] The government, too, was wary of the guild. When, in December 1955, Bord Fáilte sought permission to provide hospitality to 200 members of the Institute of Journalists who were to visit Dublin the following summer, the Department of External Affairs expressed concerns that the guild might object. It noted that, while the guild was 'comparatively small [it was] very vocal and as an Irish union is strongly opposed to the two British-based unions and loses no opportunity of attacking them'. It was, the department concluded, 'very likely to protest against official entertainment being given to a British-based union'. Nonetheless, the request for hospitality was granted.[56]

A crowded field

It was against this backdrop that newspaper proprietors had to deal with the ever-mushrooming number of organisations claiming to represent journalists. Given the bitterness with which the guild had split from the NUJ, there was no love lost between the organisations. Also still in existence was the Institute of Journalists, which represented a small number of editorial staff. In 1956, a Department of External Affairs memorandum noted that 'in Dublin its membership is almost exclusively confined to Independent Newspapers Ltd'.[57] It was with this disparate group of organisations that the Dublin Newspaper Managers' Committee (DNMC) had to deal when pay claims were periodically put forward. While the institute and the guild were prepared to work together, the NUJ, which had by far the highest number of journalists in its ranks, was determined to have nothing to do with the guild. This situation led to some very bitter exchanges. In February 1953, the guild and the institute jointly submitted a wages claim to the DNMC.[58] The following month, the claim came before the JIC, the union–employer body that adjudicated on such claims. As the proceedings began, the JIC Chairman announced that he had received a letter from NUJ headquarters in London indicating that the union, representing 183 Dublin journalists, had been in prior wage negotiations with the DNMC and that, as these negotiations were likely to resume, it did not want its claim discussed by the JIC.

In response, the manager of Independent Newspapers, John J. Dunne, declared that 'it would be futile to discuss a wage claim for Dublin journalists when 183 out of the 228 employed by the DNMC would not be affected by any decision arrived at that day'. (It emerged that the guild represented forty journalists and the institute only five.) The Chairman then ruled that all three organisations meet with the DNMC before the wage claim be resumed.[59] Despite the fact that it represented less than one-quarter as many journalists as represented by the NUJ, the guild was incensed at being upstaged: it accused the NUJ of 'using a communication conceived and dictated in London, to impose a prolongation of unfavourable working conditions on their fellow Irish workers'.[60] At the subsequent JIC meeting in April, the DNMC Secretary, Joseph C. Dann, informed the council that, although he had endeavoured to get all three representative bodies to meet the managers, he had been informed by the NUJ that it was not prepared to meet the managers' committee with the representatives of the guild and the institute; instead, the NUJ wished to meet the managers' committee separately to negotiate an agreement. He also reported that he had received communications indicating that the guild and the institute would only meet the managers' committee with the NUJ present. When the Chairman invited the NUJ representative on the council, Michael McInerney, to respond, he stated that the NUJ 'catered for a homogeneous group of working journalists with special interests and they felt that they should be allowed to finish the negotiations which they had begun'. Dann then indicated that the managers would 'work out an agreement with the NUJ … with common denominators for all three bodies'.[61] The guild thus accused the NUJ of attempting 'to stultify the efforts of their fellow workers to obtain a living wage [and] sabotaging the efforts of their fellow Irishmen at the behest of a London Executive'.[62]

The following month, the guild and the institute were informed that the DNMC had reached an agreement with the NUJ. The guild noted that the managers had accepted the NUJ's revised salary scales and that

> this English based Union, purporting to represent the views of the majority of Irish newspaper men, has once again bound it members – and other journalists who are not members of any Union – to the acceptance of a salary adjustment, conceived in an atmosphere foreign to all Irish requirements, and out of all proportion to the all too apparent realities of the present high cost of living.[63]

When, at the subsequent JIC meeting, the guild persisted in advancing its claim, John J. Dunne of Independent Newspapers declared that the agreement was the result of negotiations between the DNMC and NUJ representatives who had come 'specially from England and were experienced men who knew well the needs of Irish Newspaper men in the matter of salaries'. Similarly, Dann declared that the managers 'were going to adhere rigidly to the terms of the Agreement they had negotiated'. The guild ultimately accepted the agreement with the provision that the DNMC accept personal applications for wage increases by senior journalists not covered by the agreement.[64] Unhappy at how things had turned out, the guild noted that forty Irish journalists had been forced to accept an agreement 'negotiated in the main, by two men "from across the water" who could not possibly be *au fait* with economic conditions in Ireland'.[65]

The existence of the guild proved to be a continuous irritant to newspaper proprietors. During a Labour Court hearing on a pay claim in 1956, the Irish Printing Federation, representing newspaper proprietors, noted that such claims were complicated by the fact that the newspaper industry recognised three unions, 'each of which had submitted demands varying widely in scope'. Thus, the proprietors had to 'cut through a mass of conflicting claims' and engage in protracted negotiations with three different unions. In this instance, while they had been able to reach an agreement with the guild and were making progress with the institute, they had been unable to reach agreement with the NUJ. In response, Ronald Hallett, NUJ organiser, noted that the 220 NUJ members in Dublin were in the proportion of ten to one of the other unions. The NUJ could not, he maintained, 'be stampeded in regard to an inadequate wage offer because a minority group had cashed in and taken what it could get'.[66] In a similar Labour Court hearing in 1962, it was stated that the NUJ represented 289 journalists while the guild represented only eight.[67]

Two guilds

Alongside the Guild of Irish Journalists there existed a cohort of journalists of strong Catholic faith. In February 1955, Archbishop McQuaid indicated to his vigilance committee that 'owning to the importance of journalists' he was interested 'in the formation of a group of Catholic journalists'.[68] The committee identified suitable members, and, in November 1955, these journalists organised themselves into the Guild of St Francis de Sales (the patron saint of Catholic journalists and writers), membership of which was open to 'Catholics engaged in journalism, writing, publishing and advertising'. This neatly excluded the bulk of journalists working for the *Irish Times*. This guild described its aims as 'spiritual, vocational and social' with its activities 'directed towards the promotion of the Catholic social apostolate and the maintenance of the highest standard in the professional and personal conduct of the members'.[69] Its patron was McQuaid, who, a decade earlier, had failed in his attempts to establish a Catholic institute of writers and journalists.[70] The Knights of St Columbanus had been central to McQuaid's unsuccessful plan and were also involved in the new guild; its treasurer James

J. MacSweeney was a senior member of the Knights (and chairman of the Guild of Irish Journalists).[71]

Also joining the new guild was Peadar Ward, then editor of *The Standard*, who earlier that year had led the charge against Kerry-born journalist Liam MacGabhann for his independence of mind in accepting an invitation to visit the USSR. MacGabhann, then Irish correspondent of the *People*, was subjected to a McCarthy-like witch-hunt by *The Standard* for, as the paper put it, 'enjoying hospitality dispensed by the bloodstained hands of Kremlin murderers and persecutors'.[72] When several Russian publications mentioned that MacGabhann was a commentator on Radio Éireann, the paper declared that this description gave him 'an official or semi-official status and is presumably designed to convey the impression that State bodies in Ireland, and hence the Government, are anxious for closer co-operation with the USSR and satellite countries'.[73] This 'virtual smear campaign', as one journalist described it, ensured that MacGabhann's regular appearances on Radio Éireann were abruptly ended.[74] On his return from Russia, MacGabhann was told by a Radio Éireann official that he was 'no longer in good standing'.[75] Having been contacted by one of Archbishop McQuaid's intermediaries, Leon Ó Broin, Secretary of the Department of Posts and Telegraphs, noted that he had been 'disturbed by some talks given on Radio Éireann recently by Liam MacGabhann – "a fellow traveller" – in his opinion, including one *Topical Talk*. He had intervened to express disapproval. Steps were taken to avoid a recurrence … talks by "Liberals" and fellow travellers would be excluded as far as possible'.[76] MacGabhann was also put under police surveillance and had his home telephone tapped.[77] But, within journalistic circles at least, the campaign by *The Standard* backfired. A Vigilance Committee memo on Dublin journalists later noted that 'nearly all support Liam MacGabhann. Got great welcome at recent NUJ Dance'.[78] Such was the vitriol accorded to MacGabhann that, eighteen years later, in 1973, when presenting him with a journalism award, Taoiseach Liam Cosgrave quipped 'I hope *The Standard* has a photographer here'.[79]

Another member of both guilds was *Irish Press* sub-editor Gabriel Diskin.[80] Diskin, who was a regular correspondent with Archbishop McQuaid on matters relating to events in Dublin journalism circles, had the distinction of being named by the *Irish Times* as the only protester who had demonstrated outside Dalymount Park when, in defiance of a request for its cancellation by McQuaid, Ireland played Yugoslavia in a soccer match in October 1955.[81] The then President of the Football Association of Ireland, Oscar Traynor, welcomed the players, and, as a later minister for justice, had oversight of the censorship provisions that had been enacted in 1929. Just as McQuaid had no success in having the soccer match cancelled, the journalists of the Guild of St Francis de Sales had no success in lobbying Traynor on the issue of censorship. In December 1957, the guild passed a resolution 'protesting against the circulation of immoral literature' and forwarded it to Traynor. In a lukewarm reply, the Minister's secretary noted that 'little or no evidence of such literature had come to the notice of the Garda Síochána'.[82] Despite the guild claiming to have eighty-four members in 1958, by 1963 the Vigilance Committee noted that its membership was 'not good and the guild is not representative of the journalists'.[83] A later memo noted that 'journalists prefer to remain independent of one another and of religious authority'.[84]

In terms of professional matters, the Guild of Irish Journalists briefly revived the idea of a registration act and governing council for journalists and published its proposals in *An Glór* in June 1954. Foreign journalists would, according to its proposals, only be allowed to practise journalism 'through a licence issued by the Governing Council', while journalists in Northern Ireland could register provided they were of 'Irish nationality'. An appeal for all three representative organisations to work together to get the necessary legislation passed went unheeded as did a later appeal to the government to 'to put the Journalistic profession on the same basis as that of the Legal, Secretarial, and Accountancy professions, who enjoy state recognition'.[85] In social and educational terms, the guild took some progressive steps. It established the 'Four Masters' awards which were made annually for outstanding contributions to journalism, and in 1957 it called on Dublin's third-level institutions to 'provide degree courses in journalism for Irish journalists'. UCD replied that, having considered the matter, it had decided that the best way it could assist in the education of journalists was by means of its existing courses in literature, history, politics, and philosophy. Trinity College simply stated that it did not have the resources to initiate such a degree.[86] Nonetheless, William Redmond, who played a central role in establishing the guild, also played a key role in setting up the School of Journalism at the College of Commerce in Rathmines.[87]

But, all this activity aside, the guild never made any headway in terms of membership, and the NUJ went from strength to strength. By 1952, the NUJ had twelve branches north and south of the border, a membership of 500 journalists, and an annual subscription base of £2,500.[88] In comparison, the guild only ever represented three dozen journalists and, despite fading into obscurity, was only formally deregistered as a trade union in 1982, following the death of James J. MacSweeney the previous year.[89] The 1949 split that gave rise to the guild left a sour taste in the mouths of many Dublin journalists. For his part, Peadar O'Curry of *The Standard* remained unrepentant. In an *Irish Times* interview in 1977, he denied indulging in McCarthyism and described those who had voted for Allen Hutt as being 'grossly mistaken'. He would, he asserted, 'do it all again' because communism stood for 'jails and concentration camps, for the suppression of speech and hostility to Christianity'.[90] Cromwell, he concluded, 'was a Sunday school teacher compared to these people'. However, when he needed union membership after he joined the *Irish Times* as a sub-editor in 1963 – where, due to his temperament, he was nicknamed 'Powder' O'Curry – he was accepted back into the NUJ, which by then had become the dominant body representing journalists in Ireland.[91]

Notes

1 *Evening Mail*, 6 Mar. 1953, p. 1. The notice was inserted on behalf of the Irish Workers' League, the forerunner to the Communist Party of Ireland.

2 G. Murphy, *In Search of the Promised Land: The Politics of Post-War Ireland* (Cork, 2009), p. 18.

3 B. Fallon, *An Age of Innocence: Irish Culture, 1930–60* (Dublin, 1998), p. 258.
4 Interview with John Kelly.
5 M. Milotte, *Communism in Modern Ireland: The Pursuit of the Workers' Republic since 1916* (Dublin, 1984), p. 117.
6 *Irish Times*, 30 Aug. 1985, p. 7.
7 *Irish Times*, 8 Apr. 1977, p. 9. The union's library was sold off by its national executive in the late 1940s – see F. Devine, 'A dangerous agitator: John Swift', *Saothar*, 15 (1990), 7–19.
8 D. Greaves, *Reminiscences of the Connolly Association: An Emerald Jubilee Pamphlet* (London, 1978), pp. 14–16.
9 NAI, DFA/305/55, letter from Col. Bryan, Department of Defence, to F. Boland, Department of External Affairs, 3 Jun. 1947.
10 *Irish Times*, 28 Jan. 1980, p. 6.
11 NAI, Jus/93/4/7, notes on communism in Saorstát Éireann, 1936, pp. 16–17. The Workers' College was established in 1932 by the Revolutionary Workers' Party, the precursor to the Communist Party of Ireland.
12 NAI, Jus/93/4/7, notes on communism in Saorstát Éireann, 1936, pp. 16–17, and supplement, p. 14.
13 DDA, AB8/B/XXIII, 3.3.280, report undated.
14 *Irish Press*, 19 Oct. 1988, p. 4.
15 DDA, AB8/B/XXIII, 1.1.19, report dated Feb. 1956.
16 C. Bundock, *The National Union of Journalists: A Jubilee History, 1907–57* (Oxford, 1957), p. 191.
17 *Irish Independent*, 14 Oct. 1948, p. 2.
18 DDA, AB/8/B/XXII, 81.1.1 and 81.1.2. See also *Irish Independent*, 1 Nov. 1948, p. 6.
19 DDA, AB/8/B/XXIII, 3.3.297, letter undated; HCRC, NUJ, Dublin branch minutes, 4 Sep. 1948.
20 *The Standard*, 12 Nov. 1948, p. 1.
21 *The Standard*, 29 Oct. 1948, p. 4.
22 DDA, AB/8/B/XXIII, 3.3.280, letter undated.
23 *Irish Times*, 8 Apr. 1977, p. 9.
24 *The Standard*, 19 Nov. 1948, p. 4.
25 *The Standard*, 19 Nov. 1948, p. 4.
26 US National Archives, Department of State, 841D.OOB/12–148 cited in J. Horgan, 'Anti-communism and media surveillance in Ireland, 1948–50', *Irish Communications Review*, 8 (2000), 30–4, at pp. 32–3.
27 *Irish Times*, 21 Feb. 1949, p. 6.
28 *The Standard*, 25 Feb. 1949, p. 4.
29 *Irish Press*, 24 Mar. 1949, p. 5.
30 *Irish Press*, 23 Mar., 1949, p. 5.
31 *The Standard*, 11 Mar. 1949, p. 1.
32 S. Ward-Perkins (ed.), *Select Guide to Trade Union Records* (Dublin, 1996), pp. 208–12. Both congresses united as the Irish Congress of Trade Unions (ICTU) in 1959.
33 C. Cruise O'Brien, *Memoir: My Life and Themes* (Dublin, 1999), p. 145.
34 *Irish Times*, 23 Mar. 1949, p. 6.
35 *Irish Times*, 24 Mar. 1949, p. 8.
36 HCRC, NUJ, letter from B. Malin to branch secretaries, 29 Mar. 1949.
37 HCRC, NUJ, letter from S. B. Edgar, Branch Secretary, to guild, 5 Apr. 1949.

38 *Irish Times*, 5 Oct. 1981, p. 7; *Irish Press*, 28 Mar. 1949, p. 5. MacSweeney was later Chairman of the Catholic Housing Aid Society.
39 *Irish Times*, 28 Mar. 1949, p. 1.
40 NAI, 97/9/994, copy of guild 'Bulletin', Apr. 1949, p. 4.
41 NAI, 97/9/994, copy of guild 'Bulletin', Apr. 1949, p. 4.
42 *Irish Press*, 28 Mar. 1949, p. 5.
43 DDA, AB8/B/XXIII, 3.3.280, undated.
44 NAI, 97/9/994, copy of guild 'Bulletin', May 1949, p. 1. See also *Irish Press*, 27 Apr. 1949, p. 5. The unions were the ITGWU, the Dublin Typographical Provident Union (printers), the Stereotypers' Society and the Bookbinders' and Allied Trades' Union.
45 NAI, 97/9/994, copy of guild 'Bulletin', May 1949, p. 8.
46 NAI, 97/9/994, copy of guild 'Bulletin', May 1949, p. 9.
47 'Bulletin', Jun. 1949, p. 3.
48 *Irish Times*, 23 Jul. 1949, p. 1.
49 *Irish Press*, 3 Oct. 1949, p. 5.
50 *An Glór*, Feb. 1952, p. 1.
51 *An Glór*, Feb. 1952, p. 2.
52 *An Glór*, Feb. 1952, p. 2.
53 NAI, P 4834, letter dated 1 Aug. 1952; memo dated 20 Aug. 1952.
54 NAI, P 4834, letter dated 31 Oct. 1953. My thanks to Aoife Whelan for translating this letter.
55 *Times Pictorial*, 30 Oct. 1954, p. 14.
56 NAI, 406/561, letters dated 30 Dec. 1955 and 17 Jan. 1956.
57 NAI, 406/561, briefing note dated 17 Jan. 1956.
58 *An Glór*, Mar. 1953, p. 2.
59 *An Glór*, Apr. 1953, pp. 2–3.
60 *An Glór*, Apr. 1953, p. 1.
61 *An Glór*, May 1953, pp. 2–3.
62 *An Glór*, May 1953, p. 1.
63 *An Glór*, Jun. 1953, p. 1.
64 *An Glór*, Jul. 1953, pp. 2–3.
65 *An Glór*, Jul. 1953, pp. 1–2.
66 *Irish Times*, 8 Mar. 1956, p. 3.
67 *Irish Times*, 6 Jun. 1962, p. 6.
68 DDA, AB8/B/XXIII, 1.1.10, memo dated 28 Feb. 1955.
69 *Irish Times*, 25 Nov. 1955, p. 7.
70 J. Cooney, *John Charles McQuaid: Ruler of Catholic Ireland* (Dublin, 1997), p. 201.
71 *Irish Times*, 5 Oct. 1981, p. 7; *Irish Press*, 28 Mar. 1949, p. 5.
72 *The Standard*, 28 Jan. 1955, p. 1. See *Irish Times* 14 Jan. 1955, p. 5 for a defence of MacGabhann.
73 *The Standard*, 25 Mar. 1955, p. 1.
74 Fallon, *An Age of Innocence*, p. 258.
75 *Pictorial*, 6 Aug. 1955, p. 2.
76 DDA, AB8/B/XXVI/a/1/34, memo dated 11 Feb. 1955.
77 Information from Dorothy MacGabhann.
78 DDA, AB8/B/XXIII, 3.3.279, memo undated.
79 *Kerry's Eye*, 13–19 Jan. 1979, p. 5. Anthony Cronin, who also travelled to the USSR, wrote a series of articles – 'Behind the Curtain' – which were published in the *Irish Times*, 9–15 Feb. 1955.

80 *Irish Times*, 25 Nov. 1955, p. 7.

81 DDA, AB8/B/XXIII, 4.2.386. In his many letters, Diskin addressed McQuaid very informally as 'A Chara'. *Irish Times*, 20 Oct. 1955, p. 1; 5 Jan. 1956, p. 3. While both John Cooney (*McQuaid*, p. 312) and Tim Pat Coogan (*Ireland in the Twentieth Century*, p. 731) note that supporters had to pass large protests, according to the *Irish Independent* and the *Irish Times*, Diskin protested alone outside the venue with a papal flag.

82 *Irish Times*, 23 Dec. 1957, p. 8.

83 *Irish Times*, 4 Feb. 1958, p. 3. DDA, AB8/B/XXIII, 1.1.114, memo dated 4 Mar. 1963.

84 DDA, AB8/B/XXIII, 1.1.116, memo dated 1 Apr. 1963.

85 *An Glór*, Jul. 1954, 1; NAI, Tsch/3/S16190 A, letter from R. Bramham to Taoiseach John A. Costello, 10 Feb. 1957. Costello's reply (27 Feb. 1957) noted he was in the middle of an election campaign and could not 'give any careful consideration to the matter'.

86 *Irish Times*, 13 Apr. 1957, p. 7.

87 *Irish Times*, 10 Mar. 1977, p. 11. See Chapter 7.

88 *Irish Times*, 30 Apr. 1952, p. 6.

89 Ward-Perkins, *Select Guide to Trade Union Records*, p. 257.

90 *Irish Times*, 8 Apr. 1977, p. 9.

91 Correspondence with John Horgan.

6

Official Ireland

You need only say 'book', 'leg', 'bet', 'dance', 'wife', 'poor', 'school', not to mention a long word like 'liberty', and you at once buy a ticket for the stratosphere and the chloroform.[1]

— Seán O'Faolain on Irish society, 1944

In one of the few self-critical reflections on journalism in early to mid-twentieth-century Ireland, journalist Michael O'Toole observed that up to the 1960s journalists were generally 'a docile lot, anxious to please the proprietor, the advertiser, the prelate, the statesman'. The era was, he argued, characterised by 'an unhealthy willingness to accept the prepared statement, the prepared speech, and the handout without demanding the opportunity of asking any searching questions by way of follow-up'. The fundamental defect of Irish journalism during this time was, he concluded, 'its failure to apply critical analysis to practically any aspect of Irish life'. In his analysis, O'Toole put forward several reasons for this journalistic stagnation. These included what he described as 'the general paralysis that afflicted Irish society during those years', the lack of commitment and resources on the part of newspaper proprietors, the effects of wartime censorship, and the fact that the majority of Irish journalists were poorly educated, poorly motivated, and poorly paid.[2] When O'Toole wrote this analysis in 1988, his views were not popular with his fellow journalists: even today, the sight of a journalist critiquing fellow journalists or journalism is somewhat frowned upon in media circles. But historian Terence Brown was harsher in his summation of journalism in pre-1960s Ireland:

> Regrettably, almost all Irish journalism in the period had contented itself with the reportage of events and the propagandist reiteration of the familiar terms of Irish political and cultural debate until these categories became mere counters and slogans often remote from any actualities. Irish journalism therefore comfortably reinforced the prevailing sense that Ireland, marked, as the nationalists constantly stressed, by distinctive religious, social, and linguistic forms, was somehow different from the rest of the world. It did not challenge Irishmen and women to reflect seriously on their own reality. It allowed, by contrast, an absorption with abstractions such as Sovereignty, the Faith, Republicanism, the Language.[3]

The dominant terms of Irish political and cultural debate were 'those nationalist doctrines of an ancient Gaelic and Catholic nation rooted in the Irish Irelanders' vision of an unspoken Irish tradition which must be restored to its former glory'. Had journalism been able to challenge this received wisdom then 'that sense of Irish uniqueness so necessary to the unthinking acceptance of the dominant nationalist ideology would have been disturbed'. An objective and critical examination of Irish social life would, Brown concluded, 'have revealed as well as things unique to the country the degree to which Irish life was influenced by the world around it'.[4]

During this period, many national newspapers were effectively the organs or semi-organs of the dominant institutions within the state. In broad terms, Fianna Fáil had the uncritical support of the *Irish Press*, Fine Gael was supported by the business-oriented *Irish Independent*, and both these newspapers were wholly uncritical of the Catholic Church, which, in turn, was supported by the lay-owned weekly publications the *Irish Catholic* and *The Standard*. While there was plenty of competition for voters and readers, there was little space for diversity of opinion or impartial critical analysis. Fianna Fáil and Fine Gael may have adopted different positions on political, economic, and social issues, and these positions may have been supported respectively by the *Irish Press* and the *Irish Independent*, but in the heel of the hunt such positions first went through the filters of nationalist and Catholic ideology. Very little that challenged the dominant narrative that Ireland was a unique monoculture characterised by Catholic virtue and Gaelic ideals of ruralism and language restoration could be published in a mainstream newspaper.

Within such a relatively rigid ideological structure, it would have to be a brave or foolhardy journalist that would go against the grain of the publication that they worked for. Anyone with the nerve to challenge such orthodoxy brought odium on themselves and was cast in the public mind as a heretic, a Communist, or a West Brit.[5] But, amid this conformist society, two publications did their best to challenge the status quo – one by accident and one by design. Considered by many as the relic of southern unionism that would eventually fade away, the *Irish Times* became the only national daily title not tied or beholden to any power bloc during the period. The other publication that cast a cold eye on Irish society was the monthly periodical *The Bell*.[6]

The pre-television media landscape

While the state had established a Civil Service-controlled radio station (2RN) in January 1926, its daily news bulletin was aired at 7.30 p.m. so as not to offend the national newspapers, which had expressed concerns about a loss of circulation should the news be aired any earlier. This, combined with the fact that live political discussions were prohibited until the mid-1950s, meant that the population was almost solely dependent on newspapers for coverage of current affairs. And, in the words of novelist Frank O'Connor, those newspapers were 'intolerably dull … not trying to educate the public [and] trying to camouflage reality', much of which was, O'Connor surmised, a result of 'party ties'.[7]

For its part, the *Irish Press* was established to represent the world view of Fianna Fáil, or more accurately, the world view of Éamon de Valera, and did so most particularly during election time. As noted in Chapter 4, it played a central role in bringing Fianna Fáil to power in 1932 and keeping it there. Throughout the 1940s and 1950s, the paper's support for Fianna Fáil policies – ruralism, protectionism, restoration of the Irish language, and neutrality – was unshakeable.[8] The *Press* was also deferential towards the sensibilities of the Catholic Church, particularly in relation to what were referred to as 'indelicate' topics – as evidenced by the recollection of one *Press* journalist:

> An epidemic of gastro-enteritis was killing babies by the hundred in Dublin. I interviewed a woman doctor who told me that the death rate could be slashed, the epidemic halted, perhaps, if only mothers would breast-feed their children. The assistant editor of the newspaper changed the phrase 'breast-feeding' to 'feeding the children themselves'. When I protested, he said: 'That other phrase is indelicate'. When I said his alternative was confusing, and reminded him that lives were at stake, he walked away. 'Feeding the children themselves' it was. The blinds were as thick as that.[9]

In contrast, the *Irish Independent* remained a purely commercial enterprise characterised by its strong Catholic ethos. It had been an enthusiastic supporter of the Censorship of Publications Act in 1929, and, led by long-time editor Frank Geary, its pro-Catholic stance reached its peak during the Spanish Civil War when the paper gave its support to Franco in his revolt against the democratically elected socialist government. For the *Independent*, the conflict represented a battle between Catholicism and communism: in one leading article, it declared that 'all who stand for the ancient Faith and the tradition of Spain are behind the present revolt against the Marxist regime in Madrid'.[10] Geary was, however, enlightened enough to send a female journalist, Gertrude Gaffney, to report on the war.[11] In 1954, as the *Independent* celebrated fifty years in business, Archbishop John Charles McQuaid publicly praised its 'policy of distinctive loyalty to the church'.[12] Indeed, as Ray Raymond Smith, later a journalist with the paper, remembered, when writing about anything to do with the church 'blandness' was required:

> You wrote 'nice' copy and nice copy meant the sub-editors did not have to entertain qualms about letting it through. It was eminently suitable to the era when the Catholic Church exerted an influence in Irish life that was awesome and it extended into what went into the papers and what stayed out ... Those who made it to the top had an uncanny perception of what did not ruffle the feathers of the Hierarchy or bring blushes to the faces of the 'good nuns' as we invariably seemed to describe them.[13]

While this period may have marked the *Independent*'s conservative highpoint, up to the 1980s a statue of the Virgin Mary was located in the *Independent*'s library, where, up to the 1960s, some staff members would meet to recite the rosary.[14]

The world view of the Catholic Church was semi-officially represented by the *Irish Catholic* and *The Standard*. In a review of these publications in 1945, one critic (Conor Cruise O'Brien) expressed the view that, since Ireland was an important provider of missionaries, both publications were 'weapons in a world battle' rather than reflections of Irish Catholic opinion. The Catholicism of the average

Irishman was neither as 'demonstrative nor aggressive' as that reflected in the two papers, and the 'long tirades against Communism' were, he asserted, 'about as real as an outburst of anti-Semitism on the Blasket Islands'.[15] Established in 1888, the *Irish Catholic* was 'a conservative-national organ, supporting the Irish Hierarchy in their corporate decisions on all religious and political matters'.[16] *The Standard*, which first appeared in 1928, was equally devoted to the church line, but in a more militant way.[17] Both papers supported Franco during the Spanish Civil War, and condemnations of communism and reports on sermons and Lenten pastorals all featured prominently. In 1938, Peadar O'Curry became editor of *The Standard* and adopted a policy of 'Rahillization', whereby the paper's principle contributor was the avowedly Catholic (and later priest) Professor Alfred O'Rahilly, of University College Cork. O'Rahilly engaged in vitriolic condemnation of anyone or anything that challenged the power of the church.[18] As remembered by Patrick Kavanagh, who wrote briefly for *The Standard* in this period, writing for such an organ required a certain level of dexterity:

> He too took a job on a pious paper and wrote week after week stories about people who were defaming the name of 'our late beloved cardinal'. So eager was he to succeed as a sycophant in the pious line that he had nine names for the Pope – The Pope, Holy Father, His Holiness, Supreme Pontiff, Vicar of Christ, Invisible Head of the Church, Angelic Shepherd, Successor of St Peter, Bishop of Rome and the rest which he only could remember occasionally.[19]

One of O'Rahilly's favourite targets was the *Irish Times*, which he once described as giving publicity to 'all kinds of cranks and scoffers, sabbatarians, secularists [and] grouching intellectuals'.[20] Indeed, as remembered by Cathal O'Shannon, in the 1950s the *Times* was viewed 'as the devil incarnate by a lot of Catholics. We were the people who read banned books. To be in the *Irish Times* was almost an occasion of sin.'[21] Edited from 1934 to 1954 by Robert Smyllie, the *Times* editorialised against compulsory Irish in school, the prohibition of divorce, literary censorship, and the rise of Franco in Spain. Like the *Irish Independent*, it too sent a reporter, Lionel Fleming, to Spain in 1936. However, its critical coverage of the conflict cost it advertising revenue when the Catholic Headmasters' Association boycotted the paper.[22] The *Times* also opposed neutrality and censorship during the Second World War and, in 1951, was the only national newspaper to challenge the church's opposition to the Mother and Child healthcare scheme.

Similar to the *Times*, in that it did not blindly accept the pronouncements of politicians or clergy, was Seán O'Faolain and Peadar O'Donnell's monthly publication, *The Bell*. First published in October 1940, *The Bell* advocated O'Faolain's view that Ireland was a 'country at the beginning of its creative history, and at the end of its revolutionary history'.[23] This was a philosophy that was anathema to the political and religious institutions that depended on rose-tinted views of the past and the restoration of a past Eden for their legitimacy. Editorially, *The Bell* was infused with the searing frustration that O'Faolain and O'Donnell felt at the conservatism – or counter-revolution – that had followed Irish Independence.

While both men had hoped that an independent Ireland would be based on liberty, fraternity, and equality, what emerged post-Independence was, in the words of Donal McCartney, 'a nationalism that was exclusive, isolationist, restrictive, narrow and bourgeois in its values'.[24] This was not the Ireland that O'Faolain had envisaged while engaged in militant activity: 'We had looked forward to seeing all classes untied, all religions equal, all races welded, all ideas welcome.'[25]

The Bell's mission then was to tackle the accepted wisdom of what O'Faolain referred to as the 'bourgeoisie, Little Irelanders, chauvinists, puritans, stuffed-shirts, pietists, Tartuffles, Anglophobes, Celtophiles, *et alii hujus generis*' and steer the magazine 'between a faint star that calls itself the Spirit of Human Liberty and a vast fog compounded of the Humbug, Hypocrisy, Selfishness, and Cowardice of our ruling snob-classes'.[26] Describing itself as 'a survey of Irish life', *The Bell* set out to document the true social conditions then prevailing in Irish society. It provided a focal point for those who despaired at the state's political, economic, social, and cultural development since 1922 and allowed such people to vent their frustrations. At the very least it let them know that they were not alone. Alongside short stories, poetry, and reviews, *The Bell* published critical articles on the conditions of prisons, illegitimacy, crime, workhouses, hospitalisation, dance halls, fisheries, clericalism, public libraries, mental illness, poverty, pawnshops, TB, urban slums, the Irish language, and literary censorship. The picture of Ireland that emerged was generally not a pretty one. As one reviewer later put it, very often its best articles came from people who were 'describing the one thing they have really *felt*, really *seen*, in all their lives'.[27] Indeed, *The Bell* was the only publication that mentioned the issue of child abuse – an issue that would come to the fore in later decades. In 1944, it published a series of three articles written by Olivia Manning Robertson recounting her experiences of working as a play-leader in Dublin Corporation playgrounds, one of which hinted at paedophilia. Having encountered a crying child who told her that a man had offered her chocolates if she went home with him, Robertson brought the child to a garda station and witnessed a garda being dispatched to question the man. Robertson heard nothing more until six months later when she learnt from the child that the man concerned had been found dead in one of Dublin's canals.[28]

'Seedy, scruffy creatures'

For all the harsh words about the state of journalism in the 1940s and 1950s, the reality was that journalists were poorly trained, relatively uneducated, poorly paid, and immersed in a profession that suffered from a strong drinking culture. It was a time characterised by, as journalist and novelist Breandán Ó hEithir put it, 'repression, emigration, clerical domination, spurious patriotism and an education system that seemed to train people to be physically fearless and morally cowardly'.[29] There was no formal training course in journalism, and many journalists entered the industry through serving apprenticeships in local newspapers. This generally meant learning on the job and working all hours covering all sorts of events. With a few years' experience and good references, a move from the provincial to the national press was possible. As recalled by Brian Inglis, then with the *Irish Times*, 'there was no retirement age; most reporters stayed at their work, unless rescued by a legacy, until chronic illness or death removed them, because there was no pension scheme'.[30] At sub-editorial level, a sprinkling of graduates – 'mainly briefless barristers and former clerical students' – processed the reporters' raw copy and cleaned up factual, spelling, and grammatical errors.[31]

The public perception of the profession also left a lot to be desired. As Lionel Fleming of the *Irish Times* put it, there was 'a certain stigma on the profession; an assumption by the public that reporters are all seedy and rather unscrupulous men, with a taste for drink, an ignorance of grammar, and a capacity for never getting their facts quite right'.[32] Inglis concurred: 'reporters were indeed a despised species, I found; all the more because we were needed, if the functions were to be accorded the space their organisers considered they deserved in the paper the next morning'.[33] It seemed that those who wielded any kind of authority took a dim view of journalists and journalism. In 1941, *The Bell* carried an account of an out-of-work journalist's visit to a social-welfare office to appeal having been disallowed from claiming benefits:

> 'What about this journalism of yours?' asked the little man, leaning back in his chair. I told them. 'How much do you make?' It was easier explaining that; but I could see they did not believe me. These men are instinctively opposed to men of my vocation. I need not have said at all that I wrote for the papers, but some grain of honesty which is more a tribute to my parents than to myself, naggingly forbade me to do that. Queer, sour thoughts ran through my mind in that moment; but I fought against an emotional contraction of class prejudice … It is hard to keep cool when it is hinted that you are a liar.[34]

As Inglis recalled, reporters were viewed as 'seedy, scruffy creatures who would turn up at funerals and weddings, wanting lists of people who attended, scribbling down names on the backs of envelopes, and invariably, to judge from the next day's *Irish Times*, getting them wrong'. Much time, he noted, was spent 'reporting minor functions of the kind which had little news value' in the hope that attendees would become regular readers 'when they saw their names in the paper as having won a prize for the best sponge cake at a local fête'.[35]

Content-wise, the journalism of this time consisted almost exclusively of straight reportage and innocent features. Women's journalism still centred on recipes, fashion features, and bargain-hunting, while social-affairs journalism was non-existent. A 'Guide to Careers' series published in the *Irish Independent* in 1956 observed that 'Irish journalism offers some openings for women, but they are few. Where fashion pages, social functions, and those features with a special appeal for women readers are concerned, all the daily papers will always have work for the woman journalist: otherwise the prospects are not good'.[36] Political and business reporting was straight-laced and deferential with an absence of critical commentary, opinion or analysis. While there was the odd scoop, investigative journalism had yet to make an appearance, and, as Lionel Fleming outlined, the notion of journalism being a cut-throat profession was a misnomer:

> Reporters did not spend their time acquiring 'scoops' at the expense of their rivals; if a 'scoop' (or, more properly, a 'beat') did crop up, they would naturally make the most of it. But on the whole, their attitude to each other was the very contrary. 'Dog does not eat dog' was their motto. They tended to stick together in a self-protective, almost Masonic fraternity; sharing all, or nearly all, of what they learnt.[37]

Poor pay also hampered the development of journalism. As Michael O'Toole observed, 'in a profession which is notoriously open to corruption, impoverishment nearly always led to low standards'.[38] Bribes to keep stories out of newspapers were often offered to journalists. In 1944, the NUJ's North-West branch passed a motion 'resenting and deploring the growing tendency on the part of members of the public to attempt to secure suppression of certain types of case through personal influence and offer of financial inducements'. The motion recorded that as much as £20 had been offered to one journalist alone in the space of a few days. The resolution also asserted that it was the duty of journalists 'to present accurate and fair reports of Court proceedings' and that the branch's members would 'continue to fulfil their duties to the newspaper reading public without fear or favour and to act with a sense of responsibility to the public and in the interests of common justice'.[39]

The poor manner in which journalists were perceived by the public and treated badly by employers was mirrored in the attitude with which they were viewed and treated by the Government Information Bureau. Established in 1934 with former *Irish Independent* journalist Sean O'Keefe (Shán Ó Cuív) as its first director, the bureau was viewed with a mixture of bemusement and annoyance by journalists. Despite its best intentions, it quickly became known as 'the Bureau of No Information' due to its slow and cautious manner in dealing with information requests:

> You'd have to submit a question and they'd say ring us back at half-four and you'd have a reply back from whatever department it was. The thing was so inane and stupid and shrouded in secrecy. There was a reporter one day – there was some royal burial or death in England – and he rang up and asked whether the government would be sending a representative. The reply came back eventually; 'the procedure will be as on other occasions'.[40]

When a journalist put a request for information to the bureau, it would be passed on to the relevant government department, which would then pass it on to the relevant section; any information that was deemed worthy of release then travelled back the same channels. Many journalists felt that with the information passing through so many hands what was eventually approved had been filtered to the point of uselessness. Most journalists avoided it as much as possible because it was, as one journalist described it, a 'cumbersome, unsatisfactory, time-wasting procedure'. Other journalists had an even more dim view of the bureau, describing it at one extreme as being like 'a bicycle valve; it lets everything in but very little out', and at another extreme as being 'the state liar'.[41]

Challenging the Catholic Church was also a bad career move: writing in 1951, Seán O'Faolain observed that 'few Catholics here who have to consider their careers, not to speak of their wives and children, are going to stray far from Count Mosca's advice to the young cleric: "Believe what they tell you, or not as you prefer, but never raise any objection". '[42]

The censorship imposed by the state during the Second World War – and the shortage of newsprint – only added to the difficulties that journalists faced. As all newspapers drastically reduced their size and print runs to cope with newsprint shortages they also had to observe the provisions of the Emergency Powers Act 1939 whereby war news, home news, weather and shipping news, comment pieces, editorials, reviews, advertisements, photographs, and letters to the editor were censored to ensure content did not favour any belligerent or undermine the state's neutrality.[43] The censorship impacted hugely on the coverage of events at home. In February 1944, the censor prevented the *Irish Times* from reporting that shops in Dublin's Grafton Street had been defaced by anti-Semitic graffiti.[44] Reportage of and editorial comment on the state's execution of IRA men in Mountjoy Gaol (including IRA Chief of Staff Charlie Kerins) throughout the war years were very severely restricted.[45] Even when the war arrived, via German bombers, on Ireland's shores, caution was required. While journalists were allowed to report, in April 1941, that Belfast had been bombed and that firefighters had crossed the border to combat the flames, when, some weeks later, Dublin was bombed, journalists were prevented from identifying the culprits until the German government had publicly accepted responsibility.[46] And, as outlined by Donal Ó Drisceoil and Clair Wills, when the war ended, some journalists questioned the veracity of the audio-visual footage of concentration camps.[47] In the long term, the censorship regime left journalists in no doubt as to who had the final say on how free the press was to be in Irish society, and, in the words of one journalist then just beginning his career, 'probably had an effect on both the press and the public for some years after'.[48] The net effect was to create and perpetuate an inward-looking ideology of 'official Ireland'. Proud of its sovereignty and religious faith, the Irish people lived, as Seán O'Faolain put it, in 'a paradisal state where there are no vulgar, real obstacles to be solved or struggled with'.[49] The reality, of course, was very different: it just was not reported on.

Out of sight, out of mind

One of the key characteristics of the mainstream press during the 1940s and 1950s was the level of self-censorship that operated in relation to any topics deemed 'indelicate' or any events that could give rise to scandal or embarrassment for the Catholic Church. This self-censorship did not extend to *The Bell*, which, as Seán O'Faolain noted, had a circulation of 3,000 copies per issue, meaning that he had 'an intelligent, selective readership [and could] assume a great deal of personal liberty of expression'.[50] Indeed, throughout the 1940s and 1950s, O'Faolain acted as something of a media watchdog, constantly noting the sustained absence of any controversial material in the mainstream press. In 1942, he noted how seldom could be heard a 'frank *public* discussion of any three of the following subjects – Birth Control, Freemasonry, The Knights of Columbanus, Unmarried Mothers, Illegitimacy, Divorce, Homo-sexuality, Rhythm, Lunacy, Libel, Euthanasia, Prostitution, Venereal Disease or even Usury'.[51] As for the power of the press, O'Faolain had harsh words: in 1944, he noted that 'editors sometimes like to pretend that politicians dare not utter their whole minds, but that editors can and do. I admit I have met editors who can and do – though less in their papers than in their slippers.'[52]

In particular, crime, and specifically sexual crime, went unreported in the press – thus giving the impression that it did not exist. If it did not exist, then nothing had to be done about it. The reality was, of course, that sexual crime did exist but was airbrushed out of public discourse by its absence in the press. Writing in 1941, O'Faolain noted that 'it is a tradition in Dublin newspapers not to exploit personal scandals, however juicy the news. You can call that anything you like – Hush-Hush, Cowardice, Prudery, Decency … Whether the thing is good or bad it is an instructive approach to standards of behaviour in Journalism.'[53] Shortly afterwards, an anonymous crime reporter criticised the extent of sexual crime being perpetrated and the failure of the press to report on the issue. He noted that 'few vice cases are ever mentioned in the press [and] a screen of official secrecy seems to shroud the whole question'.[54] The situation was little different in Northern Ireland. Recalling his days reporting court cases in Belfast, James Kelly noted that if a 'dirty case … too shocking for the delicate sensibilities of our readers' was called the journalists would retire to a nearby venue for a game of snooker:

> Many of the cases in the courts went unreported in those days for reasons of good taste so that most of the population lived in blissful ignorance of what was going on in their own city. I must confess that coming from a sheltered existence in a middle-class family my experiences in my first days of reporting in the courts came as an eye-opener. Here was the steamy side of life with a vengeance as, through the dock each day, there passed in procession the unfortunates, men and women who had fallen by the wayside, the prostitutes, perverts, small-time crooks and con-men.[55]

When, in 1944, the *Irish Times* reported on a series of trials involving the sensitive issue of abortion, it felt compelled to publish a lengthy leading article justifying its coverage. While it acknowledged that the reportage 'must have pained and shocked many of our readers', it declared that it had 'a duty to the community on this matter, and in the discharge of this duty, we have been forced, strongly against our will, to print matter which, in ordinary circumstances, we should be inclined to suppress'. Vice, it concluded, was 'encouraged by the refusal of responsible persons to look at things as they are', and, for that reason, it had decided to 'focus the searchlight beam of clear and unprejudiced thought upon the startling increase of certain civil evils'.[56]

Unsurprisingly, given their institutional power, court cases involving Catholic priests were an absolute no-go area for the press. In 1941, a High Court case in which two schoolboys sued one of their teachers, Revd John Kearney, was completely ignored by the Irish press but received sustained coverage in the British press. As reported in the *Daily Mirror*, the boys alleged that 'Fr Kearney had forced them to strip and gave them each twenty lashes with a loaded sporting whip'. The description of the assault left nothing to the imagination:

> [First student] was told to take off his coat and trousers, and even his shirt was pulled up by Fr Kearney. He was told to get across a chair, and received nearly twenty fierce lashes with the whip. He called for mercy, but none was shown. Then he had to witness the same horrible exhibition of cruelty. Later he was expelled.

In the priest's defence, it was stated that 'the flogging was decided on at a meeting of the college staff and Fr Kearney was directed to administer it'. While he had 'demurred at first it was in the course of his duty as a priest and professor that he carried out his most distasteful duty'. In his direct evidence, Kearney denied that the punishment was excessive, though he admitted that he had used a hunting crop to beat the boys.[57] The following day's headline in the *Daily Mirror* – 'Flogged Boys: Priest Wins' – was succinct but telling. Summing up the verdict, Justice Martin Maguire declared that 'it had been established that the boys got what was a common case of a severe beating', and, while objection had been taken to the horsewhip, 'it was more humane than a cane, being less liable to cause a break in the skin'.[58] While the *Irish Independent* listed the case in its 'To-day's Law List', it did not report on the case. Neither did the *Irish Press*. Similarly, while the *Irish Times* listed the case in its 'Legal Diary', it did not report on it. Even that most independent of journals, *The Bell*, encountered difficulty reporting on the case. In a letter to Frank O'Connor, Seán O'Faolain wrote of the journal's printer blocking his open letter to the Minister for Justice (Gerry Boland), the banning of a radio debate on education, Boland inviting him into his office for a 'talk', the mixture of promise and threat in Boland's remarks, and his hopes (unsuccessful) of mentioning the flogging incident in *The Bell*.[59]

The same self-censorship applied when, in 1943, a case of criminal conversation involving a priest was heard in the High Court.[60] Again, the British press, in the guise of the *Daily Mirror*, led the way with sustained coverage when it reported how a County Longford solicitor, Bernard Connolly, sued Revd Thomas O'Connell for having slept with his wife.[61] Even by today's standards, the case, heard before the President of the High Court, Justice Conor Maguire, was a sensational one. It was alleged that Fr O'Connell had 'stalked and hypnotised Mrs Connolly [and then] took her to a Dublin hotel and there debauched her. On the following day he took her to Bray and had illicit intercourse with her.' Shortly after Mr Connolly found out about the affair, Mrs Connolly announced she was pregnant.[62] In her evidence, Mrs Connolly stated that Fr O'Connell had told her that 'a priest could tell by looking at a person what sins the person was capable of committing, and that the only sin he would be capable of committing would be birth control'. She also stated that they later met in a Dublin hotel where they slept together and he told her he loved her.[63] In later evidence, she stated that 'the idea of a priest guilty of adultery going off to say Mass the next morning should have appalled her, but it did not'; she had been 'swept off her feet by Fr O'Connell and he could have done anything'. She denied that she was making allegations in revenge for her husband, sometime previously, having had lunch with someone described as a 'blonde bombshell'.

Fr Connolly's solicitor stated that he denied 'every charge and foul imputation made against him' and noted that British and Northern Ireland newspapers had given the case 'so much publicity against the church'.[64] In his direct evidence, Fr O'Connell stated that Mrs Connolly had told him that her husband was 'the grandest in the world if he would keep off the drink' and that the invitation to travel to Dublin had come from her. They had stayed in the same hotel 'so that he might help her with her religious difficulties' and that evening they had merely 'said the Rosary together'.[65] Again, no national title reported on the case; the closest it got to a mention was a one-line listing in the *Irish Times*'s 'Legal Diary'. The provincial title most likely to report on the case, the *Longford Leader*, also ignored it. However, what makes this case even more interesting is that the national newspapers did not shy away from reporting other cases of criminal conversation. The previous year, all three national titles and the relevant provincial titles (the *Leitrim Observer* and the *Connacht Tribune*) had reported extensively on such a case involving a postman who was sued for damages by a soldier. The case, which also involved the postman being tried for attempted murder of the soldier, resulted in £400 being awarded to the soldier and a divorce being granted, on the grounds of adultery, to the postman's wife.[66]

Despite the acquiescence of Irish newspapers in not reporting court cases involving Catholic clergy, the reporting of the Connolly case in British newspapers prompted one Dublin councillor to call for the press 'to be henceforth prevented from reporting the details of unpleasant crimes'. The irony was not lost on Seán O'Faolain, who noted that the proposal was made 'while simultaneously, one of the most dramatic cases of *crim. con.* that we have had here for a generation was totally suppressed in all our local papers, but was appearing in full in Northern and English news-sheets, freely imported in the usual way'.[67]

The spiral of silence that surrounded court cases also extended to what occurred within the industrial schools.[68] In 1946, Fr Edward Flanagan, the founder of the famous Boys' Town reformatory in Nebraska, toured Ireland and delivered a message on child welfare that was very far removed from the system then operating in Ireland. His message that 'there are no bad boys or bad girls' seemed very much at odds with Ireland's borstals (youth prisons), industrial schools, and Magdalene laundries.[69] He declared himself against physical punishment and observed that 'one would have to be a psychologist to know that physical punishment would have the effect desired'.[70] Following a visit to a training school in Belfast, he asserted that 'in those places there was little common-sense shown in trying to get inside the mind of the child'.[71] As his tour continued, someone passed him information about what was happening in the industrial schools. In 2009, the Commission to Inquire into Child Abuse found that Fr Flanagan had been made aware of the details of a case of abuse that had occurred at St Joseph's Industrial School, Limerick, in 1945. A local councillor (later identified as Martin McGuire) had written to the Ministers for Education (Thomas Derrig) and Justice (Gerry Boland) informing them of the physical abuse suffered by a fifteen-year-old boy who was in the custody of the Christian Brothers. Having failed to convince the Department of Education of the need for a public inquiry, the councillor sent his file on the case to Fr Flanagan.[72] As his tour ended, Flanagan labelled the country's borstals 'a disgrace' and declared that the prisons were 'a disgrace to a Christian Catholic people'. He again denounced physical punishment and urged parents not to send their children to reformatories.[73] Oddly, given Flanagan's blunt criticism of Irish penal institutions, no politician contradicted him. This may have been because he was a man of the cloth or because to do so would have risked a public debate on the conditions in which children were detained. It was most likely the latter: Flanagan was, after all, just a visitor who would eventually leave. But Flanagan was not content with just airing his concerns in Ireland. On his return to the United States he told the *New York Times* that the juvenile detention system in Ireland was 'a disgrace' and that physical punishment, 'including the cat-o'-nine tails, the rod and the fist', was being used to punish children in reform schools.[74]

With Flanagan safely out of the country, politicians suddenly found their tongues. Questioned in the Dáil on Flanagan's comments, Minister Boland replied that since Flanagan had not seen, nor had he asked to see, any borstal or prison during his visit he was surprised that Flanagan used 'such offensive and intemperate language' to describe them. On his silence during Flanagan's visit, Boland declared that he 'not disposed to take any notice of what Monsignor Flanagan said while he was in this country, because his statements were so exaggerated'. Asked about Flanagan's statements in the American press, Boland, who, as Minister for Justice, would have been aware of the Limerick abuse case, declared that the reform schools were 'under the management of religious orders who are self-effacing people and who do not require any commendation from me'.[75] Such was the political oversight of children sent by the state to detention centres run by religious orders. The truth about what went on in those institutions would not emerge for many decades. Despite Flanagan's condemnation of the institutions and how they operated, there was no follow-up story by any Irish newspaper. There was, instead, a refusal on the part of the press to engage with the issue. Flanagan had given his statement to the New York press after having been told by one of his Irish contacts that none of the Irish daily newspapers were prepared to investigate the Limerick abuse case, despite being requested to do so.[76]

Only when the ill-treatment of children was raised in the Dáil did the press take notice, and, even then, not every newspaper reported the exchanges. In 1954, Peadar Cowan, then an independent TD, questioned the Minister for Education, Seán Moylan, about the punishment of a fourteen-year-old boy in Dublin's Artane Industrial School. The boy's arm had been broken by a Christian brother who had hit the child on the head, back, and arm with a sweeping brush. In reply, Moylan described the case as an isolated incident. Only the *Irish Times* reported the exchange; the *Irish Independent* and the *Irish Press* ignored it.[77] Some years earlier, the *Irish Times* had published a four-part series on child delinquency and industrial schools, written by an anonymous special correspondent, that described the schools' inhabitants as 'the unwanted, the neglected, and the outcast children of Ireland' and observed that society had 'grown accustomed to the system and cannot see how disastrously bad it is'. But it also described Artane Industrial School as, 'within its limitations, a good school [where] discipline appears to be less oppressive than in many a wealthy boarding school' and Daingean reformatory as being 'run on most enlightened lines'.[78]

In 1954, the year decreed by the Vatican as a time of special devotion to the Virgin Mary, the *Irish Times* reported on the growing phenomena of children born out of wedlock and committed to orphanages being adopted by American couples. In January of that year, it observed that church-run institutions were expecting a busy time in the subsequent twelve months as it was 'anticipated that many Americans passing through Ireland during the Holy Year will wish to take back Irish children, orphans or otherwise'. It reported that forty to fifty children had been taken to America the previous year and that, as Ireland did not have an adoption process, it was 'legitimate under present circumstances for American couples to come to Ireland, arrange to be shown over our orphanages, and to choose usually the healthiest boy or girl for adoption'.[79] The following April, George Burrows, Editor of the *Times Pictorial*, revealed that airlines were offering 'cut fares to Americans and to Irish people who are adopting Irish children from Irish orphanages and homes'. He also revealed that he had 'seen a request to newspapers that no publicity should be given to the removal of Irish-born babies from this end'.[80] Such a request was necessary as Irish newspapers were receiving information about the adoptions from news agencies such as United Press and Associated Press – a result of airlines such as TWA (Trans World Airlines) and AOA (American Overseas Airlines) seeking positive publicity from the 'cut fares' offered to adopters. In October 1951, the *Irish Times* reported that in one week alone eighteen parties of children had been flown from Shannon to America, that 500 children had been transported the previous year, and that for 1951 that number had been already been exceeded in October.[81] The *Times* was the only newspaper to criticise this practice. While *The Bell* had, in 1941, criticised what it referred to as 'the export of Irish children in the name of lonely souls elsewhere', the *Irish Independent* and *Irish Press* simply published photographs of the children arriving at their new homes in America.[82] Writing many years later, long-time journalist and political commentator James Downey concluded that it would be 'be quite wrong and foolish to exaggerate the merits of the kind of journalism practised a generation ago [because it] was gravely deficient in probing the real activities of governments or state sponsored or local authorities, as opposed to what appeared on the surface'.[83]

Pushing boundaries

There was, however, one beneficial, if short-lived, development in journalism during this period: the establishment by Seán MacBride of the Irish News Agency in 1949.[84] As Minister for External Affairs, MacBride wanted a news agency to publicise internationally the government's position on Partition. Led by its managing director, Conor Cruise O'Brien, the agency became the training ground for some of the most influential journalists of subsequent decades. Among those who worked at the agency were Douglas Gageby (Deputy Editor of the *Sunday Press*, founding Editor of the *Evening Press*, and Editor of the *Irish Times*, 1963–74 and 1977–86), Brendan Malin (former political correspondent of the *Irish Press* and later editor of the *Sunday Globe* in Boston), John Healy (later *Irish Times* political commentator, 'Backbencher'), Des Fisher (later editor of the London *Catholic Herald* and subsequently deputy head of RTÉ News), Kevin O'Kelly (later a reporter with RTÉ who, in 1972, went to prison rather than reveal a source), and Seamus McConville (later editor of *The Kerryman*). Despite providing full-time employment for over a dozen journalists and freelance work for another 100 journalists, the agency endured continuing hostility from the editors and senior journalists of the national titles who supplemented their income by acting as stringers for international newspapers. It also endured hostility from the Department of Finance, which viewed it as expensive and as duplicating the work of the Government Information Bureau and the national newspapers, all of whom were already long-standing members of the rival Press Association. Amid the economic malaise of the 1950s, the agency was closed in 1957.[85]

Despite the woeful economic conditions, there were some innovations and notable scoops within journalism and at least one direct challenge to the dominance of church over state during the late 1940s and early 1950s. In 1947, *Irish Times* journalist Dick Dowling came into possession of the diaries of Hermann Görtz, a German spy who had been interned in Ireland during the war and who had committed suicide rather than be deported back to Germany. Dowling's series, 'Mission to Ireland', which detailed Görtz's experiences in Ireland, including his attempts to work with the IRA, was a rare insight to what was really happening in Ireland during the Emergency.[86] In 1948, Hector Legge, Editor of the *Sunday Independent*, revealed that the government was planning to repeal the External Relations Act and take the state out of the British Commonwealth. The Taoiseach, John A. Costello, then on a tour of Canada, was forced to confirm the veracity of the story from abroad.[87]

In July 1949, the *Irish Times* published a four-part series on venereal disease, then a much hidden aspect of Irish society. The special correspondent who wrote the series noted the 'astonished unbelief' in official quarters when they went looking for information. Many doctors felt that the series would 'offend religious susceptibilities and direct the thoughts of clean thinking persons unnecessarily towards unpleasant matters': the vast majority, however, felt that 'a certain amount of well-reasoned and tactful publicity would be good'.[88]

In August 1950, the *Irish Press* had a worldwide scoop with its story of sixteen-year-old Aga Muller, who, along with her father Paul, tried to escape from post-war Germany by sailing their small boat to South America. Having arrived in Ireland, they sailed for the Canary Islands but were shipwrecked off the coast of Liberia, where Paul Muller died. Against worldwide interest in their story, Liam

MacGabhann of the *Irish Press* convinced Aga Muller to come to Ireland where her story was told in a thirty-one-piece series for the paper.[89]

In January 1950, following a speech by one Revd Felim Ó Briain, in which he declared that liberals and socialists advocated 'a free morality – the ethics of free love', the *Irish Times* threw its pages open to correspondents – many using pseudonyms – who wrote in on issues such as literary censorship, the special position afforded to the Catholic Church in the Constitution, and Irish society's attitudes to matters sexual. For three months, the 'Liberal Ethic' debate dominated the paper's agenda. It was a clever move by editor Robert Smyllie: by clearing space for readers to express their views he allowed for the ventilation of many alternative viewpoints on taboo topics, and, should anyone object to the views expressed, he could declare that the views being expressed were not necessarily those of the paper.[90]

The following year, Smyllie played a central role in the Mother and Child controversy that led to the downfall of the first inter-party government. As health minister, Noël Browne proposed maternity education and free medical care for all mothers and children up to the age of sixteen, with the additional stipulation that mothers be allowed to choose their own doctor.[91] The Catholic hierarchy objected because, as they saw it, the scheme encroached upon their sphere of influence, allowed the state to become involved in sex education, and, since mothers could choose their own doctor, allowed for the possibility of Protestant doctors treating Catholic mothers. In October 1950, Browne met with the hierarchy and offered to reconsider the clauses of the scheme that dealt with maternity education and to consult with them on any reformulation. Given that these provisions were not central to the scheme, he agreed to drop them if no agreement was reached.[92] This compromise was not acceptable to the hierarchy; they leaned on Browne's cabinet colleagues and warned that a critical issue of faith was at stake. One bishop later described the legislation as 'based on the Socialistic principle that children belonged to the State … and reminded one of the claims put forward by Hitler and Stalin'.[93] In April 1951, Browne was asked to resign by his party leader, Seán MacBride.

Just before Browne resigned, he sent a Civil Service friend over to the *Irish Times*. The friend entered Smyllie's office and dropped a large envelope on his desk. It contained the confidential cabinet correspondence between Browne, the Taoiseach, John A. Costello, and the hierarchy. Browne had previously met with Smyllie and had secured a promise from him that if he resigned the *Irish Times* would publish the letters in full. As Browne recalled in his autobiography, he had 'been warned that the Government might attempt to put an embargo on their publication, but Smyllie, an editor with genuine liberal beliefs, had promised me that should such an embargo be attempted, then, at the risk of going to prison, he "would publish and be damned"'.[94] It was not a decision taken lightly – by either man. The documents were protected under the Official Secrets Act 1920, and by retaining the cabinet file and passing it to Smyllie, Browne had breached the Act. By being in possession of the file and not notifying the Gardaí, so too had Smyllie. Both men could each have incurred a maximum of two years' imprisonment.[95]

True to his promise, Smyllie published the correspondence – a ground-breaking first for Irish journalism. (When the Dublin papers had been given tetchy correspondence between the government and the Governor General in July 1932, the government had put an embargo on publication, and all the papers had obeyed the order.[96]) The *Irish Times*'s publication of the letters forced the other national titles to do likewise. The initial letter of objection from the hierarchy to the Taoiseach described Browne's scheme as 'a ready-made instrument for future totalitarian aggression'. In a leading article, Smyllie noted that 'the Roman Catholic Church would seem to be the effective Government of this country'.[97] Costello seemed to confirm Smyllie's point when he declared that, as a Catholic, he had to obey the hierarchy regardless of what that meant for himself or Fine Gael.[98] One of the few journalists to support Smyllie was Mary Francis Keating, who wrote the *Irish Times*'s weekly 'Report to Housewives' column. Having described the public health system as 'something to be shuddered over as a searing experience' and as a system wherein patients suffered 'a series of indignities, of delays, and often culpable and harmful neglect', Keating was dropped from the paper following complaints from the medical profession.[99] Other supporters included David Boyd of the *Waterford Standard*, who described MacBride as a 'political careerist', and Seán O'Faolain, who noted in *The Bell* that it seemed as if the republic had 'two parliaments: a parliament at Maynooth and a parliament in Dublin' – a system that was 'certainly not an entirely democratic one'.[100] For its part, the NUJ's Dublin branch discussed 'whether it was within its power to pass a resolution in relation to the Mother and Child Scheme'. However, its officers, having 'gone carefully through the rules of the union … could find no section which would permit the branch to pass any resolution on the matter', concluded that 'any proposal on the matter would be "out of order" '.[101]

The Browne affair was, however, an isolated incident in terms of journalism challenging the status quo. Indeed, when, in 1953, Fianna Fáil and the hierarchy clashed over the provisions of a revised Health Bill, the press acquiesced in the non-publication of a statement that had been issued by the bishops criticising the legislation. When the Taoiseach, Éamon de Valera, agreed to meet the hierarchy to discuss their concerns, a senior cleric rang the *Irish Press* and the *Irish Independent* instructing them not to publish the bishops' statement. Both titles acquiesced – but it is interesting to note that the statement had not been sent to the *Irish Times* in light of its conduct in relation to the Mother and Child affair.[102] Around the same time, Desmond Williams, writing in *The Leader*, bemoaned the condition of journalism in Ireland, which he believed suffered from 'ignorance, indifference, lack of competition, and the poor payment of journalists'. This resulted in newspapers that were 'often dull, sometimes tasteless and nearly always intellectually unattractive'. There was, he declared, an acute absence of critically informed analysis: 'Irish journals have little to say, except in terms of news, on important developments at home [and] the announcements of official experts [were too] easily swallowed by newspaper commentators.' While editors probably found it difficult to improve their newspapers 'on account of the low level of education in Irish journalism', newspaper proprietors had become 'unimaginably satisfied and complacent'.[103] Less harshly, Brian Fallon of the *Irish Times* noted that while there was 'a great deal of flatness, provincialism and dullness', newspapers also 'gave a good proportion of their feature space to specialists of all kinds and even to intellectuals'.[104] However, in a report written in 1954, the German Ambassador noted that 'the Irish press in general only reaches the level of a provincial press … The papers have no foreign correspondents … The journalists are badly paid, so that they lack the incentive to improve their knowledge, and they have no resources to undertake foreign travel.'[105] All this would not change until Ireland embraced free trade and reintegrated itself with the wider world. In 1959, Seán Lemass succeeded Éamon de Valera as taoiseach; the long-running debate on the introduction of a national television service was also coming to a head. Its arrival in December 1961 changed journalism in Ireland forever.

Notes

1 S. O'Faolain, 'On editing a magazine', *The Bell*, 9:2 (1944), 93–101, at p. 99.
2 M. O'Toole, 'The Roman Catholic Church and the media in Ireland', in T. Fahy and M. Kelly (eds), *The Role of the Media in Irish Society* (Dublin, 1988), pp. 11–14.
3 T. Brown, *Ireland: A Social and Cultural History* (Dublin, 2004), pp. 192–3.
4 Brown, *Ireland*, pp. 143–4 and 192–3.
5 West Brit is a derogatory term applied to a person judged to be too Anglocentric in their culture or politics.
6 For a history of *The Bell* as a literary periodical, see K. Matthews, *The Bell Magazine and the Representation of Irish Identity: Opening Windows* (Dublin, 2012).
7 *Irish Times*, 15 Jun. 1935, p. 10.
8 For histories of the Irish Press Group, see M. O'Brien, *De Valera, Fianna Fáil and the Irish Press* (Dublin, 2001); and R. Burke, *Press Delete: The Decline and Fall of the Irish Press* (Dublin, 2005).
9 A. Bestic, *The Importance of Being Irish* (London, 1969), pp. 3–4.
10 *Irish Independent*, 22 Jul. 1936, p. 7.
11 Gaffney's series, 'In war-torn Spain', was published during Feb. and Mar. 1937. A second series was published in Oct. and Nov. 1937. For Gaffney's obituary see *Irish Independent*, 10 Dec. 1959, p. 13.
12 *Irish Independent*, 3 Jan. 1955, p. 12.
13 R. Smith, *Urbi et Orbi and All That* (Dublin, 1995), pp. 2–3.
14 I. Milne, 'Independent Newspapers as employer', in M. O'Brien and K. Rafter (eds), *Independent Newspapers: A History* (Dublin, 2012), pp. 146–56, at p. 146.
15 D. O'Donnell (Conor Cruise O'Brien), 'The Catholic press: a study in theopolitics', *The Bell*, 10:1 (1945), 30–40, at pp. 31–2.
16 O'Donnell (O'Brien), 'The Catholic press', p. 34. For more on the *Irish Catholic*, see J. Dunne, *Headlines and Haloes* (Dublin, 1988).
17 See *Irish Times*, 4 Aug. 1928, p. 14.
18 See M. O'Brien, *The Irish Times: A History* (Dublin, 2008), pp. 141–3 and 151–3.
19 P. Kavanagh, 'Diary', *Envoy*, 18 (1951), 72–3; For a review of Kavanagh's journalism, see F. Shovlin, '*Kavanagh's Weekly* revisited', *Studies*, 87:347 (1998), 282–90.
20 *The Standard*, 28 Feb. 1958, pp. 1–7.
21 Interview with Cathal O'Shannon.

22 See O'Brien, *The Irish Times*, pp. 90–2.
23 S. O'Faolain, 'Standards and taste', *The Bell*, 2:3 (1941), 5–11, at p. 6.
24 D. McCartney, 'A nationalist right enough', *Irish University Review*, 6:1 (1976), 73–86, at p. 76.
25 S. O'Faolain, 'The stuffed shirts', *The Bell*, 6:3 (1943), 181–92, at p. 192.
26 S. O'Faolain, 'Signing off', *The Bell*, 12:1 (1946), 1–4, at p. 1; 'On editing a magazine', 9:2 (1944), pp. 93–101, at p. 97.
27 V. Mercier, 'Verdict on the Bell', *The Bell*, 10:2 (1945), 156–67, at p. 160.
28 Olivia Manning Robertson, 'Deformed', *The Bell*, 9:2 (1944), 129–34. See also 'Out Patients', *The Bell*, 7:6 (1944), 510–14; and 'Court Circular', *The Bell*, 10:5 (1945), 395–401.
29 B. Ó hEithir, *The Begrudger's Guide to Irish Politics* (Dublin, 1986), p. 122.
30 B. Inglis, *Downstart* (London, 1990), p. 85.
31 O'Toole, 'The Roman Catholic Church', p. 12.
32 L. Fleming, *Head or Harp* (London, 1965), p. 127.
33 Inglis, *Downstart*, pp. 84–5.
34 Anon., 'Off the dole', *The Bell*, 2:3 (1941), 44–6, at p. 46.
35 Inglis, *Downstart*, p. 81–4.
36 *Irish Independent*, 28 Jan. 1956, p. 7.
37 Fleming, *Head or Harp*, p. 128.
38 O'Toole, 'The Roman Catholic Church', p. 12.
39 *Irish Times*, 8 Mar. 1944, p. 1. The offences referred to were mostly smuggling offences.
40 Interview with Gerry Mulvey.
41 *Irish Independent*, 8 Jul. 1969, p. 6.
42 S. O'Faolain, 'The Bishop of Galway and *The Bell*', *The Bell*, 17:6 (1951), 15–17, at pp. 16–17.
43 The most comprehensive account of censorship during the war can be found in D. Ó Drisceoil, *Censorship in Ireland, 1939–45* (Cork, 1996).
44 NAI, D/J; OCC 5, Press Censorship monthly reports 1944 (Feb.).
45 Ó Drisceoil, *Censorship in Ireland*, pp. 238–42.
46 *Irish Times*, 17 Apr. 1941, p. 2; 31 May 1941, p. 1.
47 Ó Drisceoil, *Censorship in Ireland*, pp. 128–9; C. Wills, *That Neutral Island: A Cultural History of Ireland during the Second World War* (Cambridge, Mass., 2007), pp. 408–10.
48 D. Gageby, 'The media in Ireland, 1945–70', in J. J. Lee (ed.), *Ireland, 1945–70* (Dublin, 1979), pp. 124–35, at p. 125.
49 O'Faolain, 'On editing a magazine', p. 99.
50 O'Faolain, 'On editing a magazine', pp. 95–6.
51 S. O'Faolain, 'The mart of ideas', *The Bell*, 4:3 (1942), 153–7, at pp. 153 and 155.
52 O'Faolain, 'On editing a magazine', pp. 94–5.
53 O'Faolain, 'Standards and taste', p. 5.
54 Anon., *The Bell*, 5:4 (1942), 173–83, at p. 183.
55 J. Kelly, *Bonfires on the Hillside* (Belfast, 1995), p. 40.
56 *Irish Times*, 2 Aug, 1944, p. 3. While all three national titles gave extensive coverage to the trial of nurse Mary Anne Cadden in 1956, it was covered as a murder case, despite it centring on an illegal abortion procedure that went wrong. The only mention of Cadden's activities as a backstreet abortionist was when the victim was described as having died from 'an illegal operation' performed by Cadden (see national titles between Oct. 1956 and Jan. 1957). Cadden was sentenced to death, but this sentence was commuted to life imprisonment. She died in the Central Mental Hospital in 1959.

57 *Daily Mirror*, 6 Nov. 1941, p. 8.
58 *Daily Mirror*, 7 Nov. 1941, p. 5.
59 Letter cited in M. Harmon, *Sean O'Faolain* (London, 1994), p. 148.
60 The law of criminal conversation allowed a man to sue for damages if another man had sexual congress with his wife. This law was repealed in Ireland in 1981.
61 It is unclear who, at this stage, the *Daily Mirror*'s reporter/stringer in Dublin was: the articles are unattributed.
62 *Daily Mirror*, 7 May 1943, p. 5.
63 *Daily Mirror*, 12 May 1943, p. 5.
64 *Daily Mirror*, 14 May 1943, p. 8.
65 *Daily Mirror*, 15 May 1943, p. 2. This is the last day of coverage. Given that no judgment was registered in the case we can only assume that it was settled out of court.
66 See *Irish Independent*, 10 and 18 Feb. 1942, pp. 2–3; *Irish Press*, 14 Feb. 1942, p. 3 and 10 Dec. 1942, p. 5; *Irish Times*, 10, 11, 12, 18 and 20 Feb. 1942, various pages; *Leitrim Observer*, 21 Feb. 1942, p. 3; *Connacht Tribune*, 21 Feb. 1942, p. 5.
67 O'Faolain, 'The stuffed shirts', p. 181; 'Shadow and substance', *The Bell*, 6:4 (1943), 273–9, at p. 275.
68 In 2009, the Ryan Report (Commission to Inquire into Child Abuse) critiqued press coverage of the industrial schools as spasmodic and constrained. Ryan Report (2009), vol. IV, pp. 229–32.
69 *Irish Times*, 10 Jun. 1946, p. 6.
70 *Irish Times*, 20 Jun. 1946, p. 3.
71 *Irish Times*, 24 Jun. 1946, p. 7.
72 Report of the Commission to Inquire into Child Abuse (Dublin, 2009) (Ryan Report), vol. I, paras 11.41–11.68.
73 *Irish Times*, 8 Jul. 1946, p. 6.
74 *New York Times*, 17 Jul. 1946, n/p.
75 *Irish Times*, 24 Jul. 1946, p. 7; DED, vol. 102 (col. 1134–45), 23 Jul. 1946.
76 Ryan Report, vol. I, para. 11.60.
77 *Irish Times*, 24 Apr. 1954, p. 7.
78 *Irish Times*, 2–6 Feb. 1950.
79 *Irish Times*, 14 Jan. 1950, p. 3.
80 *Times Pictorial*, 29 Apr. 1950, p. 10.
81 *Irish Times*, 8 Oct. 1951, p. 1.
82 M.P.R.H., 'Illegitimate', *The Bell*, 2:3 (1941), pp. 78–87, at p. 81; see *Irish Independent*, 4 Aug. 1949, p. 5; 16 Dec. 1949, p. 5; and 21 Mar. 1950, p. 6; *Irish Press*, 10 Nov. 1949, p. 3, and 20 Feb. 1952, p. 1. Adoption was finally introduced in Ireland in 1952, and the practice of exporting children ceased. See M. Milotte, *Banished Babies* (Dublin, 1997).
83 *Irish Times*, 20 Sep. 1983, p. 10.
84 Intriguingly, there existed a previous Irish News Agency, known as the Irish Press Agency, which was run in the 1880s by James Carew in London. It existed initially to publicise the Irish Parliamentary Party's campaign for Home Rule. Many of its leaflets are to be found in the National Library of Ireland.
85 For a comprehensive overview of the Irish News Agency, see J. Horgan, 'Government, propaganda and the Irish News Agency', *Irish Communications Review*, 3 (1993), 31–42. See also J. Healy, *Healy, Reporter: The Early Years* (Achill, 1991), Chapters 7–10; and C. Cruise O'Brien, *Memoir: My Life and Themes* (Dublin, 1999), pp. 144–52.
86 See *Irish Times*, 25, 27, and 29 Aug. 1947; and 1, 3, 5, 8, and 10 Sep. 1947.

87 *Sunday Independent*, 5 Sep. 1948, p. 1. See K. Rafter, 'A tale of womanly intuition: Hector Legge at the *Sunday Independent*, 1940–70', in O'Brien and Rafter (eds), *Independent Newspapers: A History*, pp. 119–32.
88 *Irish Times*, 21 Jul. 1949, p. 1. The series ended on 25 Jul. 1949.
89 See *Irish Press*, 5 Aug.–11 Sep. 1950.
90 *Irish Times*, 24 Jan 1950, p. 3. See also, R. Smyllie (ed.), *The Liberal Ethic* (Dublin, 1950).
91 In 1947, Fianna Fáil passed its Health Act, which included a 'Mother and Child Welfare Scheme' that proposed maternity education and free medical care for all mothers and children up to the age of sixteen. This had not been implemented due to protests from doctors that their fee-paying patients would desert them in favour of free treatment by the state.
92 N. Browne, *Against the Tide* (Dublin, 1986), p. 161.
93 *Irish Times*, 1 May 1951. The bishop concerned was Michael Browne of Galway.
94 Browne, *Against the Tide*, p. 186.
95 Official Secrets Act 1920, sections 2 and 8.
96 See O'Brien, *The Irish Times*, pp. 73–4.
97 *Irish Times*, 12 Apr. 1951, p. 1.
98 DED, vol. 125 (col. 784), 12 Apr. 1951.
99 *Irish Times*, 14 Apr. 1951, p. 5; O'Brien, *The Irish Times*, pp. 140–1.
100 *Waterford Standard*, 15 Apr. 1951, p. 4; S. O'Faolain, 'The Dáil and the bishops', *The Bell*, 17:3 (1951), 5–13, at p. 5.
101 HCRC, NUJ, Dublin Branch Minutes, 28 Apr. 1951.
102 J. Cooney, *The Crozier and the Dáil: Church and State, 1922–86* (Cork, 1986), p. 24. See also *Irish Times*, 10 June 1953, p. 1.
103 *The Leader*, 25 Oct. 1952, pp. 21–2.
104 B. Fallon, *An Age of Innocence: Irish Culture, 1930–60* (Dublin, 1998), p. 230.
105 PA AA, 2 205-00-33, Katzenberger-AA, 3 Aug. 1954, cited in J. J. Lee, *Ireland, 1912–85: Politics and Society* (Cambridge, 1989), p. 607.

7

The impact of television

Television brought with it a new brand of vigorous, questioning journalism which required politicians and even clerics to explain themselves before the cameras. The new regime was almost as traumatic for print journalists as it was for the public figures who had to face the hostile environment of the TV studio.[1]

— Michael O'Toole on the arrival of television

In the early 1960s, the country was at what one author described as 'the threshold of a delayed peaceful, social revolution'.[2] In 1959, Seán Lemass succeeded Éamon de Valera as Taoiseach, and the publication of T. K. Whitaker's *Economic Development* and a white paper on economic expansion led to free trade and a gradual re-entry into the wider global economy. The arrival of multinational corporations, attracted by low taxes, low labour costs, and an English-speaking workforce, prompted an economic boom. As the economy expanded, at a rate of 4 per cent per annum between 1960 and 1967, emigration declined and more females joined the workforce. Change also occurred in the education system, including the introduction of free post-primary education. Announced out of the blue by Minister for Education Donogh O'Malley at an NUJ seminar in September 1966, the move caught everyone by surprise – including his cabinet colleagues and the Catholic hierarchy, which controlled the education sector. The step was a bold one, given that the vast majority of children left school having completed primary level.[3] But the fact that O'Malley made the announcement in front of a room of journalists ensured that there was no going back – despite a concerted campaign by the hierarchy to kill the initiative.[4] The number of students completing second-level thus increased from 4,500 in 1950 to 19,000 in 1970 and 61,000 in 1998. Third-level numbers also increased: from 7,900 in 1950 to 25,000 in 1970 and 112, 200 in 1998.[5] The evolution of a more educated population was to have a significant impact on all aspects of society, including the practice of journalism and the relationship between journalism and society generally. The teachings of the church also came under the spotlight as the Second Vatican Council convened in Rome to examine Catholicism in the modern age.

As the state looked outwards, so too did its media. In 1960, the *Irish Times* dispatched its features editor, Jack White, on a 15,000-mile tour of Africa to bring readers 'a fresh and unbiased picture of the startling changes' that were taking place on the continent.[6] In July of that year, Irish troops were sent to the Congo on their first United Nations peacekeeping mission. When the first contingent of troops arrived, Raymond Smith of the *Irish Independent* pointedly reported on how they arrived in their 'heavy tweed uniforms' and overcoats.[7] Four months later, Smith was back in the Congo, along with Michael O'Halloran of the *Irish Press*, Cathal O'Shannon of the *Irish Times*, and John Ross of Radio Éireann, to report on the aftermath of an ambush in Niemba, in which nine soldiers were killed by Baluba tribesmen.[8] The following year, Smith was joined by Des Fisher of the *Irish Press* and Noel Conway of the *Irish Times* to report on the siege of Jadotville, where 150 Irish soldiers were besieged for a week by Katangese troops.[9]

The inauguration of a national television service (Telefís Éireann) in 1961 was another watershed.[10] Its arrival followed a torturous decade of committees and commissions to decide the format of the new service. The ultimate decision was that the service should be a public-service broadcaster, funded by a licence fee and advertising, overseen by a government-appointed authority, and required to be objective and impartial in its coverage of news and current affairs. On the broadcaster's first night of transmission, on 31 December 1961, President de Valera noted that he felt 'somewhat afraid'; while television could 'build up the character of the whole people' it could also 'lead through demoralisation to decadence and disillusion'. Striking a more positive note, Taoiseach Seán Lemass noted that Irish people were citizens of the world and there were 'standards, aims and values which transcend national frontiers and are universal in their application'.[11]

Most concern centred on the type of programmes that the new service would broadcast. While de Valera expressed concern that viewers would be persistently exposed to 'some squalid domestic brawl or a street quarrel', Cardinal John D'Alton called on the new service to provide programmes that would be 'enlightening, entertaining, reflecting high ideals'. Even Lemass acknowledged that 'in the field of entertainment there is a need to maintain proper standards and values'.[12] But there was little discussion about how television might impact on the practice of journalism. While the legislation underpinning the new broadcaster required it to be objective and impartial in its treatment of news and current affairs, there were no guidelines as to what this meant in real terms. While this requirement would, in time, provide a strong counterblast to the existing media and the constrained journalism that then existed, when the broadcasting legislation was being drafted and debated there was no appreciation that this requirement might be the catalyst for the development of critical journalism that would challenge the certainties of the power blocs that had, for decades, set the parameters of debate within society.

In the legislation's initial draft, the Broadcasting Authority was obliged to ensure that 'information and news and programmes relating to matters of political or industrial controversy or the subject of current public debate are presented objectively and impartially and without any expression of the Authority's own views on such matters'.[13] After discussion at cabinet, it was suggested to the Minister for Post and Telegraphs, Michael Hilliard, that advisory committees on religious and political matters be established, and his thoughts were canvassed on whether the advice of these committees 'should, to some extent, be binding on the authority'.[14] In his reply, Hilliard noted that such committees had been considered when the Bill was being drafted, but he had concluded that 'the Authority should be left as free as possible to arrange its proceedings in accordance with its own experience'. In his draft reply, Hilliard noted that he did not object to the authority 'being required to appoint a political advisory committee if it is thought that it will not be possible for it to obtain agreement from the parties on such matters as party political broadcasts without having such a committee'. He obviously had second thoughts on the wisdom of this idea as he struck it out of the reply.[15] Thus, in the first draft of the Broadcasting Bill, the impartiality of the new service was preserved. Section 18 (1) of the Bill stated:

> It shall be the duty of the Authority to secure that, when it broadcasts any information, news or feature which relates to matters of public controversy or is the subject of current public debate, the information, news or feature is presented objectively and impartially and without any expression of the Authority's own views.

When introducing the Bill in the Seanad, Hilliard made only a fleeting reference to the provisions of Section 18. He noted that the government had agreed 'to impose only the minimum statutory obligations and restrictions on the Authority – such as an obligation to preserve impartiality in matters of public controversy – so that it may have the maximum freedom within the broad context of its functions to formulate and implement its own policies'.[16] When the Bill moved to the Dáil, Hilliard simply observed that 'impartiality in regard to matters of public controversy is provided for in Section 18 and I do not think that there will be any opposition to the provision'.[17] But it is clear that these provisions weighed on the Taoiseach's mind. In a memorandum to his private secretary in March 1960, Lemass suggested that the government prepare for the Television Authority 'policy directives of a very general character [that] would not lay down very rigid rules but would convey the views of the Government on how particular problems likely to arise should be dealt with'. Among the subjects that such policy directives would cover were the country's image ('the avoidance of stage-Irishisms, playboyisms, etc.'), social problems ('encourage objective presentation of facts and constructive comment. The "God-help-us" approach should be ruled out') and coverage of events in Northern Ireland.[18] In reply, his secretary noted that such directives 'could be represented, both at home and abroad, as an illiberal action, calculated to hamper unduly the freedom of the Broadcasting Authority and reflecting an attitude of distrust on the part of the Government towards a body which will be appointed by themselves'.[19] There ended the idea of policy directives.

For the most part, politicians on all sides viewed impartiality as Telefís Éireann simply reporting verbatim, as happened on Radio Éireann's *To-day in the Dáil*, what the government said and what the opposition said on any given issue. They did not view the broadcaster as providing a platform for the ventilation of a multiplicity of opposing viewpoints in a contest for support.[20] This, perhaps, was unsurprising: the politicians of that era operated in a relatively closed media system that uncritically reported on or reflected the views of political parties and the Catholic Church. There was little scope for divergent views to be articulated, and what is nowadays called social-affairs journalism did not exist. But the personnel hired to staff Telefís Éireann's news and current-affairs sections were a mix of older newspaper reporters and young university graduates who viewed the obligation to be impartial as something more akin to doing what the *Irish Times* had done during the 'Liberal Ethic' debate of 1950: to represent the complexity of social reality by reflecting the diversity of opposing ideological world views that existed in society. In a report to Dublin's Archbishop John Charles McQuaid, one source noted that of the sixteen producers hired by Telefís Éireann, only four were Catholic. The producers – who were variously described as 'a Liberal', 'a Left-wing trade unionist and writer', 'a divorced actress who has been associated with numerous left-wing groups for many years', 'violently anti-clerical', 'an admirer of Joyce, Yeats, etc.', 'anti-clerical and is against all forms of censorship', 'one of the leading Liberals here', 'a divorced Jewess … associated with the production of indecent plays in Dublin for some years', 'a former member of the IRA' – appeared not to subscribe to the church's infallibility on social issues.[21] It did not take long for such diverse world views and different interpretations of impartiality to collide.

Clashes with government

As the 1960s progressed, journalism slowly became a contested terrain as broadcasters pushed at boundaries and politicians tried to restrict any interpretation of impartiality from going, in their view, too far. Although there were many minor skirmishes between the broadcaster and the government, the first major rupture occurred in October 1964 when the Minister for Agriculture, Patrick Smith, resigned and sent his letter of resignation to all media outlets. According to an NUJ statement, a government order was issued to RTÉ's news division that 'only official statements from the Government Information Bureau could be broadcast'. The order was rescinded later that day when evening newspapers published the letter.[22] In September 1966, Smith's successor, Charles Haughey, was annoyed to find that his televised interview on the government's ongoing dispute with the National Farmers' Association (NFA) was followed immediately by a rebuttal statement from the NFA leader Rickard Deasy. Three minutes after the broadcast ended, Haughey rang the RTÉ newsroom to complain about this juxtaposition of viewpoints. He asked that his complaint be made known to the Head of News, Pearse Kelly, and that Kelly get in touch with him. When contacted at home, Kelly instructed that the NFA statement be dropped from all news bulletins.[23] Again, the spat became public knowledge: at a meeting, the station's journalists pointed out that Haughey had not sought the removal of the NFA's statement; that decision had been taken by senior editorial staff. In a statement, Haughey declared that he had 'felt compelled in the public interest' to lodge his protest. He had given specific advice to farmers, and he felt that to have his advice 'followed by contradiction from an organisation could only lead to confusion and damage to the industry'. For its part, the NFA expressed amazement that 'any Minister would try to interfere with the legitimate viewpoint being expressed by another organisation whether he is in disagreement with them or not'.[24] In a speech to the Dublin

Chamber of Commerce, RTÉ's Director General, Kevin McCourt, declared that an editorial error had occurred: in his view, the error was the initial inclusion of the NFA statement, not its withdrawal following Haughey's complaint.[25]

This declaration angered the station's NUJ branch, which met in emergency session. It publicly disagreed with McCourt and declared that the NFA's statement would have run on all bulletins but for Haughey's complaint. The statement had been omitted on the orders of the Head of News, and, according to the branch, 'this was the only error of judgment involved'. It reminded McCourt that the Broadcasting Act imposed a duty on the RTÉ Authority 'to present news relating to matters of public controversy objectively and impartially'. It also quoted from the news division's staff manual, which asserted that 'no pressure from any source whatsoever will be permitted to influence the content or presentation of news bulletins in any way [and] attempts by any source, official or unofficial … to exert pressure or influence on the news, or the way the news is presented, will not be tolerated'. While it accepted the right of the head of news to make final judgements on news bulletins, it could not allow the director general to assert that the error of judgement 'was made not by the Head of News in withdrawing the NFA statement but by the editorial staff in giving it'.[26] The matter was raised in the Dáil, and the government was accused of interfering with RTÉ. In response, Seán Lemass declared that the government had a responsibility for ensuring that RTÉ's programmes did not go against the public interest (however that was defined) or conflict with national policy. He also rejected the idea that the station be completely independent of the government and again defined impartiality as being 'between political parties' without any reference to other interest groups and how their views might be represented in news or current affairs:

> Radio Telefís Éireann was set up by legislation as an instrument of public policy and as such is responsible to the Government. The Government have overall responsibility for its conduct and especially the obligation to ensure that its programmes do not offend against the public interest or conflict with national policy as defined in legislation. To this extent the Government reject the view that Radio Telefís Éireann should be, either generally or in regard to its current affairs and news programmes, completely independent of Government supervision. As a public institution supported by public funds and operating under statute, it has the duty, while maintaining impartiality between political parties, to present programmes which inform the public regarding current affairs, to sustain public respect for the institutions of Government and, where appropriate, to assist public understanding of the policies enshrined in legislation enacted by the Oireachtas. The Government will take such action by way of making representations or otherwise as may be necessary to ensure that Radio Telefís Éireann does not deviate from the due performance of this duty.[27]

In response, the NUJ sought a meeting with Lemass and the Minister for Posts and Telegraphs, Joseph Brennan, but was refused. It then issued a statement that pointedly asked how public order or the authority of the state might have been undermined by representing the government's and the NFA's view on the dispute in the same news item. It challenged Lemass's assertion that the government had responsibility for the conduct of RTÉ and his rejection of the principle that the station should be, in regard to current-affairs and news programmes, completely independent of government supervision and accused him of 'reading into the Broadcasting Authority Act far more than that Act contains'. While it conceded that Lemass and the government 'may not like some of the criticism which has been directed at them from time to time', it firmly believed that 'the right to criticise must remain together with the right of journalists to report such criticism'. It concluded by reiterating its 'determined opposition to any attempt by this Government, or any other, to stifle legitimate criticism of its policies, or to tamper with the news'.[28] As the decade progressed, such clashes increased in frequency.

In terms of current affairs, as John Horgan has pointed out, while the newsroom was primarily reactive in that it reported stories, interviewed spokespersons for competing interests and responded to events of the day, current affairs was more proactive in that it took the long view by examining underlying structural issues and identifying who benefited from certain policies and at whose expense.[29] There were plenty of institutions that were sensitive to any critical analysis being directed at them, but there were also plenty of broadcasters willing to conduct such analysis. Put most simply, the 1960s saw the entry of the first post-Civil War generation into politics; so too did it see the entry of the first batch of producers and reporters into a media environment in which objectivity and impartiality were enshrined in legislation. The station's flagship current-affairs programme, *Seven Days*, produced by Lelia Doolan, was a critical part of the questioning of received wisdom and the homogeneity of the values that shaped Irish society. An early programme questioned the influence that the oath-bound Knights of St Columbanus had in political circles; another suggested that Irish emigrants in Britain 'had lost interest in their religion'.[30] In December 1967, a revamped and renamed *7 Days* incurred the wrath of Fianna Fáil when it presented analysis that showed that, under the proposal to change the electoral system from proportional representation to the first-past-the-post system, the party would regularly win large majorities.[31] This was objectivity and impartiality (and the public interest) writ large – but no political party had ever envisaged RTÉ making programmes like this.

Television's effect on print journalism

The fact that so many of these controversies made their way into the public domain by means of political–journalist disputes over what the impartiality obligation actually meant had several knock-on effects on the print media. As Maurice Walsh aptly put it, the advent of television heralded 'a force field reconfiguring other media, the practices of politics, and culture more widely'.[32] In the first instance, the national newspapers' political journalists were given their own television programme, *Hurler on the Ditch*. Chaired by John Healy of the *Irish Times*, the weekly programme gave Michael Mills of the *Irish Press*, Michael McInerney of the *Irish Times*, and Arthur Noonan of the *Irish Independent* a platform on which to analyse and discuss the political issues of the day, sometimes in a way that was not possible in their respective newspapers. As Michael Mills, Political Correspondent of the *Irish Press*, put it:

> I had an advantage over previous political correspondents in that television had arrived and I appeared on several programmes and would often say on television what I might have difficulty saying in the *Irish Press*. There was opposition from sections of Fianna Fáil with many meetings passing resolutions trying to get the management to sack me. When the attacks came, Vivion [de Valera, *Irish Press* controlling director] resisted them and said he would stand by me. I used to get flack from TDs but I had regular access to television and radio which was a great help as I could reach a far greater audience there than by the *Irish Press*.[33]

Such analysis and commentary did not sit well with some politicians. In 1966, during a Seanad debate on broadcasting, Senator Patrick Quinlan criticised the prominent coverage given to the views of political journalists. They had, he asserted, 'been given a place of importance in this country altogether out of keeping with a democratic country'. No other democracy would, he declared, allow 'a small group to get into their hands the power to make and break politicians and to make and break Governments that Telefís Éireann have given to the political commentators here'.[34] The arrival of television also created an element of competition between broadcasters and print journalists. While one commentator noted that 'Irish print journalists suddenly found themselves in competition with a new breed of interviewer, people like Brian Farrell and John O'Donoghue [who] were often better educated, more confident and more professional than their colleagues in the newspapers', simply by their longevity in reporting politics, press political correspondents tended to have better sources.[35] This occasionally produced tensions when they were interviewed by the newer broadcasters. Reviewing one current-affairs programme in 1970, a television critic noted that

> Brian Farrell had got a bit testy with John Healy and Arthur Noonan because they seemed to him to be coy about their interpretation of Mr Ó Móráin's resignation as Minister for Justice and John Healy had, in turn ticked Farrell off for expecting them to provide sensational tit-bits specially for television.[36]

Amid a modernising society, a more open media landscape, and the growth of impartial journalism, there was an increased awareness among national newspaper proprietors that newspapers and their style of journalism had to change. There emerged a recognition that newspapers could no longer be seen to be linked to or supportive of any one political party or interest group. Writing in 1966, Tim Pat Coogan observed that 'more of the country's newspapers [were] coming to see their role as stimulators of the mind and not as retailers of received prejudices'.[37]

At the *Irish Press*, controlling director Vivion de Valera was attuned to the changing times. As remembered by Michael O'Toole, Vivion realised that the days of the slavish 'my party, right or wrong type of coverage were over and through the appointment of Michael Mills introduced a degree of impartiality that was unthinkable in the early days'.[38] Appointed political editor in 1963, Mills accepted the post on the condition that he 'would not write propaganda'.[39] Three years later,

Mills was the first to break the news of Seán Lemass's intention to resign as taoiseach. The story was denied by Fianna Fáil, and the paper came under immense pressure to retract it. Having held out for two days, the paper was on the verge of retraction when word came through of a special parliamentary party meeting having been called – the meeting at which Lemass confirmed his resignation.[40] Tim Pat Coogan, who was appointed editor in 1968, remembered that 'there were fierce rows and terrific pressure from the party, but the paper could not maintain the appearance of being aligned to Fianna Fáil'.[41] The new policy was best encapsulated in the phrase 'fair to all, friendly to Fianna Fáil', and, although the paper tried to put some critical distance between itself and the party, at election time it always called on its readers to vote for the party – a legacy of the paper's foundation but also a recognition of who its core readership was.

At the *Irish Independent*, long-time editor Frank Geary retired in 1961 and was replaced by his deputy Michael Rooney. Although never tied to Fine Gael in the same way that the *Irish Press* was tied to Fianna Fáil, the *Irish Independent* was highly sympathetic to the party's fortunes. On the eve of polling day for the 1965 general election, the paper noted that it 'existed to reflect public opinion, to inform and guide it' and would not advise its readers on how to vote. Old habits die hard, however, and it fulsomely praised Fine Gael's 'Just Society' plan, which, it noted, Fianna Fáil had scrambled to imitate. By doing so, it concluded, Lemass had 'obliquely voted Fine Gael'.[42] But, for a brief period at least, it looked as if the *Irish Independent* was about to acknowledge the changes going on around it. Appointed editor in June 1968, Louis McRedmond 'had a fondness for the eternal verities of journalism: good writing, solid research, getting it right. He was unshowy and unspectacular.' He was also a moderniser and 'had been successfully nudging the *Irish Independent* away from its predilection for the crustier Catholic values in his reports on Vatican II from Rome'.[43] However, the board of Independent Newspapers did not like McRedmond's editorial philosophy. It was of the view that the *Irish Press*, not the *Irish Times*, was the newspaper group to be competed with: that meant an emphasis on news not critically informed analysis. In December 1969, barely eighteen months into the job, McRedmond was sacked, and the *Independent* reverted to its news-dominated identity. It was, remembered one later editor, 'a powerful paper, steeped in tradition and staffed by righteous men, many of whom were slaves to what had been politically correct in the 50s'.[44]

It was the *Irish Times* that reacted most proactively to the changes occurring during the 1960s. Appointed editor in 1963, Douglas Gageby, aided in no small part by news editor Donal Foley, sensed the commercial and journalistic opportunities arising from a changing society and presided over the transformation of the paper from being the organ of the Protestant minority, albeit one with a liberal Catholic readership, to being a truly national newspaper. Women's journalism, up to then still dominated by recipes and fashion, was modernised with the appointment of journalists such as Mary Maher and Eileen O'Brien, both of whom had a brief to write on serious issues of concern to female readers. Social-affairs journalism was pioneered by another new arrival, Michael Viney; John Horgan was appointed religious correspondent and sent to Rome to report on the Second

Vatican Council; and Fergus Pyle was appointed as its Northern Ireland correspondent. The result was a vibrant, socially aware, and critically informed newspaper. Its political coverage also evolved. While Michael McInerney remained as political correspondent, it was John Healy and his 'Backbencher' column that attracted most attention. To many people, it was the most influential political column of the 1960s. It contained information, sometimes on government policy, sometimes political gossip, derived from information not available to other political writers, and it was written in a daring and irreverent style that treated politicians as individuals who were not above the temptations and mistakes of everyday life. As one commentator noted, 'until the arrival of the "Backbencher" column in the *Sunday Review* and later the *Irish Times*, which has in turn led to a similar licence in other newspapers, regular and provocative political journalism was almost unknown in Ireland'.[45]

Journalism and the Catholic Church

The development of television and the critical perspective that began to inform journalism during the 1960s resulted in journalists repeatedly asserting their independence from institutions that had once dictated the news agenda. Besides the main political parties, the other institution most affected by this development was the Catholic Church. Up to the mid-1960s, the church was above criticism or scrutiny of any sort, but television and its impact on journalism changed all that. The acquiescent relationship that the press had with the church was neatly summed up in a report presented to Archbishop McQuaid by his 'public image committee':

> Many journalists believe that the Church enjoys a special protection from criticism in the editorial and letter columns of newspapers other than the Irish Times. They believe that the clergy enjoy an immunity from unfavourable reports even in instances where the clergy figure as citizens rather than as priests, e.g. in breaking the law. It is well known among journalists that certain newspapers have a policy of keeping off issues in which the Church may be involved … Many journalists believe that the intervention of ecclesiastical authority is responsible for the cautious policies of editors or they believe that newspaper proprietors are so afraid of falling foul of the hierarchy and clergy that they always play safe … Journalists believe that all too often the Church abuses the press in attempting to control what should or should not be reported or commented on.

The report also wryly observed that 'a favourite occupation in every news-room is the writing of imaginary headlines for religious news, headlines which, of course, could never be printed'.[46] In a later report, the committee concluded that television seemed far more difficult to control:

> Television also gives a new and powerful platform to many people who never had it in the Press. What is said in the Press is mostly written by a small group of professional journalists under the supervision of an editor. Most of what is said in Public Affairs programmes does not come from professional journalists, and is

> really only controlled by them to the extent that they may have picked the people who appear in the programme. This new factor in the situation is of importance, because it means that a small group, who tend to be very critical of the Church in Ireland, are having a much greater impact on public opinion through the medium of television than was ever done previously.[47]

Immediately after the establishment of Telefís Éireann, McQuaid sought to appoint one Canon Cathal McCarthy to liaise between himself and the broadcaster. Such overtures were not reciprocated by the station's director general, Ed Roth, a Boston-born Irish-American Catholic who had been hired because of his experience of getting new stations off the ground.[48] A letter from one Fr Fehily which indicated that Roth was unaware of McCarthy's supposed role prompted an angry retort from McQuaid: 'Mr. R. was given 1½ hours of my time during which I asked Fr McC. to call over. Mr R. was at once to phone Fr McC. to see him. From that good day he has never given any sign of life. If Mr R. thinks we can take that treatment, he is mistaken.'[49] There followed a letter from McQuaid to the Chairman of the RTÉ Authority, Eamonn Andrews, informing him that he had appointed McCarthy as his 'personal liaison priest in Dublin, the City and Diocese in which is situated the Television centre [to] facilitate the necessary consultations between the Television authority and the Archbishop of Dublin'.[50] The polite response from Andrews noted that he hoped there would 'be many and fruitful contact between him and the Television Authority'.[51]

In reality, Andrews and the station's new director general, Kevin McCourt, were working feverishly to prevent McQuaid from having any involvement in the station. McCourt later recounted how he and Andrews 'spent many hours … analysing, planning against giving the Hierarchy collectively or singly, any voice in control of programme-making'.[52] McQuaid sensed such plans: writing to McCarthy in September 1962, he observed that 'we ought to move at once, for the position in TÉ is hardening every month that passes and a permanent shape is appearing in which we do not properly take our place … Our policy, in my view, is dilatory, timorous, and piecemeal'.[53] Ultimately, Andrews and McCourt succeeded in appointing a Dominican priest, Fr Romuald Dodd, to the position of religious adviser while McQuaid was in Rome attending the second session of the Second Vatican Council. As a Dominican, Dodd was outside McQuaid's sphere of influence. McQuaid's reaction to this move was telling: in a letter to McCourt, he declared himself 'the sole authority competent in matters of Faith and morals in the Diocese in which your station is situated'.[54]

McQuaid's asserted authority was refuted by the station the following month when the liberal theologian Fr Gregory Baum was interviewed on its *Newsview* programme in relation to the Second Vatican Council. This prompted a next-day missive from McQuaid's secretary, Revd James McMahon, requesting McCourt 'to state by whose authority Rev. Gregory Baum, OSA, who appeared on a Telefís Éireann programme, was invited to speak and did speak in this Diocese on matters of Faith and Morals'.[55] In a riposte, McCourt declared that while the station was responsible for using Baum's services, it assumed 'that if he required ecclesiastical clearance to participate in a programme of the kind involved, this would be a matter between him and the ecclesiastical authorities'.[56]

Documentary-making also caused McQuaid anxieties. In 1965, Brian Cleeve set out to make a programme on the Artane and Goldenbridge industrial schools. However, when the Superior of Artane insisted that he have the final say on the script, the school was dropped from the programme. Having received this news by letter, McQuaid wrote the phrase, 'Glad Artane is out' on the correspondence.[57]

The Late Late Show, hosted by Gay Byrne, also caused McQuaid anxiety. When Byrne caused a media storm after asking a quiz contestant what colour nightdress she wore on her wedding night, McQuaid wrote to McCourt describing the segment as 'vulgar, even coarse and suggestive'.[58] In his response, McCourt observed that 'television possesses some magnetism for risk-taking and for being racy, especially in the field of light entertainment'.[59] Two months later, when a Trinity College student, Brian Trevaskis, criticised McQuaid for supporting literary censorship and referred to Galway's new cathedral as a monstrosity and its bishop as a moron, McCourt wrote to McQuaid to explain that 'lapses from good taste and outbursts of bad manners on television programmes … may not necessarily be premeditated in themselves, but perhaps stem from the stimulation and exhibitionism sometimes created by television'.[60] One can only surmise whether these defining moments of Irish television would have occurred had McQuaid succeeded in having his own representative appointed to the station. Certainly, some of his own priests urged him to take action. In a letter that condemned the 'anti-Catholic, anti-Irish propaganda of the Late Late Show', they urged McQuaid 'to see to it that the suave Mr Byrne be prevented from providing a platform for the vermin of England, France, USA, or anywhere such vermin can be picked up'.[61] It was, however, too late to put the genie back in the bottle.

McQuaid also struggled with the new sense of independence demonstrated by print journalists, particularly those appointed as religious correspondents. Among the journalists who covered the early sessions of the Second Vatican Council were Des Fisher of the London *Catholic Herald*, Seán Cryan of the *Irish Press*, Liam Shine of the *Irish Independent*, and Seán Mac Réamoinn and Kevin O'Kelly of RTÉ. The church's reticence in dealing with journalists was evident from the beginning: journalists were excluded from the debates, and the scarce press releases did not associate individual bishops with the various points being made. As Louis McRedmond of the *Irish Independent* recalled, at the first session in autumn 1962, 'journalists were refused all opportunity to compile the best evidence. They were deliberately thrown back on second-rate and third-rate sources [including] the known views of certain Fathers, interviews with bishops trammelled by their oath of secrecy, and even Roman gossip.'[62] Despite this, McRedmond believed that 'using all the unsatisfactory evidence they could get [journalists] managed to piece together a narrative, which, for all its shortcomings, gave a reasonable, thorough and basically true account of what happened'.[63] McQuaid disagreed: in a note written in 1964 he recorded his opinion that 'the reporting on the Council has been very bad – deplorable'.[64]

The following year, McQuaid fulminated at what he referred to as the 'facile ignorance' of journalists who were reporting the council as a battle between progressive and conservative forces.[65] Much of this critical attitude, it seemed to those advising McQuaid, stemmed from the advent of television. In a report presented to him in 1964, his 'public image committee' noted that television had 'accustomed people to take it for granted that men who hold positions of authority and responsibility owe it to the public to explain their actions'. It described those who most frequently presented or contributed to programmes as 'Catholics of university education who make no secret of the fact that they regard themselves as having a mission to shake Irish Catholics out of a condition of lethargy, conservatism and simple Faith'. Referring to the press, it observed that

> prior to the Council most Irish lay people took it for granted that there was an official line on most, if not all problems, and that Bishops more or less all held the same views without having to arrive at them by discussion. The Vatican Council, as reported by the press, presented a very different picture … From that reporting the Irish hierarchy appears conservative.[66]

The final session of the council was reported on by McRedmond and John Horgan of the *Irish Times*. Their reportage, no longer influenced only by the Irish hierarchy but more so by their international sources and colleagues, grated with McQuaid. When, on the eve of that session, Pope Paul VI issued a strident encyclical, *Mysterium fiedi*, McQuaid praised it as 'a firm statement of the unchanged and unchanging doctrine of the church'. But he was again unhappy with its reportage: he described McRedmond's report in the *Irish Independent* as 'tolerable' while Horgan's report in the *Irish Times* was dismissed as 'lamentable in its ignorance and immaturity'. While McRedmond noted that the encyclical might have been aimed against 'new ideas that might have found champions on what could be called the extreme left-wing of the liberal fathers', Horgan observed that 'the more patently progressive bishops and council experts … are anxiously concerned to preserve and enlarge the area of free discussion and questioning which has been such a major feature of the movement for reform'.[67] Horgan had, McQuaid dismissively concluded, 'met the lightweights', a reference to the journalist having met theologians enthusiastic about the reformist nature of the council.[68] The Dublin Diocesan Press Office kept an eye on how the religious correspondents were reporting developments in Rome: writing to McQuaid's secretary, the Diocesan Press Officer, Ossie Dowling, observed that 'Horgan is leading the way [and that] McRedmond may be trying to out-Horgan Horgan.' In a letter to McQuaid himself, Dowling observed that McRedmond 'is aware of the line Horgan is taking and may colour his own dispatches accordingly, lest he be classified as a "conservative" '.[69]

When he arrived back in Dublin, McRedmond received what he called 'a shattering jolt': while 'the strenuous efforts of Irish newspapers, radio and television had borne fruit in widespread interest' in the council's deliberations, within certain sections of Irish society 'preconceived notions had hardened in such a way that the news from the Vatican had been twisted to sustain a bias instead of being allowed to mould ideas afresh'.[70] Similarly, John Horgan considered it 'astonishing, and frustrating, to discover that all the theological, historical and liturgical richness to which we had been exposed in Rome, and which had left an indelible mark on all those who experienced it, had only touched the fringes of Irish Catholicism'.[71] At its most public, such orthodoxy was represented by McQuaid's remark on his return to Dublin that while the faithful may 'have been disturbed at times by reports about the Council [and] worried by much talk of changes to come', he could tell them that 'no change would worry the tranquillity of [their] Christian lives'.[72]

Despite his misgivings, McQuaid responded to the changed media environment in a number of ways: he had established the Dublin Diocesan Press Office in May 1965 and appointed a diocesan press officer, Ossie Dowling. He also sent a young priest, Fr Joe Dunne, on a three-month broadcasting course in New York. Dunne later initiated one of Irish television's most innovative programmes. *Radharc*, which first aired in 1962, was initially a religious-affairs programme but soon spread its coverage into social affairs, covering such issues as young offenders, homelessness, Irish emigrants in Britain, and adoption.[73] As Robert Savage has remarked, 'the series helped Irish society become aware of complex political and social problems both at home and abroad'.[74] Despite such innovations, overall, as Michael O'Toole saw it, 'of all the powerful institutions, the church proved least able to cope with the new demands of TV and the fresh approaches to news-gathering and comment' that marked the arrival of a more critical media era.[75]

The GAA: coverage and controversy

The GAA was little different. The attitude of most of its county boards was that journalists should know their place or risk losing access to information. In his memoir, John Healy, then on the *Western People*, recounts being asked to leave a victory dinner in Castlebar when Mayo won the All-Ireland Football Final in 1950. His offence was to have written about 'dirty play in Mayo GAA games'. When the county board threatened to sue for libel, the paper's editor, Fred de Vere, having checked Healy's sources, challenged the board to go ahead with the action. The board backed down but passed a resolution banning Healy from all future games.[76]

As remembered by one journalist, Alan Bestic, the GAA fostered a sense that 'all Gaelic games players were clean-limbed youths, drenched with fine Irish sportsmanship and incapable of mean thought or action, while those who played "foreign" games were a bunch of scurrilous, knuckle-dustered thugs with hate in their hearts for their opponents'.[77] It was as if the GAA, as journalist Michael Finlan, put it, 'could not abide any suggestion that the national games … might not always be activities of impeccable sportsmanship and almost pristine purity'. The result was that media coverage of unpleasant aspects of the games was sanitised. As recalled by Finlan, Radio Éireann, which began broadcasting GAA games in 1926, 'conspired in the myth of unstained sportsmanship, with Michael O'Hehir describing the beautiful sunny weather whenever the players began knocking the bejaysus out of each other'.[78] The same applied to newspapers. As recalled by Alan Bestic:

> I remember, for instance, seeing members of a team, beaten in the All-Ireland Gaelic football final, thumping the starch out of the referee as they came off the

> field, while the victors tried to fight them off. This unpleasant yet understandable scene took place in front of the stand which held the President of Ireland Seán T. O'Kelly; the Prime Minister Éamon de Valéra [sic], with several members of his Cabinet; the Apostolic Nuncio, Dr Paschal Robinson, with several members of the diplomatic corps, plus a fair coterie of bishops. It was a dramatic incident; but not a line about it appeared in the newspapers next day.[79]

Those who transgressed this code of silence suffered: Bestic recalled one photographer who tried to record an altercation on the field who 'had his camera smashed to bits; and he had collected a fair hiding too'.[80] In 1961, John D. Hickey of the *Irish Independent* wrote frankly of the physical alercations involving Cork's captain Christy Ring during that year's Munster hurling final:

> The exchanges were always mercilessly hard but there was only one flare up of any consequence when John Doyle and Ring became emeshed in a catch-as-catch-can, or punch-as-punch-can on the ground eighteen minutes after the restart. That was unseemly enough but it was deplorable that Ring, after arising, should strike Tom Moloughney with his hurley, causing the Tipperary man to be assisted from the pitch with a head injury. Numerous other players became embroiled but the incident would hardly have qualified for mention but for Ring's action.[81]

In contrast, the *Irish Times* merely noted that 'displays of temper on both sides erupted into nasty incidents on two occasions'. The *Irish Press* noted that the game was marred by 'an unsavoury explosion of fisticuffs', that Moloughney was struck by a hurley and that the game 'added no lustre to Ring's reputation', but, unlike Hickey's report, it did not explicitly link Ring with the assault on Moloughney.[82] The GAA did not take such frank reporting lightly. The following month, Hickey was refused admission to the press box of the Cork athletic grounds when he showed up to report on the Cork County Senior Hurling Final. When the NUJ threated to impose a ban on reporting any games in Cork, one member of the county's GAA board described the union's attitude as 'impertinent and insolent'.[83] Threats of legal action followed – at least four libel actions were initiated on the basis of Hickey's report.[84] After several months of negotiations involving Michael McInerney of the NUJ and representatives of the Cork county board, both sides released a statement that noted Ring's name 'should not have been singled out', that all libel actions had been withdrawn, and that the union's threat of action and the county board's ban on Hickey had been lifted.[85]

But, as Alan Bestic observed, by the late 1960s, sports journalists, empowered by the televising of GAA games from 1962 onwards, were less shy in pointing out foul behaviour on the field. While RTÉ television, as recalled by Michael Finlan, initially 'chose to aim its cameras at the cheery faces of the crowd on Hill 16 [any time] tempers got out of hand in the heat of play', such tactics simply indicated that something serious was happening on the field.[86] Gradually, altercations began to be televised and reported on. In 1968, Bestic noted that 'the newspapers are writing openly that hurling in particular is becoming so dangerously dirty that it threatens to kill itself'.[87] But it took time for the GAA to adjust to such candid coverage.

In May 1968, a serious breach of relations between the GAA and the NUJ occurred. Reviewing that year's National League Hurling Final between Tipperary and Kilkenny, John D. Hickey of the *Irish Independent* noted that the game had produced 'eight scandalous minutes [of] acts of violence that must have sickened every spectator … with a shred of respect for the precepts of law and order, never mind the canons of good sportsmanship'.[88] Mick Dunne of the *Irish Press* noted that the game was 'regrettably tarnished by a half-hour that amounted to the most despicable and disgraceful exhibition of outright viciousness witnessed in Croke Park for many years'. Rivalry between the teams had 'exploded into such maliciousness that the hurling turned into sickening savagery'.[89] Similarly, Paddy Downey of the *Irish Times* noted that 'the "needle" which has marred a number of recent matches between these counties again thrust up its ugly and malicious spike'.[90] The Tipperary GAA county board responded by prohibiting selectors and players from giving interviews or information to six named sports journalists, including Hickey, Dunne, and Downey.[91]

In response, the NUJ's Dublin branch instructed its members not to report, comment on, or handle any GAA news emanating from Tipperary and declared that it deplored the county board's attempt 'to curb objective comment'.[92] The national titles did not report on Tipperary's training or preparation for that year's All-Ireland Hurling Final against Wexford, though the final itself, which Tipperary lost, was reported on. Immediately after the final, the Tipperary county board lifted its ban but, not being officially notified of this, the NUJ extended its ban to cover any game involving a Tipperary team.[93] It was December before the NUJ lifted its ban, expressing its belief that it had 'demonstrated that Irish journalists will not tolerate abuse or intimidation from any organisation or individual'.[94] Reviewing the situation some weeks later, the NUJ's Dublin branch chairman, Maurice Hickey, observed that because of a misunderstanding of the journalist's functions, people were often aggrieved at candid criticism in the press because they felt 'the side had been let down'. Such sensitivities were, he contended, at the heart of the Tipperary county board's dispute with sports journalists. Keen to disabuse organisations of these sensitivities, Hickey declared that 'the journalist is not a public relations man and it is not part of his job to present a favourable image of public men, of organisations and events all the time; the warts must be shown when necessary'. He also observed that it was the branch's intention to work more closely with management and editors in relation to professional matters.[95]

A changing profession

On a professional level, journalism modernised during the 1960s as more thought was devoted to the role of journalism: was it simply to report what politicians and the hierarchy said and did, or was it to report all this and put wider social and political contexts to such reports? If the latter applied, then journalists required an education in the liberal arts – a position strongly advocated by Louis McRedmond. Interviewed in 1967, McRedmond argued that the best education a journalist could get was 'a liberal arts degree and on to it grafted practical journalism'.[96] The education of journalists had exercised minds before. In 1945, the Knights of St Columbanus had proposed the creation of 'a school of journalism'. It sponsored a series of lectures at the Central Catholic Library in the autumn of that year and approached UCD with a proposal, but the idea went nowhere.[97] In a later memorandum to Archbishop McQuaid, Supreme Knight Dermot J. O'Flynn explained that while the NUJ 'was inclined to look upon the project with little enthusiasm ... ultimately they gave the scheme their blessing, admitting that it was a good one, even if it did not coincide exactly with their ideas'. However, when eventually consulted, the DNMC rejected the idea and complained that industry had not been consulted about the skills journalists needed. It noted that 'a Journalist's Diploma, to have any real validity, would need to show proficiency in such practical elements of journalism as shorthand, précis, interviewing techniques, and typographical knowledge'.[98]

In 1953, the NUJ's Irish council was 'authorised to prepare a draft scheme governing education and entry into journalism', while in 1959 it was noted that 'the proposal (training and education scheme) had been put before the newspaper managers and they turned it down and the union could not go ahead with the scheme without their support'.[99] Some years later, in January 1962, Pat Nolan, Father of the *Irish Times* NUJ chapel and the republic's delegate on the union's NEC, noted that a recently introduced 'training and education scheme' in Northern Ireland was 'working reasonably well'.[100] Having attended a 'training and education' meeting in London, Nolan set about securing the approval of Archbishop McQuaid before approaching the newspaper managers. Describing the managers as 'cautious', Nolan observed that 'they must be convinced that there are no ulterior motives behind this scheme, that it is absolutely altruistic, and designed solely for the improvement of the standard of journalism, that it has no union affiliation and that it will not be used as a lever for increased wages'.[101] In a memorandum, McQuaid recorded a conversation he had with Nolan. According to McQuaid, Nolan's 'intention is that this school would be a work of the union but his first care would be to submit the scheme to the Archbishop to ensure that everything would be in accordance with Catholic education. He might then approach the Taoiseach, or in some way, the government'.[102] McQuaid ran Nolan's plan past Fr Thomas Murphy, who acted as chaplain to Dublin journalists, and was informed that 'an educational move as Paddy N. [Nolan] proposes, with the push of the union behind it and the Catholic outlook expressed by him would be ideal'.[103]

Having secured the consent of McQuaid and the newspaper managers, Nolan's next step was to write to Taoiseach Seán Lemass in April 1963 to outline the rationale for a training scheme. Observing that the function of newspapers had changed with the advent of television, Nolan argued that 'nowadays the newspapers serve a public which knows the main news, at least in outline, from radio and television, and their function is tending to become the interpreting and explaining of it'. If the opportunity to educate journalists in giving context to the news was lost, then there was, Nolan concluded, 'some danger that some of the papers may be tempted, as has happened in other countries, to become artificial and superficial without aims higher than building or maintaining circulation'. Lemass forwarded the letter to the Minister for Education, Paddy Hillery. In a covering note, Lemass observed that the proposal was 'a good idea that could develop in a way which would put the profession of journalism on a sounder basis'. He also recorded his assumption that if such a scheme was desired then 'the Vocational Education Authorities in Dublin and some other cities would be prepared to institute a course in journalism leading to a diploma'. He thus suggested that the department send a representative to any discussions between the NUJ and newspaper managements 'for the purpose of conveying a general interest in the idea'.[104]

In July 1963, Nolan again wrote to Lemass – this time to invite him to speak at the inauguration of the new course at the College of Commerce, Rathmines. However, when Lemass sought advice from the Department of Education as to whether it was 'appropriate or desirable' for him to attend the formal opening, he was informed that the Department 'considered that the course ... is not of such importance as to warrant the attendance of the Taoiseach'.[105] It ultimately fell to the Minister for Social Welfare, Kevin Boland, to represent the government at the event. In his address to the first class of thirty junior reporters, sub-editors, and photographers, Boland declared that he found it discourteous that when Irish was spoken in the Dáil 'practically every notebook in the Press Gallery should automatically close'.[106] Along with Irish, students studied newspaper law, economics, government, English, and practical journalism courses such as reporting, copyreading, feature writing, and interviewing skills. The two-year course, which ran for one half-day per week, was open only to those already employed by a newspaper. In 1968, the course was replaced by a one-year full-time certificate, which was, in time, converted into a two-year full-time certificate. And, despite the NUJ having had to secure Archbishop McQuaid's approval for the course, by 1975, its director, Sean Egan, spoke of the need for aspiring journalists to have a good command of sociology, politics, psychology, literature, and economics. Journalists, he declared, were not 'inspired by the holy ghost'.[107] A newer generation of journalists – in the words of Maurice Walsh – 'did not perceive themselves as trade stenographers drilled in convention during apprenticeships on provincial newspapers but as professionals with ideas and knowledge about politics, economics, and history'.[108]

Along with playing a role in establishing journalism education in Ireland, Pat Nolan played a central role in strengthening the position of the NUJ. For many years, the Irish branches had been campaigning for the appointment of a full-time Irish official in the belief that members' issues could not be serviced properly from Head Office in London. In 1964, the union's annual delegate conference agreed to the creation of the post. However, having accepted the nomination for the position, Nolan then caused consternation by insisting that he would only take the post if the Irish membership paid a levy towards his salary so that he would not be beholden to anyone in London. The union's NEC would not agree to this, and so the position remained unfilled until 1965 when Jim Eadie, Father of the Chapel at Independent Newspapers, accepted the post after receiving Nolan's blessing.[109] Eadie took office just as all national newspapers disappeared from the streets between July and September due to a printers' strike and all journalists were put on protective notice. It was a baptism of fire for Eadie who also had to deal with the fallout from the *7 Days* programme on illegal moneylending in Dublin that provoked outrage from the Minister for Justice, Micheál Ó Móráin and eventually led to RTÉ having to defend the programme before a tribunal of inquiry. The programme, edited by Muiris Mac Conghail, was aired in November 1969, but, as it did not tag acted scenes of money changing hands as reconstructions, it looked as if the programme was presenting them as actuality. The programme very quickly provoked a war of words between the government and RTÉ. In the Dáil, Ó Móráin described the programme's claims of widespread illegal moneylending as 'grossly exaggerated' and the evidence of those interviewed as 'nothing but a tissue of lies'. He also claimed that alcohol was supplied to the participants, that the programme had been 'deliberately contrived for television', and that it was 'a phoney programme'.[110]

In its reply, RTÉ declared that 'nothing in it was contrived to present a dishonest picture' and that it rejected Ó Móráin's assertion that 'programme-makers were misled by the participants into distorting its presentation'.[111] When the RTÉ Authority met with the Minister for Posts and Telegraphs, Patrick Lalor, it reiterated that the programme's content was 'authentic' and that it 'did not present a distorted or exaggerated picture of the social problems of illegal money lending in Dublin'.[112] With no sign of RTÉ backing down, the government established a three-judge tribunal of inquiry to investigate not the extent of illegal moneylending but the programme's production process, its authenticity, whether its content amounted to a fair representation of the facts, and whether 'reasonable journalistic care' had been taken in its making.[113] The response of the print media was instantaneous. *Hibernia* described the tribunal as an attempt 'to discredit public affairs television programmes … and erode the freedom of journalistic enquiry within RTÉ', while the *Irish Times* observed that it would be 'impossible from now on for any producer to involve himself in any subject that has controversial aspects without fearing that ultimately he may be called upon to defend himself before an official tribunal'.[114] Even the Fianna Fáil-supporting *Irish Press* described the tribunal as 'the grossest, most outrageous and most indefensible interference with the freedom of the press, of the journalist's right to comment on matters of the highest public importance'.[115]

The tribunal was a searing experience for the team – Muiris Mac Conghail, Joe McCormack, Bill O'Herlihy, and Janet Moody – that had produced the programme. O'Herlihy, who endured having to give five and a half days of evidence, described the tribunal as 'a gruelling experience with a merciless attack from the state'.[116] The tribunal's report came down decidedly against RTÉ. It found that the programme team 'through hear-say evidence got a very colourful impression of the scale of illegal money-lending and of the supposed violent means associated with it'. It also found that the 'selection and editing of material for screening and the use of illustrative shots supported these subjective views rather than presented an objective picture'. Ultimately, it found the programme 'not to be authentic either in relation to the scale of the money-lending or in relation to the associated violence', but also that 'the team did not in any way try to induce exaggeration'. Of no comfort was the finding that 'the result of the programme has been beneficial' since the Garda Síochána was now fully aware of the many problems associated with illegal moneylending.[117]

Despite the 'urgent public importance' that prompted the establishment of the tribunal, some of the most interesting documents in the National Archives' files on this topic are the myriad letters to and from the Departments of Finance, Justice, the Taoiseach, and Posts and Telegraphs, each denying responsibility for establishing the tribunal and therefore seeking to be absolved of the estimated £200,000 costs associated with it.[118] The tribunal was a traumatic experience for RTÉ: looking back at this period many years later, Muiris Mac Conghail acknowledged that after the tribunal 'an edge had been dulled in the area of investigative reporting and the RTÉ Authority and management became overcautious and apprehensive about government attitudes in general and what they might herald'.[119] The outbreak of the Northern Troubles was to plunge relations even lower.

Notes

1 M. O'Toole, 'The Roman Catholic Church and the media in Ireland', in T. Fahy and M. Kelly (eds), *Media Association of Ireland Essays* (Dublin, 1988), pp. 11–14, at p. 11.
2 D. Thornley, 'Ireland: the end of an era', *Studies*, 53:209 (1964), 1–17, at p. 16.
3 In Jun. 1940, Taoiseach Éamon de Valera, who was also Acting Minister for Education, circulated a memo that noted that 'for nine-tenths of the Irish people the primary school is the sole source of secular education'. See DED, vol. 80 (cols. 1565–652), 6 Jun. 1940.
4 *Sunday Independent*, 11 Sep. 1966, p. 1; *Irish Times*, 12 Sep. 1966, p. 12. See also J. Horgan, *Seán Lemass: The Enigmatic Patriot* (Dublin, 1997), pp. 298–301. It is interesting that O'Malley announced his initiative to the media before consulting with the hierarchy – the very opposite approach to that taken by Noël Browne for his Mother and Child scheme.
5 See A. Redmond (ed.), *That Was Then, This is Now: Change in Ireland, 1949–99* (Dublin, 2000), pp. 45–51.
6 *Irish Times*, 26 Jan. 1960, p. 1.
7 *Irish Independent*, 30 Jul. 1960, p. 13.
8 *Irish Independent*, 10 Nov. 1960, p. 13.
9 The troops surrendered just as a peace accord between the United Nations and Katanga was agreed. See *Irish Independent*, 21 Sep. 1961, p. 1.
10 Telefís Éireann changed its name to Radio Telefís Éireann (RTÉ) in 1966. In 2009, Radio Telefís Éireann became Raidio Telefís Éireann.
11 *Irish Press*, 1 Jan. 1962, pp. 1 and 5.
12 *Irish Press*, 1 Jan. 1962, pp. 1 and 5.
13 NAI, TSCH/3/S16748A, general scheme of Broadcasting Bill, section 7 2 B, 3 Dec. 1959.
14 NAI, TSCH/3/S16748A, letter from government secretary to Hilliard, 4 Dec. 1959.
15 NAI, TSCH/3/S16748A, Hilliard's reply, n/d.
16 Seanad Éireann Debates (SED), vol. 52 (col. 19), 20 Jan. 1960.
17 DED, vol. 179 (col. 760), 24 Feb. 1960.
18 NAI, TSCH/S14996, memo dated 30 Mar. 1960.
19 NAI, TSCH/S14996, reply dated 4 Apr. 1960.
20 DED, vol. 180 (col. 575), 16 Mar. 1960.

21 DDA, AB8/B/XXVI/a/3/54, undated report on Telefís Éireann.
22 *Irish Times*, 26 Oct. 1966, p. 8.
23 *Sunday Independent*, 9 Oct. 1966, p. 12.
24 *Irish Times*, 3 Oct. 1966, p. 1.
25 *Irish Times*, 4 Oct. 1966, p. 9.
26 *Irish Times*, 4 Oct. 1966, p. 9. Kelly resigned in Nov. 1966.
27 DED, vol. 224 (col. 1046), 12 Oct. 1966.
28 *Irish Times*, 26 Oct. 1966, p. 8.
29 J. Horgan, *Broadcasting and Public Life: RTÉ News and Current Affairs, 1926–97* (Dublin, 2004), pp. 48–50.
30 *Irish Times*, 19 Oct. 1967, p. 10.
31 *Irish Times*, 15 Jan. 1968, p. 12.
32 M. Walsh, 'Media and culture in Ireland, 1960–2008', in R. Bourke and I. McBride (eds), *The Princeton History of Modern Ireland* (Princeton, NJ, 2016), pp. 253–70, at p. 254.
33 Interview with Michael Mills.
34 SED, vol. 60 (col. 1492), 17 Feb. 1966.
35 O'Toole, 'The Roman Catholic Church and the Media', p. 11.
36 *Irish Times*, 11 May 1970, p. 14.
37 T. P. Coogan, *Ireland Since the Rising* (London, 1966), p. 174.
38 Interview with Michael O'Toole.
39 Interview with Michael Mills.
40 Interview with Michael Mills.
41 Interview with Tim Pat Coogan.
42 *Irish Independent*, 6 Apr. 1965, p. 12.
43 J. Horgan, 'The changing of the guard at Middle Abbey Street, 1961–73', in M. O'Brien and K. Rafter (eds), *Independent Newspapers: A History* (Dublin, 2012), pp. 133–45, at pp. 136 and 141.
44 Vincent Doyle, cited in I. Kenny, 'Vinnie Doyle, *Irish Independent*', in *Talking to Ourselves: Conversations with Editors of the Irish News Media* (Galway, 1994), pp. 11–28, at p. 18.
45 D. Thornley, 'Television and politics', *Administration*, 15:3 (1967), 217–25, at p. 223.
46 DDA, AB8/B/XXVI/e/78, 'The journalist and the church', undated but most likely late 1963 or early 1964.
47 DDA, AB8/B/XXVI/e/78, report dated 5 Jun. 1964.
48 R. Savage, *A Loss of Innocence: Television and Irish Society, 1960–72* (Manchester, 2010), p. 28.
49 DDA, AB8/B/XXVI/a/3/9, memo dated 2 May 1961.
50 DDA, AB8/B/XXVI/a/3/9, letter dated 11 Oct. 1961.
51 DDA, AB8/B/XXVI/a/3/9, letter dated 17 Oct. 1961.
52 Cited in J. Bowman, *Window and Mirror: RTÉ Television, 1961–2011* (Dublin, 2011), p. 67.
53 DDA, AB8/B/XXVI/a/3/9, letter dated 16 Sep. 1962.
54 DDA, AB8/B/XXVI/a/3/9, letter dated 7 Nov. 1963.
55 DDA, AB8/B/XXVI/a/3/71 and 72, letter dated 12 Dec. 1963. McQuaid's original dictation referred to Baum as 'the stranger priest'.
56 DDA, AB8/B/XXVI/a/3/70, letter dated 17 Dec. 1963.
57 DDA, AB8/B/XXVI/c, Mon. Cecil Barrett to McQuaid, letter dated 1 Jun. 1965, cited in Horgan, *Broadcasting and Public Life*, pp. 32–3.

58 DDA, AB8/B/XXVI/a/3/98, letter dated 12 Feb. 1966.
59 DDA, AB8/B/XXVI/a/3/98, letter dated 15 Feb. 1966.
60 DDA, AB8/B/XXVI/a/3/110, letter dated 5 Apr. 1966.
61 DDA, AB8/B/XXVI/a/3/148, letter dated 13 May 1968.
62 L. McRedmond, 'Dialogue in the church: the journalist', *The Furrow*, 15:1 (1964), 3–13, at p. 6.
63 L. McRedmond, *The Council Reconsidered* (Dublin, 1966), pp. 162–3.
64 DDA, AB8/B/XXVI/e/78, note dated 24 Jan. 1964.
65 DDA, AB8/B/XXVI/a/6, letter to Fr Joe Dunn, 4 Nov. 1965.
66 DDA, AB8/B/XXVI/e/78, report dated 5 Jun. 1964.
67 *Irish Independent*, 13 Sep. 1965, p. 15; *Irish Times*, 13 Sep. 1965, p. 6.
68 DDA, AB8/B/XXVI/c/27, letter from McQuaid to Ossie Dowling, 15 Sep. 1965.
69 DDA, AB8/B/XXVI/c/27, letter from Dowling to Fr MacMahon, 20 Sep. 1965; letter from Dowling to McQuaid, 20 Sep. 1965.
70 McRedmond, *The Council Reconsidered*, pp. 7 and 180.
71 J. Horgan, 'Remembering how we once were', *Doctrine and Life*, 53:4 (2003), 241–6, at p. 241.
72 *Irish Times*, 10 Dec. 1965, p. 11.
73 For an account of *Radharc*, see J. Dunne, *No Tigers in Africa* (Dublin, 1986).
74 Savage, *A Loss of Innocence*, p. 242.
75 M. O'Toole, *More Kicks than Pence: A Life in Irish Journalism* (Dublin, 1992), p. 176.
76 J. Healy, *Healy, Reporter: The Early Years* (Achill, 1991), pp. 36–7.
77 A. Bestic, *The Importance of Being Irish* (London, 1969), p. 153.
78 *Irish Times*, 20 Dec. 1991, p. 10.
79 Bestic, *The Importance of Being Irish*, pp. 153–4.
80 Bestic, *The Importance of Being Irish*, pp. 153–4.
81 *Irish Independent*, 31 Jul. 1961, p. 13.
82 *Irish Times*, 31 Jul. 1961, p. 2; *Irish Press*, 31 Jul. 1961, p. 14.
83 *Irish Independent*, 30 Sep. 1961, p. 18; *Irish Times*, 9 Oct. 1961, p. 9; *Irish Independent*, 4 Oct. 1961, p. 14.
84 HCRC, NUJ, Dublin branch minutes, 1 Apr. 1962.
85 *Irish Independent*, 23 Apr. 1962, p. 17.
86 *Irish Times*, 20 Dec. 1991, p. 10.
87 Bestic, *The Importance of Being Irish*, p. 154.
88 *Irish Independent*, 13 May 1968, p. 11.
89 *Irish Press*, 13 May 1968, p. 16.
90 *Irish Times*, 13 May 1968, p. 3.
91 *Irish Times*, 19 Aug. 1968, p. 11 and 22 Aug. 1968, p. 3.
92 *Irish Independent*, 26 Aug. 1968, p. 5.
93 *Irish Independent*, 8 Oct. 1968, p. 11.
94 *Irish Independent*, 23 Dec. 1968, p. 1.
95 *Irish Times*, 13 Jan. 1969, p. 11.
96 A. M. Fox, 'The training of journalists in Ireland', *Journalism and Mass Communication Quarterly*, 44:2 (1967), 316–18, at p. 316.
97 DDA, AB8/B/XXVI/d/76, memo dated 23 Aug. 1955. The lecture series included 'Philosophy and the press' (11 Oct. 1945); 'Journalists at work' (18 Oct. 1945); 'Careers in journalism' (8 Nov. 1945); 'Ethics of journalism and advertising' (15 Nov. 1945), and 'Review of journalism in Ireland' (22 Nov. 1945).

98 DDA, AB8/B/XXVI/d/76, memo dated 26 Sep. 1962.
99 HCRC, NUJ, Irish council minutes, 6 Dec. 1953 and Dublin branch minutes, 6 Jun. 1959.
100 HCRC, NUJ, Irish council minutes, 9 Jan. 1962.
101 DDA, AB8/B/XXVI/d/76, undated letter from Nolan to McQuaid.
102 DDA, AB8/B/XXVI/d/76, undated memo.
103 DDA, AB8/B/XXVI/d/76, memo dated 16 Jan. 1963.
104 NAI, Tsch/3/S16190 B/95, Nolan letter dated 8 Apr. 1963; Lemass letter dated 10 Apr. 1963.
105 NAI, Tsch/3/S16190 B/95, letter dated 8 Aug. 1963.
106 See *Irish Independent*, 10 Sep. 1963, p. 9.
107 See www.rte.ie/archives/2013/0702/460070-whats-required-of-a-journalist; for more on Egan, a former editor of the *Roscommon Champion* and RTÉ reporter, see *Irish Times*, 7 Nov. 2009, p. 12.
108 Walsh, 'Media and culture in Ireland', p. 260.
109 Interview with Jim Eadie.
110 DED, vol. 242 (cols. 1263–9), 19 Nov. 1969.
111 *Irish Independent*, 20 Nov. 1969, p. 1.
112 *Irish Independent*, 29 Nov. 1969, p. 1.
113 NAI, 2000/6/518 (Nov.–Dec. 1969). The three judges were Justices Sean Butler, Denis Pringle, and Charles Flynn.
114 *Hibernia*, 19 Dec. 1969–8 Jan. 1970, p. 2; *Irish Times*, 16 Dec. 1969, p. 11.
115 *Irish Press*, 17 Dec. 1969, p. 10.
116 Bill O'Herlihy, *We'll Leave It There So* (Dublin, 2012), p. 93.
117 NAI, 2001/6/440 (Jan.–Nov. 1970).
118 NAI, 2001/6/440 (Jan.–Nov. 1970).
119 Mac Conghail, cited in Horgan, *Broadcasting and Public Life*, p. 139.

8

The Troubles and censorship

Unlike our colleagues in Belfast, we, in the north-west, thankfully did not have to report the obscenity of Catholics and Protestants shooting it out on city streets, but still we got our share of the riots and all that followed in their wake.[1]

— Martin Crowley, Derry NUJ branch, 1971

While one might not expect Northern Ireland to have featured on the southern media agenda prior to the outbreak of the Troubles in the late 1960s, for much of the previous decades the North had featured occasionally in the print media. During the 1930s and 1940s, the *Irish Press* retained the services of Patrick Scott as its Belfast correspondent: Scott reported on the Blitz for the *Press* and subsequently joined the Irish News Agency.[2] For many years, the *Irish Independent* retained the services of Belfast journalist James Kelly, who kept both it and the *Sunday Independent* supplied with news of happenings north of the border. In his memoir, Kelly recounted how he reported on the devastation that followed the German bombing of Belfast in April 1941. Despite the southern state's neutrality, his mention of southern fire units helping to fight the fires that spread through the city was not censored.[3] However, the following year, his interview of the first American soldier to disembark in Northern Ireland was stopped by the Dublin censor.[4] For the most part, the two jurisdictions maintained a wary coexistence interrupted only by Éamon de Valera's stint as MP for South Down between 1933 and 1938, his anti-Partition campaign of 1948–51, the IRA's Border Campaign of 1956–62, and the 1965 reciprocal visits north and south by Taoiseach Seán Lemass and Northern Ireland Premier Terence O'Neill. At the *Irish Press* there was a residual wariness about anything relating to the North. The group's editor-in-chief (and Éamon de Valera's son), Vivion de Valera, had decreed that 'no column of Brendan Behan's was to be published before it was vetted by him personally'. To the de Valeras, Behan's republicanism made him 'strongly suspect'.[5] As the Border Campaign kicked off, Vivion's wariness increased:

> He often used to walk through the newsroom around lunchtime and ask 'what's doing today, what's the news?' One day he came in and the main story was on one of the early border incidents and he just said to John O'Donovan [chief sub-editor] who had the page-proof, 'is that the best lead you have?' John said 'yes,

> that's what the editor and I think is the best lead'. I said 'yeah, that's the story'. He said, 'are you sure?' and I said 'do you want us to change it?' He didn't say anything, he just walked off.[6]

Given that the Border Campaign had been devised by an Irish Press Group employee, Vivion had reason to have been wary. The activities of former Irish Army officer and *Evening Press* sub-editor Seán Cronin (later an IRA chief of staff) surprised many at the newspaper group. The paper had just gone to print one day when Cronin approached Douglas Gageby for 'a quiet word'. Cronin told him that 'he had a personal problem; he wanted to go and to go now', so Gageby gave his blessing.[7] As former *Irish Press* journalist John Kelly remembered it, while 'everyone in the newsroom knew that Cronin was strongly republican, no one realised that he was as involved as he seems to have been'.[8] A subsequent garda raid on the newspaper failed to capture Cronin, who was later arrested near the border and charged with membership of the IRA.[9] As recalled by Kelly, at the Press Group 'there was an awful lot of surprise, shock and consternation when people realised what was going on'.[10]

The rapprochement marked by the visit of Taoiseach Seán Lemass to Belfast and his northern counterpart, Terence O'Neill, to Dublin in 1965 represented something of a new beginning. Similarly, the appointment of Douglas Gageby to the editorship of the *Irish Times* in 1963 marked a change in emphasis. He appointed Fergus Pyle as the paper's Northern Ireland editor – a move that puzzled so many people that Gageby found himself justifying it in almost every interview he did. In one such interview, he declared that southern newspapers 'had been largely sleeping for decades' and described the paper's coverage of the Stormont Assembly as 'a slice of Irish life'.[11] It was, however, a slice of Irish life that did not appeal to all journalists. In his memoir, Frank Kilfeather recalled having 'to spend tortuous hours listening to the most dreadful debates in the North's so called "parliament" and then send reams of copy to Dublin. It was only a glorified county council.'[12]

Whatever about cross-border journalism, in terms of media consumption the border was a real barrier: there existed no all-island newspaper, and only a fraction of newspapers printed crossed the border in either direction. The best performer in this respect was the *Irish Times*, which sold about 4,000 a day in the North. The most prominent newspapers in the North were the nationalist *Irish News*, the unionist *News-letter*, and the liberal-unionist *Belfast Telegraph*, the readerships of which were sharply demarcated along religious lines. In 1970, 93 per cent of the *Irish News*'s readership was Catholic, 87 per cent of the *News-letter*'s readership was Protestant, while the readership of the *Belfast Telegraph* was divided 68 per cent Protestant and 32 per cent Catholic. Only 5 per cent of the northern population read a Dublin newspaper, while 32 per cent read a British title.[13] Nonetheless, the appointment by the *Irish Times* of a northern editor was an ingenious move: as the Unionist government clashed with the civil-rights movement and the North descended into violence, the *Irish Times* had a head start over its Dublin competitors in having its own full-time correspondent on the ground.[14]

Also on the ground was Douglas Gageby himself: he travelled to Derry on at least one occasion to participate in a civil-rights march and was not shy in calling things as he saw them. In one leading article he described the gerrymandering of Derry as 'a travesty of democracy'.[15] Things finally came to a head in October 1968 when Northern Ireland's Minister of Home Affairs, William Craig, banned a civil-rights march in Derry, which went ahead regardless. The outcome was described by Fergus Pyle of the *Irish Times*: 'For a quarter of an hour on Saturday afternoon, police in a Derry street punched, batoned and pursued Civil Rights demonstrators in a brutal and sickening display of what can only be called concerted violence.'[16] The chaotic scenes were captured by RTÉ cameraman Gay O'Brien and soundman Eamon Hayes and beamed around the world. The widespread public revulsion that followed prompted claims from northern politicians that the disturbances had been 'magnified and distorted by press and television coverage'.[17]

Such criticism did not go unanswered: the NUJ Belfast branch declared that, since its members had been 'in the thick of the Duke Street disturbances', they had been better positioned to witness what had happened than the 'various politicians who were not there and who have since condemned press and TV coverage'. The branch resented the 'efforts by politicians to divert attention from their own inadequacies and shortcomings, and disregard for truth, by wrongly blaming newsmen'.[18] In the early years of the Troubles, this was to be a constant refrain. In 1971, the Derry and North-West NUJ branch noted that 'some people had tried to make a "whipping boy" out of the press by ascribing the reasons for street violence to exaggerated reports of incidents or to an excess of publicity being given to the people involved in the disturbances'.[19]

As conditions in the North deteriorated, the NUJ expressed concern at the dangers faced by its members. When the *Belfast Telegraph* chapel lodged a claim for 'danger money' for covering riots, management responded by issuing armoured 'deerstalker' hats. This provoked outrage from the chapel officers, who pointed out that reporters were likely to be attacked by both sides for wearing such conspicuous hats. Holiday vouchers were the ultimate compromise.[20] In January 1969, the Dublin branch chairman, Maurice Hickey, noted that journalists had suffered 'verbal and physical threats and actual assault as "innocent bystanders" during the civil rights agitation in the North'. They had also been 'abused and obstructed' by those who were 'supposed to be upholders of law and order'.[21] Despite the potent political undercurrents, the union seemed united in reporting events rather than expressing opinion on how the situation should be resolved. But, as the political temperature soared during the marching season of 1969 and the situation in Derry reached crisis point, journalists' emotions ran high. In August 1969, the Dublin branch passed a motion of support for the Irish government's request to the United Nations that an international peacekeeping force be deployed to Northern Ireland. It also called for the suspension of the Northern Ireland constitution, government, and parliament; the introduction of temporary direct rule from Westminster; the disbanding of the B Specials; and an investigation into civilian deaths. The motion was sent to the union's NEC in London with a request that it be brought to the attention of the British government.[22]

Having become aware of the motion, the union's Belfast branch issued a statement that disassociated itself from the Dublin resolution. It stressed that the NUJ was not a political organisation and that its only interest was the protection of the rights of its members. It also stated that the Belfast branch had 'a hard-and-fast rule that politics are not discussed at branch meetings' and expressed regret that its Dublin colleagues had 'allowed themselves to become involved in the politics of the current situation'.[23] The statement obviously focused minds: the following day, the *Irish Press* chapel passed a motion disassociating itself from the Dublin branch's resolution, and an *Irish Times* article quoted an unnamed chapel officer as having said that the original resolution 'was not in the best interests of journalism'.[24] This was an early indication of the long-term tension that covering the Troubles would cause within the union.

Section 31

South of the border, the eruption of the Troubles caught the government off-guard, and the Department of Foreign Affairs resorted to collecting and circulating newspaper articles on Northern Ireland written by Michael McInerney of the *Irish Times*. Having interviewed McInerney, one civil servant noted that he 'exaggerates the desire of the British Government to bring Dublin into discussions of a new solution at present or at the near future'.[25] However, McInerney seems to have been an intermediary of sorts. Writing in 1972, then British Ambassador Sir John Peck reported to London that McInerney had telephoned him to report that in a private conversation with Jack Lynch 'the latter had said that his speech at the Fianna Fáil party conference on Saturday had been principally addressed to the British government. Without using the words quote "olive branch" unquote, Mr Lynch had spoken of quote "extending a hand" unquote to the prime minister.' Peck also noted that 'Irish ministers are aware of McInerney's close relations with my information officer and that Mr Lynch would have known in advance that whatever he had to say about his speech to McInerney would be reported via Evans to me and thence to you.'[26]

The tensions within the cabinet about how to react to the escalating situation were reflected in the various resignations and sackings that shook the Fianna Fáil government. While the sudden resignation of the Minister for Justice, Micheál Ó Móráin, in May 1970 raised eyebrows, a telephone call from the Government Information Bureau asking the national newspapers to hold off printing the next day's edition until an important government statement could be released added to the suspense. The statement – that Ministers Neil Blaney and Charles Haughey had been sacked by Taoiseach Jack Lynch because they did not fully subscribe to government policy on Northern Ireland and that another minister, Kevin Boland, had resigned in protest – finally reached the newspapers at 2.50 a.m. As remembered by *Irish Independent* journalist Chris Glennon,

> in keeping with the style of the time, there was no explanation of why Mr Lynch had taken such a drastic step. It was well into the day before newspapers were

able to link the upheaval to an alleged attempt to import arms into the state for possible transfer to Northern Ireland.[27]

However, Glennon's colleagues at the *Sunday Independent* had been well aware of what had been going on. A week previously, that paper's political correspondent, Ned Murphy, had been given all the relevant information by Fine Gael leader Liam Cosgrave, who, in turn, had received the information via an anonymous note on official garda notepaper. The note, which mentioned Blaney and Haughey as being involved in 'a plot to bring arms from Germany worth £80,000 for the North', urged Cosgrave to ensure that the affair was 'not hushed up'. Having been given sight of the note, Murphy wrote what the *Sunday Independent* later referred to as 'what would have been one of the most sensational stories in the history of Irish journalism'.[28] However, having mulled over the story for two days, Murphy's editor, Hector Legge, decided not to use the story, thus depriving the paper of a sensational scoop. The following week, once the affair had become public, the *Sunday Independent* published the story of its knowledge of the affair under the headline, 'The Scoop We Didn't Publish'. Acknowledging that Murphy's account 'was a factual account of events afterwards borne out by statements in the Dáil' and that the story might have brought down the government, it explained that Legge had agonised over where his duty lay: 'to his country or to his profession'. According to the article, Legge had decided that 'the proper place to have the matter raised was in the Dáil'.[29] However, in subsequent years, Legge maintained that his decision not to publish was prompted by his desire to avoid defamation cases being taken against the newspaper.[30] Whatever the reason, the decision not to publish has been described by John Horgan as 'passing up what would undoubtedly have been one of the biggest scoops in twentieth century Irish journalism'.[31]

After the high-level sackings, the government sought to ease tensions by holding an 'absolutely off the record' meeting with the editors of the national newspapers at which the editors were told that under Section 10 of the Offences Against the State Act 1939, newspapers were prohibited from publishing statements from illegal organisations such as the IRA. Taken aback, the editors told then Minister for Justice Des O'Malley that their newspapers were only reporting, not glamorising, what was happening.[32] Such was the sensitivity surrounding the Arms Crisis that, even ten years later, when *Magill* published the diaries of Peter Berry, the Department of Justice's secretary general at the time of the crisis, RTÉ management 'instructed all areas of radio and TV that there should be no coverage of the "Magill" arms trial story'.[33]

The issue of whether or not the media were 'glamorising' the conflict took a dramatic turn in October 1971 when then Minister for Posts and Telegraphs Gerry Collins issued a directive under Section 31 of the Broadcasting Authority Act. The section, which gave a significant amount of power to the government of the day, stated: 'The Minister may direct the Authority in writing to refrain from broadcasting any particular matter or matter of any particular class, and the Authority shall comply with the direction.' In the words of Michael Hilliard, the minister who had guided the Act through parliament ten years previously, the section gave the minister 'a veto power on broadcasts which may be detrimental to the general public interest [such as] the broadcast of a particular programme or kind of programme that could be very embarrassing in our relations with another country or countries'.[34] Collins's directive required RTÉ to refrain from broadcasting 'any matter that could be calculated to promote the aims and activities of any organisation which engages in, promotes, encourages or advocates the attaining of any particular objective by violent means' and was issued after RTÉ aired pre-recorded interviews with senior IRA figures in a *7 Days* programme on Northern Ireland. This directive, along with its successors, was to cause numerous rifts between journalists and the government and among journalists themselves for the subsequent two decades.

RTÉ's initial reaction was measured: it observed that the directive did not affect reportage and analysis of violent events, the broadcasting of statements from organisations accepting or denying responsibility for violent or unlawful acts, or current-affairs programmes provided care was taken to avoid promoting the aims and activities of such organisations.[35] In November 1971, the NUJ's Broadcasting branch sought a meeting with Taoiseach Jack Lynch to discuss the directive, but Lynch refused to meet any such deputation.[36] Some days later, the branch declared that the directive had been invoked by RTÉ management to restrict presentation of 'a legitimate news item'. The item was a news conference by seven men who had escaped from Belfast's Crumlin Road Gaol. Two of the men were interviewed by an RTÉ reporter, but management had instructed that these could not be aired because of the directive.[37] At the NUJ's annual delegate meeting of April 1972, the issue of censorship was high on the agenda. The London Magazine and Book branch called on the union's NEC to 'give full support to any member who was penalised for opposing censorship' and urged the Irish government 'to withdraw restrictions imposed on Irish radio and television'. An Irish delegate, Cian O hEigeartaigh of RTÉ, stated that pressure 'must be brought to bear to ensure that the Irish Government freed journalists of the shackles placed on them'.[38] As the first anniversary of the directive approached, RTÉ journalists based in Belfast held a two-hour work stoppage though the NUJ's Broadcasting branch did not engage in any action.

The directive's ambiguity finally came to a head on 19 November 1972 when RTÉ Radio aired a report based on an interview by its news features editor Kevin O'Kelly with the IRA's chief of staff, Seán Mac Stiofáin. Two days later, the Minister for Post and Telegraphs, Gerry Collins, asked the RTÉ Authority what action it intended to take in relation to this alleged contravention of his directive. After a marathon ten-hour meeting, the authority noted that the specific technique used – interviewing persons before a broadcast and then reporting but not airing their direct replies – had been utilised previously without objection. However, in an attempt to mollify the minister, it stated that such material would in future need prior approval from the station's director general. This nuanced response did not satisfy Collins: on 24 November, the authority was sacked and replaced with nominees of the government's choice.

The following day, O'Kelly was sentenced to three months' imprisonment for contempt of court after he refused to identify the person (Mac Stiofáin) whose voice could be heard on his tape. Mac Stiofáin had been arrested outside O'Kelly's house on the day following the broadcast and charged with membership of an illegal organisation. Within two hours of O'Kelly's imprisonment, the NUJ's Broadcasting branch held an emergency meeting and informed station management of its intention to strike. The two-day all-out strike began at 6.30 p.m. on the day of O'Kelly's imprisonment. In a statement, the branch expressed its support for O'Kelly, who had 'gone to jail in defence of a principle which is basic to the free practice of journalism'. It noted that the work of journalists would 'be impossible if journalists were to co-operate with prosecutions based on information given to them in the course of their work' and also declared that, while journalists had no 'sympathy with people accused of illegal acts [they had to] protect the independence and integrity of our profession'.[39] The union's South-Eastern branch suggested that all the union's branches withdraw cooperation with government members until 'full freedom of the press, radio and television services' was guaranteed, and the NUJ's general secretary, Ken Morgan, expressed surprise at the severity of O'Kelly's sentence given that Mac Stiofáin had been sentenced to six months' imprisonment for membership of an illegal organisation.[40] O'Kelly's sentence was obviously meant to send a clear message to journalists: the previous year, BBC reporter Bernard Falk had been sentenced to four days' imprisonment after he had refused to name, in a Belfast court, a man he had interviewed for a television programme about the IRA.[41]

A general meeting of all Dublin journalists at Liberty Hall agreed on a one-day strike, and publication of all evening editions of 28 November and all daily editions of 29 November ceased. Significantly, journalists on the *Cork Examiner*, which was not an NUJ stronghold, also voted to strike. This was the first time in that paper's 131-year history that journalists withdrew their labour. There followed a march of 300 journalists from Liberty Hall to Leinster House. In a statement, the union declared that it had marched to Leinster House to tell politicians that it feared further imprisonment of journalists, if they, like O'Kelly, 'refuse to abrogate their words as journalists and to become part of public prosecutions'.[42] Having spent a night or two in prison, O'Kelly was released on bail to appeal his sentence – not on the right of journalists to protect their sources but on the severity of the sentence imposed.[43] After a full hearing at the Court of Criminal Appeal in June 1973, O'Kelly's sentence was reduced to a fine of £250, which was paid anonymously.[44] Despite the protests, the government continued its offensive. As remembered by then *Irish Press* editor, Tim Pat Coogan, Taoiseach Jack Lynch 'made a determined effort to deny the IRA the oxygen of publicity':

> He began by calling in the editors of the national daily newspapers (myself included) and senior RTÉ executives to the Taoiseach's Department where he gently suggested that we curtail IRA coverage by approaches such as: 'Just call it an IRA raid, not a daring IRA raid' … He threw a frightener into the journalists [and] brought RTÉ into line.[45]

The following month, two explosions in Dublin city centre increased the political temperature, and the NUJ backed off from its campaign. In a letter to the union's general secretary in January 1973, Irish organiser Jim Eadie noted that, given all that had happened, the last thing that was needed was 'a campaign by the NUJ on this issue, even if we are satisfied that legitimate journalism is being restricted'. The union could not, he concluded, 'afford the luxury of looking at this problem of censorship in isolation from the general political and indeed military situation in this country'.[46]

Reporting the Troubles

The ever-worsening Troubles resulted in a flurry of activity in Dublin newsrooms as journalists were sent north to cover the conflict. As Kevin Rafter has observed, there was a sense that the North was a big story, and, 'despite the dangerous environment, the importance of the news story coupled with an associated excitement acted as a magnet for many ambitious young journalists'.[47] In his memoir, Kevin Myers describes being 'desperate to get up to the North before the Troubles ended'.[48] While the *Irish Times* had Fergus Pyle in Belfast as its northern editor, as the conflict worsened, Henry Kelly, Renagh Holohan, Conor Brady, and Dermot Mullane were sent north to bolster the paper's coverage. The *Irish Independent* depended on the services of James Kelly and Denis McGrath. While the *Irish Press* had a staff reporter – Paddy Reynolds – in Belfast, in 1970 it appointed Vincent Browne as its northern editor. A few months into the job, Browne was given a sub-machine gun that his IRA source claimed was one of many made in a Belfast engineering works for distribution to loyalists. His front-page *Sunday Press* story caused a stir, but when he was later found in possession of the gun Browne was arrested and fined for possession of the firearm.[49] In 1972, Browne was succeeded by Michael Keane, who was helped by Belfast staffer Ciaran McKeown, later prominent in the 'Peace People' movement. RTÉ was represented by Liam Hourican, Frank Dunlop, and, later, Kevin Myers, who wrote a highly readable but chilling account of his time in the North. Reporting the conflict was a hazardous affair. When internment was introduced in 1971 and the disused airfield outside Belfast, Long Kesh, was hurriedly pressed into use as a detention camp, journalists were banned from visiting the facility. However, *Irish Press* Editor Tim Pat Coogan visited the camp using the assumed name of a prisoner's relative, as did Mary Cummins of the *Irish Times*.[50]

All those who have spoken or written about their time reporting from the North have recounted numerous near escapes from death or serious injury. Others were not so lucky: *Sunday World* Northern Editor Jim Campbell was shot and seriously injured by loyalists in 1984, and Martin O'Hagan, also of the *Sunday World*, was killed by loyalists in September 2001. Following O'Hagan's killing, the NUJ magazine *Journalist* ran a feature entitled 'We Name the Innocent Men' on those questioned in relation to the killing, but, ultimately, no one was charged.[51]

One interesting aspect of the Troubles was, as Diarmaid Ferriter has pointed out, 'the exploration of how ordinary people lived and reacted on both sides of the divide'. In this respect, along with Eamonn McCann, female journalists – Fionnuala

O'Connor, Susan McKay, Nell McCafferty, and Mary Holland – were paramount.[52] Writing in 1973 about life as a journalist in the North, Renagh Holohan of the *Irish Times* observed, that unlike in Dublin, the NUJ press card was essential for proving your identity and *bona fides*. It was, Holohan recalled, 'an instant introduction to the chief man on the spot, be he army, police or subversive, and it's the only way of getting any information'. Covering stories without it was problematic:

> A journalist standing beside me at a republican funeral in Milltown Cemetery some time ago was rapidly escorted from the graveyard, tape recorder, notebook and all, by a group of men because he had left his card at home. The rest of us stood by motionless. I suppose we could have walked out in protest as we knew he was genuine but the story was a good one.[53]

Not that the press card was an infallible defence: having been taken into 'custody' by the IRA, Holohan produced her NUJ card to be told 'sure you can buy that in Woolworths'. She was held for an hour's questioning in a deserted block of flats before being released after answering a series of questions about Dublin's geography.[54] The fact that, in 1976, the British Army admitted that it had issued forged press cards to intelligence operatives did nothing to enhance the integrity of press cards or the safety of journalists.[55] The revelation resulted in the British Defence Secretary, Roy Mason, issuing an order that banned the use of imitation press cards.[56]

South of the border, things were not much better. In May 1971, an *Irish Independent* photographer was arrested by military personnel at Dublin's Ringsend power plant. While the Defence Act 1954 made it an offence to photograph, draw, sketch, or paint any military installation, it did not apply to the power plant or to the other strategic infrastructure to which the government had decided to assign military protection. The paper responded by putting a photograph of two armed soldiers approaching its photographer on page one and devoting its leading article to calling on the Minister for Defence to explain the arrest.[57] Paramilitaries also sought to exert pressure. The hunger strike and forced feeding of sisters Marion and Delores Price (who had been imprisoned for car-bomb offences in London in 1973) created tensions in southern broadcast and print media. In February 1974, a planned radio interview with their sister was dropped ten minutes before it was due to be aired after RTÉ management decided that it 'could possibly' contravene the government's Section 31 directive.[58]

The tension increased dramatically when the newly appointed editor of *The Kerryman*, Seamus McConville, received a telephone call supposedly from the IRA threatening 'serious action' would be taken against him if the paper published an article written by columnist Con Houlihan that was critical of the Price sisters. As McConville recalled, 'I checked with republican sources to see if the threat was genuine or not and was told that it was. Despite pleas by friends in the republican movement not to publish I decided to stand over the paper's right to publish views whether it agreed with them or not.'[59] The paper's offices and printing plant were put under round-the-clock garda protection. On publication day, the paper led with a front-page leading article that noted that the last time it had been so threatened was during the War of Independence, when 'the newspaper did not offer either the actual support – or the silence – which the British thought their policies deserved'. What the IRA wanted, it concluded, was silence, and its motive was 'the same motive which impelled the Tans [and was] just as unsavoury'.[60] Houlihan's column (centred on a letter written to the *Irish Independent* by a Tralee-born but London-based nurse, Pauline Carmody, who had treated those injured by the Price bombs) was published on page eight. However, the following week, *The Kerryman* acknowledged that the 'nurse' had no connection with the Tralee address she had used in the letter and that the three London hospitals that had treated the bomb victims had no such nurse on their staffs.[61] A week later again, the republican newspaper, *An Phoblacht*, denied any threat had been made against *The Kerryman*, but the latter insisted that the threat it had received was real and had been substantiated by a senior IRA figure in Kerry.[62]

Later that year, the Editor of *An Phoblacht*, Éamonn Mac Thomáis, was sentenced to fifteen months' imprisonment for membership of the IRA and possession of a document that had been issued by the Republican Publicity Bureau. Since Mac Thomáis was a member of the NUJ, his arrest and imprisonment put the union in a delicate position. The Chairman of the Dublin branch, Niall Connolly, declared that since the union had never involved itself in the political beliefs of its members and had not allied itself to any political group, it could not comment on the charge of membership of an illegal organisation. However, Connolly viewed the other charge (possession of an incriminating document) as 'dubious and suspect and … a further attempt to curtail the legitimate rights of any journalist to report or comment on any matter which comes within his sphere of work, irrespective of whether it offends the State or any shade of political opinion'. The Dublin Freelance branch passed a motion expressing its concern about the confiscation of files and equipment from *An Phoblacht*'s premises and noted that such actions could be 'a means to the effective suppression of that or any paper'.[63] Although *An Phoblacht* was not banned, no Irish government department, for obvious reasons, took out a subscription with it. Instead, it fell to a civil servant to purchase a copy of it outside Dublin's General Post Office every week.[64]

Politicians, both Irish and British, also sought to exert pressure on journalists. On two occasions, March 1974 and November 1975, Fine Gael's John Kelly reminded journalists that under the Offences Against the State Act 1939 newspapers were prohibited from publishing statements from illegal organisations such as the IRA. On the latter occasion, Kelly observed that the law (which allowed for the imprisonment of newspaper proprietors for up to six months) had 'not been invoked because more harm than good could be done'.[65] The Northern Ireland Secretary of State, Roy Mason, was far blunter. In January 1977, it was reported that, at a dinner with BBC executives, he suggested a three-month blackout on reporting terrorist activities, referred to the station's reporters as 'disloyal', and criticised the station for not accepting the advice of the Northern Ireland Office on what news to carry. When the BBC executives pointed out that it was not the station's role or function to act as a propaganda arm of the government, Mason reportedly retorted that the IRA would have been defeated 'years ago' had the Northern Ireland Office been allowed to direct BBC policy.[66]

In 1973, the newly appointed Minister for Posts and Telegraphs, Conor Cruise O'Brien, also engaged with journalists. In one of his first interviews he stated that he had objected to Section 31 not because of its limitations but because it did not specify what the limitations were. He also declared his willingness to meet with the NUJ to discuss the ban.[67] While some meetings occurred, the directive remained in place, and relations soon deteriorated. In February 1974, the NUJ's Broadcasting branch instructed its members not to cooperate with O'Brien's new RTÉ Complaints Advisory Committee, which included NUJ stalwart Michael McInerney as one of its three members. The branch favoured the establishment of a press council that oversaw print and broadcast media but took most offence at O'Brien's decision that cases relating to Section 31 be excluded from the tribunal's remit. As the branch saw it, this ensured that the Section 31 directive took precedence over Section 18 of the Broadcasting Act, which required RTÉ to present news and current affairs objectively and impartially. Displaying some nimble thinking, the branch challenged O'Brien to declare whether he believed the Section 31 directive was exempt from the provisions of Section 18 and to give a legal justification for this or else to declare that objectivity and impartiality took precedence over Section 31 and include cases involving the directive within the remit of the new complaints mechanism.[68]

Relations deteriorated further when, two months later, the NUJ held its annual delegate conference in Wexford. While the Taoiseach's department viewed the conference as 'a wonderful opportunity for the Irish government … to meet top flight British, Irish and other journalists at a crucial juncture in Anglo-Irish relations' and sponsored a drinks reception, things did not turn out quite as hoped.[69] On the first day of the conference, the union's president, John Bailey, called on the government to withdraw its Section 31 directive. At the government-sponsored reception that evening, O'Brien asked Bailey whether he could address the conference.[70] The proposal that O'Brien be allowed to speak to the delegates was 'overwhelmingly defeated after a debate in which Irish and British journalists threatened to walk out of the conference or demonstrate against the Minister if he attempted to address the conference'.[71] In addition, the conference passed a motion calling for the rescinding of the directive 'and the restoration to RTÉ of a right and a duty to provide the public of Ireland with a free, impartial and balanced news and current affairs service'. Proposing the motion, NUJ General Secretary Ken Morgan declared that 'coverage of news and current affairs by RTÉ had been inhibited beyond the bounds imposed by the directive'. Seconding the motion, John Devine of the Dublin branch and later NUJ president, declared that 'although there had been an "obscenity of violence" in Ireland, journalists wanted the people to get a free, balanced news and current affairs service'. Such was the fear among journalists, he asserted, that 'a journalist would have to be able to read the mind of the current Minister in order to know who should … be allowed to state their case on RTÉ'. Cian O hEigeartaigh from the Broadcasting branch declared that the directive was 'crippling the whole range of RTÉ's analytical current affairs programmes to the point where they were no longer authentic'. The motion was passed unanimously.[72] The final straw for the NUJ came in June 1974 when reportage of the comments made by Rose Dugdale during her trial for IRA activity were excised from the report that had been prepared for the lunchtime radio news. That afternoon, the Broadcasting branch met, declared the extension of censorship to the reportage of court cases 'unacceptable', and instructed its members not to undertake any court-reporting assignments until the issue was resolved.[73] Since court proceedings are privileged in terms of reportage, the NUJ believed that such reports were not governed by the Section 31 directive and that RTÉ management was enforcing the directive too strictly. A compromise was reached after extensive negotiations: the union agreed to cease its action while management sought legal clarity. This advice ultimately supported the union's viewpoint.[74]

In October 1976, just prior to the passing of a new Broadcasting Act, O'Brien issued a more definitive directive in which he specifically named the organisations, the spokespersons of which were prohibited from being interviewed or having reports of their interviews aired on RTÉ. From then until the section's non-renewal amid the Peace Process in 1994, the directive was a bone of contention between journalists and politicians and among journalists themselves as legal battles about whether the directive encompassed party-political broadcasts within its remit, whether it infringed freedom of expression, and just who or what constituted 'a spokesman' were fought in the Irish High and Supreme Courts and the European Commission of Human Rights.

The chill factor

Overall, the 1970s and 1980s were a low point in media–state relations. As the Troubles worsened, journalists found themselves between armed insurgents and constitutional politicians seeking how best to end the violence. How to report what was happening without being defined by either party as being a part of the problem resulted in some tense stand-offs. While the Section 31 directive caused tension, so too did attempts by politicians to pressurise journalists into not reporting anything that might weaken the authority of the government. The political context in which this battle of wits was played out was, by any standard, appalling. The killing of fourteen civilians by the Parachute Regiment in Derry in January 1972 resulted in the burning of the British Embassy in Dublin city centre. In October 1973, a hijacked helicopter landed on the exercise yard of Dublin's Mountjoy Prison and whisked away three senior IRA prisoners. The escape made worldwide headlines after one of the escapees gave an interview to German newspaper *Der Spiegel*.[75] In March 1974, the IRA killed Fine Gael senator Billy Fox in County Monaghan, and two months later a series of car bombs killed thirty-three people in Dublin and Monaghan. In October 1975, the IRA kidnapped Dutch industrialist Tiede Herrema, and a two-week search was followed by an eighteen-day stand-off before Herrema was released. In July 1976, the IRA killed the British Ambassador, Christopher Ewart-Biggs, in Dublin. Amid such a torrent of atrocities it was, perhaps, inevitable that sensitivity on the part of politicians, judiciary and the Garda Síochána would put strain on the usually cordial relationship between journalists and politicians.

The killing of Ewart-Biggs prompted the Fine Gael–Labour coalition to introduce emergency legislation. While the Emergency Powers Bill increased the period of detention for suspects from forty-eight hours to seven days, Section 3 of the Criminal Law Bill sought to reinforce Section 10 of the Offences Against the State Act 1939 by creating a new offence of incitement which was ambiguous enough to encompass the print media within its remit. It was, as one editor put it, 'a Section 31 type restriction on newspapers'.[76] In an interview with Bernard Nossiter of the *Washington Post*, the section's sponsor, Minister Conor Cruise O'Brien, stated that he would use the section to prosecute the editors of newspapers that published readers' letters to which the government objected, a file of which, mostly from the *Irish Press*, he produced for Nossiter. When Nossiter told *Irish Press* Editor Tim Pat Coogan what had transpired, the paper's political correspondent, Michael Mills, was sent to interview the Attorney General, Declan Costello, who confirmed that 'if the *Irish Press* continued to print such letters then he would charge the editor'.[77] As remembered by Mills, he got the impression that within the coalition 'there was a feeling that the *Irish Press* was subversive to the state; that it was justifying and provoking IRA killings'.[78] There followed a series of bitter exchanges between the *Press* and O'Brien, with the former claiming that the section represented 'full-scale political censorship' and the latter stating his belief that newspapers were the IRA's favourite medium for 'recruitment propaganda'.[79] Growing public opposition to the section eventually resulted in the coalition amending it so that it no longer pertained to the media. Interestingly, in light of what was to follow, the NUJ's South-Eastern branch wrote to the President, Cearbhall Ó Dálaigh, to express its 'grave concern about certain aspects of the Government's proposed emergency legislation' and declared that unless amendments to 'safeguard Press freedoms and civil liberties' were made, the branch would engage in 'blacking [non-reporting] of all Government Ministers and Coalition Deputies'.[80]

When Ó Dálaigh exercised his prerogative to send the Emergency Powers Bill to the Supreme Court to test its constitutionality, the government was incensed. At a speech at Columb Army Barracks, Mullingar, the Minister for Defence, Paddy Donegan, declared that the President (and Commander-in-Chief of the Armed Forces) was 'a thundering disgrace' and that the Army 'must stand behind the state'. The only journalist present at what should have been a nondescript event – the opening of a canteen – was Don Lavery of the *Westmeath Examiner*, who now witnessed the minister for defence criticising the head of state before assembled army officers. Later that day, an army officer rang the offices of the *Westmeath Examiner* asking to speak to the Editor. Fully realising the importance of the story, Lavery passed it on to the national dailies.[81] The controversy that followed saw Donegan and Taoiseach Liam Cosgrave pitted against the President in a high-stake public stand-off. When Cosgrave refused to accept Donegan's resignation, Ó Dálaigh resigned. Despite persistent rumours over the years that Donegan had used more colourful language than 'thundering disgrace', Lavery has always maintained that that was the phrase used:

> The exact words used were 'thundering disgrace' – not 'thundering fucker' or 'fucking disgrace' or a 'thundering bollix' or any of the other permutations wrongly suggested since then. Donegan was not drunk. Sitting eight inches across from him I got no smell of drink off the minister, who was an alcoholic; he did not slur his words, and he did not stagger or sway. He had been quite definite in what he wanted to say. He asked one Army office afterwards what he thought. He replied 'Straight from the shoulder as usual, Minister.'[82]

If Troubles-related journalism claimed a president, it also, three years later, claimed a taoiseach. In August 1979, the IRA killed a member of the British royal family, Lord Louis Mountbatten, in County Sligo, and later that same day blew up a British Army bus – killing eighteen soldiers – in County Down, from the southern side of the border. When the British government demanded security concessions from Jack Lynch's government, the *Irish Press*, in the guise of Michael Mills, was first to reveal that both governments had agreed an over-flight zone along the border.[83] Having initially denied the veracity of the story to his own parliamentary party, Lynch later confirmed the new arrangements while on a visit to Washington. With a petition demanding his resignation circulating within his parliamentary party, Lynch resigned and was replaced by Charles Haughey.

For its part, the British government was equally sensitive to how Irish journalists covered the northern conflict – and equally misunderstood criticism of government action as thinly disguised support for the IRA. Tensions reached a peak during the 1981 hunger strike. In November 1981, the then Fianna Fáil Mayor of Cork, Paud Black, denounced Irish journalism at a national tourism conference. Black accused journalists – and RTÉ journalists in particular – of being sympathetic to the IRA and declared that television cameras should be withdrawn from Northern Ireland for one year so that tourists would not be afraid to visit Ireland. While RTÉ denied its broadcasts were supportive of the IRA, the NUJ condemned Black for 'endangering the lives of RTÉ staff working in Northern Ireland' and described his speech as 'a further attempt to intimidate RTÉ journalists into co-operating with censorship'.[84] Two days later, Black met with the British Ambassador to outline his concerns, but, in a report to London, the Embassy observed that RTÉ's coverage was 'reasonably balanced' and that the most influential group at the station was Sinn Féin the Workers' Party, who were 'bitterly anti-Provisional'.[85] But, like Black, the embassy tended to view any criticism of government policy as pro-IRA and provided London with a list of newspaper journalists that it believed were sympathetic towards the IRA. Those listed – Ed Moloney, Seán Cronin, Deasún Breathnach, Vincent Browne, Gene Kerrigan, Eamon McCann, Gerry Lawless, and Paddy Prendiville – were journalists who were critical of British and Irish government policy on Northern Ireland and who had frequent journalistic contact with IRA sources. But, as did the Irish government, the British Embassy confused criticism of government policy, reportage of what was happening in the North, and access to IRA sources as latent or active support for the IRA. As one embassy official blithely put it, 'the hunger strike proved to many Irish journalists that they mattered and that Ireland mattered. No wonder that they milked it for all it was worth.'[86] If anything, the correspondence indicates that journalists were no longer wary of reportage that might offend those in power – even amid a conflict as pronounced as the Troubles. As the 1970s and 1980s unfolded, the propensity of journalists to cause offence – and that of officialdom to take offence – increased dramatically.

Notes

1 *Irish Times*, 11 Jan. 1971, p. 13.
2 See *Irish Times*, 26 Jul. 1984, p. 11 for more detail on Scott.
3 *Irish Independent*, 17 Apr. 1941, p. 5.
4 J. Kelly, *Bonfires on the Hillside* (Belfast, 1995), p. 122.
5 Interview with John Kelly.
6 Interview with Douglas Gageby.
7 Interview with Douglas Gageby.
8 Interview with John Kelly.
9 *Irish Times*, 11 Jan. 1957, p. 4 and 18 Jan. 1957, p. 1.
10 Interview with John Kelly.
11 R. Kearney and D. Moran, 'Public responsibility and the press', *The Crane Bag*, 8:2 (1984), 13–23.
12 F. Kilfeather, *Changing Times: A Life in Journalism* (Dublin, 1997), p. 34.
13 R. Rose, *Governing Without Consensus: an Irish Perspective* (London, 1971), pp. 343–4. For histories of northern newspapers, see E. Phoenix (ed.), *A Centenary of Northern Life: The Irish News and 100 Years of Ulster History, 1890s–1990s* (Belfast, 1995) and M. Brodie, *The Tele: A History of the Belfast Telegraph* (Belfast, 1995).
14 Gageby also sent reporters to other global hotspots; in 1968, Dermot Mullane was dispatched to Paris to cover the student riots, and John Horgan was dispatched to Nigeria to report on its civil war; in 1969, Dennis Kennedy was dispatched to South Africa to report on the Apartheid regime.
15 *Irish Times*, 4 Oct. 1968, p. 11.
16 *Irish Times*, 7 Oct. 1968, p. 1.
17 *Irish Times*, 19 Oct. 1968, p. 13.
18 *Irish Times*, 19 Oct. 1968, p. 13.
19 *Irish Times*, 11 Jan. 1971, p. 13.
20 *Irish Times*, 8 Oct. 2011, p. 7.
21 *Irish Times*, 13 Jan. 1969, p. 11.
22 *Irish Times*, 20 Aug. 1969, p. 9.
23 *Irish Times*, 21 Aug. 1969, p. 4.
24 *Irish Times*, 22 Aug. 1969, p. 4.
25 NAI, DFA 2002/19/489 – contains 'Britain's new look at Ireland', 29 Dec. 1969–2 Jan. 1970; 'Report on the North', 27 Mar.–2 Apr. 1970; 'Political exploration', 27–30 Oct. 1970.
26 Peck to Foreign and Commonwealth Office: telegram no 82: 21 Feb. 1972 (National Archives, London, FCO 87/11), cited in D. Ó Beacháin, *Destiny of the Soldiers: Fianna Fáil, Irish Republicanism and the IRA, 1926–73* (Dublin, 2010), p. 353.
27 *Irish Independent*, 20 Oct. 2011, 'Rolling back the years' supplement, p. 170. A junior minister, Paudge Brennan, also resigned.

28 *Sunday Independent*, 8 Jun. 1975, p. 8.
29 *Sunday Independent*, 10 May 1970, p. 3.
30 *Sunday Independent*, 15 Jun. 1975, p. 7.
31 Correspondence with John Horgan.
32 Interview with Gageby on RTÉ's *7 Days*, c. 1972.
33 *Irish Independent*, 30 Jun. 1980, p. 1.
34 SED, vol. 52 (cols. 21–2), 20 Jan. 1960.
35 See D. Fisher, 'Getting tough with RTÉ', in M. Corcoran and M. O'Brien (eds), *Political Censorship and the Democratic State: The Irish Broadcasting Ban* (Dublin, 2005), pp. 61–72.
36 *Irish Times*, 20 Nov. 1971, p. 11.
37 *Irish Times*, 26 Nov. 1971, p. 9.
38 *Irish Times*, 22 Apr. 1972, p. 9.
39 *Irish Times*, 27 Nov. 1972, pp. 1 and 8.
40 *Irish Times*, 27 Nov. 1972, pp. 1 and 8.
41 *Irish Times*, 5 May 1971, p. 15.
42 *Irish Times*, 29 Nov. 1972, p. 15.
43 *Irish Times*, 28 Nov. 1972, p. 5.
44 *Irish Times*, 1 Sep. 1994, p. 11.
45 *Evening Echo*, 19 Oct. 2009, p. 10.
46 Letter dated 16 Jan. 1973, cited in J. Horgan, 'Journalists and censorship: a case history of the NUJ in Ireland and the broadcasting ban 1971–94', *Journalism Studies*, 3:3 (2002), 377–92, at p. 383.
47 K. Rafter, 'Bombers and mavericks: *Magill* magazine's coverage of Northern Ireland, 1977–90', *Media History*, 17:1 (2011), 63–77, at p. 65.
48 K. Myers, *Watching the Door: A Memoir, 1971–78* (Dublin, 2006), p. 13.
49 I. Kenny, 'Vincent Browne, *The Sunday Tribune*', in *Talking to Ourselves: Conversations with Editors of the Irish News Media* (Galway, 1994), pp. 101–30, at pp. 115–17.
50 T. P. Coogan, 'Foreword', in D. Kenny, *The Press Gang: Tales from the Glory Days of Irish Newspapers* (Dublin, 2015), pp. 1–7, at p. 3; *Irish Times*, 24 Feb. 1972, p. 10.
51 T. Gopsill and G. Neale, *Journalists: 100 Years of the NUJ* (Dublin, 2007), p. 212.
52 D. Ferriter, *The Transformation of Ireland* (New York, 2004), p. 635.
53 *Irish Times*, 17 Jan. 1973, p. 8.
54 *Irish Times*, 17 Jan. 1973, p. 8.
55 *Irish Independent*, 16 Feb. 1976, p. 1.
56 *Irish Independent*, 24 Feb. 1976, p. 18.
57 *Irish Independent*, 12 May 1971, pp. 1 and 13.
58 *Irish Independent*, 10 Jan. 1974, p. 11.
59 *Irish Times*, 27 Sep. 1983, p. 12.
60 *The Kerryman*, 8 Feb. 1974, p. 1.
61 *The Kerryman*, 15 Feb. 1974, p. 1.
62 *The Kerryman*, 22 Feb. 1974, p. 9.
63 *Irish Times*, 10 Oct. 1974, p. 1.
64 E. Delaney, *The Accidental Diplomat: My Years in the Irish Foreign Service, 1987–95* (Dublin, 2001), p. 319.
65 *Irish Times*, 14 Nov. 1975, p. 13.
66 *Irish Times*, 7 Jan. 1977, p. 26.
67 *Irish Times*, 15 May 1973, p. 5.
68 *Irish Times*, 20 Feb. 1974, p. 9.

69 NAI, 2006/7/461, memo dated 15 Feb. 1974.
70 *Irish Times*, 24 Apr. 1974, p. 8.
71 *Irish Times*, 25 Apr. 1974, p. 11.
72 *Irish Times*, 26 Apr. 1974, p. 9.
73 *Irish Times*, 26 Jun. 1974, p. 1.
74 *Irish Times*, 29 Jun. 1974, p. 1.
75 *Irish Times*, 20 Nov. 1973, p. 9.
76 Interview with Tim Pat Coogan.
77 Interview with Michael Mills.
78 Interview with Michael Mills.
79 *Irish Press*; 4 Sep. 1976, p. 8; DED, vol. 292 (col. 474), 7 Sep. 1976.
80 NAI, 2009/115/17, letter dated 28 Sep. 1976.
81 *Irish Independent*, 19 Oct. 1976, p. 1.
82 See *Irish Independent*, 6 Jan. 2007, p. 9 for Lavery's account of the event.
83 *Irish Press*, 5 Oct. 1979, p. 1.
84 *Irish Times*, 19 Nov. 1981, p. 9.
85 For a detailed analysis of this issue, particularly in relation to *Today Tonight*, see Chapter 6 of J. Horgan, *Broadcasting in Irish Public Life: RTÉ News and Current Affairs, 1926–97* (Dublin, 2004), pp. 154–79.
86 *Irish Times*, 30 Dec. 2011, p. 8.

9

Modernity comes knocking

By the mid-1960s the newsman had become a new kind of expert, a critic of society as he saw it, imbued with an intellectual and political ambition. Although to a great extent this has gone almost unnoticed, the truth is that it involved a radical and qualitative change whereby the newspaper became more like the magazine and the journalist was transformed into a commentator.[1]

— Bishop Jeremiah Newman, 1977

It was during the 1960s that the social-affairs aspect of the new journalism finally took root in Ireland. As outlined in previous chapters, the new journalism had emerged as a form of journalism concerned with social reality that had, in the early years of the state, been stymied by the Catholic Church. The moral crusade by the vigilance groups associated with the church ensured that objectionable newspapers imported from Britain were not easily sold and that what was considered 'objectionable content' was absent from indigenous newspapers. The fact that the new journalism devoted, as T. P. O'Connor put it, 'as much attention to the man in the gutter as to the man on the throne', was anathema to the church. Similarly, O'Connor's contention that the new journalism acted as 'a justice tribunal in human life [that] described life clearly and veraciously' ensured the church's hostility to it on the grounds that exposing the true conditions of everyday life would destroy the myth of a virtuous nation happy with its lot.[2] Thus, for the first half of the twentieth century, the press steered clear of 'indelicate' topics – namely anything to do with matters sexual.

But, as the state embraced free trade and enjoyed an economic boom, attitudes began to change. Helped in no small part by television chat shows such as *The Late Late Show* and, from 1973 onwards, *The Gay Byrne Hour* on RTÉ Radio 1, there emerged a determination among journalists to forge a new mode of journalistic inquiry into the reality of life and to discuss 'indelicate' issues in an open manner. The role of the 'outsider perspective' in this process was critical: the cold eye cast on Irish society by non-Irish journalists – such as Michael Viney and Mary Maher – who had made Ireland their home played a key role in challenging the insular conservative climate that had characterised Ireland since Independence.

One such outsider journalist was Honor Tracy, who worked as a correspondent for British newspapers. Born in Ipswich, Tracy moved to Dublin and worked as an editorial assistant on *The Bell* before becoming Irish correspondent on *The Observer*. In 1947, the paper sent her to Japan to report on its post-war devastation, and on her return to Dublin she acted as the *Sunday Times*'s Irish correspondent. In May 1950, she reported that a new house had been built for the parish priest of Doneraile, County Cork, and noted that the cost of the house had been borne by the parishioners. The article compared the impoverished parishioners' houses – 'without water or light' – to the 'large, modern villa with its glaring red roof and white walls' and alleged that 'the spaciousness of the thing has taken away their breath'. It also noted how the house had been funded: 'the church dues are increased, the collections multiply and the Canon's voice, so tired and confused, rises clear as the Shandon bells from the steps of the altar as he pricks the faithful on to fresh endeavours' (this was a time when priests read aloud how much each parishioner had contributed to the weekly collection of dues).[3]

The priest, Canon Maurice O'Connell, who had not been named in the report, sued for defamation on the grounds that the article implied he had abused his position as parish priest and that he was 'seeking luxury and comfort incompatible with his office'.[4] In settling the case by means of a £750 donation to the St Vincent de Paul charity, the paper apologised to O'Connell and stated that the article was 'untrue in its material facts' and that the description of him was 'inaccurate and misleading'.[5] Tracy in turn sued the newspaper for casting aspersions on her journalistic integrity. Her solicitor declared that the nature of the complaints she had heard from parishioners was in 'the oblique Irish way, with talk such as "oh Lord, it is the size of a ship"'.[6] In evidence, Tracy stated that she had attended Sunday mass and had heard O'Connell engage in fund-raising by giving a sermon about the Stock Exchange in which he told his parishioners 'not to mind the stock exchange and things of that sort, but to lay up for yourselves the unspeakable joys of heaven'.[7] After much argument about how much the house had cost, the jury found in Tracy's favour and awarded her £3,000 in damages against the paper.[8]

The case is instructive because Tracy, an outsider, had done nothing other than cast an impartial eye on how Irish society was structured – in this case the power of the church and the unwillingness of people to question the power of the clergy; something no Irish journalist could have done at the time. As demonstrated by the legal response that her article prompted, such detached, critical observation was generally not well received. Writing about her experiences afterwards, Tracy observed that Catholic clergy were 'highly sensitive to criticism and do all in their power to ensure that it never sees the light of day'.[9] Writing in 1950, Robert Smyllie of the *Irish Times* recorded his annoyance at 'Irish writers and Irish newspaper men in particular, getting all hot and bothered because some visiting journalist dares to criticise us and refuses to share the view that Ireland is what the New Zealanders would describe as the juicy onion, or the bees' knees.' Fair criticism was good for the country because, Smyllie concluded, Irish people were 'far too much inclined to think of ourselves as a kind of specially chosen people and to resent chaff of any kind'.[10] Welcome or not, the phenomenon of outsiders holding up a mirror to Irish society and, through the medium of social-affairs journalism, forcing people to view the reflection gained momentum throughout the 1960s and 1970s.

A changing media

It was in the 1960s that female journalism finally shook off the shackle of the 'feminine angle', prompted by the introduction of free trade, structural changes in the media industry, social and political change, and the rise of the feminist movement. While free trade resulted in a booming economy, more women joining the workforce and greater disposal income, the introduction of television forced newspapers to reconsider their relationship with the power blocs that dominated Irish society. In the era of impartial news and current affairs delivered by RTÉ, newspapers could no longer be tied to or be unquestionably supportive of political parties or the Catholic Church. Social change – including the emergence of the first generation of politicians unconnected with the Independence movement or Civil War and the introduction of free second-level education – helped create a more open and questioning society, while the rise of feminism put the place of women in Irish society centre stage. The response from national newspapers to these changes was varied, but the *Irish Times* unquestionably led the way.

Always regarded as the 'outsider' (Protestant) newspaper, it had never bought into the isolationist 'Gaelic-Catholic' identity-building project that had been taken to extremes after Independence. It had continually questioned the power that politicians ceded to the Catholic Church and was always prepared to cover topics considered taboo by other newspapers. In an Ireland that was changing and beginning to question the social structure, its new editor, Douglas Gageby, was determined to reinvent the paper's staid, but questioning, Protestant identity. Appointed editor in 1963, Gageby recruited Donal Foley to be news editor, and together they appointed journalists from Britain and America – adding the outsider's critical distance and perspective to the paper's coverage of social issues. One such appointment was that of Michael Viney, an English journalist with an interest in social affairs, who arrived from London's Fleet Street in 1961. Viney initially worked as a freelance contributor to the *Irish Times*, and one of his first series, 'Ireland for Sale?', dealt with the tensions in rural Ireland between locals and non-nationals who bought land. He subsequently joined the paper on a full-time basis and, over the next ten years, wrote a multitude of social-inquiry series on topics that were, up to then, invisible in terms of media coverage.

The topics addressed by Viney – 'Mental Illness in Ireland' (1963), 'Alcoholism' (1964), 'No Birthright: The Unmarried Mother and Her Child' (1964), 'A World Made Mad: A Study of Schizophrenia' (1965), 'Young Offenders' (1966), 'Broken Marriages' (1970) – were referred to by other newspapers as 'indelicate': they were not to be written about for fear of offending political or religious sensibilities. In a way, one could argue that there were no vulnerable groups or minorities in Ireland until the arrival of outsider journalists such as Viney. Since such groups did not exist in the media, they did not exist in the public imagination. By putting such material into the public domain, Viney ensured that whatever else politicians or the hierarchy could say about these groups, they could no longer deny their existence. Writing in *The Guardian* in 1965, Peter Lennon observed that Viney was able to write such articles 'because he was trained outside Ireland and had a different set of nerves and conditional reflexes to Dublin taboos'.[11] Given his interest in social affairs, Viney's work was reviewed by Archbishop McQuaid's vigilance committee. It simply noted that 'Viney, an Englishman and a non-Catholic, while presenting and writing reasonable articles on social issues is not an expert sociologist'.[12] But since this was the first time that these topics had been investigated in detail, many of Viney's series were reproduced in pamphlet form by the *Irish Times* and served as sociological texts in an Ireland in which sociology was only beginning to develop as a discipline.

Recalling his arrival, Viney remembered he 'found an Ireland virtually innocent of social inquiry or investigative journalism'. His eight-part series 'Young Offenders', published in 1966, was the first to indicate that not all was well in the industrial schools run by religious orders. Recalling the series, Viney noted he 'was aware of treading on strange cultural and historical ground and of the absence of professional secular expertise and self-scrutiny familiar from Britain'.[13] In his article on Daingean, the largest industrial school, he observed that the priests' vocation was 'unsupported by any formal training in institutional child care [and they had] made little attempt to keep up with international writing, discussion and experiment in the care of deprived and delinquent children'. Noting that such institutions had often been 'regarded within their orders as places of banishment or refuge for inadequate or misfit religious', he concluded that 'these were not the most suitable men to have the care of children'.[14]

This article prompted the longest response to Viney's series, though the respondent wrote to correct the dour description of the institution and its staff. The Christian Brothers had, the respondent contended, 'very considerable formal training, belonging to religious orders, which have been at institutional work for a century and over', while the public had 'crazy ideas about industrial schools. They imagine beating dished out as part of the day's routine.' The high walls, he continued, were not 'designed to prevent escapes' but existed 'because of the shelter they give the playgrounds from the winds', and the wire on top of the wall was there 'to prevent the boys losing balls during ball games'.[15] While tragically laughable in hindsight, the letter is illustrative of either the denial or the innocence that then existed in Irish society. In a similar vein, throughout the 1970s, Eileen O'Brien's 'A Social Sort of Column' examined social issues that were mostly ignored by society, including the elderly in nursing homes, the homeless, and the wives of alcoholics. Likewise, Nell McCafferty's 'In the Eyes of the Law' column described the often wretched circumstances of those who found themselves before the courts and the varying levels of discretion meted out to them by the judiciary.

Gageby and Foley also nudged women's journalism into the modern era. A dedicated page for women's issues was proposed by Foley but was initially rejected by another outsider journalist who had made Ireland her home. Mary Maher had begun her journalism career at the *Chicago Tribune*, but, tired of the restrictive scope of female journalism there – shopping and fashion features that attracted advertising – she moved to Ireland and in April 1965 found herself on three months' probation at the *Irish Times*. When, in early 1968, Foley suggested a dedicated women's page, Maher was 'vehemently opposed' to the idea since in her experience 'women's pages were designed by male editors with the advertising department, for housewives whom they imagined had only one interest: to buy things to bring home'. But when Foley suggested a 'women's page with serious articles, scathing social attacks and biting satire', Maher agreed, and in May 1968 'Women First' was born.[16] Under Maher's guidance, the page cast a cold and discerning eye on the patriarchal nature of Irish society and how this impacted on the day-to-day lives of women. In its early days, it advocated better training facilities for student nurses and examined such issues as divorce and women's rights under early Irish (Brehon) law, contraception, martial celibacy, equal pay, and how Dublin's housing crisis was affecting the health of mothers and children, though it alternated such articles with the more traditional shopping, cooking, and fashion columns.[17] Maher edited the page for eighteen months before handing the reigns to Maeve Binchy, who had joined the paper after initially contributing articles while teaching. Binchy was under no illusions about the battle facing women in seeking equal rights: in one article she noted that 'women demanding better conditions for women are too often and too widely dismissed as frustrated Lesbians sublimating everything nice and normal into a grotesque campaign'.[18]

The page was a first for Irish journalism, and the other national dailies scrambled to follow suit. At the *Irish Press*, Tim Pat Coogan appointed Mary Kenny as its women's editor in 1969. At this stage, the paper had one female journalist, Micheline McCormack, who later went on to be women's editor of the *Sunday World*. Kenny, who had written articles for the *Evening Press* and *Irish Times* as an eighteen-year-old in Paris, caused quite at a stir at the Press Group. Recalling her appointment, Coogan noted that she 'arrived in Burgh Quay like a comet exuding in its wake a shower of flaming particles from burning bras [and] surrounded herself with a coterie of talented young women, like Anne Harris, Nell McCafferty, Rosita Sweetman, June Levine, and Máirín de Burca'.[19] Another frequent contributor was Nuala Fennell, who later established the first refuge for women in Dublin and was elected as a Fine Gael TD in 1981 before being appointed Junior Minister for Women's Affairs in 1982.[20] Kenny's 'Woman's Press' page published articles such as a three-piece series of testimonies written by deserted wives, a feature based on an interview with two female prostitutes, a provocative (for the time) quiz so that its readers could establish whether they were an 'emancipated woman or sheltered lady', and a frank interview with the feminist Eva Figes in which the latter discussed female self-pleasure.[21] Despite Kenny's promise that she was 'not going to turn the *Irish Press* into a vehicle for feminist propaganda', the Press Group Chairman, Vivion de Valera, did not think much of this new departure in women's journalism and referred to Kenny and her contributors as 'the wild wild women'.[22]

At the *Irish Independent*, things were not quite as radical. Its dynamic female journalist, Mary McCutchan, wrote series on the experiences of female gardaí, troubled children, the experiences of blind people, emigrants in Britain, and orphans, before becoming the paper's women's editor and establishing the 'Independent Woman' page, helped by Mary Anderson, Nuala Fennell, and Janet Martin, in 1970.[23] However, given that the *Irish Independent* was the newspaper of conservative middle Ireland, its women's page was somewhat tamer than those of its counterparts. Its first outing featured a 'peace plan for the sex war', a piece on the experience of Spanish au pairs in Dublin, and an article on 'the lethal side of electric blankets'.[24] When it did tackle contentious issues, readers usually protested. In an October 1970 article entitled 'The Facts about Women's Wrongs', staff writer (and later women's editor) Janet Martin criticised 'the Government's downright refusal to look at the question of contraception [and] this country's insular approach to abortion, unwanted babies and unmarried motherhood'.[25] This prompted a 'regular reader' to ask whether Martin was advocating that Ireland 'follow England's example [and] allow the sale of contraceptives and legalise abortion, despite the fact we would be breaking God's law by doing so?'[26] A subsequent report that Senator Mary Robinson planned to introduce a private member's bill to legalise contraception also prompted a backlash.[27] One reader advised the page to 'stop trying to putrefy the women of this country, lest God takes a direct hand against you' while another claimed that 'the Catholic Irishwoman is appalled by such publicity to subjects which are against our Church's teaching'.[28] Sometime later, another reader accused the page of 'brainwashing married women to have careers outside the home and pressing for a change in the law relating to contraceptives'. This, the reader concluded, was 'all part of a plan to prepare the ground for "permissive" legislation, directly contrary to the teaching of the Catholic Church'.[29]

Despite the conservatism at the heart of the newspaper industry and Irish society, it was unthinkable that such features as those published in the new women's pages would have been published ten years earlier. Indeed, the fact that the women's pages were features and not straight news gave the female editors greater scope in terms of not only the topics that could be covered but also the commentary provided. As Fianna Fáil senator Neville Keery noted, 'the days of the woman's page or magazine programme devoted exclusively to knitting patterns and recipes have gone [and] problems of sex and marriage, politics and education are now the dominant themes'. This, Keery concluded, was no bad thing as the reports and commentary of the women's pages had 'an accuracy and depth' that was lacking in general media coverage.[30] But not everyone thought so: in a letter to the *Irish Times*, one reader criticised Mary Maher and Michael Viney as 'outsider journalists poking about in the shaded (for outsiders) corners of our community and producing conclusions to disturb our supposed complacency'. The population was, the writer declared, 95 per cent Catholic, and 'the Viney and Maher writings leave one wondering whether their own religious biases colour their observations'.[31] But Ireland, and journalism, was changing: by 1968, the year in which *Humanae vitae* reconfirmed the Catholic Church's ban on contraception, even the *Irish Press*'s religious correspondent, T. P. O'Mahony, could freely describe the church as being 'on the threshold of one of the greatest crises in its history' and predict the encyclical's 'widespread rejection by clergy and laity'.[32]

Campaigning journalism

As the 1970s began, topics that had once been considered taboo featured increasingly in women's journalism, helped in no small part by the emergence of the global women's rights movement and the part played by journalists in spreading its tenets in Ireland.[33] As remembered by Mary Maher, by this time 'the women's pages were an open forum for the [equality] campaign ... it was certainly helpful to the cause that those of us organising the crusade had such prominent platforms'.[34] The recruitment by the *Irish Times* of several more female journalists – Mary Cummins and Renagh Holohan in 1969, Nell McCafferty in 1970, and Christina Murphy in 1972 – added to the impetus for change in relation to the status of women and the ban on contraception. In April 1970, Mary Kenny's 'Women's Press' page profiled Senator Mary Robinson, who declared that 'for many people divorce and contraception are part of their civil rights'.[35] Later that year, Kenny and her *Irish Times* counterpart, Maeve Binchy, addressed clerical students at the National Seminary in Maynooth and were not shy in stating their views. While Binchy told them that the day was gone when women were 'going to take advice from celibate priests', Kenny condemned the legislation 'which makes you a criminal if you want to plan your family'.[36] Despite the clamour for change, the country's (male) political correspondents were not optimistic. On RTÉ's *The World This Week*, they (Michael McInerney, Michael Mills, and Arthur Noonan) agreed that politicians recognised that 'there was some public demand for change' but also believed 'there would be no votes – there might even be a loss of popularity – for anyone who pressed for admission of divorce and contraception'. Such contentious issues, they concluded, would be tacked 'by omission rather than commission when we entered the EEC [European Economic Community]'.[37]

But the push for change continued. In October 1970, Mary Maher, June Levine, and Mary Kenny appeared on RTÉ's *The Late Late Show* and called for the establishment of 'a liberation movement for women'.[38] The following week, the *Irish Times*'s 'Women First' page ran a series on 'Women's Lib'. Written by Mary Maher, Nell McCafferty, Maeve Binchy, Mary Cummins, and Theodora FitzGibbon, the series examined the origins of the Women's Liberation Movement in America, its emergence in Britain, the Irish experience, and case studies of what different Irish women thought of it, the journalists' personal views on it, and how advertisers targeted women as consumers.[39] It also published a page of readers' responses that were supportive and critical of the series.[40] In November 1970, Mary Kenny's 'Women's Press' page published a full page on 'The Case for and Against Contraception', while the following month Maeve Binchy's 'Women First' page published a column on the topic written by an anonymous priest who pointedly asked when would the church recognise 'that there are circumstances, in case of birth control, as in all other spheres of morality, which can lessen, and at times even remove, the guilt of those who break the law?' It also asked its readers to take part in a postal poll on whether the ban should be repealed.[41] The following week, it revealed that 424 readers had voted 'yes' while only two readers had voted 'no'.[42] Over at the *Sunday Independent*, June Levine occasionally wrote on the nascent women's movement; one such article contended that patriarchal governments emerged 'because women have not come forward to take their share of the political burden'.[43]

The formation of the Irish Women's Liberation Movement (IWLM) and the publication of its reform manifesto 'Chains or Change' led to another invitation to its leaders to discuss its demands – equal pay, equality before the law, equal education, an end to the ban on contraception, and rights for deserted wives, unmarried mothers and widows – on *The Late Late Show* in March 1971. While the panel consisted of Senator Mary Robinson, historian Mary Cullen, television producer Lelia Doolan, Máirín Johnson, and Nell McCafferty, others such as June Levine, Mary Maher, Nuala Fennell, and Mary Kenny contributed from the audience. The unexpected appearance of Garret FitzGerald, who dashed from his home to the studio to rebut some of the arguments made by Mary Kenny, ensured that the debate descended into chaos, or, as Brian Devenney, the *Irish Independent*'s television critic, described it, 'an ebullient shout-in'.[44] The following month Maher, McCafferty, and Kenny played central roles in the official formation of the IWLM at Dublin's Mansion House and in the organisation of the 'contraception train' from Belfast to Dublin on World Communications Day (22 May 1971) that led to a stand-off in Dublin's Connolly Station between members of the organisation and customs officers.

The unsuccessful attempt in 1971 by Senators Mary Robinson, John Horgan, and Trevor West to introduce a private members bill in Seanad Éireann to lift the ban on contraception prompted much comment that sought to link the issue with wider issues such as divorce and abortion.[45] A statement by the Catholic hierarchy declared that there was discontent among the public at the 'pressures being exerted on public opinion on questions concerning the civil law on divorce, contraception, and abortion', and Cardinal William Conway complained to RTÉ's head of news, Jim McGuinness, about what he viewed as the station's tendency to 'put forward the advocacy of change or the progressive viewpoint to the detriment of the conservative, establishment, or status quo attitude'.[46] The backlash prompted Mary Kenny of the *Irish Press* to declare that the legalisation of contraception would not 'instantly pave the way for divorce, abortion, euthanasia, mass prostitution of 11-year-old children and epidemic VD [venereal disease]' and to observe that people were 'running around the place in a state of fevered hysteria as though the whole thing was a mandate for the statutory introduction of the Permissive society'. She also called on readers to recognise the reality of marriage breakdown: divorce Irish-style, she concluded, amounted to 'desertion … no alimony, no legal custody of the children, no protection whatever'.[47] A week later, when Archbishop McQuaid issued a pastoral letter that described the possible legalisation of contraception as 'a curse upon the country', many members of the IWLM walked out of the masses at which it was read and held a protest outside the archbishop's palace in Drumcondra.[48] Mary Kenny later led a protest group that entered the grounds of Leinster House and sang 'We shall not conceive' to the tune of 'We Shall Not Be Moved'.[49]

However, Kenny's journalism and her actions irritated many people, not least some of her colleagues in the IWLM, who expressed concerns about her headline-grabbing antics.[50] The Catholic hierarchy also upped the ante: in May 1971, the Bishop of Clonfert, Thomas Ryan, declared that 'probably never before, certainly not since the penal days was the Catholic heritage of our country subjected to so many insidious onslaughts on the pretext of conscience, civil rights, and women's liberation'.[51] Politicians also reacted: in the Dáil; Fianna Fáil's David Andrews declared that they 'did not need an organisation led by her [Kenny] to tell us about our obligations to deserted wives, to the unmarried mother, or to the position of the illegitimate child in our society'. Politicians on all sides had, he concluded, 'spoken forcefully in favour of this deprived section of our community'.[52] This exchange prompted a somewhat heated interview by Kenny of Andrews in which he observed that, while he sympathised with some of the aims of the women's movement, Fianna Fáil wanted 'a proper social security structure brought about in an evolutionary fashion rather than in a revolutionary fashion'. By 'stunting on *The Late Late Show*' and engaging in campaigning journalism, Kenny had, he concluded, 'abused [her] position in this country as woman editor of one of our national newspapers and as a member of Women's Lib'. In response, Kenny described Andrews as 'a classical example of the threatened male'.[53] Fine Gael politicians also viewed Kenny with suspicion: in his speech to Fine Gael's 1971 Ard Fheis, party leader Liam Cosgrave took a dig at Kenny by noting that while 'he could get publicity for his deputies, should he send them out in hot pants', he would not do so. That Ard Fheis also heard one delegate call on the party to resist the 'sex-tyranny' represented by Kenny and her IWLM colleagues.[54]

Andrews and Cosgrave were not the only people who kept an eye on Kenny and her colleagues. In June 1968, a new Catholic lay organisation, the Lausanne Group, was established by former *Irish Press* journalist Joe Foyle to combat those who were propagating 'fashionable left-wing ways'. Such people were, according to Foyle, 'active on RTÉ programmes and in some journals … and in the general revamping of our cultural and economic situations'.[55] The subsequent appearance of the group's journal, *Guide*, which asserted to be 'Under the Patronage of Our Lady, Queen of Angels', brought a new dimension to the debate about the role of journalists in society. Edited by Foyle, *Guide* was distributed to private subscribers and, often unprompted, to public figures and politicians. It sought to critique the role that media and journalists played in society – but from the position that there existed an objective moral law that was being undermined by new technology (television) and subjective journalists and editors who used 'bias techniques' to frame or 'warp' coverage towards a particular understanding of an issue.[56] First published in 1969, *Guide* printed 'analyses of a selection of RTÉ TV programmes, noting the way in which issues are analysed, and moral/religious beliefs related to them'. According to Foyle, the discussions on such programmes reflected 'progressive thinking in Dublin circles and it [was] important to be able to assess such thinking critically'.[57] Most journalists viewed Foyle's self-appointed media watchdog activities as annoying rather than dangerous. While John Healy of the *Irish Times* noted that Foyle 'has a good file on the media men [and] he knows the marital status of most of the crowd, in the abstract and the concrete', Tom O'Dea of the *Irish Press* observed that Foyle circulated views that 'in the old days – in another Ireland that is now dead – could have dislodged a man from his job'.[58]

In October 1970, Foyle's activities were discussed on *The Late Late Show* on which, as interpreted by Foyle, he was labelled 'a muckraker' by Gay Byrne.[59] The following month, he was given a seven-minute right of reply on the show.[60] Reviewing his performance, *Irish Press* television critic Tom O'Dea compared him to American Senator Joe McCarthy: while McCarthy 'saw in every dissenting or questioning remark by his fellow-countrymen a threat to the political fabric of his country [Foyle] investigates Irish people who do not propound his narrow view of things. He conducts witch-hunts as cunningly as the senator did, and with the same talent for self-propagation.'[61] Foyle also wrote a television-review column for the *Irish Catholic* and was a prolific letter-writer to national newspapers. Many of his letters criticised named journalists for not considering the existence of objective moral law in their reportage of the contraception issue.[62] On the place of women in Irish society, Foyle was somewhat at odds with the women's movement. Interviewed in the *Irish Press*, he noted that females operated 'on more of a feeling, intuitive plane' and that a university education 'definitely reduces a girl's marriage prospects because men do like their wives to be less markedly intelligent than they are themselves'.[63]

Reaction and retrenchment

Despite such reactions, the women's pages maintained their promotion of female activism, with varying degrees of success. The abrupt departure of Mary Kenny from the *Irish Press* to the London *Evening Standard* in 1971 saw its 'Women's Press' page lose its edge. Tired of 'Vivion [de Valera] harping on about her', Tim Pat Coogan appointed a man, Liam Nolan, in her stead. Nolan, a broadcaster with RTÉ, was, according to Coogan, 'alert to what was happening in society, but compared with Mary he could justly be termed a conservative [and] his sojourn put an end to Vivion's fixation with the women's page'.[64] But the *Irish Times*'s 'Women First' page continued to push boundaries. In the run-up to the 1973 general election, it made a concerted effort to put equality on the political agenda. It published an open letter to politicians calling for the introduction of legislation on child maintenance payments, listed a fantasy all-female cabinet that included Senator Mary Robinson as Taoiseach, and profiled all sixteen female electoral candidates.[65] It also published a questionnaire on social issues and women's rights that it had distributed to all political parties and subsequently devoted two days of its space to publishing the responses it had received, outlining the various parties' views on equal pay, discrimination in the workplace, the legalisation of contraception and divorce, and the right of women to sit on juries.[66] Reviewing the impact of the women's pages in September 1974, Olivia O'Leary observed that 'some of the most influential, far-seeing and truthful examples of journalism at its best appeared under women's page headings' and that such journalism represented 'a brave and unapologetic onslaught on social shibboleths of all kinds'. But, O'Leary concluded, such journalism should never have had to be grouped under women's pages because female readers 'had a right to see their particular problem or interest included in the general assessment or presentation of any question of human rights, politics, sport, labour relations, social change, foreign affairs, finance or social satire'.[67] O'Leary's comments were prescient: at the *Irish Times*, the 'Women First' page continued to be published until October 1974. In a farewell note, its editor, Christina Murphy, observed that women's affairs had become 'such a focus of public and political attention' that it could move from 'the cosy confines of the women's page and onto the front page of the newspapers where it belongs'.[68]

Women's affairs also finally made it onto the airwaves with RTÉ's *Women Today* radio show, led primarily by Clare Duignan, Betty Purcell, Doireann Ní Bhriain, and Marian Finucane. First aired in May 1979, the programme continued the coverage of issues pioneered by the women's pages and, as remembered by Betty Purcell, despite complaints about the programme's content and 'constant pressure at Editorial Board and Authority levels to rein in the programme's controversial aspects', there was no attempt by management to influence content.[69] A less successful experiment was the launch by Vincent Browne of a monthly women's magazine, *Status*, in 1981. Declaring its mission to 'break away entirely from the stereo-type women's magazine and appeal directly to the thousands of Irish women who have been influenced by the women's movement in the last decade', *Status* was edited by Marian Finucane.[70] Its first edition carried reports on the lack of female representation in politics, the work of the Council for the Status of Women, the marginalisation of women within the Irish Farmers' Association, the safety concerns surrounding use of the contraceptive pill, and legislation that affected women, but, as remembered by Deputy Editor, Pat Brennan, 'the antipathy towards the magazine was stunning'.[71] Reviewing the magazine's precarious history, Kevin Rafter noted that 'the concept of a current affairs magazine for women met with strong resistance from advertisers' and that the magazine's identity was often compromised by its sister title, the hard-core news monthly, *Magill*:

> The dramatic cover images [for *Status*] in August 1981 came from the H-Block riots at the British embassy in Dublin. The demonstration on 18 July 1981 happened ahead of the next issue of *Magill* but just prior to the *Status* publication deadline. Following an intervention by Browne, a profile of Mother Teresa and a feature on night-cleaners were thrown out to make way for a five-page report on the embassy riots and analysis of the garda response.[72]

Ultimately, *Status* never sold more than 18,000 copies a month, well below its 30,000 circulation target, and it ceased publication after ten issues.

Regardless of the medium used by female journalists, two issues, contraception and abortion, remained highly contentious. In 1973, following a challenge to the ban on contraception by Mary McGee, the Supreme Court ruled that there existed a constitutional right to marital privacy which also allowed for the use of contraception, but the Court also ruled that the ban on the sale and importation of contraception was not unconstitutional. How to legislate for the fact that Irish people could legally use contraception but not legally purchase it resulted in Charles Haughey's infamous phrase, an 'Irish solution to an Irish problem'.[73] In 1979, as Minister for Health, Haughey introduced a Bill that allowed for the availability of contraception for 'family planning or for adequate medical reasons', provided the purchaser had a doctor's prescription.[74] For some, even this restricted availability was too much. Responding to Haughey's initiative, Fine Gael's Oliver J. Flanagan expressed 'great fears in regard to the continuance into the 1980s of parliamentary democracy as we know it' and criticised journalists for pushing for social change. As Flanagan saw it:

> There has not been any widespread demand for legislation of this kind but it has been the subject of agitation by certain liberal-minded people, certain liberal-minded journalists in the Press, on radio and television, all anxious to help to establish a completely materialistic State without any regard for the need to maintain some reasonable degree of moral standards. When wildcat, crazy, daft journalists put their pens to paper it is to advocate a society in which marriage would be pushed into the background, in which abortion is not to be decried, in which countries are described where economic progress and abortion are portrayed side by side. These liberal-minded journalists think it is part of their modern obligation to pen articles which are evilly designed, an attack on family life and on the family as we have known it.[75]

Haughey's legislation was, according to Flanagan, 'an attack on marriage as well as on human life and its creation'. As the years progressed, the notion of rights granted on the grounds of privacy engendered bitter division within journalistic circles on the issue of abortion.

In the mid-1970s, the NUJ sought to construct a 'working women's charter' – a move that brought the different status of abortion in the union's three jurisdictions – Britain, Northern Ireland and the Irish Republic – into focus. In a letter to the union's newspaper, *Journalist*, eight Irish journalists observed that in Ireland 'where sex education is non-existent, the sale and advertising of contraceptives illegal, and divorce impossible, unwanted pregnancies and unwanted children are even more likely than in Britain'. While conceding that it would be preferable that contraception and family-planning advice be freely available, the letter concluded by noting that abortion 'needs to be available as a last resort, if pregnancy is not to be a penalty'.[76] At its 1976 annual delegate meeting, the NUJ adopted a pro-choice stance, but it was not until its 1980 meeting, when it reaffirmed that position and agreed to campaign for the extension of British abortion law to Northern Ireland, that twelve Irish members resigned from the union in protest. The context, as always, was crucial. While the union's position was driven by its support for Britain's National Abortion Campaign (a campaign that sought to mitigate the effects of the so-called 1979 'Corrie Bill', the aim of which was to tighten up abortion law in Britain), the timing, from an Irish perspective, could not have been worse. When the ban on contraception was struck down by the Supreme Court in 1973 on the grounds of privacy, many feared that the ban on abortion would be similarly struck down. When the NUJ agreed to seek the extension of British abortion law to Northern Ireland, a split was all but inevitable.

The twelve resignations from the NUJ and moves by the relatively inactive Institute of Journalists to reorganise and recruit disaffected NUJ members resulted in the union's Irish delegates meeting at Liberty Hall and agreeing to request the union's NEC to cease the union's activities in terms of extending British abortion law to Northern Ireland. It also passed a motion that declared abortion 'a private and personal matter with no direct connection with the profession of journalism' and agreed to seek the deletion of the issue from union policy at the subsequent annual delegate meeting. But for some it was too little too late, and the resignations from the union were to become a lightning rod for disaffection, much of which centred around one journalist, Billy Quirke, who was also President of the Adoptive Parents' Association of Ireland. After he resigned from the NUJ and joined the Institute of Journalists, Quirke's colleagues were instructed by the NUJ to 'black' him as the union operated a 'closed shop' at the newspaper group that employed him. For over two weeks, his colleagues refused to process or publish his articles. Claiming that the union's actions were unconstitutional because they breached his right of association, Quirke secured a one-week High Court injunction against the NUJ that restrained the union from interfering with his articles or his work as a journalist. A subsequent continuation order was granted for three months, at the end of which no defence had been lodged by the NUJ.[77] In June 1981, the union withdrew its 'blacking' order and paid Quirke £1,000 in damages plus legal costs.

At the union's 1981 annual delegate meeting, the aforementioned Irish delegates' motion to delete any reference to abortion from NUJ policy was defeated. Instead, the union reaffirmed its right to choose policy and also pledged its backing for the newly formed 'Women's Right to Choose' group in Ireland. By this time, fears of a constitutional challenge on the grounds of privacy against the ban on abortion had culminated in a campaign by groups such as the Society for the Protection of the Unborn Child (SPUC), headed by Billy Quirke, and the Pro-Life Amendment Campaign to circumvent this possibility by inserting a 'pro-life' clause into the Constitution. This clause sought to make unconstitutional any attempt by legislators to rescind the ban on abortion. In a speech at a protest meeting of 2,000 people outside Dáil Éireann, Quirke criticised the 'aetheistic trend-setters who are in public life today and who control the media [which gave] disproportionate air time and newspaper space to those trying to undermine the traditional morality of Ireland'. Quirke described those who supported his position as 'the great silent majority of Ireland' and warned that those in the media and public life 'had better look out'.[78]

In September 1983, following a bitterly divisive referendum campaign – described by Gene Kerrigan as Ireland's 'moral civil war' – the electorate, in a poll characterised by a low 54 per cent turnout, voted in favour of inserting an anti-abortion clause in the Constitution.[79] As polling day approached, *Sunday Tribune* journalist Helen Lucy Burke left her seat at Sunday morning mass and accused Dublin's Archbishop Dermot Ryan of misusing 'his authority and office to make a political statement to a captive audience'.[80] To do this in 1983 required a remarkable degree of conviction and bravery. The last edition of *In Dublin* prior to polling day was a special 'Vote No' edition that carried articles by Nell McCafferty, Monica Barnes TD, Senator Catherine McGuinness, Mary Raftery, and Helen Shaw. Raftery's article detailed the intimidation endured by politicians – such as Alan Shatter, Nuala Fennell, Monica Barnes, Maurice Manning, Catherine McGuinness, and Ruairí Quinn – who advocated a 'no' vote.[81] The constitutional amendment heralded, as Nell McCafferty described it, 'a lousy decade for Irishwomen'. What she described as 'the gulf between the lip service – paid by priest, politician, and lay fundamentalist to their own notion of womanhood – and the reality of women's lives' became more and more apparent as the years unfolded.[82] There emerged some in-house criticism of how journalists covered the referendum; *Irish Press* journalist Tim O'Sullivan contended that 'the anti-amendment views of many Dublin-based reporters strongly coloured their presentation of the pro-amendment case'.[83] Despite the criticism, journalists continued to devote considerable attention to the position of women in society, particularly in relation to the sensitive topic of crisis pregnancy.

In early 1984, the *Sunday Tribune*'s reportage of the death of teenager Ann Lovett and her baby within the grounds of a church in Granard, County Longford, drew condemnation and commendation in equal measure. Having been tipped off about the tragedy, the paper's news editor, Brian Trench, assigned reporter Emily O'Reilly to verify the facts. The paper exclusively broke the story on 5 February 1984 – a full five days after the deaths. The report broke new ground in that it named Lovett and reported that she 'had apparently concealed her pregnancy and had attended school in the local convent until the day of her death'.[84] The reaction to the story from small-town Ireland was immediate: the paper was inundated with letters criticising it for reporting the tragedy and for naming the victims, though some supportive letters also arrived. The following week, the *Sunday Tribune* defended its coverage by stating that its editorial team had 'thought long and hard about naming the girl involved' and that naming Lovett had 'fixed the image of her tragedy much more clearly in people's minds'.[85] While the reporters who travelled to Granard were accused of bringing shame on the town, the tragedy was the catalyst for those who had, similar to Lovett, been forced by social mores to hide a pregnancy, give birth in secret, and, in a few cases, commit infanticide. Hundreds of letters from such women descended on RTÉ Radio 1's *Gay Byrne Show* and were read out by actors. The result was, in Colm Tóibín's words, 'the most relentless assault which has ever been presented to a mass audience on the accepted version of reality in this country'.[86] Looking back at these events twenty years later, Emily O'Reilly noted that 'Ann Lovett's death, in a sense, marked an end to all that. It told not just its own story, but also the story of one part of a generation before it, a shameful story of terror and hypocrisy and misogyny.'[87]

Shortly afterwards, the Kerry Babies case – centred on the deaths of two newborn infants, one in Abbeydorney and one in Cahersiveen – prompted some searching journalism on the position of women in Irish society and the power of state bodies.[88] Having admitted to killing her own (Abbeydorney) infant, Joanne Hayes was charged with murder in relation to both infants in May 1984. But the following October, the charge against Hayes was dropped, and the saga would have faded from public view had it not been for reporters Don Buckley and Joe Joyce. Having seen confidential garda records of the case, Buckley and Joyce revealed that blood tests had indicated that Hayes 'could not have committed the crime for which she was charged' (the killing of the Cahersiveen infant). Their in-depth report examined the history of what they referred to as the 'bizarre murder investigation' – including how the Gardaí were now in a quandary by having a confession for a killing that Hayes did not commit.[89]

The subsequent tribunal of inquiry, established to investigate the circumstances surrounding the preferment and withdrawal of the murder charge and allegations of misconduct against the investigating gardaí, became, in the words of Nell McCafferty, who covered the tribunal for the *Irish Press*, 'about the mattresses and the men in Joanne Hayes's life, and her private behaviour with them'.[90] The tribunal report's 'banal inadequacy' was summed up succinctly by Mary Holland of the *Irish Times*: it found that 'women were to blame because women tempt men, conceive children, and make an unholy mess of things when nobody wants to be left holding the baby'.[91] It is no consolation that, in spite of its unpleasantness and misogyny, the saga prompted some of the best journalism of the 1980s: Gene Kerrigan's analysis of the episode and his searing critique of the tribunal's report, published in *Magill*, stand the test of time as exemplars of critically informed public-service journalism.[92]

As the 1980s unfolded, there remained sensitivities within the NUJ on the issue of matters sexual. In October 1985, a consultative conference of NUJ members criticised attempts by SPUC 'to obstruct and deny women access to information on fertility control and pregnancy counselling' by initiating legal action against the Dublin Well Woman Centre, which offered information on termination services available in Britain. Before the motion was voted on, one journalist noted that 'this was an area about which some members felt so strongly that they would leave the union rather than support it'.[93] Nonetheless, some journalists – particularly Mary Holland of the *Irish Times* – were at the forefront of ensuring that Ireland faced up to the reality of abortion. Holland, who in 1983 fronted a Channel Four television documentary, *Ireland: The Politics of Abortion*, was very much to the fore in raising funds to enable the pregnancy advisory agencies to defend themselves in court.[94] But the fact that the abortion debate took place at all and that the Lovett and Kerry Babies tragedies were being reported on – and were being discussed in terms of what they demonstrated about Irish society as a whole – was indicative of how much Ireland, and journalism in Ireland, was changing.

Notes

1 J. Newman, *The State of Ireland* (Dublin, 1977), p. 99.
2 *Irish Times*, 14 Apr. 1911, p. 5.
3 *Irish Times*, 9 Dec. 1950, p. 10.
4 *Irish Times*, 3 Jul. 1951, p. 7.
5 *Irish Times*, 7 Jul. 1951, p. 5.
6 *Irish Times*, 1 Apr. 1954, p. 3.

7 *Irish Times*, 2 Apr. 1954, p. 3.
8 *Irish Times*, 9 Apr. 1954, p. 4.
9 H. Tracy, *Mind You, I've Said Nothing! Forays in the Irish Republic* (Washington, DC, 1968), p. 93.
10 *Irish Times*, 14 Oct. 1950, p. 7.
11 *The Guardian*, 19 Jan. 1965, p. 8.
12 DDA, AB8/B/XXIII, 1.1.124, report dated 22 Jan. 1964.
13 *Irish Times*, 12 Jun. 2009, p. 15.
14 *Irish Times*, 4 May 1966, p. 12. Viney's eight-part series was published between 27 Apr. and 6 May 1966.
15 *Irish Times*, 17 May 1966, p. 8.
16 M. Maher 'Introduction', in E. Gillespie (ed.), *Changing the Times: Irish Women Journalists, 1969–81* (Dublin, 2003), pp. 11–12.
17 *Irish Times*, 11 Jun. 1968, p. 6; 13 Jun. 1969, p. 8; 14 Mar. 1968, p. 8; 1 Aug. 1968, p. 6; 12 Sep. 1968, p. 6; 9 Jun. 1970; 18 and 19 Sep. 1969, pp. 6.
18 *Irish Times*, 13 Nov. 1969, p. 8.
19 T. P. Coogan, *A Memoir* (London, 2008), p. 145.
20 See N. Fennell, *Political Woman: A Memoir* (Dublin, 2009).
21 *Irish Press*, 30 Sep.; 1 and 2 Oct. 1969; 6 Jul. 1970, all p. 6; 29 Oct. 1970, p. 8.
22 *Irish Press*, 31 Aug. 1970, p. 6; Coogan, *Memoir*, pp. 148–9.
23 *Irish Independent*, 19–20 Feb. 1969, p. 3; 16–22 Apr. 1969, p. 3; 28–30 May 1969, p. 3; 8–16 Oct. 1969, various pages; 22–4 Dec. 1969, various pages.
24 *Irish Independent*, 1 Sep. 1970, p. 7.
25 *Irish Independent*, 15 Oct. 1970, p. 8.
26 *Irish Independent*, 24 Oct. 1970, p. 8.
27 *Irish Independent*, 27 Oct. 1970, p. 6.
28 *Irish Independent*, 4 Nov. 1970, p. 6.
29 *Irish Press*, 4 May 1971, p. 6.
30 *Irish Press*, 2 Mar. 1970, p. 12.
31 *Irish Times*, 1 Nov. 1966, p. 12.
32 *Irish Press*, 30 Jul. 1968, p. 1.
33 For a contemporary account of the development of the women's movement in Ireland, see P. Brennan, 'Women in revolt', *Magill*, Apr. 1979, 34–46.
34 *Irish Times*, 27 Mar. 2009, p. D37.
35 *Irish Press*, 20 Apr. 1970, p. 8.
36 *Irish Press*, 26 Sep. 1970, p. 3.
37 *Irish Times*, 25 May 1970, p. 10.
38 *Irish Press*, 13 Oct. 1970, p. 10.
39 *Irish Times*, 4–10 Oct. 1970.
40 *Irish Times*, 15 Oct. 1970, p. 6.
41 *Irish Press*, 3 Nov. 1970, p. 8; *Irish Times*, 15 Dec. 1970, p. 6.
42 *Irish Times*, 22 Dec. 1970, p. 6.
43 *Sunday Independent*, 7 Feb. 1971, p. 10. See also J. Levine, *Sisters* (Dublin, 1982).
44 *Irish Independent*, 10 Mar. 1971, p. 10.
45 *Irish Times*, 16 Mar. 1971, p. 9.
46 *Irish Times*, 12 Mar. 1971, p. 1; programme policy committee minutes, 4 May 1971 cited in J. Horgan, *Broadcasting and Public Life: RTÉ News and Current Affairs, 1926–97* (Dublin, 2004), p. 92.
47 *Irish Press*, 22 Mar. 1971, p. 6.

48 *Irish Press*, 29 Mar. 1971, p. 4.
49 *Irish Press*, 1 Apr. 1971, p. 1.
50 A. Stopper, *Mondays at Gaj's: The Story of the Irish Women's Liberation Movement* (Dublin, 2006).
51 *Irish Times*, 24 May 1971, p. 13.
52 DED, vol. 254 (col. 85–6), 25 May 1971.
53 *Irish Press*, 31 May 1971, p. 6.
54 *Irish Times*, 18 May, 1971, p. 6.
55 *Irish Times*, 18 Jun. 1968, p. 13.
56 J. Foyle, *Ten Media Bias Techniques* (Dublin, 1969).
57 NLI, *Guide*, no. 1, 25 Mar. 1969, 2. *Guide* later changed its name to *Receiver*.
58 *Irish Times*, 3 Apr. 1971, p. 10; *Irish Press*, 21 Nov. 1970, p. 11.
59 *Irish Times*, 9 Apr. 1971, p. 9.
60 See *Irish Catholic*, 16 Oct.–27 Nov. 1970 for more on this controversy.
61 *Irish Press*, 21 Nov. 1970, p. 11.
62 *Irish Times*, 9 Apr. 1971, p. 9 and 15 Apr. 1971, p. 11.
63 *Irish Press*, 21 Apr. 1972, p. 13.
64 Coogan, *Memoir*, pp. 148–9.
65 *Irish Times*, 29 Jan. 1973, p. 12; 14 Feb. 1973, p. 6; 26 Feb. 1973, p. 12.
66 *Irish Times*, 7, 27 and 28 Feb. 1973, p. 6.
67 *Irish Times*, 30 Sep. 1974, p. 9.
68 *Irish Times*, 26 Oct. 1974, p. 6.
69 B. Purcell, *Inside RTÉ: A Memoir* (Dublin, 2014), pp. 41–62, at p. 49.
70 *Irish Times*, 12 Aug. 1980, p. 16.
71 *Status*, Mar. 1981, p. 4; P. Brennan, 'Publish and be damned', *Magill Special* (2000), 34–6, at p. 34.
72 K. Rafter, 'The passion of peculiarity: *Magill*, 1977–90', in M. O'Brien and F. M. Larkin (eds), *Periodicals and Journalism in Twentieth Century Ireland* (Dublin, 2014), pp. 219–34, at pp. 232–3.
73 DED, vol. 312, col. 335 (28 Feb. 1979).
74 Health (Family Planning Act) 1979, section 4.
75 DED, vol. 313 (cols. 1258–9), 5 Apr. 1979.
76 *Journalist*, Oct. 1975, cited in D. Manly, L. Browne, V. Cox and N. Lowry, *The Facilitators* (Dublin, n/d, c. 1983), p. 118.
77 *Irish Independent*, 26 Jul. 1980, p. 9.
78 *Irish Times*, 25 Dec. 1981, p. 5.
79 G. Kerrigan, 'The moral civil war', *Magill*, Sep. 1983, 6–15.
80 *Irish Times*, 10 Sep. 1983, p. 14.
81 *In Dublin*, 25 Aug. 1983, pp. 14–15.
82 N. McCafferty, *Goodnight Sisters* (Dublin, 1987), p. 1.
83 T. O'Sullivan, *Fair and Accurate? The Amendment and the Press* (Dublin, 1984), p. 7. In particular, O'Sullivan mentions P. Brennan's 'Backlash and blackmail' article in *Magill*, Jul. 1982, 14–24 as helping to frame media coverage of the referendum.
84 *Sunday Tribune*, 5 Feb. 1984, p. 1
85 *Sunday Tribune*, 12 Feb. 1984, p. 4.
86 C. Tóibín, 'Gay Byrne: Irish life as cabaret', *The Crane Bag*, 8:2 (1984), 65–9, at pp. 68–9.
87 *Sunday Times*, 30 Mar. 2003, p. 20. See also N. McCafferty, 'The death of Ann Lovett', *In Dublin*, 24 Feb. 1984, pp. 10–12.

88 See T. Inglis, *Truth, Power and Lies: Irish Society and the Case of the Kerry Babies* (Dublin, 2003); and N. McCafferty, *A Woman to Blame: The Kerry Babies Case* (Cork, 1985).
89 *Sunday Independent*, 14 Oct. 1984, p. 1 and pp. 4–5.
90 *Irish Press*, 16 Jan. 1985, p. 5.
91 *Irish Times*, 9 Oct. 1985, p. 8.
92 See G. Kerrigan, 'The Kerry Babies Case', *Magill*, 30 May 1985, 16–51; Nov. 1985, 16–34, and 14 Nov. 1985, 36–41.
93 *Irish Times*, 21 Oct. 1985, p. 8. The NUJ's Dublin Branch later disassociated itself from the motion; see *Irish Times*, 5 Nov. 1985, p. 7.
94 *Irish Times*, 19 Feb. 1983, p. 5 and 4 Oct. 1986, p. 3.

10

Lifting the lid

There is no tradition of dissent or outspokenness in the Irish culture. Irish society tends to be closed and introvert with a strong authoritarian streak to which, among other institutions, the Catholic Church contributes greatly. There is a great deal of hypocrisy in our society. And, journalism, of course, is influenced by the general cultural climate.[1]

— Anonymous editor, 1987

In October 1979, shortly after Pope John Paul II had concluded his visit to Ireland, the President's secretary, Micheál Ó hOdhráin, summoned the editors of the national daily newspapers and RTÉ's head of news to Áras an Uachtaráin for a meeting with President Patrick Hillery.[2] As Aidan Pender of the *Irish Independent*, Tim Pat Coogan of the *Irish Press*, Douglas Gageby of the *Irish Times*, and RTÉ's Head of News Wesley Boyd assembled in the Áras, they were aware of rumours that had been circulating in media and political circles throughout the Pope's visit. The rumours had, as recalled by Tim Pat Coogan, been 'ignited and fuelled by the descent on the country of a hoard of British tabloid journalists' assigned to cover the Pope's tour.[3] The rumours were as varied as they were detailed: Hillery had had an affair with a secretary; he was having an affair with a French woman who had worked for him during his time as a European Commissioner; there were photographs of him in a compromising position on a boat off the Isle of Man; he had been spotted giving his bodyguards the slip while his car was stopped in traffic lights so that he could meet his mistress; he had been seen climbing in a window of the Áras late at night after a rendezvous with his mistress; a foreign publication was about to reveal that he was leaving his wife to live with another woman; he and his wife had ceased to function as a couple and were enjoying independent lives with other people; a legal separation was imminent; and, ultimately, that he intended to resign as president.

When Hillery entered the room where the editors had assembled, he announced he had no intention of resigning. The rumours were, he insisted, untrue, and, as recalled by Wesley Boyd, Hillery declared that he believed the rumours were being deliberately promoted and that there were 'some people working out the succession stakes on the possibility of [his] resignation'.[4] The editors suggested that he issue a statement covering three areas – his non-resignation, his healthy family life, and a denial of an affair – to their political correspondents. When the political correspondents assembled in the Áras sometime later, Hillery duly issued them with the statement that had been drafted with the aid of the editors. The correspondents then had the unenviable task of informing the Irish people that their President's marriage was intact and that he was not resigning.[5] As the rumours had been circulating primarily in media and political circles, the news would have been surprising and confusing to most people.

What is interesting about the episode is that Hillery decided to call in the editors and deny the rumours *only* after a Dublin periodical, *Hibernia*, had telephoned Áras an Uachtaráin for comment. It had decided to publish a story on the rumours – observing that there had been 'evidence for some time that his marital relations were none too happy' and that Mrs Hillery, 'who owns a house in Spain, has been conspicuous by her absence on all but the most important of the President's public appearances' – and Hillery had decided to issue a denial prior to publication.[6] The following week, *Hibernia*'s Darach MacDonald noted that 'for perhaps the first time since the founding of the State, the question of private morality in public life has been raised, though the press, at least, has so far dodged the issue carefully'. MacDonald noted that 'all of the Irish daily papers rallied to the President [and] not one of them gave any details of the rumours that had led to the exceptional presidential statement and editorially they backed the President'. Hillery 'had sought and got the uncritical backing of the Irish papers, but in doing so he added enormously to the circulation of the rumours concerning his personal life'. Hillery had, MacDonald concluded, chosen 'or at least felt it necessary to defend his marital relations as if they were indeed a matter for the proper concern for the public'.[7] This was new territory and an indication of how some parts of Irish journalism were changing: the idea of a publication contacting a president for comment on rumours about his marriage was unprecedented. But the saga also indicated continuities in that the summoned editors accepted Hillery's interpretation of events without reservation and advised him on the contents of his statement for their political correspondents. It also illustrated a central tenet of Irish journalism that prevailed for many decades: the love lives of public figures were out of bounds for journalism.[8]

Apart from this tenet, which persisted up to the 1990s, Irish journalism developed dramatically during the 1970s. It was during this decade that another critical element of the new journalism – investigative journalism – finally began to be incorporated into Irish journalism. As Brian Trench has noted, it was during the 1970s that the notion of journalism giving offence to those in power – or rather those in power taking offence at the work of journalists – became commonplace. Up to the late 1960s, it seemed there was a conscious effort on the part of journalists to avoid giving offence, however inadvertent. But in the 1970s there was a marked increase in people taking offence at the work of journalists. This arose not out of journalists being gratuitous or setting out to deliberately offend. Instead, it arose out of them being more curious and out of individuals and institutions being offended by the notion of journalists seeking transparency and accountability in public life. If, as Trench put it, journalists were 'offenders', there was a long list of 'offendees' who took exception to more sharply focused journalistic scrutiny.[9] Among those who took offence were those who, arguably, had never before been subject to demands for public accountability. As the 1970s unfolded, the Garda Síochána, the judiciary, politicians, and the clergy were to take offence at the work of various journalists.

In 1968, all three national titles reported on a court case in which a Christian brother was sued by the parents of a nine-year-old disabled boy who had been repeatedly beaten with a leather strap and a stick. The headlines, 'Boy Tells of Beating by Christian Brother' (*Irish Times*), 'Boy Sues Christian Brother for Assault' (*Irish Independent*), 'Beaten with Strap and Stick' (*Irish Press*), would have been unthinkable only a few years previously.[10] But, while media attitudes towards covering such cases had changed, public attitudes towards the power of the Catholic Church had not: the jury found that the brother had administered 'an excessive amount of punishment' but awarded only one shilling in damages.[11] Later that year, the *Irish Press* published a five-part series, 'Drugs in Ireland'.[12] Written by Andy Bushe, it was billed as 'a thorough investigation of drug-taking in this country'. This was the first time that a journalist had investigated the issue, and it did not go down well in some quarters. Having telephoned the Department of Health for comment, he was invited to visit the department. Upon Bushe's arrival, he was shown into a room where three senior civil servants sat behind a table. Refusing to answer questions, they demanded to know from where he had got his information and accused him of seeking to create a problem where none existed. Bushe had, it seemed, offended the department's hierarchy. Interestingly, three months later, the Minister for Health, Seán Flanagan, announced the launch of a working party on drug abuse.[13] Journalism was no longer, or at least was becoming less, susceptible to officialdom's ability to kill stories through blanket denial. Some of the key drivers for this incremental change – such as the advent of television and greater access to education – have been outlined in earlier chapters, but throughout the 1970s there were further factors that propelled journalism to be more questioning – and more 'offending'. These included a greater penetration of British media, new newspaper titles determined to be different, and, crucially, the development of a vibrant and crusading periodical press.

A changing media landscape

The activities of the British press pack during the papal visit was, in many ways, a result of increased British media interest in Ireland that had begun as both countries geared up for entry into the EEC. As part of the preparations, both states signed the Anglo-Irish Free Trade Agreement of 1965, one section of which provided for the removal of duties on imported newspapers that had existed since 1932. Whatever their merit, the duties had afforded an element of protection to Irish newspapers for nearly forty years. The duties were firmly aimed at the imported daily press: the Finance Act 1933 imposed a duty of two-fifths of a penny on imported daily newspapers that had a circulation in excess of 1,000 copies.

Subsequent legislation increased the duty to a full penny by 1941.[14] The situation was somewhat different for Sunday titles: the Finance Act 1932 imposed a duty of one penny (excluding daily titles) on all newspapers and periodicals, but they remained exempt from the duty if the surface area of their pages did not exceed 320 square inches.[15] This, according to Clann na Poblachta TD, Seán Ó Tiománuidhe, 'was an easy matter for the newspapers to arrange and so they got in free of duty'. As Ó Tiománuidhe saw it, Fianna Fáil had constructed the regulations in this way so as to hamper the circulation of the *Sunday Independent* – Ireland's only Sunday title until the arrival of the *Sunday Press* in 1949.[16] Either way, the impact of these duties was dramatic. The circulation of imported daily newspapers declined in value from £216,000 in 1932 to £99,000 in 1934.[17] Post-war, circulation stood at 4,571,556 daily newspapers in 1947 and 5,335,020 in 1949: this represents respective average daily sales of 14,747 and 17,210 for all the imported daily titles. This, in the context of average daily sales in 1953 of 203,206 for the *Irish Independent*, 198,784 for the *Irish Press*, and 35,421 for the *Irish Times*, was a drop in the ocean.[18]

However, the sales of Sunday titles were more substantial. In 1947, annual sales of imported Sunday titles stood at 15,704,988; by 1949, annual sales stood at 20,268,360.[19] This equates to weekly sales of 302,019 and 389,776 respectively. This compares with weekly sales, in 1953, of 395,507 for the *Sunday Independent* and 378,454 for the *Sunday Press*.[20] By 1955, Irish newspaper companies were describing the market penetration of imported Sunday titles as 'a matter of grave anxiety'. Appearing before the Prices Advisory Board in 1955, the General Manager of Independent Newspapers, John J. Dunne, described the British drive for Irish circulation as 'a most intense one' and observed that Irish newspapers 'were in a state of great danger because of the terrific fight going on by British newspapers to capture Irish circulation'.[21] Throughout the 1960s, this competition intensified: the value of imported daily titles rose from £114,000 in 1964 to £409,000 in 1969, and the value of imported Sunday titles rose from £363,000 to £775,000, which, adjusted for price fluctuations, amounted to a 62 per cent increase in volume. It was estimated that between 1963 and 1969 the share of the overall newspaper market held by Irish newspapers (both daily and Sunday) declined from 88 per cent to 82 per cent.[22] By 1976, concerns were being expressed that 'British newspapers were being dumped on to the Irish market at a lower price purely to boost circulation figures for ABC audit purposes, which in turn, would help them sell more advertising'.[23]

The greater presence of British Sunday titles seemed to suggest that a similar, indigenous product would be successful – hence the arrival of the *Sunday World* in 1973. Although the *Sunday World* is often referred to as Ireland's first tabloid newspaper, the *Sunday Review*, published by the *Irish Times* between 1957 and 1963, holds that distinction. The *Sunday Review*, edited by John Healy, had a simple approach: 'if you had a good story you hit the reader with it by professional use of print and clever illustration. And you were not afraid to say what you meant.'[24] The *Sunday Review* is most remembered for Healy's irreverent 'Inside Politics' column, written under the pseudonym 'Backbencher', which later transferred to the *Irish Times*. Although the *Sunday Review* had a circulation of 190,000 copies per week and had colour pages, as one executive recalled, 'it didn't grab the advertisers' and was, in many ways, before its time.[25] No such constraints applied to the *Sunday World*. Launched in March 1973, it broke new ground in terms of layout, content, and suggestive imagery. With access to colour printing, as one commentator noted, it 'absorbed many insights from its UK competitors, notably a cheeky willingness to engage in sexual innuendo'.[26] With its suggestive slogan – 'We go all the way' – and catchy advertising – 'Are you getting it every Sunday?' – it was characterised by a tabloid sensibility and an investigative zeal. Edited by Joseph Kennedy, and ably assisted by Liam MacGabhann, the first edition of forty pages had a 'colour girl' on its front page. It specialised in short, snappy stories over large headlines and sought to appeal to as wide a demographic as possible: alongside its news pages, the first edition carried three pages of cartoons, seven pages of sport, a woman's page (edited first by Terry Keane and then Micheline McCormack), and placed an emphasis on the entertainment world, especially the live music scene, and extensive television listings. In terms of layout and design it was a million miles away from the staid *Sunday Independent* and *Sunday Press*. Its first edition carried a one-page special on 'the year of the bikini' – accompanied by two photographs that would, only a few years earlier, have brought denunciations from the Archbishop's palace. A subsequent edition posed the question 'Who's the Sexiest Man in the Cabinet?' – its two-page spread awarded the honours to Garret FitzGerald and Justin Keating.[27] It announced its intention to help its readers with their personal problems and advised that it had retained 'the services of a marriage counsellor, a social worker, and a theologian'. The second issue's 'Dear Linda' column marked a radical departure in terms of sexual advice to readers – both in terms of the advice given and the frankness with which it was delivered – and contrasted sharply with the more conservative advice dispensed by the *Sunday Press*'s agony aunt, Angela McNamara, the advice of whom 'was strongly influenced by the Catholic discourse governing sexuality that emanated from the Vatican'.[28] The *Sunday World* was also marked by an investigative zeal – its first edition carried a two-page spread on 'Irish drug addicts in London'.[29] Its first leading article set the tone:

> In this newspaper, common objects like spades will be known as spades. They are used to dig with and we intend to dig. For the news and the facts behind the news … The Irish media have been much at fault because they have communicated according to their politics and policies. They have been trammelled with strings. They have been manipulated like puppets. We have no strings … Where we can discover hypocrisy or corruption our job will be to expose it. And we will do this so that it will be easily seen by as many people as possible, written as clearly as we can, graphically and with an economy of words.[30]

Its intention to dig yielded results: in September 1975, it published an article, headlined 'Find This Evil Man', in which it identified one John Grey (formally John Halford) as being a major organiser of prostitution in Dublin.[31] When Grey sought (unsuccessfully) a High Court injunction to prevent the publication of further stories about him, the paper admitted that it had 'published extremely defamatory statements about Mr Grey and they wished to publish more extremely defamatory statements' as it could 'justify these statements to the hilt'.[32] In November 1976, the paper was back in the High Court to successfully fight injunctions from two Dublin 'health centres' that it intended to expose as brothels.[33]

Circulation-wise, the *Sunday World* was an outstanding success: between July and December 1973 it established weekly sales of 206,442.[34] By 1977, it had overtaken the *Sunday Independent*, selling 293,004 copies per week compared to the *Independent*'s 272,359, though it remained far behind the *Sunday Press*'s sales of 381,611.[35] Not everyone was impressed with the journalism offered by the *Sunday World*. In 1976, Bishop (later Cardinal) Cahal Daly observed that journalists were 'no more exempt than others from the danger of being prepared to do anything for the sake of money [by] writing the cheapest form of pulp journalism for circulation and readership'.[36] The following year, the paper's new editor, Kevin Marron, defined its approach as 'enterprise journalism':

> It didn't wait for things to happen. It made them happen. It goes out there and turns over a few stones and says 'Look what we've found.' It is a time-consuming, expensive, and highly dangerous type of journalism and could teach one an awful lot about our tangled legal system.

Irish newspapers were, he argued, 'snobbish and took themselves far too seriously'. In contrast, the *Sunday World* sought to 'stimulate and entertain [in the] era of gossip journalism'.[37] As its circulation continued to increase, Independent Newspapers acquired 58 per cent of the title in 1978 and completed the acquisition in 1983. At the following year's annual meeting of Independent Newspapers, one shareholder complained about the decreased space devoted by the group's titles to religious matters. In response, company chairman Tony O'Reilly defended the 'somewhat prurient nature' of the *Sunday World* and noted that most Irish people now had 'an increasingly flexible approach to the practice of religion'.[38]

'Where the Sweep Millions Go'

O'Reilly's acquisition of the *Sunday World* had followed his acquisition of Independent Newspapers in 1973 in the wake of that year's Sweepstake controversy. In January 1973, the *Sunday Independent* published 'one of the most remarkable pieces of investigative journalism that had ever appeared in an Irish newspaper up to that time'.[39] The story would also herald a change in ownership of Independent Newspapers and effectively end the careers of the paper's editor and the journalist who wrote the story. The Irish Hospital Sweepstake was a government-sanctioned lottery run by the McGrath family ostensibly for the benefit of Irish hospitals. However, a significant number of tickets were sold in Britain, America, and Canada – jurisdictions that classed such lotteries as illegal.[40] In 1972, the *Sunday Independent*'s editor, Conor O'Brien, assigned reporter Joe MacAnthony to investigate the Sweepstake on foot of previous critical reports in the *Reader's Digest* in 1959, *Fortune* magazine in 1966, and RTÉ's *7 Days* current-affairs programme in September 1969.[41] As MacAnthony recalled, 'Conor suggested that I do a story on the Sweeps. I think Conor had a whiff of something though he never said anything, or gave me anything.'[42] Thus began twelve months of investigation into one of the most secretive operations in the state. As part of his research, MacAnthony travelled to New York and Canada to interview police, postal, and customs officials about how tickets were smuggled in and how money was smuggled out of those jurisdictions. His findings – under a front-page headline 'Where the Sweep Millions Go', beside a photograph of Sweepstake Chief Executive Joe McGrath and his wife – were startling. Describing McGrath as 'one of the richest men in Europe as a result of his work in the Irish Sweeps', MacAnthony revealed that Irish hospitals received less than 10 per cent of the value of the tickets, with the other 90 per cent disappearing in 'expenses'. He also revealed that hospitals received only 75 per cent of the sum described as the 'Hospitals Fund' as taxation was collected from the hospitals, not the organisers, and that organisers were involved with a bookmaking group in buying ticket shares that, ultimately, allowed them to win their own prizes.[43]

As recalled by MacAnthony, 'Conor read the story and immediately passed it to the paper's lawyers. The lawyers said we could run it if we were certain that we had all the facts straight.' On 21 January 1973, the paper published the story over three pages. Although originally planned as a two-part series, O'Brien decided to run it all in one go to ensure there would be no interference with the second half. As recalled by MacAnthony, 'We were planning to run the story over two Sundays, roughly 4,000 words in each story. But Conor said that we would never get the second part out. It would be stopped. So he decided the run the whole story at once.'[44]

The outcome was immense. The McGrath family, which ran the Sweep, was incensed. The majority shareholder in Independent Newspapers, T. V. Murphy, was equally upset, as he and Joe McGrath were friends. The business community was also upset: the following day, Murphy's stockbroking firm lost a substantial number of clients, and the Sweep curtailed its advertising in the Independent titles for two months afterwards. On the subsequent Wednesday, when Murphy encountered McGrath's son Patrick at a race course, the latter 'publicly abused the older man calling him amongst other things a fucking traitor'.[45] One senior Independent executive recalled seeing Murphy shortly afterwards in his office at Independent House: 'he was emotionally drained and clearly deeply wounded by the consequences of the report on him'.[46] There was, *Hibernia* magazine noted sometime later, 'scarcely a single parallel in Irish journalistic history'. In the *Hibernia* Press Awards of that year, MacAnthony won the award for best investigative article, while O'Brien, who 'originated the idea and showed the courage to publish', received a special mention.[47] Despite the accolades, the Sweepstake continued, albeit in ever declining monetary terms, until 1986, and, arguably, MacAnthony's story had most impact not on the future of the Sweepstake but on the future of Independent Newspapers.[48]

In late February 1973, a still unhappy T. V. Murphy was approached by businessman Tony O'Reilly at a rugby match at Lansdowne Road. When O'Reilly expressed an interest in acquiring a controlling stake in Independent Newspapers, Murphy 'showed enough reluctance to keep the price up and enough interest to keep him bidding'. When word got out that O'Reilly was bidding for the company, one senior editorial executive visited Murphy at his home to express concern 'that the Indo was going to become some sort of vehicle for O'Reilly's financial manipulations and/or an instrument of instructing public opinion'. Both men discussed alternative bidders, and Murphy agreed 'that [a] McGrath bid in some form could not be ruled out, but was emphatic that [the] McGraths were too smart to take any action that might be construed as revenge for [the] Sweeps article'. Murphy also revealed that he had insisted on 'hard cash and that he wasn't going to accept Fitzwilton or any other paper money'.[49] By mid-March, it was confirmed that O'Reilly had acquired the company's voting shares; ultimately, O'Reilly would own just under 30 per cent of Independent Newspapers. As rumours of a takeover abounded, the company's NUJ chapel held a meeting that resulted in the non-appearance of the *Irish Independent* – an action that led to all 180 journalists being sacked.[50] The *Independent* remained off the streets for five days, and production only resumed when O'Reilly stated that there would be no redundancies.[51]

But prompting people to leave or promoting them out of harm's way was another story altogether. In June 1974, an investigation by Joe MacAnthony and Paul Murphy into planning motions at Dublin County Council revealed that county councillor and North Dublin TD Ray Burke had benefited to the tune of £15,000 after a parcel of land in his constituency was rezoned, against the wishes of planners, from agricultural to industrial use. MacAnthony had gone digging in the Companies Registration Office and, while looking through the files of the development company, had found a memorandum of agreement that included a fee of £15,000 to Burke under the heading 'professional fees'. When contacted for comment, Burke declared that he regarded the zoning motion and the payment as 'entirely unrelated'.[52] Responding to the story, the Minister for Local Government, Jim Tully, announced that he had referred the issue to the Attorney General.[53] As an investigation got under way, the document on which the story had been based disappeared from the file at the Companies Registration Office. When interviewed by the detective investigating the affair, MacAnthony was told that, most likely, the investigation would go nowhere. Looking back on the affair some decades later, MacAnthony concluded:

> Certainly, if I had stayed with the *Sunday Independent*, I would have stayed on his tail, and on those who made contributions to his phantom political fund, including Tony O'Reilly. I put down the welter of corruption in Irish politics to Burke's escape from retribution after that exposure in 1974. It gave everybody in the game a licence to steal.[54]

By this stage, MacAnthony's time at Independent Newspapers was drawing to a close. As he recalled, 'first I lost what was called merit money. It was the first clear signal that I had to get out of the newspaper. There were other signals and ultimately words of advice from Conor O'Brien that I should go and find my future elsewhere.'[55]

In October 1974, MacAnthony, accompanied by his wife and four young children, emigrated to Canada where he worked as an award-winning producer-director with the Canadian Broadcasting Service. Conor O'Brien's career also suffered. In 1976, he was 'moved upstairs' as editorial manager and replaced as editor by Michael Hand. He died, prematurely, in 1985 at just fifty-seven years of age.[56] Circulation, rather than public transparency, was, it seemed, more important to the company's new chairman. In an interview, O'Reilly stated that his takeover was 'primarily commercial' and that he wished for the company to 'continue its aggressive commercial standards'.[57] In 1998, *Magill* magazine revealed that in June 1989 O'Reilly's company Fitzwilton had given a £30,000 cheque to Ray Burke, then Minister for Communications.[58] In late 1989, Burke had announced that an Independent Newspapers subsidiary, Princes Holdings, had been awarded the bulk of government licences to supply a multi-channel television service around the country.[59] There was, Fitzwilton later maintained, no connection between the payment and the allocation of licences: the £30,000 had been intended as a political donation to Fianna Fáil and not to Burke himself.[60]

The *Irish Times* also underwent a change of ownership. In April 1974 it announced that it was to become ownerless and be administered as a trust committed to publishing 'an independent newspaper primarily concerned with serious issues for the benefit of the community throughout the whole of Ireland free from any form of personal or of party political, commercial, religious or other sectional control'.[61] The trust would ensure that news would be as accurate and as comprehensive as practicable and be presented fairly; that comment and opinion would be informed and responsible, and would be identifiable from fact; and that special consideration would be given to the reasonable representation of minority interests and divergent views.[62] While there were some misgivings about the financial manoeuvres that facilitated the creation of the trust, the consensus among its journalists was that it at least prevented the paper being taken over by a media magnate.[63]

It was within this new dispensation that the paper – under the editorship of Fergus Pyle – published one of the most significant pieces of investigative journalism of the 1970s. On 14 February 1977, under the headline 'Gardaí Using North-Style Brutality in Interrogation Techniques', the *Irish Times* initiated a week-long series of articles by Don Buckley, Renagh Holohan, and Joe Joyce that revealed the activities of a 'heavy gang' of interrogators within the Garda Síochána. The series was based on extensive interviews with victims, lawyers, doctors, social workers, and gardaí, and its first instalment left nothing to the imagination: 'The "Heavy Gang", as the group has been nicknamed within the force, physically assaults and applies severe psychological pressure on suspects. The pressure includes threats, lies, and psychological tricks and is intensified by depriving suspects of sleep, food and water over long periods.'[64] As the week progressed, the series dominated the front page, and detailed case histories of ill-treated suspects were printed in the 'News Focus' page.[65] Responding to the series, the Minister for Justice, Paddy Cooney, denied the existence of a garda squad specialising in interrogation. But this neatly sidestepped the issue as the *Irish Times* had not alleged the existence of such a squad; it had alleged that a squad within the force was exceeding its legal limitations.[66] In a subsequent interview on RTÉ, Cooney declared that while he was not stating that the story was untrue, he believed 'there were journalistic tricks which could be employed to make things sound something a bit different from what they were'.[67] Such was the political oversight of Ireland's police force.[68] There was, of course, no shortage of people willing to take offence at the story. The coincidental fact that the paper broke the story at the same time as the state was pursuing a case against Britain in the European Court of Human Rights over the use of unorthodox interrogation methods in Northern Ireland prompted some politicians to attack the paper's heritage and question its loyalty to the state. One government TD accused the *Irish Times* of being 'traditionally hostile to Irish institutions'; another accused it of 'doing the dirty work for John Bull'.[69] Such reactions did not deter the paper: the following month it revealed that fingerprint evidence had been falsified in a failed attempt to convict a suspect of murder.[70] However, such hard-hitting stories came at a price: the *Irish Times* found itself cut off from receiving information from the force's press office, and the Garda Commissioner, Edmund Garvey, ordered the force's intelligence unit to investigate the leaking of information to the paper.[71]

Giving offence

A key factor in the development of critical, inquiry-led journalism from the 1970s onwards was the emergence of a vibrant periodical press. As has been noted elsewhere, early and mid-twentieth-century Ireland was serviced by periodicals, weekly or monthly, that were characterised by adherence to particular causes such as the Irish language, trade unionism, and religion.[72] However, in the latter forty years of the century, the most prominent journals were those that concentrated on current affairs, promoted investigative journalism, and exposed the often opaque interaction between the worlds of business and politics. This burst of activity was helped in no small way by the advent of colour advertising. Having invested heavily in large-scale printing plant the national newspapers could not take immediate advantage of the innovation of colour printing. This left the lucrative field of colour advertising open to others before the national newspapers finally integrated colour printing into their plant and introduced weekend supplements that very much usurped the function of the weekly or fortnightly periodical. It was these periodicals that Brian Trench had in mind when making the observation that it was during the 1970s that the notion of journalism giving offence to those in power – or rather those in power taking offence at the work of journalists – became commonplace. Among these periodicals were *Hibernia*, *Magill*, *Hot Press*, and *In Dublin* – all of which were associated with a strong-willed proprietor or editor. Their tone was distinctly crusading and investigative, and they all made insisting on greater accountability and transparency in public life their *raison d'être*.

This insistence on accountability and transparency was effectively built into the business models of these periodicals – they were born not from a desire to make a profit but from a keen frustration of how public life operated in Ireland and a determination to articulate views absent from mainstream media. They *existed* to interrogate the relations between business and politics, to shed light on the machinations of state bodies, and to demand accountability on behalf of the public. This is not to say that they did not need to make a profit – every media outlet needs to do this – but, crucially, their unique selling point was their determination to demand public accountability and to express dissatisfaction at the *status quo*. Their influence on the ideas of the intellectual elite who were the makers of public opinion in Ireland – in politics, the public service, and the universities – ensured that these journals helped shape the thinking that led to the emergence of a more open Irish society from the late 1960s onwards.[73] As part of the media sphere, but standing apart from mainstream media, these periodicals often acted as an echo chamber for the daily and weekly newspapers and RTÉ news and current-affairs programming, and, with a more generous deadline than conventional media, they often had the time (though not necessarily adequate resources) to devote considerable attention to topics not covered, or not covered in depth, by daily media. Very often these topics were picked up by mainstream media, thus bringing them into mainstream discourse. As recalled by Brian Trench, this was very much the case with the fortnightly *Hibernia*.[74]

Established in 1937 with the support of the Catholic lay order, the Knights of St Columbanus, it was acquired by John Mulcahy in 1968. Prior to the acquisition, Mulcahy was, Trench noted, a contributor to the publication 'on business and economy, taking a sceptical view of many prevailing orthodoxies and dominant business personalities and groups'. This sceptical view was magnified under Mulcahy's proprietorship–editorship as *Hibernia* developed a strong presence as 'an independent, frequently dissenting voice [providing] a platform for a wider range of opinion than was represented in daily and weekly newspapers and in broadcasting'.[75] As recalled by Trench:

> From 1973 *Hibernia* gave particular attention to stories of bad planning, illegal property development, councillors' conflicts of interests, and related issues. Mulcahy's guidance to his staff in using the resources in the planning departments of Dublin city and county councils and in the Companies Records Office was crucial to *Hibernia* unearthing many stories that, with the exception of a single but famous report in the *Sunday Independent*, the big press turned away from.[76]

In his work, Trench indicates some major pieces that give a flavour of the investigative nature of *Hibernia*'s journalism: 'Planning: Widening the Loopholes' (30 November 1973), 'Making a Fortune in Tallaght: Was Bribery Involved?' (21 June 1974), 'The Councillors' Interests' (5 July 1974), 'Illegal Little Boxes' (21 February 1975), and 'Reduced to Rubble' (2 May 1975). One of these stories ('Making a Fortune in Tallaght: Was Bribery Involved?') resulted in *Hibernia* journalists being interviewed by detectives investigating suspected corruption in local government. Along with investigating misconduct on the part of the security services in Northern Ireland, it also reported debates and conflicts in the left and in republicanism 'not just for its value as controversy but also out of recognition of the substantive interest in the various positions'.[77] In February 1978, during the controversial Sallins train robbery case in the juryless Special Criminal Court,

Hibernia was the only publication to point out that one of the three judges fell asleep regularly at the bench. As recalled by Trench, 'despite cautions from journalist colleagues to Niall Kiely that reporting the observable facts would be risky, *Hibernia* gave precise times on a particular day when the judge was seen to nod off'.[78] When defence lawyers challenged the conduct of the trial, a challenge that included an affidavit from Kiely, they were unsuccessful. On day sixty-five of the trial, Justice John William O'Connor died, and a retrial was ordered.

A similar crusading tone was present in *Magill*. As recalled by former editor, Kevin Rafter, the monthly *Magill* 'was very much shaped by the particular interests of its proprietor and founding editor, Vincent Browne'.[79] Indeed, John Waters has written of Browne having 'through the force of his personality, created a whole new model of Irish journalism'.[80] Browne had previously edited the short-lived student magazine turned current-affairs magazine, *Nusight*, in the late 1960s, and followed this with stints as a reporter with the *Irish Press* and the *Sunday Independent*. Determined to run his own publication, *Magill* first appeared in October 1977 with Browne identifying five dominant themes for the magazine: civil liberties, Northern Ireland, women's rights, the redistribution of wealth, and the issue of accountability. In focusing on these areas, Browne also defined the kind of journalism he envisaged for *Magill*:

> The whole purpose of journalism is to enforce accountability on the part not just of public bodies but on the part of all institutions of power in society. Thus journalism is concerned not just with Governments but also with police forces, bureaucrats, courts, big business, trade unions, churches, even newspapers themselves.[81]

As outlined by Rafter, during its first publication span from 1977 to 1990, alongside political and business news and analysis, *Magill* examined issues that other publications shied away from. These included a series of interviews with senior members of the Provisional IRA from 1978 onwards – significant in a period when, due to Section 31 broadcasting restrictions, 'republican voices were silent on most media outlets'.[82] In 1980, *Magill* caused a sensation when it published extensive abstracts from the diaries of Peter Berry, the Secretary General of the Department of Justice at the time of the Arms Crisis of 1970. In his diaries, Berry recorded having informed then Taoiseach Jack Lynch of the plot to import arms in October or November 1969. Lynch always maintained that he first heard of the plot in April 1970 when he acted immediately by sacking the ministers concerned.[83] Another seminal piece was the extensive two-part series on Sinn Féin the Workers' Party which investigated its links with the Official IRA and the influence of the party within RTÉ's current-affairs division.[84] As already mentioned (see Chapter 9), its analysis of the Kerry Babies saga in 1985 was peerless.

From 1983 to 1990, *Magill* was edited by Colm Tóibín, Fintan O'Toole, Brian Trench, and John Waters. One theme that ran through *Magill* in the early 1980s was its investigations of lay-religious groups that sought to exert pressure on politicians and in-depth features such as 'The Secret World of the Anti-Divorce Lobby' (May 1986), 'The Moral Civil War' (September 1983), 'The Secrets of Opus Dei'

(May 1983), and 'Abortion: Blackmail and Backlash' (July 1982) did much to expose the opaque relationship between politics and religion. Another theme related to malpractice within the Garda Síochána, and again, in-depth investigations such as 'The Death of Fr Molloy' (August 1986), 'Chaos in the Gardaí' (April 1986), 'The 11-Year-Old Who Confessed to a Murder He Didn't Commit' (December 1984), 'The Garda Scandal' (November 1984), and 'Criminal Conspiracy Within the Gardaí' (September 1983) indicated that all was not well within the force. Crime and its social implications also received significant attention. In November 1983, it published an exposé by Mary Raftery on the Dunnes – the Dublin criminal family widely blamed for introducing heroin into Ireland. The following month, it published a major piece by June Levine on prostitution in Dublin. Entitled 'A Woman in Gangland', the piece had been subject to a High Court injunction that *Magill* successfully appealed to the Supreme Court. In a similar vein, the pressures (from advertisers, the temptation to sensationalise) on journalists were also scrutinised through features such as 'Two Weeks in the Life of the Media' (September 1985), 'Crime Hysteria' (18 April 1985), and 'Trial by Television' (August 1984). With a circulation that declined from 30,000 in its initial years to 13,000 in 1989, *Magill* was, according to Rafter, eventually outflanked by 'the national newspapers that had adapted their editorial offerings to include longer articles, many by names who had first emerged in *Magill*'.[85]

Coming from a slightly different angle in that they initially concentrated on youth culture before articulating a jadedness with the existing political, social, and cultural orders, both *Hot Press* and *In Dublin* sought to speak to a distinct demographic: the generation that had grown up in post-protectionist Ireland, that had been afforded the opportunity of free secondary education, that had involved itself in a reinvigorated student movement, that had benefited from an expanding third-level sector and a reduction of the voting age from twenty-one to eighteen years of age, and that was coming of age in an Ireland that no longer recognised the 'special position' of the Catholic Church.[86] This was also the first generation to grow up with television – 83 per cent of all homes had a television set in 1977.[87] In his work on *Hot Press*, Joe Breen described this generation as 'more knowledgeable, more opinionated, and less patient with the old ways'.[88] Launched a week before the 1977 general election, in which the newly enfranchised group would vote for the first time, *Hot Press* founder Niall Stokes noted that the campaign had been 'dominated by the same boring old faces that have been popping up on posters since any of us can remember'.[89] As recalled by Stokes, *Hot Press* was launched 'in the belief that there was an audience for a politically aware, counter-culturally inclined magazine'. In particular, he felt that 'the deference shown to the Roman Catholic Church in all areas of Irish life, including the media, was entirely inappropriate'.[90] As outlined by Breen, *Hot Press* was modelled very much on *Rolling Stone* in that it had deep roots in the then counterculture, flagged its uniqueness as the voice of that culture, published ground-breaking journalism, discovered major journalistic figures, and broadened its coverage into politics and lifestyle as its reader profile extended beyond the under-twenty-fives. As its readership matured, *Hot Press* turned 'its liberal spotlight on many of the country's pressing social problems, such as drug abuse, sexual mores and the lot of the marginalised while questioning the institutions and shibboleths that governed social life'.[91]

A similar path was adopted by *In Dublin*, which first appeared in 1976. As recalled by its founding editor, John Doyle, he was determined to protect *In Dublin*'s original function – as a listing magazine – and build circulation before expanding its remit. Doing otherwise, he observed, had collapsed previous magazines such as *Buck Out* and *Pushbike*. Their determination to attack 'the Church, the Establishment, and Conor Cruise O'Brien' had, Doyle contended, ensured they attracted no advertising.[92] *In Dublin* initially followed a more cautious path, but nine months into its first year it ran a cover story on 'lonely hearts'.[93] The response it received prompted it to open its advertising columns to personal contact adverts, some of which may have brought blushes to the cheeks of more innocent readers. One of its first crusades – 'the Fighting Cock Fund' – was launched after Dublin City Council withdrew its grant to Dublin's Project Art Centre in protest at a visiting English theatre group, Gay Workshop. Contributions from readers topped over £1,000, and the council eventually reinstated the grant.[94] In 1978, it spearheaded a petition to stop the destruction of Dublin's Wood Quay and the following year expanded its format and editorial content to include reviews, interviews, and features. By the early 1980s, it had gone from a humble listings magazine to a current-affairs-led listings and review magazine. It now carried news, a major current-affairs feature, and an interview with a politician or social activist, with reviews and listings located at the back. It was, in many ways, a more accessible and youth-oriented *Magill*. It also carried the first hint of the abuse scandal that would later engulf the Catholic Church. In August 1984, Nell McCafferty attend the Merriman Summer School in Lahinch, County Clare, at which one female participant made an angry reference to the 'furtive lechery of priests'. Over the course of the week, several female conference participants confided in each other about the clerical abuse they had suffered. 'How widespread', McCafferty's article asked, 'is this molestation of girls and women by priests?' She concluded that it was 'widespread, damnable, destructive, and ought to be stopped'.[95]

Among those who wrote for *In Dublin* in the 1980s were Nell McCafferty, Eamonn McCann, Derek Dunne, Mark Brennock, Colm Keena, Sam Smyth, Declan Lynch, Mary Raftery, Jonathan Philbin Bowman, Kate Holmquist, Fintan O'Toole, Pádraig Yeates, Michael Dwyer, Helen Shaw, and Ann Marie Hourihane, while it was edited at different stages by Colm Tóibín, John Waters, David McKenna, Ferdia Mac Anna, and Fiona Looney.[96] Looking back at his involvement with all three magazines, John Waters concluded that 'together they amounted to an Irish counter-culture'. As he saw it, 'whether they were explaining pop music or police brutality, the magazines brought, for the first time to Irish journalism, a thing called *attitude* [as …] a new generation of writers began to deal with issues in ways that defied the journalistic handbooks'. Ultimately, they helped that new generation to rebel 'against the orthodoxy of the Ireland into which they were born, and against the orthodoxies of those who could see only one direction in which it could go'.[97] As the 1980s and 1990s unfolded, this journalistic counterculture would, gradually, be incorporated into mainstream journalism.

Notes

1 Newspaper editor quoted in M. Doornaert and H. Larsen, *Censoring the Troubles: An Irish Solution to an Irish Problem – Report of an IFJ Fact-Finding Mission to Ireland* (Brussels, 1987), p. 9.
2 Hillery had assumed office without an election in 1976 following the resignation of Cearbhall Ó Dálaigh.
3 T. P. Coogan, *A Memoir* (London, 2008), p. 226.
4 *Irish Times*, 20 Jan. 2009, p. 15. Hillery's thinking was that Charles Haughey was behind the rumours in an attempt to force Hillery to resign, force Taoiseach Jack Lynch to stand for president, and allow Haughey to assume the leadership of Fianna Fáil. But the origins of the rumours remain a matter of speculation: Tim Pat Coogan attributed them to 'the dark arts sections of the Northern security services' (*A Memoir*, p. 226). Gene Kerrigan and Pat Brennan pointed the finger at the Garda Síochána; Gene Kerrigan and Pat Brennan, *The A–Z of Irish Scandals and Controversies* (Dublin, 1999), p. 156. Another rumoured source was the KGB (*Sunday Independent*, 26 Apr. 1981). Hillery's biographer, John Walsh, states that Hillery believed they came from the Haughey wing of Fianna Fáil; John Walsh, *Patrick Hillery: The Authorised Biography* (Dublin, 2008), p. 460.
5 See *Irish Independent*, *Irish Press*, *Irish Times*, 4 Oct. 1979, p. 1.
6 *Hibernia*, 4 Oct. 1979, pp. 1 and 5–6.
7 *Hibernia*, 11 Oct. 1979, pp. 1 and 5.
8 John Walsh notes that Douglas Gageby asked then *Irish Times* European correspondent, John Cooney, to investigate the rumours in Brussels, a request Cooney rejected. See Walsh, *Patrick Hillery*, p. 454.
9 B. Trench, 'Hibernia, dissent, and causing offence', paper presented at 'Periodicals and Journalism in Twentieth Century Ireland', National Library of Ireland, 28 Feb. 2015.
10 *Irish Times*, 27 Jun. 1968, p. 7; *Irish Press*, 27 Jun. 1968, p. 7; *Irish Independent*, 27 Jun. 1968, p. 8.
11 *Irish Times*, 28 Jun. 1968, p. 13.
12 *Irish Press*, 16–20 Sep. 1968.
13 S. Flynn and P. Yeates, *Smack: The Criminal Drugs Racket in Ireland* (Dublin, 1985), p. 8.
14 Finance Act 1933, section 8; Finance Act 1934, section 16; DED, vol. 83 (col. 90), 7 May 1941. By the time the duty was abolished in 1971 it stood at 1.2 pence.
15 Finance Act 1932, schedule 2.
16 DED, vol. 121 (col. 994), 31 May 1950.
17 D. O'Donnell (Conor Cruise O'Brien) '*The Irish Independent*: a business idea', *The Bell*, 9:5 (1945), 386–94, at pp. 392–3.
18 DED, vol. 121 (col. 994), 31 May 1950; vol. 137 (col. 651–3), 19 Mar. 1953. Averages are based on 310 publishing days per annum.
19 DED, vol. 121 (col. 994), 31 May 1950.
20 DED, vol. 137 (col. 651–3), 19 Mar. 1953.
21 *Irish Times*, 19 Nov. 1955, pp. 5 and 10.
22 Committee on Industrial Progress 1971; see *Irish Times*, 7 Jan. 1971, p. 4.
23 *Irish Times*, 9 Nov. 1976, p. 11.
24 D. Foley, *Three Villages* (Waterford, 2003), p. 113.
25 Interview with Louis O'Neill.

26 J. Horgan, *Irish Media: A Critical History since 1922* (London, 2001), pp. 108–9. The *Sunday World* was published by Sunday Newspapers Ltd. (owned by Hugh McLoughlin, Gerry McGuinness, and Tom Butler) and printed by the Creation Group, which published several women's magazines.
27 *Sunday World*, 15 Apr. 1973, pp. 16–17.
28 P. Ryan, 'Asking Angela: discourses about sexuality in an Irish problem page, 1963–80', *Journal of the History of Sexuality*, 19:2 (2010), 317–39, at p. 319.
29 *Sunday World*, 25 Mar. 1973, pp. 12–13.
30 *Sunday World*, 25 Mar. 1973, p. 10.
31 *Sunday World*, 21 Sep. 1975, p. 1.
32 *Irish Times*, 14 Oct. 1975, p. 13. See *Sunday World*, 19 Oct. 1975, p. 1
33 *Irish Times*, 18 Nov. 1976, p. 13. See *Sunday World*, 7 Nov. 1976, p. 1 and 21 Nov. 1976, p. 2.
34 *Irish Times*, 20 Oct. 1976, p. 12.
35 *Irish Times*, 31 Aug. 1977, p. 12.
36 *Sunday World*, 16 Aug. 1976, p. 6.
37 *Irish Times*, 30 Sep. 1977, p. 14. Kevin Marron was one of four Irish journalists who died in an air crash in 1984. The others were Niall Hanley, John Feeney, and Tony Hennigan. For obituaries, see *Irish Times*, 15 Nov. 1984, p. 8. Marron had been succeeded as editor by Colin McClelland in 1981.
38 *Irish Times*, 29 Mar. 1984, p. 12.
39 Horgan, *Irish Media*, p. 105.
40 For detailed accounts of the Sweepstake, see M. Coleman, *The Irish Sweep: A History of the Irish Hospitals Sweepstake 1930–87* (Dublin, 2009) and D. Corless, *The Greatest Bleeding Hearts Racket in the World* (Dublin, 2010).
41 Conor O'Brien was a former editor of the *Evening Press*; he became editor of the *Sunday Independent* in 1970. MacAnthony began his career at the *Irish Times* and joined the *Irish Independent* in 1968. By the early 1970s, he was working at the *Sunday Independent*. A review of the *7 Days* programme noted that it 'said nothing; they just delivered the facts and figures and if there were any inferences to be drawn that was left to you', *Irish Times*, 29 Sep. 1969, p. 12.
42 *Irish Echo*, 18 Feb. 2011, n/p.
43 *Sunday Independent*, 21 Jan. 1973, p. 1. See also pp. 8, 9, 10, and 12.
44 *Irish Echo*, 18 Feb. 2011, n/p.
45 Coogan, *A Memoir*, p. 166.
46 Private source.
47 *Irish Times*, 18 Jan. 1974, p. 5.
48 A later investigation by RTÉ into the Sweeps was canned after it was deemed too sensitive an issue to tackle: see J. Horgan, *Broadcasting and Public Life: RTÉ News and Current Affairs, 1926–97* (Dublin, 2004), pp. 151–3.
49 Private source. Fitzwilton was O'Reilly's private holding company.
50 *Irish Times*, 14 Mar. 1973, p. 1.
51 *Irish Times*, 19 Mar. 1973, pp. 1 and 13.
52 *Sunday Independent*, 23 Jun. 1974, pp. 1 and 4.
53 *Sunday Independent*, 30 Jun. 1974, p. 4.
54 Interview of Joe MacAnthony conducted by David Manning and Miriam Cotton, dated 15 Apr. 2008, available at www.mediabite.org.

55 *Irish Echo*, Feb. 2011, n/d. See www.irishecho.com/2011/02/swept-under-the-rug-2. 'Merit money' refers to the differential package that MacAnthony earned as an investigative reporter.
56 *Sunday Independent*, 10 Feb. 1985, p. 22.
57 *Irish Times*, 19 Mar. 1973, pp. 1 and 13.
58 V. Browne, 'O'Reilly's Fitzwilton gave a £30,000 cash cheque to Ray Burke in June 1989', *Magill*, Jun. 1998, 16–22.
59 *Irish Times*, 29 May 1998, p. 8.
60 While the payment was referred to the Mahon Tribunal, in Jul. 2007, Fitzwilton secured a Supreme Court ruling that prevented the tribunal from holding public hearings into the payment. The tribunal had investigated the affair in private but had, the Supreme Court ruled, not followed proper procedure in its attempts to initiate a public hearing.
61 Companies Registration Office (CRO), Irish Times Trust Ltd, memorandum of association, article 2.d.ii.a.
62 CRO, Irish Times Trust Ltd, memorandum of association, article 2.d.ii c 1–3.
63 For a detailed account of the creation of the trust, see M. O'Brien, *The Irish Times: A History* (Dublin, 2008).
64 *Irish* Times, 14 Feb. 1977, p. 1.
65 See *Irish Times*, 15 and 16 Feb. 1977, p. 10.
66 *Irish Times*, 18 Feb. 1977, pp. 1 and 9.
67 *Irish Times*, 19 Feb. 1977, p. 5.
68 Amnesty International's subsequent investigation into the allegations confirmed their veracity: see Report of Amnesty International Mission to Ireland, 1977.
69 *Irish Times*, 19 Feb. 1977, p. 5.
70 *Irish Times*, 1 and 2 Mar. 1977, pp. 1.
71 *Irish Times*, 5 Mar. 1977, p. 1.
72 M. O'Brien and F. M. Larkin (eds), 'Introduction', *Periodicals and Journalism in Twentieth Century Ireland* (Dublin, 2014), pp. 9–15.
73 O'Brien and Larkin, 'Introduction'.
74 B. Trench, '*Hibernia*: voices of dissent, 1968–80', in O'Brien and Larkin (eds), *Periodicals and Journalism in Twentieth Century Ireland*, pp. 187–202. Trench was assistant editor of *Hibernia* for many years. It ceased publication in 1980 after a succession of libel actions.
75 Trench, '*Hibernia*', pp. 190 and 187.
76 Trench, '*Hibernia*', p. 194.
77 Trench, '*Hibernia*', p. 201.
78 Trench, '*Hibernia*', p. 196; see *Hibernia*, 3 Feb. 1978, p. 6. O'Connor died on 6 Jun. 1978.
79 K. Rafter, 'The passion of particularity', in O'Brien and Larkin (eds), *Periodicals and Journalism in Twentieth Century Ireland*, pp. 219–34, at p. 219.
80 J. Waters, *Jiving at the Crossroads* (Belfast, 1991), p. 115.
81 V. Browne, 'Editorial', *Magill*, Jan. 1985, 4–15, at p. 13. (This is *Magill's* 100th edition.)
82 K. Rafter, 'Bombers and mavericks: *Magill* magazine's coverage of Northern Ireland, 1977–90', *Media History*, 17:1 (2011), 61–75, at p. 64.
83 V. Browne, 'Arms Crisis 1970: the inside story', *Magill*, May, Jun., and Jul. 1980.
84 V. Browne, R. McGuigan, and C. Coulter, 'The secret world of SFWP' (parts 1 and 2), in *Magill*, Apr. and May 1982.
85 Rafter, 'The passion of particularity', pp. 231–2. *Magill* ceased publication in 1990 but re-emerged in 1997 for eleven issues under Browne's editorship before the title was sold. Thereafter, it appeared intermittently under several owners including Mike Hogan and Ian Hyland.

86 The franchise had been extended in 1973 but took effect for general elections in 1977; the constitutional reference to the Catholic Church was altered in 1973 prior to entry to the EEC.
87 D. Fisher, *Broadcasting in Ireland* (London, 1978), p. 58.
88 J. Breen, 'A tilt at all those windmills', in O'Brien and Larkin (eds), *Periodicals and Journalism in Twentieth Century Ireland*, pp. 203–18, at p. 207.
89 *Hot Press*, 9 Jun. 1977, p. 3.
90 Quoted in Breen, 'A tilt at all those windmills', pp. 206–7.
91 Breen, 'A tilt at all those windmills', pp. 204 and 213.
92 *Irish Times*, 9 Jul. 1977, p. 12.
93 *In Dublin*, 10 Dec. 1976–6 Jan. 1977, pp. 4–5.
94 *In Dublin*, 17–30 Apr. 1986, p. 5.
95 *In Dublin*, 6–19 Sep. 1984, p. 9.
96 *In Dublin* became part of the Tribune Group in 1988 and was eventually acquired by Mike Hogan. It was banned by the Censorship Board in 1999 in relation to its advertising of massage parlours and ceased publication in 2003.
97 J. Waters, *Race of Angels: The Genesis of U2* (Belfast, 1994), pp. 102–3.

11

Spirit of the nation

That question assumes I am a wealthy man, but I would not necessarily assume that, if I were you. Ask my bank manager.[1]

— Charles Haughey, responding to a reporter's question, 1979

In the July 1982 edition of *Magill*, Vincent Browne published a profile of Taoiseach Charles Haughey in which he noted that Haughey had, for some time, been the subject of numerous rumours. These rumours alleged that Haughey had 'gone broke', that he was 'badly in hock to a merchant bank', and that he was 'involved in an affair with a well-known journalist'.[2] As time would eventually prove, these rumours were more accurate than untruthful. It would, however, take over a decade of journalists investigating Haughey and his finances – and a host of tribunals of inquiry – to finally expose the truth. In many ways, the phenomenon that was Charles Haughey helped to push journalism in Ireland in a more questioning direction. For the first time since Éamon de Valera, the country had a taoiseach that very sharply and very publicly divided the nation. There was no middle ground: in the political and public spheres, Haughey was revered and feared in equal measure. He also divided journalists, and his image – that of a politician who had lied during the Arms Crisis to save his political career, of a man who would do anything to attain power, and of a politician who displayed ostentatious but unexplained wealth – ensured he became the focus of sustained journalistic scrutiny.

In addition, his rise to power came at, and contributed to, a time of systemic political and economic instability and a time of distrust between journalists and senior Fianna Fáil politicians. Three general elections occurred between June 1981 and November 1982, and these, combined with the continuous anti-Haughey heaves within Fianna Fáil, the inability of successive governments to manage the economy effectively, and the 1981 hunger strike in Northern Ireland, created a prevailing atmosphere of crisis. The fracturing of the old 'united behind one leader' consensus that had long prevailed within Fianna Fáil provided journalists with ample opportunity to shed light on the inner workings of Irish democracy – but also provided many instances of political intimidation of journalists. As the 1980s and 1990s unfolded, journalism slowly, laboriously, and torturously revealed the web of relationships between politics and business and the systemic political and financial corruption that existed at the heart of Irish public life. It was, in many ways, the time that journalism finally came of age in Ireland in that it was during this period that investigative journalism became a central and continuous feature of Irish journalism. This process was not, by any means, a one-way street, and not every investigation yielded results. The body politic and the business lobby strongly resisted the notion of journalists acting in any investigative capacity. Along with journalists' telephones being tapped, allegations of bias became the standard defence against journalistic inquiry. But this defence gradually and then very rapidly lost its effectiveness as the rotten practices at the heart of politics were finally exposed for all to see.

Telephone tapping

First elected in 1957, Charles Haughey began his political career at a time when journalism was passive, constrained, and reverential to those who represented church and state. Despite his early and avid willingness to use the media to heighten his public profile by courting the attention of political correspondents such as John Healy and Michael McInerney, and despite his awareness from his altercation with RTÉ while Minister for Agriculture in 1966 that journalism was becoming less reverential, Haughey never accepted the idea of journalism acting as a public-accountability mechanism. As one observer put it, once a proficient poacher of media attention, by the 1980s Haughey was 'a middle-aged game-keeper [who] sets out to muzzle those young poachers and plug the ears of their chosen scribes'.[3] Given his rumoured but unconfirmed financial and extramarital circumstances, it is, in retrospect, easy to understand why he sought to control the journalistic agenda. His tenuous grip on power only increased his wariness of journalists, while his remarkable ability to cling on to power against all odds only increased journalistic interest in him. The continuous heaves against his leadership, his deal-making skills in securing votes to ensure his election as taoiseach, and the continuous scandals that engulfed his administrations ensured that media scrutiny was never far away. Haughey's role in the Arms Crisis also imbued him with a whiff of sulphur, and it is arguable that the Arms Crisis influenced not only the trajectory of Irish politics for the subsequent twenty years but also the trajectory of political journalism in that the majority of political journalists placidly accepted Jack Lynch's version of the events of 1970. This faith in Lynch's account of the Arms Crisis undoubtedly influenced the attitude of journalists such as Michael Mills, Dick Walsh, Stephen Collins, and Bruce Arnold towards Haughey. For other journalists, it was Haughey's ostentatious lifestyle and unexplained wealth that dominated their interest and determined their approach. All of this culminated in a fraught, and dangerous, game of cat and mouse between Haughey and journalists in the 1980s.

It was Haughey's second term as taoiseach, from March to December 1982, that prompted most controversy and provided the material for what many view as the defining text on modern Irish politics, Joe Joyce and Peter Murtagh's *The Boss*. Written when both men wrote for the *Irish Times* and published as a contemporaneous record of events, *The Boss* is a searing critique of Haughey's 1982 administration and the turmoil within Fianna Fáil over his leadership.[4] So unhappy was Haughey with the publication that when asked to comment on the book on RTÉ Radio, he replied that he would not 'justify that particular publication with the title "book"'.[5] The persistent attempts to remove Haughey as party leader were played out in the full glare of the media, and this was pointed to by the Haughey camp as evidence of media bias against him.[6] As the heaves persisted, things took a sinister turn as verbal and physical intimidation became part of the political process and Haughey involved his government and the Garda Síochána in inappropriate attempts to determine who was providing journalists with information about the internal party feuding.

Haughey's activities in this period were indelibly intertwined with the country's newest weekly newspaper, the *Sunday Tribune*. Established by Hugh McLaughlin and John Mulcahy, the *Sunday Tribune* made its debut in November 1980. Although it incorporated the staff of the recently defunct *Hibernia*, McLaughlin declared that he was 'not interested in a radical political weekly' and that any resemblance to *Hibernia* would be 'nil'.[7] However, under Conor Brady's editorship from 1981 onwards, the paper's political coverage sharpened with the appointment of the country's first female political correspondent, Geraldine Kennedy. As a reporter with the *Irish Times*, Kennedy had secured Haughey's first interview when he became party leader and taoiseach in 1979. However, as the dissent against Haughey developed, she reported on the internal opposition to his leadership for the *Sunday Tribune*. In December 1981, Haughey opponent Charlie McCreevy gave an interview to Kennedy in which he declared that a considerable number of the party's TDs were 'less than satisfied with the direction of Fianna Fáil in opposition'. When Kennedy asked him whether there was disillusionment with Haughey within the party, McCreevy replied 'no comment'.[8] In February 1982, the *Sunday Tribune* reported that a challenge to Haughey's leadership was under way. In an interview on RTÉ's *This Week* radio programme, Haughey declared that if he worked for the *Sunday Tribune* he would 'be inclined to look after my own future'. The report of the impending challenge had been written by Kennedy, and, although Haughey later stated that he had been referring to the paper (which was losing money) rather than an individual, his uncharacteristic slip of the tongue presaged the fraught times ahead.[9]

Kennedy was not the only journalist of whom Haughey was wary. Bruce Arnold, a British-born political journalist with the *Irish Independent*, was also trusted by the anti-Haughey camp, and, in an attempt to determine who Arnold's sources were, Haughey requested his justice minister, Seán Doherty, to instruct the Garda Síochána to place a tap on Arnold's home telephone. In May 1982, Doherty instructed Assistant Commissioner (and head of the force's intelligence and security branch) Joe Ainsworth to put a tap on Arnold's telephone. The Garda Commissioner, Patrick McLaughlin, subsequently signed the order that justified the tap as being necessary to gather 'useful information concerning subversive activity' that could not be gathered in any other way. When the head of the justice department's security section, Jim Kirby, rang Garda Headquarters to enquire about the necessity of the tap, he was told that Arnold was 'politically against this country' and that suspicions existed that Arnold was being briefed by the British Embassy.[10] While Kirby recommended that the tap not be approved, Minister Doherty (who had requested the tap in the first place) ignored his department's advice and approved the tap.[11] Arnold's telephone was tapped from 10 May to 12 July 1982.

In July 1982, Haughey's office invited Hugh McLaughlin, the proprietor of the *Sunday Tribune* and an old acquaintance of Haughey, to visit the Taoiseach. At the meeting, Haughey complained about being victimised by Geraldine Kennedy and told McLaughlin that he wanted to know who her sources were. McLaughlin then contacted the *Sunday Tribune*'s editor, Conor Brady and told him of Haughey's complaint. But when McLaughlin asked Brady who Kennedy's sources were, Brady refused to reveal anything.[12] Around the same time, Brady was also approached by the former head of a semi-state body who claimed to represent 'concerned businessmen': he asked Brady to 'curb the activities of Geraldine Kennedy'.[13] Shortly afterwards, a tap was placed on Kennedy's telephone in the exact same manner as Arnold's, although this time the rationale for the tap was on the grounds of 'national security'. Kennedy's telephone was tapped from 28 July to 16 November 1982; it was lifted twelve days after Haughey's government fell after a Dáil vote on 4 November. Of the eight transcripts known to have been made of Kennedy's telephone conversations, five related to calls with other journalists, one related to a source within Fine Gael, one related to a Fianna Fáil TD, and one related to a Fianna Fáil source.[14]

Kennedy was certainly the preferred recipient of information from the anti-Haughey wing of the party: a transcript of a call between her and Fine Gael press secretary Peter Prendergast in late September 1982 indicated that she was the first journalist to be told of a renewed – and again unsuccessful – attempt to oust Haughey that would take place the following month.[15] Her story, published on 5 October 1982, predicted that it would be preceded by a resignation from cabinet. In the heel of the hunt, two ministers – Des O'Malley and Martin O'Donoghue – resigned the day before the parliamentary party meeting to decide on Haughey's leadership.[16] That same day, 5 October 1982, Assistant Garda Commissioner Joe Ainsworth passed the transcript of the call between Kennedy and Prendergast to Seán Doherty.[17] On the day of the meeting (6 October 1982), Haughey supporter Pádraig Flynn complained that the leadership challenge played into the hands of Fine Gael, the British, and their 'media collaborators' – whom he named as Kennedy, Arnold, and John Feeney of the *Evening Herald*.[18] When Haughey survived as leader, Kennedy was approached at the subsequent press conference by a member of the Haughey family: 'Miss Kennedy', he said to her, 'you will pay for this.' Over the following days, several anonymous and threatening telephone calls were made to her home, and a broken bottle – with a note with the message, 'We are watching you' – was left on her car. Eventually she spoke to a party official about the intimidation. He later told her he had spoken to one of Haughey's close associates who had said he would 'call the boys off'.[19] Such was the level of hostility that Kennedy went so far as to invite George Colley – whom Haughey had defeated to become party leader in 1979 – to her home to tell him that if she ever went missing and was found in the nearby river she would not have gone there voluntarily as she did not swim.[20]

By this time, word of the Minister for Justice putting pressure on the Garda Síochána in relation to personal and constituency issues had reached the ears of Kevin O'Connor, then News Editor of the *Sunday Independent*. Among the instances of Doherty's interference were the so-called 'Dowra Affair' wherein charges against his brother-in-law were dropped after the Royal Ulster Constabulary detained the main witness in Northern Ireland at the request of the Garda Síochána, and the 'Tully Affair' wherein he unsuccessfully attempted to have a sergeant in his constituency transferred after he had raided a pub owned by a friend of Doherty's and had resisted pressure from Doherty to drop charges against those found drinking after hours. Having travelled to Doherty's constituency and interviewed local gardaí, O'Connor returned to Dublin and received a message from one of his garda sources to make urgent contact – but only through means of a public phone box. When O'Connor did so, his contact told him that his telephone was being tapped, he was being followed, and that every effort would be made to stop publication of his investigation. The source obviously knew something O'Connor did not: even though the *Sunday Independent*'s legal team passed his investigation, the paper's editor, Michael Hand, refused to publish it. When O'Connor argued for publication, Hand told him he was 'crucifying the minister on flimsy evidence'.[21] The following week, Hand suspended O'Connor as news editor. In later years, O'Connor established that Haughey had requested a government minister to contact Hand to get the story spiked, and Hand had acceded to the request.[22] Sometime later, O'Connor decided to give his research material – including signed statements from gardaí in Doherty's constituency – to RTÉ.[23] With rumours growing in journalistic and political circles that the *Sunday Independent* had a big story on Doherty but would not print it, Peter Murtagh of the *Irish Times* contacted his garda sources – all of whom would only speak in person at clandestine meetings and never on the telephone. Shortly before Haughey's government fell, the *Irish Times* published the story of Doherty's regular interference in policing matters.[24] Such was the sensitivity surrounding what one of Murtagh's sources described as 'a take-over of the force by people who saw it as an extension of their own political rule' that it was only *after* Haughey's government fell in November 1982 that RTÉ's flagship current-affairs programme, *Today Tonight*, presented a lengthy report on political interference in the Garda Síochána.[25] Just four days prior to polling day on 20 November, the tap on Kennedy's telephone was lifted, and during the campaign Haughey accused unnamed journalists of 'working for Fine Gael'.[26]

In January 1983, the newly installed Fine Gael–Labour coalition government revealed that the previous Haughey-led government had instructed the Garda Síochána to bug Kennedy's and Arnold's telephones. While legislation allowed for tapping in relation to investigations into subversive activity, the new Minister for Justice, Michael Noonan, declared that there had been 'no justification' for the tapping of the journalists' telephones since neither of them 'could be thought likely either to be engaged in serious criminal activity or activities affecting security or to be in touch with persons who might be so engaged'.[27] While the senior garda officers – Ainsworth and McLaughlin – immediately resigned, Haughey denied any knowledge of the tapping, a stance buttressed by Seán Doherty's insistence that he alone had ordered the taps because 'national security was endangered through leaks of highly confidential Government papers and memoranda'. The taps had, he declared, never been discussed at Cabinet.[28] Doherty also revealed that Vincent Browne's home and office telephones had been tapped by previous governments and that he had continued those taps.

The revelations prompted another unsuccessful heave against Haughey (during which the *Irish Press* published what amounted to Haughey's political obituary) and the allocation of armed detectives to protect Kennedy who continued to report on Fianna Fáil's internal divisions.[29] By this time, Kennedy was writing for the *Sunday Press*, and despite, or perhaps because of, the paper's Fianna Fáil heritage, she was advised by Haughey's press officer, P. J. Mara, not to attend the party's 1983 Ard Fheis which occurred shortly after Haughey survived as leader:

> P. J. Mara wasn't always the nice guy presented. He advised me that I should not attend the 1983 Fianna Fáil ard fheis in the RDS in Dublin because the party could not guarantee my security. My response was that I was a journalist covering politics in Dáil Éireann. Fianna Fáil was the biggest party and, in a democratic state I had a right to cover their annual conference. I attended. I noted the Nazi salutes from the audiences and I thank colleagues for accompanying me to and from the door of the ladies' toilet.[30]

For his part, Seán Doherty adopted a menacing tone towards journalists who wrote about the tapping controversy. Asked to comment on the publication of *Survivor: Charles J. Haughey* by the *Sunday Independent*'s Raymond Smith, Doherty declared that he would advise Smith 'to keep in close contact with his doctor and not be alone in his own house because he may not be able to take care of himself'. Asked whether he would be prepared to be interviewed by Geraldine Kennedy or Bruce Arnold, Doherty replied that the only thing he 'would talk to those people about would be the weather'. Kennedy was, he declared, 'probably a nice little girl [who, he hoped] has learned from her mistakes'. She might, Doherty concluded, 'even yet become a journalist of some status in the future'.[31]

In 1987, Kennedy and Arnold were awarded damages in a High Court case against the state, the judgment of which described the tapping as 'an attack on their dignity and freedom as individuals and as journalists [that] cannot be tolerated in a democratic society'.[32] Doherty's revelation that Vincent Browne's telephones had been tapped by several governments prompted Browne to seek legal redress also. However, in this instance, the state adopted a tougher stance and argued that the tapping was justified because Browne was in regular journalistic contact with subversives – as illustrated by interviews with senior IRA figures in *Magill*. In 1995, Browne accepted a private settlement from the state on that basis.[33] However, when Browne discovered that the bulk of the surveillance related to non-subversive contact, he went public on the settlement. Of the eighty-five surviving transcripts, only four could be construed as relating to subversive activity: three related to conversations with IRA gunrunner Jim McCann, and the fourth related to a conversation with former IRA leader Dáithí Ó Conaill. As Browne revealed:

> All 81 of the other transcripts had nothing remotely to do with 'useful information concerning subversive activities which could not be obtained in any other way'. These conversations were with *Magill* staff, printers and distributors, journalists, public servants, lawyers, judges, defendants in the 1970s arms trial, family, friends, and politicians.[34]

Among those who had their telephone conversations with Browne transcribed were barrister (and later judge) Kevin O'Higgins, judges Liam Hamilton and Barra O'Briain, editors Michael Hand and Vincent Doyle, Geraldine Kennedy, government press secretary Frank Dunlop, Taoiseach Charles Haughey, former attorney general Colm Condon, and, ironically enough, Minister for Justice Seán Doherty.[35] Sixty of the transcripts related to the four-month period around *Magill*'s publication of its ground-breaking Arms Crisis series in 1980.[36] Among the many conversations transcribed were those between the magazine and its printers and distributors, all of whom had refused to print or distribute the relevant issues after receiving legal letters from Jim Gibbons, who had been Minister for Defence in 1970.[37] Many years later, Gene Kerrigan observed that 'knowing now that every phone call concerning the printing and distribution of the magazine was listened to by the State, one begins to wonder if anyone was getting threatening visits from dour men with their collars turned up'.[38]

The manner in which the state concluded the deal with Browne – in effect a deal to prevent the disclosure that the tapping of his telephone related to matters beyond his journalistic contacts with subversives – prompts the question as to whether the telephones of other journalists were 'justifiably' tapped during this period. Indeed, the diary entry of Jim Kirby, the head of the justice department's security section, notes that, in his conversation with Ainsworth about the request for a tap on Bruce Arnold's telephone, Ainsworth had said that it had 'been suggested in conversation why should he not be covered, others are'. The 'others', it was later revealed, included Tim Pat Coogan, Editor of the *Irish Press*.[39] Many years later, in January 1992, Seán Doherty recanted his statement that he had acted alone ten years previously. In a seemingly innocuous interview with Shay Healy on RTÉ's irreverent and satirical chat show *Nighthawks*, Doherty insisted that others – meaning Haughey – had known about the telephone taps of 1982 and had seen the transcripts that had emanated from them. Although Haughey continued to deny any involvement in the tapping, he resigned as taoiseach – and was succeeded by Albert Reynolds – in February 1992.

'Charlie Haughey's money'

As with his political manoeuvrings, Haughey's financial affairs attracted the interest of journalists. As one article, published just after he became taoiseach in 1979, put it, he was 'the wealthiest man in Dáil Éireann, with an estimated net worth approaching £3 million'. The source of this wealth was unclear despite the persistent attempts by journalists over several decades to identify how it was that Haughey was 'the richest man to hold the office of Head of Government since the foundation of the State, far outstripping in wealth any of his six predecessors'.[40] Put simply, the journalism of the period failed to penetrate the secrecy that surrounded the sources of Haughey's extravagant lifestyle. As asserted by one journalist, Dick Walsh, despite Haughey's strong belief in media bias against him, in actual fact he enjoyed 'the support of the most influential people in the media' in the early 1980s. Among those identified by Walsh as strongly supporting Haughey were *Irish Times* columnist John Healy, *Irish Press* Editor Tim Pat Coogan, and *Sunday Independent* Editor Michael Hand. As Walsh put it, the non-investigative stance towards Haughey's finances was justified by the argument that 'Irish newspapers did not stoop to the levels of the British press.' Journalists were thus stuck in a bind: they did not have evidence of wrongdoing but at the same time were prevented from looking for that evidence.[41] Oddly, Walsh did not include former *Irish Times* editor Douglas Gageby in his list of journalists that were supportive of Haughey. Gageby took his cue on Haughey from his lifelong friend John Healy, who was a stalwart Haughey supporter. Over several decades, Gageby discouraged several journalists from investigating the source of Haughey's wealth. In the 1960s, Michael Viney found that, although his inquiry-led journalism was breaking new ground, politics and Haughey's finances were no-go areas:

> He (Gageby) was less prepared, however, (and probably right) to trust my judgment about politics, always his central preoccupation. Even in the 1960s, the Haughey lifestyle evoked intense gossip. I rashly suggested that, with six months' assistance from a solicitor and an accountant, I might arrive at something safe to print, but Douglas rather doubted this. My attempt at a biographical series on Haughey was taken away by him and John Healy and largely rewritten by them: it must have seemed very naïve.[42]

In the 1970s, Frank McDonald encountered similar resistance:

> Gageby disliked a heavily researched piece I wrote on Haughey's wealth in December 1979, after he became Taoiseach, so he 'buried' it on page seven … he basically didn't want stuff that was 'damaging' to Haughey to appear in the paper – other than the usual political stuff. He also, probably, thought it was wrong to be delving into people's personal affairs.[43]

And, in the early 1980s, when 'An Irishman's Diary' columnist Kevin Myers turned his attention to Haughey's finances, Gageby spiked two articles and strongly rebuked him for crossing into territory that belonged, as he saw it, strictly to the paper's political correspondents.[44] But by the late 1980s, the *Irish Times* – under new editor Conor Brady – was far more questioning of Haughey's wealth. As recalled by Brady, in this period, several of the paper's journalists, including Frank McDonald, Dick Walsh, Mark Brennock, and Brady himself, devoted significant time and resources to investigating the source of Haughey's wealth, but to no avail. This focus caused much friction: while Dick Walsh 'was like a dog with a bone about Haughey's unexplained money', columnist and Haughey supporter John Healy dismissed the reportage as 'piss-and-vinegar stuff'.[45]

Vincent Browne's *Magill* also expended much energy in seeking to identify the source of Haughey's wealth. As Browne observed in June 1982, Haughey had 'made a considerable personal fortune while holding ministerial office and has steadfastly refused to divulge any information on how he came by such wealth'.[46] As recalled by John Waters, Browne was obsessed with discovering the source of Haughey's wealth:

> For years, the monthly planning meetings in *Magill* were distributed with lists of stories to be attempted, the first of which was, 'Charlie Haughey's money'. From time to time, someone would volunteer, or be browbeaten into volunteering, to attempt the story. The result would always be the same. After weeks of research, they would come back and report that nobody was able to say how much money Charlie Haughey had, never mind how he had acquired it. Browne would interrogate them rigorously, often flying into a rage of frustration. Had they tried such and such? Perhaps so and so knew something? In the end it would come to nothing, but the 'story' would stay at the top of the list.[47]

As journalists struggled to investigate the source of Haughey's wealth, there were three essential elements to the story that remained impenetrable: the donations from wealthy businessmen and developers channelled mostly through Haughey's accountant, Des Traynor; the corruption within the planning process that enriched many of Haughey's most loyal supporters; and, lastly, the offshore Ansbacher accounts run by Traynor whom Frank McDonald had accurately described as 'Haughey's bagman' in his book *The Destruction of Dublin* – before legal advice forced the term to be changed to 'close personal friend and financial advisor'.[48] As Conor Brady put it, these activities 'cross-fertilised and reinforced each other', behind all of which lay the influence of Traynor and Haughey.[49] Throughout the 1980s, fragments of information came to light, but there was never enough to tell the full story.

In 1981, while editor of the *Sunday Tribune*, Brady received an anonymous package in the post that contained what looked like photocopies of Haughey's personal bank statements from Allied Irish Banks (AIB). They showed an overdraft of £200,000. After making some informal queries with the bank, Brady was told that it would not discuss the affairs of any customer with a third party. Ultimately, believing that the documents might relate to only one account of many, Brady, against the advice of the paper's business editor, Des Crowley, declined to publish any details of the leak.[50] Two years later, in January 1983, a new publication, *The Phoenix*, revealed that sources had 'suggested that by early 1981, [Haughey] had run up an overdraft of at least £1 million on his personal account at the Allied Irish Banks branch in Dame Street'. It also revealed that Haughey had received £1.4 million in a land sale that had been disguised through the transactions of a multitude of companies owned by his associates.[51] That same month, Des Crowley, now writing for the *Evening Press*, reported that it had been 'rumoured in discreet financial circles for years that Mr Haughey owed £1 million to a major bank and that the bank had held its hand because of his elevated political position'. Crowley then revealed that 'sources close to Allied Irish Banks insist that he owed them around this sum last year'.[52] While the story was correct in substance, the chronology was askew: while Haughey had indeed owed the bank £1.14 million in late 1979, £750,000 had been paid against the debt in January 1980, and the bank had written off the balance.[53] Three days later, AIB issued a statement denouncing the story as so 'outlandishly inaccurate' that it felt 'bound as a special matter, to say so positively and authoritatively'.[54] This denial effectively killed the story. Faced with the prospect that Haughey might sue for defamation and use the bank's statement as proof of his claim, the *Press* backed off – although, as Crowley later noted, the *Press* simply printed AIB's statement, it did not publish a retraction or an apology.[55] Many years later, the former head of AIB's Press and Public Relations Office, Bob Ryan, declared that the statement had not emanated from his office but conceded that, given that there was a heave against Haughey ongoing at the time of Crowley's story, the statement 'probably killed off further questions and helped to secure Haughey's position'.[56] For its part, the Moriarty Tribunal, which investigated payments to Haughey, declared the AIB statement as 'disingenuous in the extreme'.[57]

Six years later, while investigating the collapse of developer Patrick Gallagher's property empire for RTÉ's *Today Tonight* programme, producer Mary Raftery discovered a documented financial link between Gallagher and Haughey. A liquidator's report on one of Gallagher's distressed businesses listed a loan of £15,000 to Haughey. The programme, due to be aired in November 1989, was delayed as the Director of Public Prosecutions considered charges against Gallagher. It was finally aired in February 1990 and made no mention of the financial relationship between Gallagher's company and Haughey, who was then taoiseach, on the grounds that to do so was 'potentially libellous'. Indeed, when Raftery asked him to comment on the matter, Haughey warned that if the matter was raised in the programme he would sue for defamation.[58]

There were also attempts to penetrate the corrupt world of planning. In 1982, Frank McDonald and Frank Kilfeather of the *Irish Times* produced a series on land rezoning in County Dublin 'highlighting otherwise inexplicable decisions, but of course without being able to produce proof that money changed hands'.[59] In July 1989, Brian Dowling and Tom Brady of the *Irish Independent* reported that a Fianna Fáil TD, five councillors, six developers, and five planning officials were under investigation for alleged corruption.[60] In February 1993, it reported on a speech made by former councillor and then minister of state Joan Burton who declared that observers of council business were frequently 'shocked at the sight of developers, their agents and lobbyists … ticking off lists of councillors as they arrive and vote for decisions that multiply at a stroke the value of lands they own or control'. For reporting on the speech, the *Irish Independent* received legal demands from forty-one councillors, some demanding a retraction and an apology, other seeking financial compensation. While the *Irish Independent* did not retract the story or apologise or pay damages, it did remove the story from later editions of the paper.[61]

In July 1993, Frank McDonald of the *Irish Times* wrote a series of reports that alleged councillors had received money from lobbyists acting for developers in return for supporting controversial land rezoning schemes in County Dublin. One report revealed that a deceased councillor, Fianna Fáil's Seán Walsh, had left almost £250,000 in several bank accounts after his death in 1989. The report described Walsh, a full-time public representative, as 'one of the most active councillors in earlier rezoning controversies'.[62] Predictably, Dublin City Council passed a motion condemning the *Irish Times* for 'impugning the reputation' of Walsh.[63] As outlined by McDonald, journalists investigating corruption were stuck between a rock and a hard place: 'the problem in Ireland is that you can't libel the living without being sued, nor libel a deceased person without being accused of speaking ill of the dead'.[64] McDonald again fell afoul of the second offence when he wrote the report of the death of Des Traynor in May 1994. In it, he mentioned financial transactions between Traynor and disgraced Australian politician, and former Australian ambassador to Ireland, Brian Burke, and aroused a storm of protest from Traynor's friends in the business community. Given that the full extent of Traynor's role in facilitating the political and financial corruption that was endemic in 1980s Ireland was not then fully known, the *Irish Times* permitted publication of a letter from a Dublin solicitor that criticised McDonald's report as 'grossly misrepresenting' Traynor.[65]

Despite the persistent and determined attempts by numerous journalists to identify the source of Haughey's wealth, it was a freak incident in February 1992 that eventually exposed all. Just nine days after Haughey resigned, in the wake of Seán Doherty's phone-tapping revelations, retail magnate Ben Dunne was arrested after a drug-induced panic attack on a hotel balcony in Orlando, Florida. After his siblings ousted him as head of Dunnes Stores, Dunne threatened legal action to break up the family trust and in legal documents stated he had given money to Charles Haughey. While the action was settled and Dunne left the business, a report commissioned by the Dunne family into the company's finances outlined several financial transactions between Ben Dunne and Fine Gael TD (and then minister) Michael Lowry. Somewhere along the way someone leaked this information – along with copies of the cheque and invoices – to Sam Smyth of the *Irish Independent*. In November 1996, under the headline 'The Minister, a Tycoon and the £200,000 House Bill', Smyth outlined the series of transactions between Dunne and Lowry, leading to the latter's resignation from cabinet.[66] Two weeks later, a report by Cliff Taylor in the *Irish Times* reported that Dunne had also given money [£1.1 million] to 'a Fianna Fáil politician'.[67] It fell to *The Phoenix* magazine to name the 'Fianna Fáil politician' as Charles Haughey.[68] More revelations followed. In August 1997, Frank Connolly of the *Sunday Business Post* revealed that developers had made numerous payments to Ray Burke, ultimately prompting his resignation as minister for foreign affairs.[69] And in September 1998, Jody Corcoran of the *Sunday Independent* revealed that another Haughey loyalist, former minister Pádraig Flynn, had received £50,000 from a building contractor in 1989.[70]

What followed in the wake of these journalistic revelations was a succession of government-appointed tribunals of inquiry to investigate payments to politicians and planning matters. While the McCracken Tribunal outlined the payments from Dunne to Haughey and Lowry and uncovered the tax-evading offshore Ansbacher accounts (whereby Des Traynor moved money for Haughey and many other wealthy individuals out of Ireland to the Cayman Islands and then back again), the Moriarty Tribunal found that Haughey had accepted money in return for political favours.[71] In its final report in 2012, the Mahon Tribunal, which inquired into planning and payments, found that corruption in Irish political life was 'both endemic and systematic … and its existence was widely known and widely tolerated'.[72] In his memoir, Conor Brady observed that, despite the best efforts of journalists, no media organisation succeeded in exposing the political corruption that was endemic in 1980s Ireland. As he noted,

> it took three sworn tribunals, invested with the powers of the High Court, six judges, 20 senior counsel, approximately 40 other lawyers and any number of court-authorised officials, working over 5 years, to find out what we now know about Haughey, his money and the circle of people who bankrolled him.[73]

Indeed, while the Moriarty Tribunal found that Haughey had received £9.1 million between 1979 and 1996, many of the donors were never identified.[74] In his take on the failure of journalism to expose Haughey and the systemic corruption and tax evasion in 1980s Ireland, Colm Tóibín noted that the near-absolute invisibility of this corruption created a consensus 'among certain journalists, economists, and a few politicians that the public debt and the annual budget deficit could only be dealt with by cuts in public spending'. As this consensus became political and economic orthodoxy, rumours about tax evasion were dismissed as left-wing fantasising.[75]

Haughey's humiliation was completed when, in May 1999, socialite Terry Keane appeared on RTÉ's *The Late Late Show* and told the nation that she and Haughey had been having an extramarital affair for nearly three decades. For many years, Keane had alluded to 'Sweetie', a prominent politician with whom she was supposedly involved, in her weekly *Sunday Independent* gossip column 'The Keane Edge'. But despite the affair being an open secret among politicians and journalists, it remained unknown to the public. As recalled by former government press secretary Frank Dunlop, 'from a media point of view the liaison was forbidden territory – not by diktat of Charlie but because nobody at the time believed that the relationship had anything to do with the day-to-day running of the country'.[76] The nearest it came to being revealed was when Joe Joyce and Peter Murtagh referred to Haughey's 'lengthy liaison with a married woman' in *The Boss*; the British gossip magazine *Private Eye* also made constant references to the affair.[77] The affair most likely influenced Haughey's decision to allow Fianna Fáil TDs to vote according to their conscience in the 1986 divorce referendum: compelling them to vote against the introduction of divorce risked exposure of his affair as a story of legitimate public interest.[78] Keane's *Late Late Show* revelations and her sale of the story to the *Sunday Times* were prompted by rumours that Kevin O'Connor – who had been prevented from publishing his investigation into Seán Doherty in the *Sunday Independent* – was writing a book that would expose the affair.[79]

'Zero risk'

In seeking to explain the failure of journalism to expose Haughey and his associates' behaviour, former *Irish Times* editor Conor Brady observed that 'some will blame the libel laws [or] the culture of secrecy in Irish public life'.[80] For her part, Mary Raftery observed that business in Ireland – and it was businessmen who had facilitated Haughey's lifestyle – operated behind an 'effective and fully functioning cloak of secrecy, and virtually all the doors are closed against anybody getting even the basic information concerning commercial activities'.[81] As with Raftery's attempt to highlight Haughey's financial relationship with Patrick Gallagher, any reportage that even mentioned suspicions of wrongdoing risked getting journalists into trouble. And, in the late 1980s, it was RTÉ that was in the firing line.

Having been returned as Taoiseach in 1987, Haughey appointed Ray Burke as minister for justice and communications. Unhappy at how RTÉ had covered the 1987 general election, on the night of the election count, Burke 'promised RTÉ personnel, off the air, that he would, to use his words, screw RTÉ'.[82] He subsequently introduced a cap on the amount of advertising revenue that the station could raise. Ostensibly, this was to facilitate the introduction of private broadcasting, but it crucified RTÉ financially. This attempt to batter RTÉ into submission created, as remembered by Mary Raftery, a situation where journalists 'were frequently frustrated by what we perceived as a lack of will by the station to stand up for itself and its journalism in the legal arena'. While this attempt to reach what one station executive described as a position of 'zero risk' could be viewed as 'refusing to squander public funds on court cases', in Raftery's view it led the station to be 'timid journalistically, shying away from stories which might land it in the courts in the first place'.[83]

This timidity – or political bullying of RTÉ – led to a situation where even the mere report of an ongoing investigation by statutory bodies led to libel threats against the station and disciplinary action being taken against journalists. In February 1989, the station's radio show *Farm Diary* reported that an unnamed Irish company had 'become involved in a meat fraud investigation' in the Middle East and that the government's export credit insurance scheme may have been misused to cover non-Irish meat. The programme's reporter, Pádraig Mannion, had spoken to sources in the meat and insurance industries in Ireland, New Zealand, and Australia and had – unsuccessfully – asked the company concerned for a comment.[84] The report provoked a letter from a legal firm acting on behalf of Anglo-Irish Beef Processors, part of Larry Goodman's beef-processing empire, Goodman International. Despite the fact that no company had been named in the report, Anglo-Irish Beef Processors claimed that it had been defamed. The 'zero risk' strategy at RTÉ immediately swung into operation, and the station aired a detailed retraction that described the story as 'completely false and without any foundation in fact'. It declared that there was 'no fraud investigation whatsoever' being carried out into the unnamed company and concluded with an apology to the unnamed company for 'the damage that has been caused by the untrue statements broadcast'.[85] RTÉ also initiated disciplinary proceedings against Pádraig Mannion and his editor, Joe Murray. Both were initially suspended without pay for a week; on appeal, this was altered to a reduction in their salary increments.[86] Similar to many such stories in the 1980s, Mannion's report was more accurate than inaccurate in that while the state export credit insurance scheme was being abused, the fraud investigation was occurring in Ireland, not in the Middle East.

It subsequently emerged that other media outlets, including the *Financial Times*, *Business and Finance*, and the *Irish Farmers Journal* had been investigating the same story but that they backed off after RTÉ's apology.[87] Ultimately, it would take a British television station to tell the full story. In May 1991, nearly two years after RTÉ's retraction, ITV aired a programme from Granada Television's *World in Action* series that levelled charges of fraud and malpractice against Goodman International. The programme was led by Irish journalist Susan O'Keeffe, who had worked as agri-business correspondent with the *Sunday Business Post* and had spent much of her time reporting on the fortunes of the beef sector. Having been alerted to irregularities within the Goodman Group, O'Keeffe was given time by the *Sunday Business Post* to dig deeper, but ultimately the paper declined to publish what she had unearthed at the time. Having met a Granada producer while he was in Dublin investigating the beef industry, O'Keeffe decided to join forces with Granada. While she was initially hired on a one-month contract, the programme took seven months and 120 interviews to complete. Entitled *Where's the Beef?* and illustrated with images of politicians and beef barons hanging from meat hooks, the programme alleged, among other issues, that bogus stamps were used in Goodman International processing factories to regrade substandard meat to qualify for EC subsidies and export to the Middle East.[88]

Called to give evidence at the tribunal of inquiry that was initiated after the programme, O'Keeffe was asked by tribunal chairman Liam Hamilton to reveal her sources. She declined to do so and observed that it was a journalist's job to 'air the information publicly and the authorities could then decide what to do with it'.[89] The Director of Public Prosecutions subsequently levelled charges of contempt of court against her. At the hearing, her defence team argued that the state had no evidence to present in support of the contempt charge since evidence given to a tribunal of inquiry could not be used against a person in a subsequent prosecution. In response, the prosecution sought to have the charge sheet amended and, when this was refused, to have the court stenographer, who had heard and recorded O'Keeffe's refusal to reveal her sources, compelled to give evidence of the alleged contempt. However, the relevant stenographer could not be located, and the judge hearing the case, Justice Dominic Lynch, eventually directed the jury to find O'Keeffe not guilty.[90]

As observed by Elaine Byrne, the Beef Tribunal was where 'the reciprocal relationship between politics and vested interests was placed under intense political, public, judicial and media scrutiny … when questions about political corruption, golden circles and the integrity of public officials were raised in a meaningful way'.[91] It also provided what then *Irish Times* editor Conor Brady termed as 'one of the most complex yet effective exercises in Irish journalism' – the appointment of that paper's theatre critic, Fintan O'Toole, to cover the tribunal:

> Fintan installed himself in Dublin Castle. There, day after day, week in week out, he cut through the proceedings like a hot knife through butter. He reduced complex arguments to simple English and summarised tortuous evidence in a way that somehow rendered it palatable. His coverage changed what might have been a dull, impenetrable and boring process into daily, accessible theatre. And it set a standard for others to follow – which they did.[92]

The tribunal's report vindicated Mannion's and O'Keeffe's investigations. It found that Goodman International had perpetrated a substantial abuse of export credit insurance by including large quantities of non-Irish beef in its exports to Iraq, that a major fraud investigation had been launched into two Goodman plants in Ireland, that the age and quality of much of the meat exported to Iraq was not as stated on the commercial contracts, and that the group had a deliberate policy to evade paying income tax by paying staff under the counter.[93] Referring to the political and business climate that tolerated and facilitated such corruption, O'Keeffe observed that Irish people were conditioned to accept 'a kind of silent situation [where] it's much more comfortable to say nothing than it is to stand up and speak out'.[94] But in the 1990s, this situation was to change gradually and then dramatically. While the various tribunals of inquiry that emanated primarily from journalistic endeavours delivered damning verdicts on the behaviour of the political and business establishments during the 1980s, that other bastion of twentieth-century Ireland – the Catholic Church – also began to witness more journalistic scrutiny directed towards it. The appalling vista that was revealed was beyond belief.

Notes

1 *Irish Times*, 8 Dec. 1979, p. 8. In 1986, Haughey and his adviser Martin Mansergh produced a book of Haughey's speeches entitled *The Spirit of the Nation* (Cork, 1986).
2 V. Browne, 'What's bugging Haughey', *Magill*, Jul. 1982, 6–9, at p. 6.
3 *Irish Times*, 24 Dec. 1983, p. 12; from Breandán Ó hEithir's review of *The Boss*.
4 Haughey served as taoiseach from Dec. 1979 to Jun. 1981, Mar. 1982 to Dec. 1982, and Mar. 1987 to Feb. 1992. J. Joyce and P. Murtagh, *The Boss* (Dublin, 1983).
5 Joyce and Murphy, *The Boss* (1997 edition), inside blurb.
6 G. Kerrigan, 'Charlie and the press gang', *Magill*, Feb. 1983, 6–8.
7 *Irish Times*, 12 Sep. 1980, p. 1. The paper was acquired by Vincent Browne and Tony Ryan in 1983, Independent Newspapers acquired 29.9 per cent ownership in 1990, and it ceased publication in 2011.
8 *Sunday Tribune*, 27 Dec. 1981, p. 1.
9 *Irish Times*, 22 Feb. 1982, p. 10.
10 *Irish Times*, 29 Sep. 2012, p. B1.
11 Joyce and Murtagh, *The Boss*, pp. 194–5. For differing perspectives on the appropriateness of the tapping of Arnold's and Kennedy's telephones, see *Irish Times*, 29 Sep. 2012, p. B1, and 10 Oct. 2012, p. 14.
12 *Irish Times*, 26 Jan. 1983, p, 1.

13 C. Brady, *Up with the Times* (Dublin, 2005), p. 192.
14 *Irish Times*, 11 Jun. 2005, p. C3.
15 The *Sunday Independent* published excerpts from the transcript on 11 Mar. 1974, pp. 1 and 2.
16 *Sunday Tribune*, 3 Oct. 1982, p. 1.
17 *Sunday Independent*, 11 Mar. 1974, p. 2.
18 Joyce and Murtagh, *The Boss*, p. 263. For more on John Feeney, see G. Kerrigan, 'The magic of John Feeney', *Magill*, December 1983, 16–24.
19 Joyce and Murtagh, *The Boss*, p. 266.
20 *Irish Times*, 27 Dec. 2013, p. 12.
21 K. O'Connor, *Sweetie: How Haughey Spent the Money* (Dublin, 1999), p. 29.
22 O'Connor, *Sweetie*, p. 28. Hand was replaced as editor by Aengus Fanning in Jan. 1984. Hand played a part in the ending of the hijacking of an Aer Lingus flight at Le Touquet airport in France in 1981. The hijacker, an ex-Trappist monk, demanded that the 'Third Secret of Fatima' be published in the *Sunday Independent*. Hand arranged for a special edition of the paper to be flown to Le Touquet. When the hijacker opened the door of the plane to receive the paper, French troops stormed and secured the plane. See A. Reynolds, *My Autobiography* (Dublin, 2009), pp. 122–4.
23 O'Connor, *Sweetie*, p. 32.
24 Joyce and Murtagh, *The Boss*, pp. 271–5. See *Irish Times*, 28 Oct. 1982, pp. 6, 8 and 13.
25 Joyce and Murtagh, *The Boss*, pp. 272 and 302.
26 *Sunday Independent*, 11 Mar. 1974, p. 2.
27 *Irish Times*, 21 Jan. 1983, p. 4.
28 *Irish Times*, 22 Jan. 1983, p. 6.
29 Joyce and Murtagh, *The Boss*, p. 340. For the 'political obituary', see *Irish Press*, 27 Jan. 1983, pp. 4–5.
30 *Irish Times*, 19 Jan. 2015, p. 14.
31 *Irish Times*, 7 Apr. 1984, p. 1. Kennedy was elected as a TD for the Progressive Democrats in 1987 but lost the seat in 1989.
32 *Irish Times*, 13 Jan. 1987, p. 8.
33 As a result of this settlement, the minister for justice who had authorised the initial tap on Browne's telephone (Paddy Cooney) took legal action against the state on the basis that the settlement may have implied wrongdoing on his part. This case was settled by the state; see *Irish Times*, 29 Oct. 1998, p. 4.
34 *Irish Times*, 2 Apr. 1997, p. 14.
35 *Sunday Independent*, 6 Apr. 1997, p. 15.
36 V. Browne, 'Arms Crisis 1970: the inside story', *Magill*, May, Jun., and Jul. 1980.
37 *Irish Times*, 23 May 1983, pp. 1 and 6.
38 *Sunday Independent*, 13 Apr. 1997, p. 31.
39 *Sunday Business Post*, 13 Sep. 1992, pp. 1 and 5.
40 *Irish Times*, 14 Dec. 1979, p. 7.
41 *Irish Times*, 22 May 1999, p. 14.
42 M. Viney, 'Y', in A. Whittaker (ed.), *Bright Brilliant Days: Douglas Gageby and the Irish Times* (Dublin, 2006), pp. 155–8, at p. 157.
43 Correspondence with Frank McDonald. See *Irish Times*, 14 Dec. 1979, p. 7, and 9 Feb. 1983, p. 8.
44 K. Myers, 'By that sin fell the angels', in A. Whittaker (ed.), *Bright Brilliant Days: Douglas Gageby and the Irish Times* (Dublin, 2006), pp. 119–21.
45 Brady, *Up with the Times*, p. 191.

46 V. Browne, 'What's bugging Haughey?', *Magill*, Jul. 1982, 6–9, at p. 6.
47 J. Waters, *Jiving at the Crossroads* (Belfast, 1991), pp. 117–18.
48 *Irish Times*, 20 Oct. 2003, p. 14.
49 Brady, *Up with the Times*, p. 189.
50 Brady, *Up with the Times*, p. 188.
51 *The Phoenix*, 7 Jan. 1983, pp. 25–6. Modelled on *Private Eye*, *The Phoenix* was established by John Mulcahy and was so named because it arose from the ashes of *Hibernia* and the *Sunday Tribune*.
52 *Evening Press*, 28 Jan. 1983, p. 7.
53 *Irish Times*, 5 Mar. 1999, p. 7. The money used to pay off the debt came from Haughey's business contacts.
54 *Evening Press*, 1 Feb. 1983, p. 3.
55 *Sunday Business Post*, 24 Dec. 2006, p. 8.
56 B. Ryan, *With a Tap on the Knee: Memoirs of an Irish Banker* (Dublin, 2001), p. 144.
57 *Irish Times*, 20 Dec. 2006, p. 6.
58 *Irish Times*, 15 Jun. 2006, p. 16 and 18 Jan. 1993, p. 4. See *In Dublin*, 19 Mar. 1982, pp. 12–17 and *Irish Times*, 23 Mar. 2006, p. 18 for Raftery's profiles of Gallagher.
59 Correspondence with Frank McDonald. See *Irish Times*, 27 Sep.–28 Oct. 1982.
60 *Irish Independent*, 31 Jul. 1989, pp. 1 and 8.
61 *Irish Independent*, 21 Apr. 2000, p. 9. The story was withdrawn from the city special edition of 22 Feb. 1993.
62 *Irish Times*, 12 Jul. 1993, p. 1.
63 *Irish Times*, 14 Jul. 1993, p. 7.
64 Correspondence with Frank McDonald.
65 *Irish Times*, 17 May 1994, p. 13.
66 *Irish Independent*, 29 Nov. 1996, p. 1. See S. Smyth, *Thanks a Million, Big Fella* (Dublin, 1997).
67 *Irish Times*, 14 Dec. 1996, p. 1.
68 *The Phoenix*, 6 Dec. 1996, p. 3.
69 *Sunday Business Post*, 10 Aug. 1997, p. 1.
70 *Irish Times*, 8 Oct. 1997, p. 1; *Sunday Independent*, 20 and 27 Sep. 1998, pp. 1.
71 The tribunal found that Haughey had encouraged the Revenue Commissioners to meet Dunne to discuss the tax liability of the Dunnes Stores Trust; it also found that Haughey had granted passports to people connected to Saudi Arabian businessman Mahmoud Fustok, who had paid him £50,000.
72 *Irish Times*, 23 Mar. 2012, p. 1. For more on the tribunals, see G. Murphy, 'Payments for no political response? Political corruption and tribunals of inquiry in Ireland, 1991–2003', in J. Garrand and J. Newell (eds), *Scandals in Past and Contemporary Politics* (Manchester, 2006), pp. 91–105.
73 Brady, *Up with the Times*, p. 188.
74 *Sunday Business Post*, 24 Dec. 2006, p. 6.
75 *Sunday Independent*, 10 Oct. 1999, p. 18.
76 F. Dunlop, *Yes, Taoiseach* (Dublin, 2004), p. 182.
77 Joyce and Murtagh, *The Boss*, p. 102; for *Private Eye* references, see Dunlop, *Yes, Taoiseach*, pp. 182–3.
78 In reality, the party campaigned against divorce. In a statement, Haughey declared himself 'personally against' the introduction of divorce: see *Irish Independent*, 21 May 1986, p. 1.
79 O'Connor, *Sweetie*, pp. 44–51 and 85–90.

80 Brady, *Up with the Times*, p. 187.
81 *Irish Times*, 18 Jan. 1993, p. 4.
82 DED, vol. 399 (col. 1585), 7 Jun. 1990. The speaker was Fine Gael TD, Jim Mitchell.
83 *Irish Times*, 5 Jul. 2007, p. 16.
84 *Irish Times*, 20 Oct. 2003, p. 14.
85 *Irish Times*, 5 Aug. 1994, p. 10.
86 The Labour Court later ruled that RTÉ had acted 'too harshly' given the 'unquestioned record of the staff involved'. *Irish Times*, 30 Jun. 1990, p. A12. RTÉ apologised for its actions after Murray had died. *Irish Times*, 16 Jun. 2012, p. 5.
87 *Irish Times*, 20 Oct. 2003, p. 14.
88 *Irish Times*, 3 Sep. 1994, p. 2 and 14 May 1991, p. 1.
89 *Irish Times*, 3 Dec. 1992, p. 1.
90 *Irish Times*, 28 Jan. 1995, p. 13. O'Keeffe was elected as a Labour Party senator in 2011.
91 E. Byrne, *Political Corruption in Ireland: A Crooked Harp?* (Manchester, 2012), p. 107.
92 Brady, *Up With the Times*, p. 223.
93 For a summary of the tribunal's findings, see *Irish Times*, 6 Aug. 1994, p. 4. See also *Sunday Independent*, 7 Aug. 1994, p. 14. For an account of the Beef Tribunal, see F. O'Toole, *Meanwhile Back at the Ranch: The Politics of Irish Beef* (London, 1995).
94 *Irish Times*, 3 Sep. 1994, p. 2.

12

An appalling vista

Journalism operates on the assumption that almost nothing is known, that everything has to be found out [while] the church operates on the opposite assumption: that everything that matters in known, has been revealed to us, and needs only to be interpreted correctly and acted upon.[1]

— Fintan O'Toole in the *Irish Times*, 1991

The seemingly endless revelations of wrongdoing that flowed from Ben Dunne's escapade in Florida exposed what many people – not least journalists – had suspected all along: that there existed a golden circle of politicians and professionals who viewed themselves as above the law. Indeed, they operated as a shadow state, out of sight of regulatory authorities and protected by the omertà of loyalty and silence that was crucial to keeping their activities invisible. It was this omertà of loyalty and silence that had prevented journalists from exposing corruption for many years. No matter how many journalists suspected that corruption existed in Irish society, there was simply no evidence – or not enough *hard* evidence – to expose what was really going on. And, when questions were asked, institutions simply closed ranks and denied everything. Corruption was, it seemed, at best a journalistic conspiracy or, at worst, journalistic bias against senior politicians and businesses. The tribunals of inquiry that flowed from the Dunne incident in 1992 finally exposed all – and, arguably, gave an impetus to whistle-blowers to provide more and more information to journalists. As the 1990s unfolded, more attention was focused on the banking institutions that had facilitated tax evasion for over a decade. In many ways, the 1990s was a decade when crime – in all its guises – came to dominate the journalistic agenda. To state that the political and banking scandals prompted a sense of cynicism and distrust of basic institutions among the public would be an understatement – but worse was to follow.

That other institution central to Irish society – the Catholic Church – also witnessed its relationship with journalism change utterly. In the early 1990s, the revelations that a priest and a bishop had fathered children were greeted with incredulity, with much anger being directed towards the media in the guise of journalists being accused of pushing an anti-church agenda. But, by the mid-1990s, these transgressions paled into insignificance as the appalling vista of child rape, and its systemic concealment by senior church figures, was revealed. The catalogue of abuse and cover-up that unfolded was followed by a tidal wave of public revulsion. The questions directed at journalists were similar to those directed at them at the time of the Haughey revelations: how had such misbehaviour remained hidden for so long and why had journalists not uncovered and exposed it? The answers were the same: the omertà of loyalty and silence that had long protected Haughey and his ilk was also present in the higher echelons of the church. Any critical journalism in relation to the church was inevitably denounced as church-bashing and met with a closing of ranks. And, while many members of the hierarchy were aware of the abuse, they consciously chose to hide its existence. The church was, after all, the definer of behaviour and morality: if its priests were seen to be abusing children, how could it credibly preach on matters sexual? However, this gamble backfired dramatically: while the existence and extent of the abuse appalled many, it was the systemic institutional cover-up of the abuse – with the result that abusers were free to continue abusing children elsewhere – that spelled the death knell for many people's faith in the church. As pews emptied, income plummeted, and the credibility of the hierarchy dissipated, there still existed the notion in some quarters that all this was somehow the fault of journalists: if they had not revealed the abuse then everything would have carried on as normal. But the 1990s in Ireland were anything but normal.

Dishing the DIRT

Whatever factors had ensured the invisibility of corruption in Ireland up to the advent of the tribunals of inquiry in the 1990s, it seems that the unveiling of wrongdoing by those tribunals encouraged greater candour on the part of whistle-blowers. The 1990s was a *decennium horribilis* for Irish banking, with insiders passing information to journalists on the myriad tax-evasion techniques used by banks to defraud the state of tax revenue. In January 1998, RTÉ's Special Correspondent, Charlie Bird, was contacted by a trade-union official who told him that the National Irish Bank (NIB) was offering access to an offshore investment scheme through an Isle of Man company called Clerical Medical International (CMI). According to the source, while customers' money initially moved offshore, it returned shortly afterwards to accounts identified only by a number. The net effect of this was that while customers could easily access their money (much of which was undeclared income), the Revenue Commissioners were prevented from establishing who owned the money. By August 1994, some £30 million had been invested in the scheme via 173 accounts, with NIB charging a hefty commission to facilitate the tax evasion. Having discussed the tip-off with RTÉ's director of news, Ed Mulhall, Bird teamed up with RTÉ's economics editor, George Lee, and found a source in the bank willing to talk. From documents supplied by this source, it quickly became clear that the bank had been targeting 'high net worth individuals' among its customer base – particularly those with undeclared income. The story, aired on RTÉ News's *Six-One* on 23 January 1998, revealed that NIB had approached around 180 of its wealthiest customers, offering them access to the tax-evasion scheme. It also revealed that the Revenue Commissioners were investigating the bank's activities.[2]

The bank's response was telling: it went straight to the High Court and secured an interim injunction that prevented RTÉ from making any more disclosures. While NIB argued that RTÉ's reports could damage customer confidence in the bank, RTÉ argued that tax-evasion activities should be exposed to public scrutiny. When the High Court later ruled in RTÉ's favour, NIB appealed to the Supreme Court, which again found that the story was in the public interest. While the station was awaiting this Supreme Court verdict, Bird and Lee continued their investigations. Their NIB source had given them documents that showed that not only was NIB defrauding the state, it was also stealing from its own customers by means of loading accounts with increased interest rates and fees. By this stage, the source was willing to give an interview – provided anonymity was secured through facial and vocal alteration. During the course of the interview, the source confirmed that NIB had deliberately targeted customers it suspected of having undeclared income for the CMI scheme. In the course of a second interview, the source confirmed that interest-loading and fee-adding activities were commonplace at the bank, with league tables of high and low performing branches being circulated by senior management. Even for an industry not renowned for its tact, league tables of theft from customer accounts was a new departure. This report, aired on 25 March 1998, prompted a special cabinet meeting that convened one hour after the broadcast. Later that evening, the government announced a series of investigations into NIB.

But, just as it seemed as if RTÉ had concluded its NIB exposé, it made one more revelation, one that moved the story into the political realm. Access to the CMI tax-evasion scheme had been provided by NIB's Financial Advice and Services division. It just so happened that newly elected Fianna Fáil TD, Beverley Cooper-Flynn, daughter of former minister, Pádraig Flynn, had worked as a manager in this division. In June 1998, RTÉ alleged that Cooper-Flynn had told retired farmer James Howard that if he invested in a CMI product, the Revenue Commissioners would never find his undeclared income. Cooper-Flynn immediately sued RTÉ for defamation. During the case, RTÉ produced three NIB customers who testified that Cooper-Flynn had encouraged them to invest in CMI investment products as a tax-evasion mechanism. The jury found that, while RTÉ had not proved that Cooper-Flynn had advised Howard about tax evasion, it had demonstrated that she had so advised others and so her reputation had not been damaged by the report. Legal costs – estimated at €2.4 million – were awarded against Cooper-Flynn. She subsequently lost a Supreme Court appeal, and RTÉ sought to have her declared bankrupt, which, if granted, would have forced her to vacate her Dáil seat.[3] In June 2007, she paid a settlement of €1.2 million to RTÉ, and the bankruptcy proceedings were dropped. Ultimately, NIB was forced to pay €64 million in back taxes, penalties, and compensation to customers while customers who had invested in CMI products paid an additional €60 million in charges and penalties to the Revenue Commissioners.

At the same time as RTÉ was revealing the inner workings of one bank, Liam Collins of the *Sunday Independent* was preparing to expose the activities of another. On no less conspicuous a day than 1 April 1998, Collins was contacted by a whistle-blower who provided him with documents that demonstrated the level of tax evasion being facilitated by AIB – this time by means of bogus non-resident accounts. In 1986, the government had introduced the inelegantly named DIRT (Deposit Interest Retention Tax) measure that compelled banks to collect a 10 per cent tax, payable on interest that accrued on people's savings. However, a clause included in the measure exempted the accounts of people, such as emigrants, who were not resident in the state. Thus began the phenomenon of the 'bogus non-resident account' as tens of thousands of ordinary citizens, who carried out daily or weekly transactions in their local banks, declared themselves non-resident in the state. This fallacy was facilitated by all the major banks so as to ensure that none of them lost market share. The height of farce was reached when one AIB customer declared their address as 'Main Street, New York'.[4]

Collins's story – supported by News Editor Willie Kealy and Editor Aengus Fanning – was headlined 'AIB Had £600m in "Bogus" Accounts' and revealed that the bank's 53,000 bogus non-resident accounts contained £600 million, which was described in internal bank documents as 'funny money'.[5] It subsequently transpired that while the Revenue Commissioners and the Central Bank were aware of the problem for several years, no investigation had been initiated because of a fear that the money would simply be moved out of the country. During August and September 1999, the Dáil's Public Account Committee – chaired by Fine Gael's Jim Mitchell – held hearings into the evasion at which it emerged that while AIB was the biggest offender, bogus non-resident accounts were widespread across all financial institutions. Shamed into action, the Revenue Commissioners were forced to act: while the financial institutions paid €225 million in interest and penalties, those who held the bogus accounts were also pursued and paid €613 million. All in all, Collins's story netted €838 million for the state and exposed the tax-evasion techniques practised by middle-class Ireland. It was, it seemed, open season on financial institutions – courtesy of whistle-blowers. That same year, Ursula Halligan of *Magill* revealed that insurance company Irish Life had engaged in turning over or 'churning' customer accounts over a protracted period of time. 'Churning' – the creation of excessive transactions on an account for the purpose of generating commission – was revealed to have occurred from 1983 onwards, and *Magill* published internal Irish Life documents that indicated that while management knew of the practice since 1992 it had continued for another two years.[6] In response, Irish Life denied that 'churning' was endemic within its business and undertook to compensate any affected customers. All these revelations indicated that institutions once almost impenetrable to journalists were, in the tribunal climate of the 1990s, susceptible to journalistic scrutiny.

Law-and-order news

Also more susceptible to journalistic scrutiny during the 1990s was the Garda Síochána. Throughout the 1980s, more space and airtime had been devoted to crime – particularly the type of crime that stemmed from the problems of social exclusion and disadvantage caused by the clearance of inner-city Dublin tenements and the creation of inadequately serviced sprawling suburban estates. Anti-social behaviour, joyriding, and the growing problem of heroin became the focus of much crime journalism, as did the emergence of criminal gangs involved in the drugs trade. The activities of the Dunne family – widely credited with introducing heroin to Ireland – were profiled in *Magill*, as was Martin Cahill, the Dublin criminal known as 'The General'.[7] This prompted RTÉ's flagship current-affairs programme, *Today Tonight*, to also profile Cahill. The footage, preserved for prosperity on YouTube, shows reporter Brendan O'Brien pursuing Cahill around the street of Dublin, with the two men in turn being followed by detectives on foot and in an unmarked police car.[8] This new approach to crime reporting – profiling and doorstepping criminals for comment – was a tactic that gained much traction in 1990s.

Another tactic adopted by crime journalists in the 1990s was the acknowledged use of criminals as sources of information. The two journalists who led the field in this regard were Paul Williams of the *Sunday World* and Veronica Guerin of the *Sunday Independent*. For many journalists, the Garda Síochána was their only source of information on crime – a dependency that was brought into sharp relief in December 1995 when the *Irish Times* revealed that a multimillion drugs consignment that had been portrayed by the force as a drugs bust was actually a compromised entrapment operation. Having engaged in a 'controlled importation' of the consignment, the force – as agreed with the targeted gang – placed thirteen tonnes of cannabis in a parked lorry on the outskirts of Urlingford, County Kilkenny. When the gang failed to show up to collect the consignment, the force decided to call in journalists and 'seize' the drugs – without telling them that it had imported the drugs in the first place. The initial headlines – '£150m Drug Swoop as Dublin Gang Foiled' (*Irish Independent*), '£150m Cannabis Haul May Have Been Bound for UK' (*Irish Times*) – were positive.[9] But the following month, John Maher of the *Irish Times* revealed that the force itself had imported the cannabis and then staged the seizure for the benefit of the media after the Dublin gang had not shown up to collect the consignment.[10]

This overdependence on the Garda Síochána for information on crime led some journalists to talk to criminals as well as the police as a matter of routine. This, in turn, led to a new genre of crime reporting that centred on reports of the interaction that took place between journalist and criminal. This had the unfortunate effect of sometimes situating the journalist as a participant in events, rather than an observer of them. The use of the first person ushered in a more intimate and involved style of writing that was very different to the detached style of crime reporting that had dominated crime journalism until then. This new genre also involved the use of code names to write about criminals without naming them. Thus the public became accustomed to reading and hearing about the nefarious activities of such individuals as the General, the Viper, the Coach, the Penguin, the Badger, the Warehouseman, the Gambler, the Monk, and the Boxer. While these code names were justified in terms of safeguarding newspapers from libel proceedings, they tended to bring a touch of drama to the reportage of organised crime. However, the 'code names as libel defence' argument was shown to have merit in 2006 when two Dublin criminals sued the now-defunct *Star Sunday* for defamation. The men claimed that the code names used by the newspaper in relation to them were the nicknames they had been known by in their school days. The men's case – that people would identify them by remembering them from school, thus damaging their reputation – was not accepted by the jury.[11]

Whatever about code names glamorising crime, the shifting focus of crime reporting away from the traditional angle of reporting crime as event – with the attendant question of who was responsible – towards reporting what criminals did with their ill-gotten gains was more dangerous. While journalists had investigated the wealth of certain politicians, doing the same for violent criminals was a new departure. Similarly, the inclusion of personal and intimate details of the lives of criminals – their relationships, their love lives, where they lived, the type of cars they drove, what schools their children attended, and where they went on holidays – was untested territory and was resented within the criminal underworld.

The brutal murder of *Sunday Independent* journalist Veronica Guerin in June 1996 by the very criminals she was writing about was a watershed moment. Between 1990 and 1996, Guerin had worked on a freelance basis for the *Sunday Business Post*, the *Sunday Tribune*, and the *Sunday Independent* and was responsible for breaking a series of exclusive stories. In September 1992, she came into possession of a recording of illegally intercepted telephone calls between Fine Gael leader John Bruton and his party colleagues Maurice Manning, Deputy Leader Michael Noonan, and the party's press officer, Peter White. For publishing excerpts of the calls – which related to Seán Doherty's revelation that Charles Haughey had been aware of the tapping of journalists' telephones in 1982 – the *Sunday Business Post*'s editor, Damien Kiberd, and Guerin herself, were fined a total of £1,000.[12] Having moved to the *Sunday Tribune*, Guerin discovered that Bishop Eamon Casey, who had left Ireland in controversial circumstances, was living in Quito, Ecuador. Having tracked him down, he agreed to grant her a series of interviews. Published over three weeks, the series caused a 40 per cent surge in the paper's circulation.[13] It also enabled Guerin to move to the higher-profile *Sunday Independent*, where she broke the story of the delay within the office of the Attorney General in processing the extradition of Fr Brendan Smyth to Northern Ireland to face charges of paedophilia – a scandal that would eventually bring down a government.[14] It was at the *Sunday Independent* that Guerin developed a public profile as a crime journalist – a profile that was utilised by the paper in its marketing strategy.[15]

Guerin's murder prompted a belated debate on the function of crime journalism. Was it to personally confront violent criminals on their doorsteps on the basis of information received from sources with their own agenda, namely other criminals and the Garda Síochána? Was it to bring criminals to justice via the media if the Garda Síochána was incapable of securing the evidence to convict them in court? Or was it, as Vincent Browne argued, to hold public institutions, the police, the court system, and the prison system to account in their handling of the crime issue?[16] Whatever the answer, whether crime journalism – a potent mix of detective work, intelligence gathering, and writing about dangerous individuals – should be the preserve of one high-profile journalist or be carried out by an anonymous investigative team to diffuse the risks involved was a debate that got lost in the heat of accusation and counter-accusation in the aftermath of Guerin's murder by a Dublin criminal gang in June 1996.[17]

It is, however, possible to conclude that the new genre of crime journalism that developed in the 1990s had one blind spot: the misconduct of some members of the Garda Síochána. It is instructive that the corruption within the Donegal division of the force was revealed not by crime journalists but by two Dáil deputies – Jim Higgins of Fine Gael and Brendan Howlin of the Labour Party – who used Dáil privilege to bring the matter to public attention. The attempted framing of individuals for the killing of cattle dealer Richie Barron, the planting and 'discovering' of drugs in a public house, the imprisonment of the pub owner on trumped-up charges, and the planning and 'discovering' of explosives to boost the promotion prospects of officers in the division all escaped the attention of the country's crime journalists.[18] The findings of the Morris Tribunal – set up to investigate the affair – that 'proper discipline has been lost from An Garda Síochána' was taken by many as an indicator that crime journalism had taken its eye off the ball.[19] As John Waters put it, newspapers had opted for 'certain "sexy" and potentially sensational elements in order to steal an edge over the competition … Crime exposés sell newspapers; exposés of injustice, as a rule, do not.'[20] But, as the century came to a close, one injustice was dramatically righted by the intervention of a crime journalist.

In February 1999, Barry O'Kelly of *The Star* revealed how two judges – Hugh Flaherty of the Supreme Court and Cyril Kelly of the Circuit Court – had, in a very unorthodox fashion, facilitated the early release of Philip Sheedy, an architect who had been convicted of dangerous driving causing death but who had served only thirteen months of a four-year sentence. O'Kelly's story prompted a public outcry: both judges resigned, and Sheedy returned voluntarily to prison.[21] Looking back on the saga, O'Kelly noted that '*The Star* deserves a lot of credit for giving me the time to work on the story, running with such legally sensitive material and for giving it such prominence.'[22] Other journalists who broke controversial stories were not so lucky. Some years previously, Richard Balls of the *Sunday Press* revealed that gardaí had, on two occasions, instructed an unnamed junior minister to leave a cruising area of Dublin's Phoenix Park. While the politician – Emmet Stagg – subsequently identified himself, much criticism was directed at Balls and the *Sunday Press* for breaking the story. While the paper's editor, Michael Keane, defended it on the basis that while Irish journalism did 'not delve into the private lives of politicians when there is no public interest factor involved [this was] a public act in an area of a public park', Balls felt the story 'haunted' him in his later career.[23]

Clerical errors

It was, however, the exposé of historical injustices that had most impact in the 1990s. Since the late 1970s, the Catholic hierarchy was much aware of the changing relationship – sometimes imperceptible, sometimes starkly obvious – that was evolving between the church and journalism. Editors were also aware of the scepticism towards the church that was present among a younger generation of journalists. Addressing reporters prior to the visit of Pope John Paul II to Ireland in 1979, *Irish Times* Editor Douglas Gageby warned them that he did not want any 'fashionable liberals sneering at the Pope', and, as recalled by Olivia O'Leary, most journalists 'tried to give the Pope a chance'. O'Leary's own resolve broke when – at a rain-soaked racecourse in Limerick – the Pope 'effectively told married women to go back to their homes and have children'.[24] In her report in the following day's paper, O'Leary noted the Pope's 'uncompromising approach to divorce, to contraception, to the position of woman as mother and child-bearer'.[25]

Such reportage did not go unchallenged. In 1981, Bishop Brendan Comiskey (then an auxiliary bishop of Dublin) hinted at the disquiet felt among the hierarchy that journalists were beginning to treat the church as it did other institutions: with objectivity and not with deference. As Comiskey put it, journalists were 'likely to view any spokesperson for the government or the Catholic Church as handing out propaganda, something in favour of the government or the Catholic Church. The journalist then sees his or her task as that of bringing a note of "objectivity" into the proceedings'.[26] Throughout the early to mid-1980s, several issues – the sacking of teacher Eileen Flynn for becoming pregnant outside of wedlock (1982), the insertion of an anti-abortion clause into the Constitution (1983), family-planning legislation (1985), and a referendum on divorce (1986) – strained church–state and church–media relations.[27] By this time, many of the generation of journalists who had begun their careers at *In Dublin*, *Hot Press*, and *Magill* had migrated to mainstream media. Less deferential towards politics and religion than previous generations of journalists, they had a different perspective on church–media relations, best summed up by Fintan O'Toole, who observed that 'journalism operates on the assumption that almost nothing is known, that everything has to be found out [while] the church operates on the opposite assumption: that everything that matters is known, has been revealed to us, and needs only to be interpreted correctly and acted upon'.[28]

It was a generational clash – represented by a greater journalistic willingness to discuss many formally taboo topics – that the hierarchy sought to counter. In 1983, Bishop Kevin McNamara (Kerry) criticised the manner in which 'certain topics … are regarded as suitable topics for chat shows on radio and TV, in which speakers of little or no qualifications parade with confidence the most varying and contradictory opinions'.[29] The following year, Bishop Jeremiah Newman (Limerick) observed that there existed 'a cancer of criticism and dissent, a cynicism about the faith' within the media.[30] But, throughout the 1980s, it was the Bishop of Ferns, Brendan Comiskey – chair of the hierarchy's Commission for Communication – that led the charge against what he viewed as irresponsible journalism. In 1985, he noted that several journalists to whom he had spoken had 'expressed grave concern about the state of the profession in Ireland'.[31] He also observed that the press ranked second-last in a survey that measured people's confidence in national institutions, and that two-thirds of people – surveyed for a separate study on religious beliefs – believed that 'the Catholic Church is often wrongly criticised in the media'.[32] Every institution was, he commented, 'constantly reminded by the media of the need for self-appraisal, self-criticism': it was time, he concluded, 'that the press in Ireland took as critical a look at its own profession and its operation as it does at all other aspects of life in Ireland'. Comiskey also queried how journalists could be objective on the issue of abortion after the NUJ had passed a motion criticising the legal action initiated by SPUC against Dublin's Well Woman Centre.[33] The only journalist to publicly counter Comiskey's statement was Michael O'Toole of the *Irish Press*. In a letter to the *Irish Times*, O'Toole queried whether Comiskey 'would regard membership of, say, Opus Dei or the Knights of Columbanus as interfering with the objectivity of a journalist's report on Church and political matters to *all* the citizens of Ireland?' Not mincing his words, O'Toole described Comiskey's analysis of journalism in Ireland as 'shallow, repetitive, and in many cases unconvincingly argued': he was, O'Toole concluded, 'an apologist and propagandist for the Roman Catholic Church'.[34]

In 1988, Comiskey accused the media of being 'determined to use the Church as it uses all other organisations and individuals, in the relentless pursuit, not of truth, but of money'. Comiskey's outburst was occasioned by several national newspapers publishing photographs of prominent church leaders leaving a private viewing of Martin Scorsese's film *The Last Temptation of Christ*, which Film Censor, Sheamus Smith, had come under pressure to ban for its supposedly blasphemous content. The result of the photographs being published was, as Comiskey saw it – 'with the unwilling co-operation of Church people' – huge publicity for the film. There existed, he concluded, 'a conspiracy by the entertainment and media industries to use the Church in an attempt to increase box office receipts and newspaper sales'.[35]

By the beginning of the 1990s, other bishops were stressing the idea that there existed a journalistic bias against the church. In February 1991, Bishop Joseph Duffy (Clogher) declared that too often in the media the church was represented 'as a kind of an old fashioned power system which rams dogmas down people's throats [and that] the values and the support systems of the Church needed to be protected against the onslaught of mass media values'.[36] To the newer generation of journalists the message was clear: as Fintan O'Toole put it, 'since the privileged interpreters of traditional wisdom are the Pope and his bishops, the message is clear: those who do not agree with us should shut up'.[37] Later that year, the *Irish Press*'s television critic, Declan Lynch – who had previously written for *Hot Press* – prompted a near boycott of the paper when, in reviewing an interview of pop singer Madonna by the BBC's Terry Wogan, he noted that she had 'incurred the displeasure of the Vatican over some of her imagery, but then those men, no slouches at iconography themselves, must look to their own interests'. Lynch concluded his piece by expressing the hope that 'if the singing Madonna ever has a son, he will give less trouble than the precocious Nazarene'.[38] What began with a handful of readers writing to the paper to complain, and the *Irish Press* printing an apology to readers for any offence caused, took on a new dimension when

Bishop Comiskey suggested a boycott of the paper in his weekly column in the *Irish Catholic*. Comiskey denounced Lynch and the *Irish Press* as 'blasphemers' and suggested that one way of objecting was for people to withdraw support from the paper 'by ceasing to purchase it or advertise in it'.[39] The belt of the crozier could still command a response in the early 1990s. *Irish Press* management instructed Lynch's department head to respond personally to every letter of complaint received.[40] Responding to the affair, Nuala O'Faolain, writing in the *Irish Times*, criticised the 'vehemence' of Comiskey's call and observed that 'mockery is the weapon of the powerless. Maybe if one side didn't bully the other, the other wouldn't mock in return.'[41]

Fears of a similar backlash prompted extreme caution when, in 1992, the *Irish Times* investigated allegations that a prominent bishop had fathered a child. The *Irish Times* had, earlier that year, risked legal sanction when Niall Kiely and Carol Coulter revealed that the Attorney General, Harry Whelehan, had – by virtue of the 1983 anti-abortion constitution clause – secured a High Court interim injunction to prevent a fourteen-year-old female rape victim from leaving the state to secure a termination. The case had been heard *in camera*, and, if it published details, the *Irish Times* risked a heavy fine or the imprisonment of its editor, Conor Brady. Nonetheless, the details of the hearing were published under the byline of Niall Kiely, as a low-key, one-column story below the fold on page one.[42] By the time the case proper came before the High Court, it was a matter of public controversy. When the court, again *in camera*, acceded to the request from the Attorney General that 'Miss X', as the child came to be known, be compelled, under threat of imprisonment, to remain in the state for ten months, the public outcry was deafening.[43] Protesters marched on the Dáil, and one Fianna Fáil deputy telephoned Brady to berate him 'for causing the whole thing'.[44] Despite the determination of the *Irish Times* to report on the X Case, taking on the might of the Catholic Church in terms of exposing the familial activities of a popular bishop was a quite different proposition.

The bishop in question, Eamon Casey (Galway), was a well-known member of the hierarchy – primarily for his work on Third World issues, his work with Irish emigrants in London, and the fact that he, along with another member of the clergy, Fr Michael Cleary, had led the singing of songs prior to the arrival of Pope John Paul II to Galway Racecourse for a papal mass in 1979. When the *Irish Times* was contacted in January 1992 by the partner of Annie Murphy, who lived in Connecticut and was claiming to have fathered Casey's child, the paper's North American correspondent, Conor O'Clery, interviewed Murphy and believed she was telling the truth. But there was no corroborative evidence. As then editor, Conor Brady put it:

> We had the greatest of difficulty in establishing the facts in relation to Annie Murphy and her son Peter. Anything that we were going to say or report would have been deniable if we had nothing more than hearsay. A lot of the witnesses who were prepared to give us information off the record were not prepared to go on the record. It was a very, very difficult story to verify.[45]

Nonetheless, Brady assigned a team of journalists – John Armstrong, Conor O'Clery, Andy Pollak, Lorna Siggins, Deaglán de Bréadún, and Geraldine Kennedy – that spent twelve weeks investigating the claims. Eventually, the oldest rule of journalism – follow the money – provided a breakthrough. When Murphy directed O'Clery to a New York priest who, over the years, had been the conduit of payments from Casey to her, O'Clery met the priest and was given details of various payments that had been made by Casey over the years. He also established that in 1990 a payment of £70,669 had been made out of a reserve account operated by the Diocese of Galway.[46] While the payments did not prove paternity, they gave the paper a reason to request an interview with Casey. The paper's religious-affairs correspondent, Pollak, telephoned Casey – who was out of the country – and arranged a meeting for when he returned. The arrangement was that Casey would meet two journalists – Pollak and O'Clery – at a hotel near Dublin Airport. While the two reporters showed up, Casey did not: in the background, both men heard RTÉ's main evening news report that the Vatican had just announced Casey's resignation as bishop of Galway 'for personal reasons'. The following day's *Irish Times* led with a story about how it had been seeking to interview Casey about money he had paid to a woman in Connecticut, and its leading article called on Casey to make 'an honest acknowledgment of the facts' that would clear the air and comfort others 'who have found themselves caught between what the law of the Church requires and what real life may actually throw up'.[47] Two days later, its leading article noted that Murphy had made serious allegations against Casey, but it did not detail what these allegations were.[48] When Casey issued a statement acknowledging that he had fathered a child with Annie Murphy and it emerged that the *Irish Times* had been aware of the paternity allegation, other media organisations accused the paper of timidity in its approach to the story.[49] The point that paternity remained an allegation until acknowledged or proved was lost on most critics. But, as Pollak put it:

> This was the biggest story to hit Ireland for decades. It involved the Catholic Church, which was still extremely powerful (this was before the clerical sex abuse scandals which so undermined its authority). The *Irish Times*, as a traditionally 'Protestant' paper, could easily be portrayed as gunning for the Church if we got anything wrong.[50]

The revelations sent shockwaves through the faithful. Ireland, it seemed, had crash-landed in the twentieth century. As Conor Brady recalled, 'You have to bear in mind that this was 1992. The sheer incredibility of the story at the time was on a scale that people wouldn't understand in today's world.'[51]

Less than three years later came the equally shocking revelation that Casey's 1979 singing partner – Fr Michael Cleary – had fathered children. Cleary, like Casey, had a high media profile. A regular panellist on television shows such as *The Late Late Show*, he wrote a weekly column, 'Reflections', for the *Sunday Independent* and also presented a nightly phone-in talk show on Dublin radio station 98FM. Dogmatic on theological issues but viewed as a champion of the disadvantaged and dispossessed, he aroused much controversy in 1993 by describing the X Case as being 'planned deliberately to test' the 1983 anti-abortion constitutional amendment.[52] After he died, in December 1993, *The Phoenix* reported that he had fathered a child in the 1970s.[53] The story was criticised by Cleary's friends – one priest described it as 'extraordinary, nasty, and cruel' (though interestingly, not as 'untrue') – though the church refused to comment on the revelation. Defending his decision to publish the story, *The Phoenix*'s editor, Paddy Prendiville, noted that Cleary had 'made a public practice of preaching about sexual morality in a strident way'.[54] The story eventually died off, but in 1995 the mother of his children, Phyllis Hamilton, decided to tell her story to Paul Williams of the *Sunday World*. The revelations were stark: she disclosed that she had had two children with Cleary: one son was given up for adoption while another, Ross Hamilton, continued to live with them as her 'love child'.[55] Despite strong denials about the veracity of the story from Cleary's family, the disjuncture between Cleary's public and private life – staunchly orthodox and vehement in his denunciation of contraception, family-planning, abortion, and divorce while being sexually active in a clandestine relationship with a woman with whom he had children – was, in mid-1990s' Ireland, hard for many people to take and seriously undermined the church's credibility on these issues. Seemingly missing the point, the church declared it 'difficult to see what honest purpose can be served by reportage of this kind' but stressed it was not challenging the story's veracity.[56] The paternity issue remained unresolved until 1999 when a twenty-minute court case confirmed the veracity of *The Phoenix*'s story: a DNA test proved conclusively that Ross Hamilton was Cleary's son.[57] But by that stage the revelations about Casey and Cleary had paled into insignificance amid the revelations of the sexual and physical abuse of children by religious personnel and the systemic cover-up of that abuse by senior church figures.

The moral abyss

The issue of sexual abuse had long been invisible in Irish society and Irish journalism. One notable exception was an eleven-page article in *Magill* by Fintan O'Toole in 1986. Based on an unpublished report commissioned by the Department of Health to examine the scale and extent of child sexual abuse in Ireland, the report found that the pattern and level of abuse was the same as that in Britain and America. It found that prior to reaching eighteen years of age, 25 per cent of female and 10 per cent of male children were subject to sexual abuse by an adult; that most cases took place within the home and were mostly unreported; that priests, teachers, doctors, and gardaí were unsure about how to handle the issue; and that, ultimately, the abuse was well hidden.[58] By 1993, the issue was very much in the public eye after a victim of abuse gave evidence against her father. The 'Kilkenny Case', as it came to be known, was the first such case given sustained media coverage. In March 1993, the perpetrator was sentenced to seven years' imprisonment having pleaded guilty to six charges of rape, incest, and assault from a total of fifty-six charges covering the period 1976 to 1991. In an interview with Kieron Wood of RTÉ, the anonymous victim gave a detailed account of the abuse she had endured at the hands of her father.[59]

Worse was to follow, but, as was the case in the development of social-affairs journalism, critical female journalism, and the revelations that led to the Beef Tribunal, it would take 'outsiders' to initially lift the veil and reveal the true extent of child abuse in Ireland. In October 1994, UTV's *Counterpoint* programme revealed the activities of Fr Brendan Smyth, a member of the Norbertine Order, who in March 1991 had been charged with sexual assault against minors in Northern Ireland. Smyth had then crossed the border and had spent nearly three years living in his order's abbey in County Cavan. In January 1994, he returned voluntarily to Northern Ireland and in June of that year received a four-year prison sentence, having pleaded guilty to seventeen charges of indecent assault. While this sentence was reported prominently in the national newspapers, it was Chris Moore's *Counterpoint* documentary *Suffer Little Children*, aired on UTV in October 1994, that prompted public debate.[60] Amid the searing first-hand testimony from Smyth's victims, it revealed that his abuse of children had been something of an open secret within the church: both his order and Cardinal Cahal Daly had for many years been aware of his activities.[61] It also revealed that the policy of reassigning Smyth to new parishes – in the hope of ending the abuse – had simply presented him with new opportunities for offending. The programme thus detailed a litany of abuse that continued for over forty years and that stretched from Ireland to Scotland, Wales, and America.[62] As Nuala O'Faolain succinctly put it, 'children were sacrificed to keep the truth about a priest hidden'.[63]

The Smyth Affair caused much public disquiet – and a change of government. In October 1994, Veronica Guerin of the *Sunday Independent* revealed that an extradition warrant from the Northern Ireland authorities seeking the return of Smyth had lain unprocessed in the office of the Attorney General for seven months.[64] The explanation offered, that the request required careful handling because the alleged offences had taken place twenty-nine years earlier and no precedent existed to guide the office's decision-making, came unstuck when it emerged that a similar request (involving an ex-monk named John Anthony Duggan) had been processed speedily in 1992. Amid claim and counterclaim about who knew what and when, the Labour Party withdrew from cabinet, and the Taoiseach, Albert Reynolds, resigned, to be succeeded as Fianna Fáil leader by Bertie Ahern, with whom Labour was prepared to re-enter government. But when *Irish Times* political correspondent Geraldine Kennedy revealed that all Fianna Fáil ministers had been aware of the Duggan case before Reynolds had defended the Attorney General in a controversial Dáil speech, Labour ended negotiations with Ahern and formed a coalition government with Fine Gael and Democratic Left – the first time a new government was formed without an election.[65]

Having served his sentence in Northern Ireland, Smyth returned to the republic, where he pleaded guilty to seventy-four charges of abuse over a thirty-five-year period.[66] As noted by Colum Kenny, Smyth 'came to be regarded by many Irish people as the personification of sexual abuse within the Catholic Church'.[67] Indeed, while Smyth became, as Michael Breen put it, 'the poster boy for all that is wrong with the Catholic Church in Ireland', he was, in fact, the first of a litany of clerical abusers revealed in the late 1990s.[68] In quick succession, the public became familiar with the unspeakable activities of, among many others, Fr Seán Fortune, Fr Ivan Payne, and Fr Tony Walsh.[69] The culture of silence that had been constructed around such activity – by moving errant priests to different parishes, by paying compensation to victims, and by insisting that victims who received compensation signed confidentiality agreements – was finally broken. The arguments put forward by church advocates that health, education, and legal professionals had also not tackled the abuse and that the church did not understand paedophilia quietly avoided the reality that, for many decades, the church had towered over those professions and that the church had an understanding – usually conservative and condemnatory – of every other aspect of human sexuality. The revelation that the church had, in the mid-1980s, taken out an insurance policy to protect itself against future abuse claims also ensured that its protestation of innocence rang hollow. As the country reeled in revulsion, journalists were not universally thanked for revealing the abuse or for reporting on associated court cases. As then *Irish Times* Editor Conor Brady recalled, 'for our court reporting of the sexual abuse cases we drew a lot of hostility … abusive telephone calls and threatening letters were not infrequent … Envelopes containing excrement were posted to me. On two occasions members of extremist pressure groups picketed the office.'[70]

Broadcast journalism also played a crucial role in revealing the past, and the personal testimony of abuse victims, related through emotionally charged interviews, proved a potent force. In September 1995, the Archbishop of Dublin, Desmond Connell, contacted the Attorney General about an upcoming *Prime Time* programme that was to reveal that Connell had approved a diocesan loan of £27,500 to Fr Ivan Payne to secretly settle a claim for compensation from abuse victim Andrew Madden. While the settlement had initially been revealed by Colm Kenna in the *Irish Press* in April of that year, in a television interview with RTÉ's religious-affairs correspondent, Joe Little, in May, Connell had stated that diocesan funds 'are not used in any way' to compensate abuse victims.[71] With *Prime Time* set to reveal the inconsistency, Connell turned to the Attorney General, who, in turn, wrote to the RTÉ Authority suggesting that any broadcast might prejudice ongoing investigations.[72] Despite this intervention, the programme aired as planned and was followed by much comment from the hierarchy about how the money constituted a loan to a priest and not a compensation payment from the archdiocese. Responding to the programme, Connell declared that he had been 'libelled', but no action was taken against RTÉ.[73] In February 1996, RTÉ screened Louis Lentin's documentary *Dear Daughter*. Through the use of reconstructions and interviews, it examined the conditions endured by children who resided at the Sisters of Mercy's Goldenbridge Orphanage in Dublin during the 1950s and 1960s. Focusing primarily on the testimony of former resident Christine Buckley, the programme revealed how residents were frequently beaten, deprived of food, and made to spent endless hours making rosary beads.[74]

In a similar vein, Channel 4 aired Steve Humphries' documentary *Sex in a Cold Climate* in March 1998. It revealed the harsh conditions and the gruelling and unpaid labour performed by residents of the Magdalene laundries for 'fallen women' – those viewed as promiscuous or who had given birth outside wedlock.[75]

In April and May 1999, RTÉ screened the ground-breaking three-part documentary series *States of Fear*. Produced and directed by Mary Raftery (and researched by her long-time collaborator Sheila Ahern), the series laid bare the physical and sexual abuse perpetrated in religious-run orphanages and industrial schools such as Goldenbridge and Artane. The powerful testimony of the victims ensured that the programmes received substantial media coverage. In his weekly column in the *Irish Independent*, Bruce Arnold observed that Raftery's programme 'presented a picture of unlimited and deliberate damage visited upon countless lives in the name of Christian charity and under the direct care of the State' and that it was 'no longer possible to entertain the idea that what went on was the result of ignorance or mistake'.[76] This was, by any measure, a far cry from the *Irish Independent* of old, and, for his trouble, Arnold was threatened with legal action by the hierarchy.[77]

Raftery's series prompted Brian Quinn, former journalist and editor of the *Evening Herald* between 1969 and 1976, to write an eloquent letter to the *Irish Times* in which he noted the failure of his generation of journalists to expose the abuse. In his letter, Quinn admitted that journalists of the 1940s and 1950s 'had their suspicions of the industrial schools' and knew in particular that the Christian Brothers had a 'reputation for excessive corporal punishment'. Quinn's letter paints a picture of 'one of the worst of the Christian Brothers break[ing] into the office of the manager and demand[ing] that a court case that mentioned Artane should not be used'. While Quinn now believed that journalists 'should have tried harder to find out the real truth', he felt that they 'would not have been believed and managements and editors would never have held out against a massed attack by the all-powerful Irish Catholic Church'. There was also, he observed, the issue of ignorance: 'that the Christian Brothers were indulging their passion for sexual abuse on their captive boys' was something that would never have occurred to Quinn or his colleagues. But while journalists of the time 'were trapped in a carefully designed plot that mixed lies with official evasion and ecclesiastical terror', ultimately he believed they had 'allowed cowardice to rule'.[78] While this may be true, even in the mid-1990s editors and journalists were still erring on the side of caution when it came to reporting clerical misconduct. In 2005, Justine McCarthy of the *Irish Independent* revealed how, in 1994, in the context of an interview with an inebriated Bishop Brendan Comiskey, he had threated to rape her if she wrote anything negative about him. While McCarthy reported the threat to her editorial superiors, it was decided that the newspaper would not report the threat.[79] On 11 May 1999, as the last of Raftery's three programmes was about to be aired, the Taoiseach, Bertie Ahern, apologised on behalf of the state to those who had been abused as children in the institutions. He also announced the establishment of a commission of inquiry into abuse within those institutions.[80]

However, it was not all plain sailing. The torrent of revelations, coupled with the breaking of the institutional power of the church to keep the abuse hidden, risked all religious personnel being tarred with the same brush and the possibility of a rush to judgement. In July 1999, two individuals, Nora Wall, a former Sisters of Mercy nun, and Paul 'Pablo' McCabe (a homeless man with mental-health issues), were convicted of the alleged rape of a ten-year-old girl many years previously at St Michael's Child Care Centre in Cappoquin, County Waterford. Wall received a sentence of life imprisonment while McCabe received a twelve-year sentence. The headlines in the tabloid press – such as the *Sunday World*'s 'Rape Nun's Abuse Pact with Smyth' – left nothing to the imagination.[81] Although the paper alleged that Wall had 'secretly provided children for the sick paedophile priest Fr Brendan Smyth [and] was part of a religious-based paedophile ring', no evidence was advanced to back up the story, which was based entirely on anonymous sources.[82] However, both convictions were quashed days later by an appeal court after it found that the state had not disclosed statements by third parties that fundamentally undermined the evidence of the victim and the chief prosecution witness.[83] As the *Irish Times* later pointed out, the case had been heard within a month of the *States of Fear* programmes, and 'the jury could not but have been affected, it seems, by the horrific abuse exposed in that series and by the complaints of the child victims that no-one listened to them'.[84]

Post *States of Fear*, there followed a near avalanche of television-led investigations. In October 1999, TV3 aired two Louis Lentin documentaries – *Our Boy's Stories* and *We Were Only Children* – that focused respectively on the experiences of male and female residents of industrial schools. A third Lentin documentary, *Philomena's Story*, aired in November 2000 and featured an interview with a former resident who claimed to have been gang-raped by a group that included nuns and a priest. This programme prompted a strong statement of denial by the Sisters of Mercy, the order that ran the home at which the incident was alleged to have taken place.[85] As the years passed, the revelations kept coming. In March 2002, BBC2 aired *Suing the Pope*, which focused on the abuse perpetrated by Fr Seán Fortune and the response of his bishop, Brendan Comiskey, to those activities. Shortly after the programme's airing, Comiskey resigned as Bishop of Ferns, and the government established an inquiry into the diocese.[86] In October of that year, RTÉ aired the game-changing *Cardinal Secrets*. Produced by Mary Raftery and presented by Mick Peelo, the programme catalogued the abuse perpetrated by eight sample priests in the Dublin archdiocese and the failure of Archbishop (and now Cardinal) Desmond Connell and other senior clergy to report the abuse to the Garda Síochána. The policy of moving offending priests to new parishes to avoid scandal was sharply illustrated by the case of Fr Noel Reynolds, who was moved from the parish of Glendalough only after locals threatened to go public. Reynolds was then transferred by the archdiocese to the National Rehabilitation Hospital.[87] The response to the programme was deafening: amid calls for Connell to resign, the government established an inquiry, chaired by Justice Yvonne Murphy, to examine how Dublin bishops had handled allegations of child abuse made known to them.[88]

Although the reports of both commissions of inquiry prompted by Raftery's documentaries – *States of Fear* and *Cardinal Secrets* – lie outside the timeline of this study, it is worth recording their findings, which do not make for easy reading. In May 2009, the report of the Commission to Inquire into Child Abuse (Ryan Report) found that in relation to the industrial schools, 'physical and emotional abuse and neglect were features of the institutions [and that] sexual abuse occurred in many of them, particularly boys' institutions'. It also found that 'the deferential and submissive attitude of the Department of Education towards the Congregations compromised its ability to carry out its statutory duty of inspection and monitoring of the schools'. In frank terms, it noted that the institutions 'depended on rigid control by means of severe corporal punishment and the fear of such punishment', that 'sexual abuse was endemic in boys' institutions', that 'cases of sexual abuse were managed with a view to minimising the risk of public disclosure and consequent damage to the institution and the Congregation', and that, 'when confronted with evidence of sexual abuse, the response of the religious authorities was to transfer the offender to another location where, in many instances, he was free to abuse again'.[89]

The following November, the Commission of Investigation into the Catholic Archdiocese of Dublin (Murphy Commission) found that 'clerical child abuse was covered up by the Archdiocese of Dublin and other church authorities [and that] the structures and rules of the Catholic Church facilitated that cover-up'. It also found that state authorities 'facilitated the cover up by not fulfilling their responsibilities to ensure that the law was applied equally to all and allowing the church institutions to be beyond the reach of the normal law enforcement processes'. Damningly, it found that the church's focus was 'on the avoidance of scandal and the preservation of the good name, status and assets of the institution and of what the institution regarded as its most important members – the priests'.[90] The report also expressed concern at the hierarchy's use of a theological concept known as 'mental reservation', which it described as permitting 'a clergyman knowingly to convey a misleading impression to another person without being guilty of lying', to knowingly mislead the media about the archdiocese's dealings with abuse victims.[91] In his evidence to the Murphy Commission, Cardinal Desmond Connell described the concept as 'circumstances in which you can use an ambiguous expression realising that the person who you are talking to will accept an untrue version of whatever it may be'.[92] In their use of the concept, the hierarchy had attempted to frustrate journalistic inquiry. In his evidence to the commission, abuse victim Andrew Madden testified that he had challenged Connell on his denial to journalists about the use of diocesan funds to compensate abuse victims. According to Madden, Connell

> explained that when he was asked by journalists about the use of diocesan funds for the compensation of complainants of child sexual abuse, he had responded that diocesan funds **are** not used for such a purpose; that he had not said that diocesan funds **were** not used for such a purpose. By using the present tense, he had not excluded the possibility that diocesan funds had been used for such purpose in the past.[93]

To many commentators, such linguistic parsing indicated the lengths to which the church was prepared to go to protect its reputation and assets. It had been amid such a culture that Irish society and its journalism had endured what journalist Brian Quinn referred to as 'the edifice of lies and evasion that flourished for so long'.[94] But no more: by the beginning of the twentieth-first century, the relationship between Irish society and its political and religious institutions – and between journalism and those institutions – had undergone a remarkable transformation that is, in the digital age, still unfolding.

Notes

1 *Irish Times*, 21 Feb. 1991, p. 10.
2 G. Lee and C. Bird, *Breaking the Bank* (Dublin, 1998). See also S. Carswell, *Something Rotten: Irish Banking Scandals* (Dublin, 2006).
3 Cooper-Flynn served as a Fianna Fáil and an independent TD for Mayo from 1997 to 2011. She reverted to her maiden name – Flynn – during this period but for consistency is herein referred throughout as 'Cooper-Flynn'.
4 L. Collins, *The Great Irish Bank Robbery* (Dublin, 2007), p. 32.
5 *Sunday Independent*, 5 Apr. 1998, pp. 1 and 4.
6 U. Halligan, 'Irish Life in multi-million pound rip-off of customers', *Magill*, Jul. 1998, 24–37.
7 M. Raftery, 'The Dunnes', *Magill*, Nov. 1983, 6–14; M. O'Higgins, 'The General', *Magill*, Mar. 1988, 14–23.
8 See www.youtube.com/watch?v=VN8aOK5CV5A (accessed 14 Jul. 2016).
9 *Irish Independent*, 9 Nov. 1995, p. 1; *Irish Times*, 9 Nov. 1995, p. 1.
10 *Irish Times*, 9 Dec. 1995, p. 1.
11 *Irish Times*, 23 Feb. 2006, p. 4.
12 *Irish Times*, 29 Jul. 1993, p. 2. Other media outlets (including the *Sunday Independent* and 98FM) that picked up and ran the story were also fined. The story appeared in the *Sunday Business Post*, 13 Sep. 1992, p. 1.
13 The series appeared in the 14, 21, and 28 Nov. 1993 editions.
14 *Sunday Independent*, 23 Oct. 1994, p. 1.
15 See *The Phoenix*, 1 Jul. 2016, pp. 3–4.
16 *Irish Times*, 28 Jun. 1996, p. 6.
17 See U. Halligan, L. Walsh, V. Browne, and C. O'Keefe, 'The Real Veronica', *Magill*, May 1998, 24–37; and E. O'Reilly, *Veronica Guerin: The Life and Death of a Crime Reporter* (London, 1998). The paper's editor, Aengus Fanning, later expressed regret about letting her take such high risks. See *Hot Press*, 5 Nov. 2008, pp. 52–5 and 125.
18 For more, see G. Cunningham, *Chaos and Conspiracy: The Framing of the McBrearty Family* (Dublin, 2009).
19 *Irish Times*, 20 May 2006, p. 1. See www.morristribunal.ie for full report.
20 *Irish Times*, 22 Oct. 1996, p. 14.
21 *The Star*, 11 Feb. 1999, p. 1. For full context, see B. O'Kelly and E. O'Reilly, 'Freeing Philip', *Magill*, May 1999, 6–10.
22 Correspondence with Barry O'Kelly.
23 *Sunday Press*, 6 Mar. 1994, p. 1, and 13 Mar. 1994, p. 13; R. Balls, 'Locking horns over Stagg with the gardaí', in D. Kenny (ed.), *The Press Gang: Tales from the Glory Days of Irish Newspapers* (Dublin, 2015), pp. 343–7.
24 O. O'Leary, 'Mr Gageby's republic', in A. Whittaker, *Bright Brilliant Days: Douglas Gageby and the Irish Times* (Dublin, 2006), pp. 45–8, at p. 47.
25 *Irish Times*, 2 Oct. 1979, p. 8.
26 B. Comiskey, 'Should Christians always lose?', *Irish Broadcasting Review*, 12 (1981), 7–11, at p. 10.

27 For more on the Flynn case, see *Irish Times*, 13 Mar. 1985, p. 8. For more on the divorce referendum, see E. O'Reilly, 'The secret world of the anti-divorce lobby', *Magill*, May 1986, 8–14; and G. Kerrigan, 'After the referendum', *Magill*, Jul. 1986, 10–13.
28 *Irish Times*, 21 Feb. 1991, p. 10.
29 *Irish Times*, 5 Apr. 1983, p. 10; 30 Sep. 1985, p. 9; 21 Feb. 1991, p. 10. See also F. O'Toole, 'An apostle's creed', *Magill*, Jun. 1986, 17–36.
30 *Irish Times*, 29 Sep. 1984, p. 7.
31 *Irish Times*, 4 Nov. 1985, p. 13.
32 *Irish Values and Attitudes: The Irish Report of the European Value System Study* (1984) found that 55 per cent of the population had 'not very much' or 'no' confidence in the press. The second report cited by Comiskey was *Religious Beliefs, Practice, and Moral Attitudes: A Comparison of Two Irish Surveys 1974–84* (Report No. 21 of the Council for Research and Development).
33 *Irish Times*, 4 Nov. 1985, p. 13. See Chapter 9.
34 *Irish Times*, 29 Nov. 1985, p. 9. See also Chapter 11 of M. O'Toole, *More Kicks than Pence: A Life in Irish Journalism* (Dublin, 1992), pp. 176–92.
35 *Irish Times*, 1 Oct. 1988, p. 1. In his memoir, Smith recalls how 'letters containing prayer pamphlets, rosaries, holy medals and various publications on the lives of the saints poured through our letterbox'. See S. Smith, *Off Screen: A Memoir* (Dublin, 2007), p. 220.
36 *Sunday Tribune*, 17 Feb. 1991, p. 5.
37 *Irish Times*, 21 Feb. 1991, p. 10.
38 *Irish Press*, 27 Jul. 1991, p. 17.
39 *Irish Catholic*, 1 Aug. 1991, p. 9.
40 R. Burke, *Press Delete: The Decline and Fall of the Irish Press* (Dublin, 2005), pp. 372–5.
41 *Irish Times*, 12 Aug. 1991, p. 10.
42 *Irish Times*, 12 Feb. 1992, p. 1.
43 'Miss X's' parents immediately appealed the decision to the Supreme Court which lifted the injunction.
44 C. Brady, *Up with the Times* (Dublin, 2005), p. 159.
45 Interview with Conor Brady.
46 Brady, *Up with the Times*, p. 147.
47 *Irish Times*, 7 May 1992, pp. 1 and 11.
48 *Irish Times*, 9 May 1992, p. 13.
49 *Irish Times*, 12 May 1992, p. 1.
50 Correspondence with Andy Pollak.
51 Interview with Conor Brady. Soon after the exposé, Casey left for a missionary appointment in Ecuador, and the £70,669 of diocesan funds was repaid by his friends.
52 *Irish Times*, 1 Jul. 1995, p. 7.
53 *The Phoenix*, 14 Jan. 1994, p. 3.
54 *Irish Independent*, 13 Jan. 1994, p. 1.
55 *Sunday World*, 25 Jun. 1995, pp. 1–8.
56 *Irish Times*, 26 Jun. 1995, p. 7.
57 *Irish Independent*, 8 Feb. 1999, p. 1.
58 F. O'Toole, 'The betrayal of the innocents', *Magill*, Jul. 1986, 16–27.
59 See *Irish Times*, 3 Mar. 1993, p. 1 for the text of the interview.
60 *Irish Times*, 25 Jun. 1994, p. 3; *Irish Press*, 25 Jun. 1994, p. 5; *Irish Independent*, 25 Jun. 1994, p. 3.

61 In 2010, it was revealed that Cardinal Seán Brady had, in 1975, whilst then a priest, investigated claims of abuse involving Fr Brendan Smyth. Brady did not report the abuse to the Garda Síochána and swore the victims to secrecy. See *Irish Times*, 19 May 2010, p. 14.
62 *Irish Times*, 8 Oct. 1994, p. A5.
63 *Irish Times*, 17 Oct. 1994, p. 12.
64 *Sunday Independent*, 23 Oct. 1994, p. 1.
65 *Irish Times*, 5 Dec. 1994, p. 1.
66 In Jul. 1997, Smyth was sentenced to twelve years' imprisonment but died in prison in Aug. 1997. He was buried in a secretive pre-dawn ceremony in his order's grounds in County Cavan.
67 C. Kenny, 'Significant television: journalism, sex abuse and the Catholic Church', *Irish Communications Review*, 11 (2009), 63–76, at p. 65.
68 M. Breen, 'The good, the bad, and the ugly: the media and the scandals', *Studies*, 89:356 (2000), 332–8, at p. 335.
69 Fortune abused children in Counties Wexford and Louth and committed suicide in 1999 while awaiting trial; Payne abused altar boys and children in his capacity as chaplain to Our Lady's Hospital for Sick Children, Dublin, and was sentenced to six years' imprisonment in 1998; Walsh was sentenced to a total of 123 years imprisonment for child abuse in Dec. 2010.
70 Brady, *Up with the Times*, pp. 162–3.
71 *Irish Press*, 7 Apr. 1995, p. 1.
72 J. Horgan, *Broadcasting and Public Life: RTÉ News and Current Affairs, 1926–97* (Dublin, 2004), p. 207.
73 *Irish Times*, 7 Oct. 1995, p. 12.
74 Despite some debate about whether the programme constituted journalism or drama documentary (see *Irish Times*, 19 Mar. 1996, p. 12), in 2004, the Sisters of Mercy confirmed the allegations were 'credible' (see *Irish Independent*, 2 Jul. 2004, p. 10).
75 The report of an interdepartmental committee, chaired by Martin McAleese, set up to examine state involvement with the Magdalene laundries found that the state facilitated the transfer of women to the laundries. See report at www.justice.ie/en/JELR/Pages/MagdalenRpt2013 (accessed 14 Jul. 2016).
76 *Irish Independent*, 1 May 1999, p. 34. See also B. Arnold, *The Irish Gulag: The Irish State and the Industrial Schools* (Dublin, 2009).
77 *Irish Times*, 12 Aug. 1999, p. 1.
78 *Irish Times*, 11 May 1999, p. 15.
79 *Irish Independent*, 29 Oct. 2005, pp. 4–5 of *Weekend Review* magazine. McCarthy agreed with this decision on the grounds that she believed it 'wrong to hold an alcoholic up to ridicule for a single transgression'.
80 The commission was originally led by Justice Mary Laffoy and later by Justice Seán Ryan. Its report is available at www.childabusecommission.ie/rpt (accessed 14 Jul. 2016).
81 *Sunday World*, 11 Jul. 1999, pp. 1 and 6.
82 In 2002, the *Sunday World* paid Wall €175,000 in damages and printed a miniscule apology on page three. See *The Phoenix*, 8 Nov. 2002, p. 8. In Dec. 2005, the Court of Criminal Appeal certified that Wall had been the victim of a miscarriage of justice. McCabe had died in Dec. 2002.
83 *Irish Times*, 28 Jul. 1999, p. 4.
84 *Irish Times*, 17 Dec. 2005, p. 17.

85 *Irish Times*, 6 Nov. 2000, p. 6.

86 The inquiry, chaired by retired Supreme Court judge Justice Francis Murphy, recorded the failure of several bishops to report allegations of abuse to the Garda Síochána and the failure of the force to investigate properly those allegations it became aware of prior to 1990.

87 *Sunday Tribune*, 20 Oct. 2002, p. 9.

88 For more on Raftery's journalism, see M. Raftery, *Do They Think We're Eejits?* ed. S. Ahern (Dublin, 2013).

89 Ryan Report (Dublin, 2009), vol. IV, pp. 451–9.

90 Report of the Commission of Investigation into the Catholic Archdiocese of Dublin (Murphy Report) (Dublin, 2009), Part 1, pp. 1–28. The Commission's report is available at www.justice.ie/en/JELR/Pages/PB09000504 (accessed 14 Jul. 2016).

91 Murphy Report, part 2, p. 643 (par. 58.19).

92 Murphy Report, part 2, p. 643 (par. 58.20).

93 Murphy Report, part 2, p. 644 (par. 58.21); emphasis in original report.

94 *Irish Times*, 11 May 1999, p. 15.

Conclusion

In seeking to map how, over the course of the twentieth century, the prevailing conditions – political, social, economic, technological, and cultural – facilitated or constrained the work of journalists and how their work impacted on the processes of social stasis and social change, it is possible to discern three periods – or waves – of journalism that characterised an ever-evolving Ireland. Despite possessing key characteristics, these waves are not mutually exclusive – more so, they flow in and out of each other, and their fluidity is, in itself, typical of the oft-times gradual, and sometimes rapid, social change characteristic of any society.

Amid the advent of the new journalism in the late 1880s, journalism in Ireland came under sustained pressure not to report on certain topics – a process that, post-Independence, was greatly intensified within a paternalistic state that was heavily influenced by the teachings and moral-guarding activities of the Catholic Church and its multifarious lay groups. In many ways, the first half of the twentieth century can be construed as a time of constructing 'Catholic Ireland'. Within this period, the social, cultural, and political power of the church was at its strongest and the power of journalism at its weakest. As the church emerged as a major power broker in the nascent Free State, there emerged a close-knit relationship between church and state, a relationship that went unchallenged by any political party. With this relationship towering over every aspect of Irish life, journalism was, by and large, constrained in terms of the topics it could report on and the reality that it could convey.

The acute reaction by the church to the new journalism of the late nineteenth century – one of horror and puritanism – set the tone for much that followed. This reaction retarded the development of journalism in the first half of the twentieth century by curtailing and delaying the advent of social affairs and investigative journalism until the 1960s and 1970s. As newsvendors came under pressure not to sell publications that carried offending material, proprietors, editors, and journalists took note. 'Indelicate' topics – to use the phrase from the time – were not to be reported on. Similarly, the effects of the Censorship of Publications Act 1929 went far beyond the banning of books and ushered in an era of sanitised crime and court reporting that allowed for the perpetuation of the myth that Ireland was a unique nation characterised by virtue, charity, and chastity.

But it would be erroneous to neglect the fact that the Free State was, demographically and culturally, a predominantly Catholic country or to neglect to mention that many press owners – such as William Martin Murphy and Éamon de Valera – were devout believers. There was also the issue of religious capital: being seen to be on the side of the church in its campaigns against social ills (however they were defined) or the spectre of communism was good for business. Within such an orthodox Catholic culture it was virtually impossible for independently minded journalism to exist. However, amid low education levels and poor employment conditions, there were some positive developments as greater organisation, particularly the establishment of the NUJ, provided a degree of solidarity and support. But even this was challenged by the church as a front for communism. The church's lay vigilance committees kept a close eye on the union, and the formation of church-inspired alternative representative groups indicates just how aware the church was of the importance of exerting control over journalists.

Thus the period from the 1880s to 1961 was a period of constrained journalism. In particular, the deference accorded to the church (even if this deference was culturally engrained and not simply crozier avoidance) was overwhelming. With the exception of *The Bell* and, occasionally, the *Irish Times*, nothing that might challenge the position of the church as the great arbiter of social, cultural, and political life could be published. Court cases involving clergy were strictly out of bounds as was any critical examination of the institutions run by the church. It is difficult not to conclude that this deference – on the part of the political, media owning, and editorial classes (and among some journalists too) – inadvertently facilitated the invisibility of the crimes of the church and allowed a pernicious evil to go unaccounted for.

If the first half of twentieth-century Ireland can be characterised as a time in which 'Catholic Ireland' was constructed, then the second half of that century can be characterised as a time in which 'Catholic Ireland' was deconstructed. And, just as the construction of 'Catholic Ireland' took place over several decades, its deconstruction also took time – decades characterised by a power struggle between church, state, and journalism. The period from 1959 onwards was characterised by an interventionist state as successive governments steered economic policy away from protectionism and towards free trade. As the economy grew and a consumer society emerged, the state reintegrated itself into the wider global community. Amid a society that quickly embraced the trappings of modernity, the balance of power in Irish society began to change, though not without a struggle from the church to retain its position as the arbiter of Irish life. This changing power dynamic is perhaps best illustrated by the decision of Minister for Education Donogh O'Malley to announce the introduction of free second-level education at an NUJ event – without first consulting those who effectively controlled the education sector – the Catholic hierarchy. This notion of an interventionist state was mirrored by the emergence of an interventionist media industry, and, by extension, interventionist journalism – in the guise of social-affairs journalism – that examined areas of life not previously accorded media attention.

Thus the period from 1961 to the late 1970s was a period of contested journalism in which journalists sought to extend the boundaries of their remit and church and state sought to push back such endeavours. The establishment of a national television service, RTÉ, required by law to be objective and impartial in its coverage of news and current affairs, changed everything. As a new generation of journalists, many of them university graduates, helped the station find its feet, the power blocs of old slowly realised that the days of visiting a newsroom to demand that contentious news items be dropped were coming to an end. There unfolded a power play as politicians, such as Seán Lemass and Charles Haughey, and members of the hierarchy, including Archbishop John Charles McQuaid, sought to impose their will on the station and, in the case of some politicians, to row back on the impartiality granted to RTÉ. There also dawned the realisation that this new medium had the effect of making people increasingly aware that 'men who hold positions of authority and responsibility owe it to the public to explain their actions'.[1]

The determination of journalists and management to prevent RTÉ being converted into a vehicle for the transmission of uncontested government or church viewpoints was not lost on their colleagues in the press who realised that it was no longer sustainable for newspapers – or journalists – to be viewed as the organ of a political party or sectional interest. There followed attempts by some national newspapers, with varying degrees of success, to put distance between themselves and their traditional affiliations. In particular, the church – most notably in the guise of Archbishop McQuaid – was dismayed at press coverage of the Second Vatican Council which made people aware that far from there being consensus on every contentious issue, there existed contrasting viewpoints within the church. The fact that the social reality within which people lived their lives was, literally, man-made and subject to debate was a revelation to many. The reinvention of the *Irish Times* most successfully captured the *zeitgeist* of a changing nation through its pioneering of social-affairs reporting and women's journalism. The integration of these elements of the new journalism into Irish journalistic practice – several decades after their integration into British journalism – did not go unchallenged. For covering taboo topics, such as the ban on contraception, the pioneering female journalists endured criticism and odium from clerical and political figures who publicly contested their journalism and accused them of undermining Irish Catholic life. Broadcast censorship in relation to the Northern Troubles also strained relations between journalists and the body politic, and among journalists themselves. In the highly charged and emotive atmosphere engendered by the Troubles, the issue of how to cover the conflict was a sore that never properly healed. Despite the contested nature of journalism from 1961 to the late 1970s, the overall sense was one of journalism establishing a critical space for itself – not altogether free from the constraints of church and state – but establishing ever greater critical distance.

One major outcome of the state's intervention in education was a tripling of third-level places between 1965 and 1985.[2] As this more educated population matured into voters, there emerged a sense of 'two Irelands' – one in which citizens had grown up in an insular and isolated state wherein the vast majority left school after primary level and in which the church was all-powerful and unquestioned, the other in which a newer generation had grown up in an outward-looking and globally connected state wherein the vast majority had completed second-level education and in many cases had progressed to third-level, and in which the church's teachings were being ever more contested. By the early 1970s, almost half the population was aged under twenty-five, and in 1972 the voting age was reduced from twenty-one to eighteen years of age. By the late 1970s, this young and well-educated demographic was entering the workforce, with some opting for careers in journalism.[3] These would be journalistic careers far removed from those that had existed in the earlier part of the century. Thus, the period from the late 1970s onwards was one characterised by challenging journalism in which the certainties of old were overtly and directly challenged by a new generation of journalists, first in specialised publications and then within mainstream media.

The advent of new outlets – such as *Hibernia*, *Magill*, *Hot Press*, and *In Dublin* – provided vital training grounds for a new generation of journalists and allowed them to question the nature and structure of Irish society through long-form journalism. It also allowed them to cast a critical eye on institutions that had never before experienced critical scrutiny. It was during this period that another element of the new journalism – that of investigative journalism – was integrated into Irish journalistic practice, again several decades after its integration into British journalism. This notion of journalism acting as a watchdog for the public and holding institutions to account was not universally welcomed and did not go unchallenged. There was, it seemed, no shortage of individuals or institutions willing to take offence at, and challenge the nature of, journalistic scrutiny. By the 1980s, this new generation of journalists had migrated to mainstream media outlets – thus upping the ante in terms of challenging institutions to be accountable and transparent.

That this new mode of journalistic inquiry coincided with a period of political instability, an economic crisis, and a push-back by the Catholic Church against what was viewed as secularising forces only heightened its impact. There emerged a growing sense of frustration among political parties, the Catholic hierarchy, the Garda Síochána, and the business community at this growing criticality on the part of journalists. The varied responses to this new mode of journalistic inquiry – telephone tapping, allegations of pushing an anti-church agenda, charges of undermining state security, and of being anti-business – was instructive. These institutions had, for much of the twentieth century, been beyond public scrutiny and in the closing decades of the century were prepared to fight to keep things that way. But, for all its faults, journalism in Ireland had moved beyond being the placid preserver of an idealised Ireland. In the late 1990s, this gradual but systematic chipping away at the carefully constructed edifice of an island of saints and scholars finally revealed endemic corruption in the political and business worlds and unspeakable horrors within institutions that had been conspicuously ignored or carefully concealed for many decades. While it is justifiable, in hindsight, to ask why it took journalism so long to reveal this malfeasance, it is crucial to consider how centres of power related to journalists – and the conditions under which journalism was practised – over the period in question.

By the end of the twentieth century, journalism in Ireland had, it seemed, come full circle – just as journalism and its delivery platforms were again changing. Amid the digital revolution of the early twenty-first century, as journalism migrated, in Joe Breen's memorable phrase, 'from the stone to the server', a whole host of new challenges and opportunities opened up, the potentialities and consequences of which are still unfolding and revealing themselves.[4]

Notes

1 DDA, AB8/B/XXVI/e/78 (public image committee), final report dated 5 Jun. 1964.

2 Third-level registration increased from 16,692 in 1965 to 51,341 in 1985. See E. Hazelkorn, A. Gibson, and S. Harkin, 'From massification to globalisation: reflections on the transformation of Irish higher education', in K. Rafter and M. O'Brien (eds), *The State in Transition: Essays in Honour of John Horgan* (Dublin, 2015), pp. 235–60, at p. 246.

3 One study, published in 1997, found that 67 per cent of journalists had completed a third-level qualification. See M. Corcoran, 'The political preferences and value orientation of Irish journalists', *Irish Journal of Sociology*, 13:2 (2004), 22–42.

4 J. Breen, 'How the *Irish Times* moved from hot metal to cold type: the impact of technological change on journalists and journalism and the ending of the power of the caseroom', paper presented at the Nov. 2010 conference of the Newspaper and Periodical History Forum of Ireland.

Sources and select bibliography

Interviews/correspondence

Over the years, the following generously granted interviews, engaged in correspondence or both: David Andrews, Conor Brady, John Brophy, Maureen Brown, Tim Pat Coogan, James Downey, Vincent Doyle, Jim Eadie, Brian Fallon, Ronan Fanning, Douglas Gageby, Patrick Geary, Paul Gillespie, Renagh Holohan, John Horgan, Michael Keane, Richard Keatinge, John Kelly, Dennis Kennedy, Geraldine Kennedy, Joe Kennedy, Hugh Lambert, Dorothy MacGabhann, Mary Maher, Brendan Malin, Seamus Malin, Frank McDonald, Michael Mills, Gerry Mulvey, Donal Nevin, Mildred O'Brien, Barry O'Kelly, Louis O'Neill, Emily O'Reilly, Mary O'Rourke, Cathal O'Shannon, Etain O Siochain, Michael O'Toole, Andy Pollak, Don Reid, Lorna Siggins, Michael Viney, Jim Walsh, Andrew Whittaker, Pádraig Yeates.

Archival sources

Chris O'Sullivan Audio Interview (National Library of Australia)
Conor Cruise O'Brien Papers (UCDA)
Desmond Ryan Witness Statement (Bureau of Military History)
Douglas Gageby Papers (Historic Collections Research Centre [HCRC])
Éamon de Valera Papers (UCDA)
Frank Gallagher Papers (National Library of Ireland [NLI])
John Charles McQuaid Papers (Dublin Diocesan Archives)
Joseph Dennigan Papers (UCDA)
Michael Knightly Witness Statement (Bureau of Military History)
Michael O'Toole Papers (HCRC)
NUJ Papers (HCRC)
Patrick Barry Moloney Papers (UCDA)
Piaras Béaslaí Papers (NLI)
Piaras Béaslaí Witness Statement (Bureau of Military History)
R. M. Fox Papers (NLI)
T. R. Harrington Papers (National Archives of Ireland)
William O'Brien Papers (University College Cork Library Special Collections)

Government publications

Dáil Éireann Debates and Seanad Éireann Debates
Report of the Commission to Inquire into Child Abuse (2009)

Report of the Commission of Investigation into the Catholic Archdiocese of Dublin (2009)

Trade periodicals

An Glór, *Bulletin*, *The Irish Journalist*, *Newspaper Press Directory and Advertisers' Guide*

Newspapers and periodicals

The Bell, *Connacht Tribune*, *Daily Express* (Dublin), *Daily Mirror* (London), *Evening Herald*, *Evening Mail*, *Evening Press*, *Freeman's Journal* (Dublin), *Freeman's Journal* (Sydney), *Glasgow Herald*, *The Guardian*, *Hibernia*, *History Ireland*, *In Dublin*, *Irish Catholic*, *Irish Echo*, *Irish Independent*, *Irish Press*, *Irish Times*, *Irish Weekly Independent*, *Kerry's Eye*, *The Kerryman*, *The Leader*, *Leitrim Observer*, *Magill*, *New Review*, *New York Times*, *Ottawa Citizen*, *The Phoenix*, *Saothar*, *The Standard*, *The Star*, *Status*, *Sunday Business Post*, *Sunday Independent*, *Sunday Press*, *Sunday Tribune*, *Sunday World*, *Times Pictorial*, *Waterford Standard*, *Weekly Irish Times*, *West Australian* (Perth)

Academic journals

Administration, *Australian Journal of Politics and History*, *Crane Bag*, *Doctrine and Life*, *Furrow*, *Historical Research*, *Irish Broadcasting Review*, *Irish Communications Review*, *Irish Ecclesiastical Record*, *Irish Political Studies*, *Irish Studies Review*, *Irish University Review*, *Journal of the History of Sexuality*, *Journalism and Mass Communication Quarterly*, *Journalism Practice*, *Journalism Studies*, *Media History*, *New Hibernia Review*, *Studies*

Books

Adams, Michael, *Censorship: The Irish Experience* (Tuscaloosa, Ala., 1968).
Ballin, Malcolm, *Irish Periodical Culture, 1937–72: Genre in Ireland, Wales and Scotland* (London, 2008).
Bance, Michael, *Smokey Joe: The Life and Times of a Provincial Newspaper Editor* (Dublin, 1994).
Bell, Desmond (ed.), *Is the Irish Press Independent? Essays on Ownership and Control of the Provincial, National and International Press in Ireland* (Dublin, 1986).
Bird, Charlie and Kevin Rafter, *This Is Charlie Bird* (Dublin, 2006).
Bowman, John, *Window and Mirror: RTÉ Television, 1961–2011* (Dublin, 2011).
Brady, Conor, *Up with the Times* (Dublin, 2005).
Brown, Stephen, *The Press in Ireland: A Survey and a Guide* (Dublin, 1937).
Brown, Terence, *The Irish Times: 150 Years of Influence* (London, 2015).
Bundock, C. J., *The National Union of Journalists: A Jubilee History, 1907–57* (Oxford, 1957).
Burke, Ray, *Press Delete: The Decline and Fall of the Irish Press* (Dublin, 2005).
Byrne, Gay, *To Whom It Concerns: 10 Years of The Late Late Show* (Dublin, 1972).
Clarke, Paddy, *Dublin Calling: 2RN and the Birth of Irish Radio* (Dublin, 1986).
Clear, Caitriona, *Women's Voices in Ireland: Women's Magazines in the 1950s and 1960s* (London, 2016).
Coogan, Tim Pat, *A Memoir* (London, 2008).

Corcoran, Farrel, *RTÉ and the Globalisation of Irish Television* (Bristol, 2004).
Corcoran, Mary P. and Mark O'Brien (eds), *Political Censorship and the Democratic State: The Irish Broadcasting Ban* (Dublin, 2005).
Cronin, Anthony, *No Laughing Matter: The Life and Times of Flann O'Brien* (New York, 1998).
Cullen, L. M., *Eason & Son: A History* (Dublin, 1989).
Devane, R. S., *The Imported Press: A National Menace - Some Remedies* (Dublin, 1950).
Doolan, Lelia, Jack Dowling and Bob Quinn, *Sit Down and Be Counted: The Cultural Evolution of a Television Station* (Dublin, 1969).
Downey, James, *In My Own Time: Inside Irish Politics and Society* (Dublin, 2009).
Doyle-O'Neill, Finola, *The Gaybo Revolution: How Gay Byrne Challenged Irish Society* (Dublin, 2015).
Dungan, Myles, *Mr Parnell's Rottweiler: Censorship and the United Ireland Newspaper, 1881–91* (Dublin, 2014).
Dunlop, Andrew, *Fifty Years of Irish Journalism* (Dublin, 1911).
Dunne, John J., *Headlines and Haloes* (Dublin, 1988).
Dunne, Joseph, *No Tigers in Africa* (Dublin, 1986).
Fahy, Tony and Mary Kelly (eds), *The Role of the Media in Irish Society* (Dublin, 1988).
Fanning, Bryan, *The Quest for Modern Ireland: The Battle of Ideas, 1912–86* (Dublin, 2008).
Farrell, Brian (ed.), *Communications and Community in Ireland* (Dublin, 1984).
Fisher, Des, *Broadcasting in Ireland* (London, 1978).
Fleming, Lionel, *Head or Harp* (London, 1965).
Foley, Michael, *Death in Every Paragraph: Journalism and the Great Irish Famine* (Hamden, Conn., 2015).
Gayle Backus, Margot, *Scandal Work: James Joyce, the New Journalism and the Home Rule Newspaper Wars* (Notre Dame, Ind., 2013).
Gillespie, Elgy, *Changing the Times: Irish Women Journalists, 1969–81* (Dublin, 2003).
Glandon, Virginia, *Arthur Griffith and the Advanced Nationalist Press, Ireland, 1900–23* (New York, 1985).
Gopsill, Tim and Greg Neale, *Journalists: 100 Years of the NUJ* (London, 2007).
Gorham, Maurice, *Forty Years of Irish Broadcasting* (Dublin, 1967).
Gray, Tony, *Mr Smyllie, Sir* (Dublin, 1991).
Greene, Roger, *Under the Spotlight: Conversations with 17 Leading Irish Journalists* (Dublin, 2005).
Hall, John B., *Random Records of a Reporter* (Dublin, 1928).
Healy, John, *Healy, Reporter: The Early Years* (Achill, 1991).
Horgan, John, *Irish Media: A Critical History since 1922* (London, 2001).
—— *Broadcasting and Public Life: RTÉ News and Current Affairs, 1926–97* (Dublin, 2004).
—— (ed.), *Great Irish Reportage: Ground-breaking Irish Journalism, Eyewitness Accounts and Dispatches since 1922* (Dublin, 2013).
Horgan, John, Barbara O'Connor and Helena Sheehan (eds), *Mapping Irish Media: Critical Explorations* (Dublin, 2007).
Inglis, Brian, *West Briton* (London, 1962).
—— *Downstart* (London, 1990).
James, Dermot, *From the Margins to the Centre: A History of the Irish Times* (Dublin, 2008).
Kelly, James, *Bonfires on the Hillside* (Belfast, 1995).
Kenneally, Ian, *The Paper Wall: Newspapers and Propaganda in Ireland, 1919–21* (Cork, 2008).
Kennedy, Dennis, *Square Peg: The Life and Times of a Northern Newspaperman South of the Border* (Dublin, 2009).

Kenny, David (ed.), *The Press Gang: Tales from the Glory Days of Irish Newspapers* (Dublin, 2015).
Kenny, Ivor, *Talking to Ourselves: Conversations with Editors of the Irish News Media* (Galway, 1994).
Kiberd, Damien (ed.), *Media in Ireland: The Search for Diversity* (Dublin, 1997).
—— (ed.), *Media in Ireland: The Search for Ethical Journalism* (Dublin, 1999).
—— (ed.), *Media in Ireland: Issues in Broadcasting* (Dublin, 2002).
Kilfeather, Frank, *Changing Times: A Life in Journalism* (Dublin, 1997).
Larkin, F. M., *Terror and Discord: The Shemus Cartoons in the Freeman's Journal, 1920–24* (Dublin, 2009).
Legg, Maire-Louise, *Newspapers and Nationalism: The Irish Provincial Press, 1850–92* (Dublin, 1999).
Lennon, Peter, *Foreign Correspondent: Paris in the Sixties* (London, 1994).
Lindsay, Paul (ed.), *The Media and Modern Society in Ireland* (Celbridge, 1993).
Mansfield, F. J., *Gentlemen, The Press! Chronicles of a Crusade* (London, 1943).
Martin, Peter, *Censorship in the Two Irelands, 1922–39* (Dublin, 2006).
Martin, Séamus, *Good Times and Bad* (Dublin, 2008).
Matthews, Kelly, *The Bell Magazine and the Representation of Irish Identity: Opening Windows* (Dublin, 2012).
Maume, Patrick, *D. P. Moran* (Dundalk, 1995).
McCafferty, Nell, *Nell* (Dublin, 2004).
McDonnell Bodkin, Matthais, *Recollections of an Irish Judge: Press, Bar and Parliament* (London, 1914).
McLoone, Martin and John MacMahon (eds), *Television and Irish Society: 21 Years of Irish Television* (Dublin, 1984).
McRedmond, Louis (ed.), *Written on the Wind: Personal Memories of Irish Radio, 1926–76* (Dublin, 1976).
Morash, Christopher, *A History of the Media in Ireland* (Cambridge, 2010).
Morrissey, Thomas, *William Martin Murphy* (Dundalk, 1997).
Mulryan, Peter, *Radio Radio: The Story of Independent, Local, Community and Pirate Radio in Ireland* (Dublin, 1988).
Myers, Kevin, *Watching the Door: A Memoir* (Dublin, 2006).
O'Brien, Mark, *De Valera, Fianna Fáil and the Irish Press: The Truth in the News?* (Dublin, 2001).
—— *The Irish Times: A History* (Dublin, 2008).
O'Brien, Mark and F. M. Larkin (eds), *Periodicals and Journalism in Twentieth Century Ireland* (Dublin, 2014).
O'Brien, Mark and Kevin Rafter (eds), *Independent Newspapers: A History* (Dublin, 2012).
O'Clery, Conor, *May You Live in Interesting Times: Memoirs of a Foreign Correspondent* (Dublin, 2008).
O'Donovan, Donal, *Little Old Man Cut Short* (Bray, 1998).
O Drisceoil, Donal, *Censorship in Ireland, 1939–45, Neutrality, Politics and Society* (Cork, 1996).
O'Reilly, Emily, *Veronica Guerin: The Life and Death of a Crime Reporter* (London, 1998).
O'Toole, Michael, *More Kicks than Pence: A Life in Irish Journalism* (Dublin, 1992).
Oram, Hugh, *The Newspaper Book: A History of Newspapers in Ireland, 1649–1983* (Dublin, 1983).
—— *Paper Tigers: Stories of Irish Newspapers by the People Who Make Them* (Belfast, 1993).
Orr, Charles, *Splash! Drama and Comedy in a Newspaperman's Career* (Braunton, 1989).

Pine, Richard, *2RN and the Origins of Irish Radio* (Dublin, 2002).
Purcell, Betty, *Inside RTÉ: A Memoir* (Dublin, 2014).
Rafter, Kevin (ed.), *Irish Journalism before Independence: More a Disease than a Profession* (Manchester, 2011).
Rafter, Kevin and Mark O'Brien (eds), *The State in Transition: Essays in Honour of John Horgan* (Dublin, 2015).
Reynolds, Paddy, *The Late Paddy Murphy: Memoirs of an Irish Journalist* (Belfast, 2004).
Ryan, Louise, *Gender, Identity and the Irish Press, 1927–37: Embodying the Nation* (New York, 2002).
Savage, Robert, *Irish Television: The Political and Social Origins* (Cork, 1996).
—— *A Loss of Innocence? Television and Irish Society, 1960–72* (Manchester, 2010).
Shovlin, Frank, *The Irish Literary Periodical, 1923–58* (London, 2003).
Smith, Raymond, *Urbi et Orbi and All That* (Dublin, 1995).
Steele, Karen, *Women, Press and Politics during the Irish Revival* (Syracuse, NY, 2007).
Steele, Karen and Michael de Nie (eds), *Ireland and the New Journalism* (New York, 2014).
Uí Chollatáin, Regina, *An Claidheamh Soluis agus Fáinne an Lae, 1899–1932* (Dublin, 2004).
Walsh, Maurice, *The News from Ireland: Foreign Correspondents and the Irish Revolution* (London, 2011).
Waters, John, *Jiving at the Crossroads* (Belfast, 1991).
Watson, Iarfhlaith, *Broadcasting in Ireland: Minority Language, Radio, Television and Identity* (Dublin, 2003).
Whittaker, Andrew (ed.), *Bright Brilliant Days: Douglas Gageby and the Irish Times* (Dublin, 2006).
Woodman, Kieran, *Media Control in Ireland, 1923–83* (Galway, 1985).

Index